Automated Machine Learning and Industrial Applications

Scrivener Publishing
100 Cummings Center, Suite 541J
Beverly, MA 01915-6106

Publishers at Scrivener
Martin Scrivener (martin@scrivenerpublishing.com)
Phillip Carmical (pcarmical@scrivenerpublishing.com)

Automated Machine Learning and Industrial Applications

Edited by

E. Gangadevi

Department of Computer Science, Loyola College, Chennai, India

M. Lawanya Shri

School of Information Technology and Engineering, Vellore Institute of Technology, Vellore, India

Balamurugan Balusamy

Shiv Nadar University, Delhi-NCR, India

and

Rajesh Kumar Dhanaraj

Symbiosis Institute of Computer Studies and Research (SICSR), Symbiosis International (Deemed University), Pune, India

Scrivener Publishing

WILEY

This edition first published 2025 by John Wiley & Sons, Inc., 111 River Street, Hoboken, NJ 07030, USA and Scrivener Publishing LLC, 100 Cummings Center, Suite 541J, Beverly, MA 01915, USA

For more information about Scrivener publications please visit www.scrivenerpublishing.com.

Wiley Global Headquarters
111 River Street, Hoboken, NJ 07030, USA

For details of our global editorial offices, customer services, and more information about Wiley products visit us at www.wiley.com.

The manufacturer's authorized representative according to the EU General Product Safety Regulation is Wiley-VCH GmbH, Boschstr. 12, 69469 Weinheim, Germany, e-mail: Product_Safety@wiley.com.

Library of Congress Cataloging-in-Publication Data

ISBN 978-1-394-27239-6

Cover image: Generated with AI using Adobe Firefly
Cover design by Russell Richardson

Set in size of 11pt and Minion Pro by Manila Typesetting Company, Makati, Philippines

Printed in the USA

10 9 8 7 6 5 4 3 2 1

Contents

Preface

The field of Machine Learning (ML) has rapidly advanced in recent years, driving exploration and experimentation across various domains. As businesses refine their strategies and leverage data-driven insights, the demand for efficient machine learning models continues to grow. Developing and optimizing these models requires extensive expertise in data science, particularly for industries seeking to implement cutting-edge solutions at scale.

This is where Automated Machine Learning (AutoML) comes into play, bridging the gap between machine learning and real-world challenges. AutoML eliminates barriers by enabling industries to harness advanced analytics without requiring deep knowledge of underlying algorithms. This book, *Automated Machine Learning and Industrial Applications*, aims to provide a clear understanding of how AutoML can be applied in industrial settings to deliver optimal solutions. It serves as a practical guide for engineers and data scientists while also offering valuable insights for decision-makers looking to integrate ML into their workflows.

The book covers a wide range of topics, including applications of AutoML in healthcare, next-generation industries, sustainable agriculture, customer support, cybersecurity, and more. It also explores the AutoML ecosystem, its integration with blockchain, and various open-source tools available on the AutoML platform. Each chapter illustrates different aspects of the technology, addressing the unique challenges of real-time applications. Additionally, numerous case studies demonstrate how AutoML enhances performance, reduces time and costs, and improves decision-making.

We would like to extend our heartfelt gratitude to all the authors who contributed their time and expertise to this book. Their dedication has been instrumental in bringing this project to fruition. We also appreciate the invaluable feedback and suggestions from our reviewers, which have helped enhance the quality of each chapter. Furthermore, we express our deepest thanks to Martin Scrivener and the team at Scrivener Publishing for their guidance and support throughout the publication process.

Finally, we are grateful to our readers for their interest in this book. We hope the insights shared here will inspire further exploration and innovation in the exciting field of Automated Machine Learning. We are excited to embark on this journey together, exploring AutoML's transformative potential across industries.

The Editors
June 2025

1

Design and Architecture of AutoML for Data Science in Next-Generation Industries

E. Gangadevi[1]*, K. Santhi[2] and M. Lawanya Shri[2]

[1]Loyola College, Chennai, India
[2]Vellore Institute of Technology, Vellore, India

Abstract
Automated Machine Learning (AutoML) acts as a key that accelerates the next-generation industries for automation process and algorithms. It simplifies the process involved in designing and deploying machine learning techniques by incorporating the accessibility feature to users in data science and machine learning models. AutoML implies the use of automated tools and techniques to expedite and automate the process of constructing, training, and deploying machine learning models. This chapter provides an insight of design and architecture of AutoML for data science in next-generation industries.

Keywords: AutoML, industries, data science, machine learning, model training, types of AutoML, feature selection, data scientist

1.1 Introduction

AutoML has gained popularity among researchers and industries due to its potential for democratizing machine learning models through the process of automation. The aim is to make ML frameworks more accessible and streamline the workflow by reducing the time for developing high-quality frameworks [1]. The techniques involved, such as data preprocessing, model evaluation, feature engineering, selection of model, and hyperparameter tuning through automation enable industrialists to effectively develop

**Corresponding author*: smgangadevi@gmail.com

E. Gangadevi, M. Lawanya Shri, Balamurugan Balusamy and Rajesh Kumar Dhanaraj (eds.) Automated Machine Learning and Industrial Applications, (1–16) © 2025 Scrivener Publishing LLC

high-quality ML models without requiring a deep study of the algorithms. Automated machine learning system models focus on efficiency, scalability, robustness, and flexibility to manage and handle large datasets [2].

1.2 Modular Design

A modular design in AutoML is crucial for developing an extensible model that supports diverse requirements, data types, and procedures.

- **Component-Based Model**
This component based architecture is the process of dividing the system into individual components in which each subcomponent is responsible for performing specific work like preprocessing, feature engineering, parameter tuning, and model evaluation. Each component encompasses various functionalities enabling well-defined interactions among related components and supporting an effective interface for performing connections.

- **Flexibility**
The model provides flexibility and reusability to achieve optimal results. The design components used across various models are capable of handling various types and sources of data with different sizes and formats. The abstraction layer is mainly used for decoupling the components enabling efficient substitution or extension for the functionality to evaluate the machine learning models without creating impact on the subsystems.

- **Dynamic Composition**
Combining the components dynamically by supporting various tasks based on their system requirements is followed. The preferences and the type of components to be combined will be decided by the user for evaluating the model. Implementing the configuration mechanism to define custom pipelines of individual component is very effective.

- **Plug and Play Architecture**
New components can be efficiently added into the existing hierarchy of the component system without modifying or reconfiguring the model. Defining standard interfaces for communicating the components enabling interoperability feature for effective utilization of individual components in an isolated manner.

- **Modular Testing and Validation**

Designing and developing an efficient testing model for validating the functions involved and evaluating the performance metrics of each component effectively. Integration testing ensures that the components work together properly for large data sets.

- **Dependency Management**

Managing dependency among various components is crucial to avoid conflicts and maintain consistency. Dependencies among various components are tested by various testing mechanisms and enable isolation mechanism to ensure the effectiveness of the model.

- **Scalability and Performance**

The components that are designed should be scalable, especially for workflows with large datasets, by utilizing distributed or parallel processing mechanisms to dynamically leverage the required computing resources.

1.3 Data Handling

Data handling in AutoML is essential for managing and maintaining data flow throughout various phases of the machine learning pipeline as shown in Figure 1.1. Data ingesting support is required to fetch various sources of data like data lakes, cloud storage, databases, and external APIs. Connectors are implemented to combine various data sources in different formats. Data preprocessing is essential for machine learning model quality and to avail optimal results. Data cleaning is one of the preprocessing

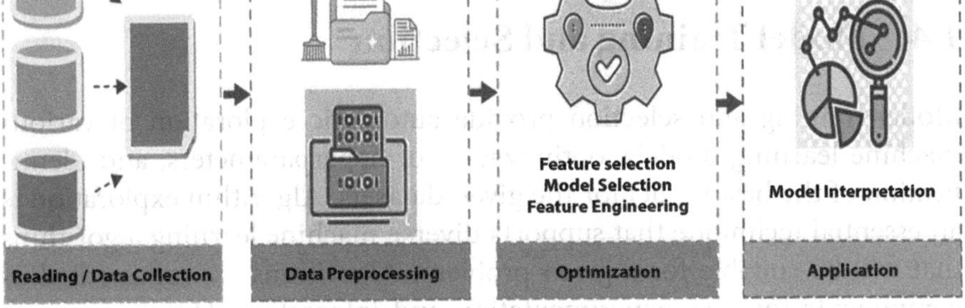

Figure 1.1 Machine learning model phases.

techniques used for handling missing data, duplication, and managing inconsistent data [3].

Data transformation is a preprocessing method that transforms the input for scaling, encoding, and normalizing and handles skewed distributions. AutoML supports automatic feature generation from existing data using various methods. Feature selection and scaling is important for selecting relatable features and ensuring uniformity to stabilize the features among various feature ranges. Data augmentation is very important for generating synthetic samples of data to train data sets and improve accuracy level. This plays a vital role when the available size of data is small. Data mirroring, cropping, rotating, and flipping are some of the techniques involved in augmenting the data samples. Tracking the lineage and maintaining version history of data sets are recommended to improve the reproducibility and auditability of various models [4].

Data quality assessment is one of the important methods that perform the quality checks of the data sources to mitigate various issues involved in addressing data issues like schema changes, anomalies, inconsistency, and data drift. Triggering alerts when deviations happen in the norms by monitoring qualitative metrics is essential. Streaming data processing support is required for real-time data ingestion, which deals with collecting data from various sources such as IoT devices and sensors. The captured data are sent to the repository for evaluation using streaming processing [5]. There are various effective stream processing frameworks available for handling high throughput and low latency data. Data privacy and security are among the most important components in data handling model to ensure compliance with standards and implement privacy regulations. Encryption and access control policies are widely used for preserving privacy and confidentiality of data. Data visualization provides various tools for exploring and analyzing the data set and to manage the relationships among various data sources.

1.4 Model Training and Selection

Model training and selection provide automatic exploration of various machine learning models, optimization of hyperparameters, and identification of the best model for the given datasets. Algorithm exploration is an essential technique that supports diverse machine learning algorithms that will be suitable for a given problem. Algorithms are represented as components for easy experimentation and integration. Hyperparameter selection is very crucial for the model performance. Configuring the hyperparameters based on the behavior of the algorithm improves accuracy results. Automatic hyperparameter optimization and parameter tuning are added advantages in AutoML [6].

Cross validation methods are used to assess the generalization process of various models by splitting the given data set into multiple folds and evaluating them to estimate the performance accurately. Ensemble learning is used to combine the predictions among various models to improve the performance. Bagging, boosting, and stacking are examples of ensemble methods used to combine predictions. Performance metrics are basic parameters used for testing a model. Various evaluation metrics are used to evaluate machine learning models in both the training and testing of datasets [7].

AutoML in Data Science

AutoML refers to the structure guidelines and techniques to automate any or all of the steps in the machine intelligence process. It offers easily accessible components and tools to expedite and improve the machine process of learning. Understanding the machine learning pipeline is helpful before utilizing AutoML.

Data scientists might concentrate on more difficult jobs using AutoML for automating time-consuming testing, sparing them some of their burden and responsibility. It also ensures enhanced efficiency and usability in traditional predictive modeling frameworks [8].

Although data science is an extensive field, a data scientist involves several kinds of skills that are not completely represented by a single tool or software. The domain requires an exhaustive knowledge of the topic as well as the recognition and formalization of the problem in a specific way to discuss alternative solutions. Information from the real world is usually noisy and unstructured. It includes errors in spelling, mismatched labeling, missing values, replication, inconsistent units, and abnormalities. The data must be adequately prepared and treated before any mathematical calculations are carried out on it.

The AutoML techniques that have been examined, so far, have limitations to certain challenges such as classification and regression. It is not strong enough to handle unsupervised machine learning techniques. The objective of AutoML is to support data scientists in their roles, not to replace them. It is a good option for creating models and enabling people who are not experts to engage with machine learning. However, compared to data scientists, AutoML is unable to express business problems or use domain expertise for extracting useful features from the data.

The three main categories of enterprises that offer AutoML solutions are as follows:

1. **Open Source:** With significant corporate backing, a number of well-known IT companies make their AI/ML research results publicly available. These easily obtainable outcomes contribute to the creation of openly available concepts.
2. **Start-Ups:** The computerized predictive forecasting company which is developed progressively is considered mainly. An increasing number of businesses are setting up in an attempt to profit.
3. **Tech Giants:** Google introduced Google Could AutoML, one of the first AutoML tools from a tech giant, claiming to be an "AI-first" firm. Numerous AutoML tools are now available through IBM's SPSS modeler.

Data Scientist vs AutoML

While speed and risk reduction are two areas where AutoML technologies outperform human data scientists, there are still areas where the human brain excels over technology. AutoML just cannot match the degree of complexity, intelligence, and creative problem solving that a data scientist brings to the process. Based on the analysis, approximately 43% of the work performed by data scientists can be completed by machines entirely, while 28.57% of the work can be completed by humans and machines working together. The remaining 28.57% of the work will require human labor only. It is also clear from the fact that firms' most recent job descriptions list AutoML solutions as a preferred skill for data scientists, for instance, Polaris and Growth Analytics. To help new data scientists develop this

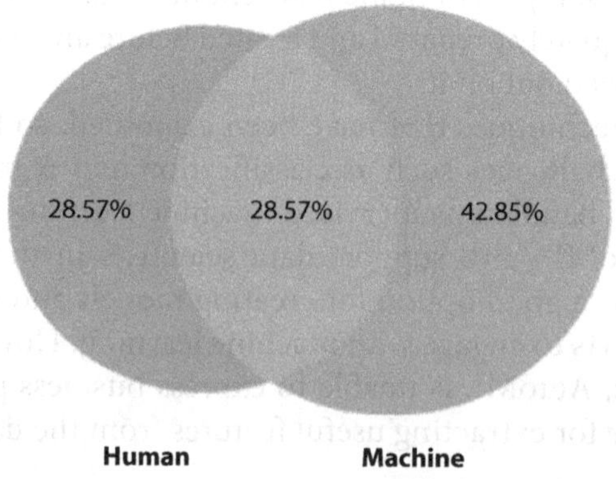

developing skill and join the revolution, online learning platforms, such as Udemy and Coursera, have started to offer courses in AutoML, such as AutoML Bootcamp, Machine Learning on Google Cloud (Vertex AI and AI Platform), Analyze Datasets, and Train ML Models using AutoML [9].

More Data Scientists Are Required

As data science grows increasingly embedded in everyday life, enterprises want additional data scientists to deliver the assistance they demand. Despite the application of data science tools, companies may not be able to comprehend their operations, evaluate their achievements, or take precise action to stop major losses [10].

Between 2021 and 2031, the number of data scientist employees will continue to grow by 36%, while the typical rate of growth for all occupations is 5%. Given the lack of data analysts and the time required for developing data science solutions, AutoML solutions may assist businesses meet their need for data scientists. Data scientists are responsible for applying machine learning algorithms into practice and selecting the approach that best fits the business case. However, bias and mistakes created by humans can occur during the implementation process. In addition to automating this process, AutoML systems can run a larger variety of machine learning algorithms to choose the best one, some of which data scientists may not have previously thought it.

To enhance its machine learning procedures, Facebook currently trains about 300,000 machine learning models. The company even hired an AutoML engineer named Asimo to automatically construct better copies of its current models. AutoML solutions will increase the return on investment (ROI) of machine learning projects because these capabilities will speed up the machine learning operations [11]. For model building, data scientists offer two benefits over the current automated ML methods: Compatibility with specific requirements: Although most AutoML structures optimize for model performance, practical problems machine learning applications demand much more than that. For example, if storage and computation constraints need a model to be embedded in edge devices, enterprises must use simpler models. Certain types can only be applied in instances wherein extension will be needed.

Model Performance: On Kaggle, an open platform for machine learning challenges, individuals are still readily overcoming models made by AutoML techniques. AutoML tools are yet to compete in any data science challenges.

These benefits are expected to fade or disappear as AutoML technologies get more powerful over time. More significantly, data scientists and their supervisors are in charge of significant duties that go beyond modeling, such as the following:

- **Decide which models need to be produced.** In data science, the initial step is also the most crucial. Understanding the company, data that are accessible through internal and external resources, concerns about data quality, computing and privacy needs, and organizational difficulties are all necessary.
- **Handling the human elements of the model's deployment.** Subject-matter specialists and management have been convinced that the model is better than the current solution. They list any potential weaknesses of the model and take steps to fix them.

These are the more basic skills of data scientists, and it will take some time before machines can solve these kinds of issues. That does not imply, however, that data scientists are especially equipped to tackle these problems.

The fundamentals of data science should eventually be as widely known as the fundamentals of statistics. Even though not everyone understands complex statistics, important ideas, like distributions, variance, and mean, are widely understood and influence business choices. Similar to how Excel made data processing and storage more accessible to all white-collar workers, AutoML tools have the ability to democratize data science for businesses [12].

AutoML in Next-Generation Industries

The application of Auto Machine Learning (AutoML) to next-generation industries is becoming more and more important as it solves problems associated with the deployment and use of machine learning models. Many of the techniques that AutoML is affecting in many businesses are as follows:

Accelerated Growth of the Modeling Development Process:

Organizations could speed up the establishment of machine learning models via using AutoML, which streamlines a lot of the modeling process, including feature design, model selection, hyperparameter tuning, and data preprocessing.

Democratizing Artificial Intelligence:

Machine learning becomes more widely available cheers to AutoML, which enables users of all skill levels, including domain experts with little experience with machine learning, to take advantage of sophisticated analytics and insights.

Falling Resource Requirements:
By automating tedious and repetitive operations, AutoML technologies can assist organizations in maximizing the use of their resources. As a result, less substantial manual intervention is required freeing up data scientists to concentrate on more tactical aspects of model building.

Enhancing Decision Making:
Future industries will often deal with massive, complex datasets. To support data-driven decision-making processes, AutoML helps extract useful insights from these datasets.

Boosting Efficiency and Precision:
AutoML frameworks use methods, such as model ensemble approaches and hyperparameter tuning, to enhance the accuracy and performance of machine learning models.

Adapting Dynamically to Data Changes:
Future businesses often operate in environments of change wherein information attributes are able to modify over time. AutoML systems can adapt to these developments and ensure that models remain useful and effective by continuously assessing and revising them.

Promoting Edge Computing and IoT:
As industries increasingly embrace edge computing and Internet of Things (IoT) technologies, AutoML can be used at the edge to automate the construction of machine learning models tailored for specific edge devices and data sources.

Retaining the Interpreting of the Model:
AutoML foundations are constantly evolving by including functions that increases the easy understanding and illumination of models. This is particularly vital in industries where compliance with regulations and confidence among stakeholders depend on recognizing the logic behind model estimates.

By Adapting to Industry-Specific Constraints
AutoML tools are being researched to tackle industry-specific obstacles such as industrial maintenance prediction, fraud in finance detection, and medical diagnostics. This modification helps improve the significance and efficacy of automated learning remedies in particular industry sectors.

Despite all of AutoML's incentives, it is necessary to remain mindful that there may not be one AutoML solution suitable for all circumstances. Companies ought to carefully consider the benefits and drawbacks of AutoML techniques and adopt a comprehensive strategy that brings together domain knowledge with automated machine learning. Additionally, compliance with regulations, moral challenges, and information privacy should be the primary concerns when using AutoML systems across categories.

Architecture of AutoML

In recent trends, deep learning has started wide application across diverse fields choosing amazing success in addressing complex AI problems [13]. Its implementation stands within areas, such as image classification, object detection, and language modeling, where it has brought attractive results.

The revolution moment occurred in 2012 when AlexNet outshined in the ImageNet Large Scale Visual Recognition Challenge (ILSVRC) processing traditional methods. However, more complex and deeper neural networks were introduced with models, like ResNet-50, featuring 50 layers and approximately 25.6 million parameters [1]. The architecture consists of steps with varying filter sizes, beginning with 64 filters in the initial stage and completing with 1,024 filters in the fifth stage. Each stage contains residual blocks, each of which contains two 3×3 convolutional layers and a crosscut connection.

The intensifying costs connected with model development have given a chance to a novel concept called the automation of the complete machine learning (ML) pipeline. Referred to as automated machine learning (AutoML), this approach improves the burden of development costs [14]. In modern times, AutoML systems can integrate many techniques making a straightforward and user-friendly end-to-end ML pipeline system. Our focus is to create a way of personalized AutoML methods directing to the development of the most comfortable AI system.

The AutoML workflow covers many stages like feature engineering, data preparation, model generation, and model evaluation as shown in Figure 1.2. The process of model processing can be divided into search space exploration and optimization methods. The basic design principles of ML models are consistent within the search space and divided into two types as follows: traditional ML models and neural architectures. For classification, optimization techniques can be classified into hyperparameter optimization (HPO) and architecture optimization (AO) [15]. HPO aims to optimize parameters related to training, such as learning rate and batch size, while AO aims to enhance parameters linked with the model itself. For example, the optimization of the number of layers in neural architectures

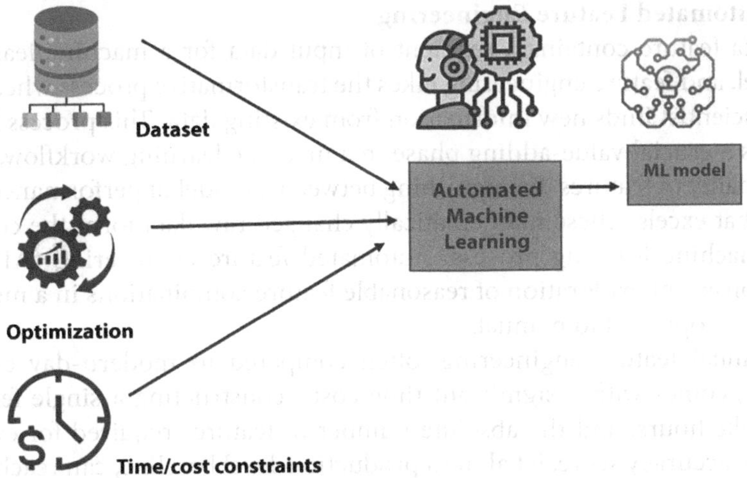

Figure 1.2 Basic architecture of AutoML.

and the number of neighbors in KNN are instances of parameters given in architecture optimization (AO) techniques.

AutoML signifies an important leap forward in the world of robotics presenting an efficient and streamlined approach to crafting machine learning models and algorithms for robotic systems [16]. This creation minimizes the manual effort and expertise traditionally required in model development. In the context of robotics, AutoML involves automating various stages of the machine learning pipeline, encompassing data preprocessing, feature engineering, model selection, hyperparameter tuning, and even deployment.

Types of AutoML

In a data science pipeline, various steps must be started by a data science team to create a predictive model. Even experienced teams of data scientists and ML engineers can find data with the improved speed and transparency given by AutoML. A data scientist typically starts the process with a hypothesis, acquires the appropriate dataset, creates data visualization, engineers additional features to store all available signals, and then follows to train a model with hyperparameters. For state-of-the-art deep learning, they also need to design an efficient architecture for a Deep Neural Network possibly leveraging a GPU if it is at their disposal [17]. The different types of AutoML are as follows:

1. Automated Feature Engineering
2. Automated Hyper Optimization
3. Neural Architecture Search

1. Automated Feature Engineering

A data feature contains a segment of input data for a machine learning model, and feature engineering takes the transformative process wherein a data scientist finds new information from existing data. This process looks out as a crucial value-adding phase in a machine learning workflow, with the quality of features distinguishing between a model of performance and one that excels. These mathematically changed raw data form the core of the machine learning process. Automated feature engineering (AFE) is the consistent exploration of reasonable feature combinations in a mechanized, as opposed to manual.

Manual feature engineering, often compared to modern-day experiment, comes with a significant time cost—constructing a single feature can take hours, and the absolute number of features required for even a simple accuracy score, let alone a production-level baseline, can reach into the hundreds [17]. By automating the exploration of the feature space, AutoML dramatically minimizes the time a data science team spends on this process, from days to mere minutes.

The benefits of automated feature engineering spread beyond time savings for data scientists. The generated features are inherently interpretable. In regulated industries, like healthcare or finance, interpretability is vital, as it reduces barriers to AI adoption. Moreover, the simplicity of these features enhances the application and actionability of high-quality models for data scientists. Automatically generated features also have the potential to determine new key performance indicators (KPIs) for an organization to monitor and act upon. Following feature engineering, data scientists progress to optimize their models through planned feature selection.

2. Automated Hyper Optimization

Hyperparameters in machine learning algorithms can be compared to devices for fine-tuning model performance, where even small adjustments can have a substantial impact. In small-scale data science modeling, hyperparameters can be manually established and optimized through trial and error.

However, for deep learning applications, the number of hyperparameters rises exponentially increasing the feasibility of manual optimization within a reasonable timeframe for a data science team. Automated hyperparameter optimization (HPO) improves this challenge by permitting teams to explore and optimize across the full hyperparameter space in an automated manner allowing them to focus on iterating and experimenting with features and models [18].

Automating the machine learning process also allows data scientists to shift their focus from the "how" of model creation to the "why." With huge amounts of available data and numerous questions to address, analytics teams can now concentrate on defining which aspects of the model to optimize for. For instance, they can address classic problems like minimizing false negatives in medical testing.

3. Neural Architecture Search (NAS)

The most complicated and time-consuming method of deep learning is in structuring the neural architecture. Data science officials invest reasonable time in choosing appropriate sections and learning rates by mostly focusing on weights in models, especially proven in language models. Neural Architecture Search (NAS), stated as "making use of neural nets for designing neural nets," reaches out as a major candidate for automation in the arena of machine learning.

NAS explores by finding architectures to learn, with the result determined by the metric against which every architecture is measured. Many algorithms can be used in a neural architecture group [19]. For example, if the required number of architectures is less, random options for testing can be done. Gradient-based approaches, transforming the discrete search space into a continuous illustration, have proven very effective. Alternatively, data science officials may practice with traditional algorithms, where architectures are measured and changes are slowly applied, developing more successful child architectures while reducing unsuccessful ones.

While neural architecture searches are a significant component of AutoML, using the democratization of AI, they frequently come with a considerable carbon footprint. An examination of these compromises is still pending, and an ongoing study in NAS methods is exploring optimization for environmental costs.

The Journey of Automated ML in the Industry

The workflow of the machine learning segments are automated by AutoML using some set of methods and practices. The tools used for automated ML focus on automating many stages of a typical machine learning pipeline to make the process easier for non-experts to create machine learning models. This pipelining removes the repeated tasks and creates seasoned machine learning engineers for building the models faster [20].

Artificial Intelligence highly creates an impact in fields like education, healthcare, agriculture, industry, and environmental challenges. However, many areas still face challenges in deploying machine learning models effectively due to time, resources, talent, and trust. There was a huge requirement for human expertise in traditional machine-learning processes. Before starting to work with machine learning algorithms, the company seeks data scientists, mathematicians, statistics experts, and researchers. There is a shortage of trained data scientists and experienced industrialist workers.

The important constraint is time. When many solutions are taken using machine learning models, it is difficult to get quick results. Few ML results take months to deploy, which is not helpful for the company. Due to high manual dependence, there may be errors during the workflow. Many companies find it difficult to transform the predicted model into to easily understandable format for stakeholders. Even by using the explainability and interpretability of ML systems, the lack of knowledge and experience does not help during implementation.

Conclusion

AutoML reduces manual dependencies and time to create models within a few weeks or days. As AutoML takes care of the repetitive task, humans concentrate on designing, understanding the problems, preparing data, and deploying the model. AutoML produces more accurate results that can be achieved in less time when working with data scientists.

References

1. Karmaker, S.K., Hassan, M.M., Smith, M.J., Xu, L., Zhai, C., Veeramachaneni, K., Automl to date and beyond: Challenges and opportunities. *ACM Comput. Surv. (CSUR)*, *54*, 8, 1–36, 2021, https://doi.org/10.1145/3470918.
2. He, X., Zhao, K., Chu, X., AutoML: A survey of the state-of-the-art. *Knowledge-Based Syst.*, *212*, 106622, 2021.
3. Wever, M., Tornede, A., Mohr, F., Hüllermeier, E., AutoML for multi-label classification: Overview and empirical evaluation. *IEEE Trans. Pattern Anal. Mach. Intell.*, *43*, 9, 3037–3054, 2021.
4. Namburu, A., Sumathi, D., Raut, R., Jhaveri, R.H., Dhanaraj, R.K., Subbulakshmi, N., Balusamy, B., FPGA-based deep learning models for analysing corona using chest X-ray images. *Mobile Inf. Syst.*, 2022, 1–14, 2022.
5. Li, Y., Wang, Z., Xie, Y., Ding, B., Zeng, K., Zhang, C., Automl: From methodology to application, in: *Proceedings of the 30th ACM International Conference on Information & Knowledge Management*, 2021, October, pp. 4853–4856.
6. Truong, A., Walters, A., Goodsitt, J., Hines, K., Bruss, C.B., Farivar, R., Towards automated machine learning: Evaluation and comparison of AutoML approaches and tools, in: *2019 IEEE 31st international conference on tools with artificial intelligence (ICTAI)*, 2019, November, IEEE, pp. 1471–1479.

7. Zheng, R., Qu, L., Cui, B., Shi, Y., Yin, H., Automl for deep recommender systems: A survey. *ACM Trans. Inf. Syst.*, *41*, 4, 1–38, 2023.
8. Milutinovic, M., Schoenfeld, B., Martinez-Garcia, D., Ray, S., Shah, S., Yan, D., On evaluation of automl systems, in: *Proceedings of the ICML Workshop on Automatic Machine Learning*, 2020, July, vol. 2020.
9. Feurer, M., Eggensperger, K., Falkner, S., Lindauer, M., Hutter, F., Practical automated machine learning for the automl challenge 2018, in: *International workshop on automatic machine learning at ICML*, 2018, July, pp. 1189–1232.
10. Drozdal, J., Weisz, J., Wang, D., Dass, G., Yao, B., Zhao, C., Su, H., Trust in AutoML: exploring information needs for establishing trust in automated machine learning systems, in: *Proceedings of the 25th international conference on intelligent user interfaces*, 2020, March, pp. 297–307.
11. Tsiakmaki, M., Kostopoulos, G., Kotsiantis, S., Ragos, O., Implementing AutoML in educational data mining for prediction tasks. *Appl. Sci.*, *10*, 1, 90, 2019.
12. Bahri, M., Salutari, F., Putina, A., Sozio, M., AutoML: state of the art with a focus on anomaly detection, challenges, and research directions. *Int. J. Data. Sci. Anal.*, *14*, 2, 113–126, 2022.
13. Salehin, I., Islam, Md. S., Saha, P., Noman, S.M., Tuni, A., Hasan, Md.M., Baten, Md.A., AutoML: A systematic review on automated machine learning with neural architecture search. *J. Inf. Intell.*, 2, 1, 52–81, 2024, Elsevier BV. https://doi.org/10.1016/j.jiixd.2023.10.002.
14. Waring, J., Lindvall, C., Umeton, R., Automated machine learning: Review of the state-of-the-art and opportunities for healthcare. *Artif. Intell. Med.*, 104, 101822, 2020, Elsevier BV. https://doi.org/10.1016/j.artmed.2020.101822.
15. Krau, J., Pacheco, B.M., Zang, H.M., Schmitt, R.H., Automated machine learning for predictive quality in production. *Procedia CIRP*, 93, 443–448, 2020, Elsevier BV. https://doi.org/10.1016/j.procir.2020.04.039.
16. Nagarajah, T. and Poravi, G., A Review on Automated Machine Learning (AutoML) Systems. *2019 IEEE 5th International Conference for Convergence in Technology (I2CT)*, Bombay, India, pp. 1–6, 2019, doi: 10.1109/I2CT45611.2019.9033810.
17. Balusamy, B. and Krishna, P.V., Simplified and efficient framework for managing roles in cloud-based transaction processing systems using attribute-based encryption. *Int. J. Comput. Sci. Eng.*, 14, 2, 135–149, 2017.
18. Musigmann, M., Akkurt, B.H., Krähling, H., *et al.*, Testing the applicability and performance of Auto ML for potential applications in diagnostic neuroradiology. *Sci. Rep.*, 12, 13648, 2022, https://doi.org/10.1038/s41598-022-18028-8.
19. Stephan, T., Al-Turjman, F., K, S.J., Balusamy, B., Energy and spectrum aware unequal clustering with deep learning based primary user classification in cognitive radio sensor networks. *Int. J. Mach. Learn. Cybern.*, 12, 3261–3294, 2021.
20. Gudzius, P., Kurasova, O., Darulis, V., Filatovas, E., AutoML-Based Neural Architecture Search for Object Recognition in Satellite Imagery. *Remote Sens.*, 15, 1, 12 91, 2022, MDPI AG. https://doi.org/10.3390/rs15010091.

2

Automated Machine Learning Model in Secure Data Transmission in Sustainable Healthcare Sensor Network Using Quantum Blockchain Architecture

Kaavya Kanagaraj[1], A. Sheryl Oliver[1], Kavitha V.P.[2], S. Magesh[3] and R. Manikandan[4]*

[1]Department of Computational Intelligence, School of Computing, College of Engineering and Technology, SRM Institute of Science and Technology, Chennai, Tamil Nadu, India
[2]Department of ECE, SRM Institute of Science and Technology, Vadapalani, Tamil Nadu, India
[3]Department of Computer Science and Engineering, Dr. M.G.R. Educational and Research Institute, Chennai, India
[4]School of Computing, SASTRA Deemed University, Thanjavur, Tamil Nadu, India

Abstract
Body sensor network (BSN), a monitoring system utilized in a healthcare setting based on Internet of Things (IoT) technology, consists of wearable or implanted devices. Due to the limited battery capacity and energy supply for sensors in BSN, extending the service cycle of the network is a significant challenge. Increasing energy efficiency and energy collection is essential for the network to remain sustainable. Operators are looking to automate network diagnosis and management using machine learning (ML) to operate complex optical communication networks cost effectively. This research proposes a novel, sustainable, network-secure data transmission technique based on automated machine learning (AutoML). Here, the healthcare network monitoring uses a Reinforcement Bayesian Regressive Vector Machine. The secure data transmission uses quantum blockchain automated transfer machine graph learning. The experimental analysis of throughput, scalability, packet delivery ratio, and data integrity is carried out.

**Corresponding author*: srmanimt75@gmail.com

E. Gangadevi, M. Lawanya Shri, Balamurugan Balusamy and Rajesh Kumar Dhanaraj (eds.) Automated Machine Learning and Industrial Applications, (17–40) © 2025 Scrivener Publishing LLC

New functionalities are needed to enable cognitive, autonomous management of optical network security to achieve these goals.

Keywords: Optical network, secure data transmission, AutoML, network monitoring, machine graph learning

2.1 Introduction

Information and communication technology (ICT)-based health surveillance systems connect people and infrastructure to improve overall quality of life. In addition to supporting the fundamental requirements of health monitoring systems, industrial stability, sustainable development, quick accessibility, and access to dependable medical care are targets that are reached by mandating and appropriately transmitting data from dedicated networks [1]. Wireless body area networks (WBANs), which scientists and researchers have developed, are made up of tiny sensors with wireless communication capabilities that can be put inside patients' bodies. The devices continuously gather biological signals from patients in hospitals and quarantine facilities using various sensors and then transmit the data collected to the local analysis unit (LPU). To improve health warnings so that healthcare practitioners can quickly respond by taking preventative measures when they see patients' falling health conditions or any emergency, LPUs should be robust and capable of processing health data in real time. LPU data may also be transferred to distant databases (DB) for long-term study and preservation [2]. WBANs have several advantages, including enabling doctors to monitor patient-specific parameters remotely, improving diagnostic accuracy and efficacy, and lowering healthcare costs per patient by giving doctors a convenient way to track patients' well-being all the time. The utility of the hybrid DL method for classifying health data using hybrid deep learning is improved in this research.

Today's industry output is affected by a current problem called "Industry 4.0." Industry 4.0 is all about connectivity, not the mass production method that predominated the first and second industrial revolutions, the steam engine, and other machinery that ran our factories during the first or even the emergence of new computer-driven methods during the machine age, which is the one we are currently living through. It is a chance to fundamentally alter how business responds to social demands. The development of Industry 4.0 is fueled by a networked, futuristic environment [3]. The potential for significant upheaval exists, and those left behind feel it intensely. Industry 4.0 refers to developing autonomous robots, intelligent inventory management methods, and intelligent supply chain management through sensors, networking, AI, ML, CPS, and other methods [4]. The development and prosperity of small- and medium-sized businesses are anticipated to be significantly impacted by the usage of Internet technology and I4.0 strategies. The results of AI are based on data utilized in ML. AI is utilized in machine learning algorithms for healthcare applications. CNNs, a type of Artificial Neural Network (ANN), form the basis for deep learning models used in image visualization applications [5]. The study of genes using deep learning makes identifying common diseases, like Turner's syndrome, hemophilia, sickle cell anemia, and others simple. It enables doctors to develop future treatments as well as medication. Doctors can determine patients' status utilizing DL and ML to find regular and aberrant patient data [6].

Research Objectives

- To propose automated machine learning (AutoML) with secure network data transmission technique.
- To develop health monitoring using Reinforcement Bayesian Regressive Vector Machine model.
- The secure network data transmission uses quantum blockchain automated transfer machine graph learning.
- The parametric analysis is carried out regarding throughput, scalability, packet delivery ratio, and data integrity.

2.2 Related Works

Numerous methods exist for examining, managing, and tracking human activity in healthcare. These methods offer solutions from a range of viewpoints. To understand how ambient assisted living encourages and supports patients with heart disease in self-management for lowering related mortality and morbidity, the author [7] published a systematic literature review covering the entire literature on the subject. The study is divided into four categories as follows: self-monitoring, wearable technology; clinical management systems; ambient assisted living for the elderly; and deep learning-based methods for diagnosing heart disease. In the beginning, Work [8] conducted an extensive survey on ubiquitous networks and smart healthcare systems to monitor a patient with chronic and lifestyle diseases. The method introduced a novel framework based on cloud-based analytics and deep learning for smart patient monitoring and recommendations. An imbalanced dataset, collected on a patient with chronic blood pressure issues, was the subject of a case study, and the patient's condition was assessed. Based on the outcomes of the experiments, the study demonstrated the strategy's efficacy. The author described the uses of deep learning in healthcare [9]. Deep learning was concentrated in seven areas. These fields include data from wearable devices, electrocardiography, electronic health records, community healthcare, electroencephalogram, genome analysis, and medication analysis. The benefits and drawbacks of the current studies are examined, and future trends and research problems are considered. The application of fuzzy logic to industrial advancements is discussed in the paper [10]. The language control protocol for skilled operations uses FL (fuzzy logic) to close the gap between theoretical and mathematical processes. This approach is used in pilot-scale plants and real-world industrial settings. In this paper, the benefits of employing fuzzy logic are highlighted. It also provides information on the potential of fuzzy logic. Alternation for Mamdani inference is explored in the paper [11]. This is used for timing sporting events. The benefits of combining Takagi Sugano and Mamdani make it better than the original system since it may minimize complexity and response time while still producing accurate results. This modified system can be utilized for many other things, including sports and strenuous exercise. The paper describes the remote health monitoring method [12]. In this method, wearable technology is utilized to measure fundamental indicators of health state such as body temperature and pulse rate. Regularly measure these parameters and archive them in the cloud for future use and reference. Their family or carers are immediately informed if there are any variations in temperature or pulse rate or if either parameter exceeds the limit. The position of the individual wearing the device is also obtained.

Additionally, it produces daily reports and data that are transferred to the cloud. This makes it easier for the doctors to compile patient reports weekly or monthly and review patient information as needed. According to Work [13], manufacturers should welcome the digital shift toward Industry 4.0 since it increases their flexibility, agility, and ability to respond to customers. This study aims to determine the variables affecting manufacturing organizations' adoption of I4.0 and create a triadic conceptual method to describe these phenomena. In-person interviews were employed as part of the qualitative exploratory study technique for this study, which was based on various case studies (n = 15) from Malaysia's manufacturing sector. NVivo was utilized to analyze data. According to research, predictive maintenance uses information from monitoring instruments and process performance indicators to identify future issues [14]. Machine learning algorithms are typically trained using data from equipment monitoring. The increase in computer accuracy is aided by the machine learning process, which entails collecting and analyzing large volumes of data. Supervised learning is commonly used in machine learning techniques, in which labeled data are sent into a method to train the algorithm [15].

Deep Belief Network (DBN) and CNN are standard DL techniques [16, 17]. DBN uses restricted Boltzmann machines, which significantly speed up the preparation process compared to a standard huge neural network. Most often, image feature extraction scenarios use CNN. These approaches, however, do not account for pattern sequences or remember changes in pattern sequences due to the length of the gaps between these sequences. Recurrent neural networks (RNNs), which have internal memory capabilities, are employed in numerous applications to address these problems and show promise [18]. In several time-series applications for prediction and classification, deep learning based on RNNs obtained great accuracy.

Three different RNN architectures are based on the recurrent units used to construct them. The primary and quick, simple recurrent units (SRUs) form the foundation of the initial RNN architecture [19]. The second RNN design is based on gated recurrent units (GRUs), which employ two gates to address gradient vanishing and accuracy instability [20]. Enterprise management is starting to place more and more emphasis on financial risk management. To reduce the risk of fierce market competition and encourage the achievement of maximum enterprise value economic goals, operators should improve their understanding, prediction, and control of financial risks; actively conduct financial analysis; prevent financial risks; and establish an early warning indicator analysis system appropriate for the business. In addition to raising risk awareness, an enterprise's long-term survival and growth depend on integrating risk assessment with performance assessment to create a single measuring system. The simulation of credit risk in corporate financial management is the subject of this research. It attempts to offer a fresh line of inquiry for an existing corporate financial management credit risk problem based on machine learning algorithms.

2.3 Proposed Model

This section discusses the proposed body sensor model based on secure data transmission with network monitoring using machine learning techniques. The proposed monitoring with data transmission model is shown in Figure 2.1.

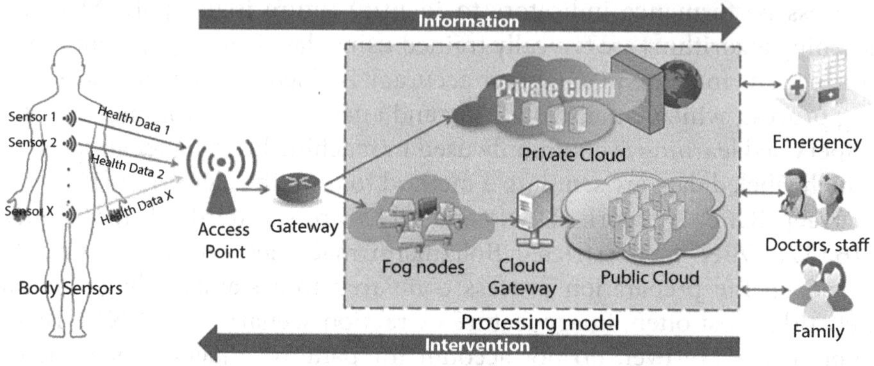

Figure 2.1 Proposed secure data transmission with network monitoring model.

A typical patient monitoring method deployment in a fog-cloud environment is shown in Figure 2.1. MIoT devices gather patient data and send it to a GW via an access point after being felt. The GW is primarily utilized for IoT devices and processing model communication. Following the first in, first out principle, the incoming requests for health data are accumulated in a buffer and delivered to the GW. The GW should decide how long the requests for health data continue. Two routes for health data traffic are proposed in the architecture: as (i) The GW can send some of sensed data to a private cloud, which is entirely separate as it does not sync with a public cloud. (ii) The public cloud can see the state and health information of the fog nodes, and the GW can transfer some of the sensed data to fog computing (FC) nodes that communicate with it. A public or private FC layer is possible. Local telecom service providers may offer FC nodes, or the public cloud may offer them through a point of presence. To further decrease the reaction time of the cloud datacenter, localized processing and storing are also carried out on the FC layer installed between MIoT devices and the cloud. Many physical machines (PMs) in public cloud datacenters are often virtualized to form a resource pool of virtual machines (VMs). VMs offer discrete running environments and share PM resources. Authorized users, including doctors, staff, emergency personnel, patients, hospitals, carers, and health ministries, have access to, and are given, the data obtained from both the private and public sectors. Any device, including a smartphone, a personal digital assistant, or a web browser, can access the recorded data.

Preprocessing of data: Using the tools at our disposal, we improve the effectiveness of data prediction in this stage of data preprocessing. These methods aid in enhancing the caliber of data preparation. Preprocessing data is necessary to make the data more accessible to users. Through this procedure, undesired data are transformed into fresh, adjusted datasets. If data are not entirely converted, they report problems in the first step or even findings that are not accurate, and the entire phase is then repeated. In some circumstances, algorithms may function well, but the outcome will not be as expected. The following are the steps to preprocess a dataset: 1. Superfluous data are removed, and relevant data are accurately stored. 2. Proper dataset layout is essential for formatting. 3. The entire process is repeated if the information does not match the user's expertise. 4. Undesirable information needs to be removed at this point. 5. Here, we may find the missing values and note them to keep them in mind for future use. 6. We will try to identify the user's transactions that were confusing by Equation 2.1.

$$\lambda = \sum_{i=1}^{X} \lambda_i \tag{2.1}$$

To simplify things, consider that incoming health data are handled in a first-come, first-served fashion at each component of the overall system. GW sends health data to Probability PC private cloud datacenter and Probability PCloud public cloud datacenter. The CG's load balancing capability distributes incoming health traffic among several VMs in a public cloud datacenter. Processing times at the GW and CG have mean rates of 1/GW and 1/CG, respectively, and are independent exponential random variables with the same distribution. Since almost infinite computing power is accessible in the cloud, we assume an M/M/C queue with an infinite waiting buffer for every fog computing node with the same service time FC. Each virtual machine instance can serve an amount of health data. An M/M/c/K queue describes every private cloud node in a private cloud datacenter. We can dynamically add and remove computer resources based on the services needed to scale up or down because incoming workloads of health data vary over time.

Network Monitoring Using Reinforcement Bayesian Regressive Vector Machine (RBRVM)

Reward functions play an essential role in traffic prediction. Additionally, relative incentives were computed for the various forms of network traffic. Using the network dataset, this reward calculation improves traffic prediction. Equation 2.2, as shown below, serves as an example of this QL process.

$$Q_L(s_i, a_i) = R_F\left(\max\left(Q(s_i + 1, a_i + 1\right) + R(s_i, a_i)\right) \quad (2.2)$$

Equation 2.3 is an expression for this QL.

$$Q(s_i, a_i) = (\Delta - 1)Q(s_i + 1, a_i + 1) + \Delta\left(R(s_i, a_i) + R_F\left(\max\left(Q(s_i + 1, a_i + 1\right)\right)\right) \quad (2.3)$$

The network traffic dataset is trained using Monte Carlo QL based on Equations 2.4.

$$X_t = Q_L\left(x_{low}, X_{high}\right) \quad (2.4)$$

To anticipate the value xi t and determine the associated prediction error xi t xi tp, where p indicates normalized Frobenius norm, for instance, Ap = 2 = [Tr(AA)]1/2. To determine the true value of data flow X produced by node i in the Bth data collection round, we define the value factor Fi B as follows by Equation 2.5:

$$F_B^i = \delta_t^i * \lambda_t^i$$

$$\text{s.t. } \delta_t^i = \frac{\sum_{t=j}^{j+m-1} \|x_t^i - \hat{x}_t^i\|_p}{m}$$

$$\lambda_t^i = \left\| \left(\sum_t o_t^i - k_{th}\right)^+ \right\|_p$$

$$o_t^i = \begin{cases} 1, & \|x_t^i - \hat{x}_t^i\|_p > \delta_t^i \\ 0, & \text{otherwise} \end{cases}$$

$$(\cdot)^{+} = \max(\cdot 0);$$

$$t \in \mathbf{T}_B, i \in \mathbf{V}, \forall x_t^i \in \mathbf{X}, j \in \mathbb{Z}^{+}, k_{\text{th}} \in \mathbb{Z}^{+}, p = 2 \quad (2.5)$$

As kth gets larger, the anti-interference capacity gets stronger. Historical forwarding records of data flow X during the Bth data collection cycle must be retrieved from the switch's flow table to analyze link status data and evaluate BWU after forecasting data flow X. In light of this, the real-time state component for RL is found as Equation 2.6.

$$\theta_B^i = \left\| \left(\frac{F_B^i}{e_B^{k_i}} \right) \right\|_p$$

$$\text{s.t. } e_B^{k_1} = \frac{N_B^{k_j}}{l_B^{k_i}}$$

$$l_B^{k_j} = \frac{1}{\left|O^{(n)}\right|} \sum_h l_B^{(i/h)}$$

$$\forall i \in \mathbf{V}, k_i = \langle i, h \rangle \in \mathbf{L}, h \in O^{(i)} \subset \mathbf{V}, t \in \mathbf{T}_B, e_B^{k_i} \in \mathbf{E}, p = 2 \quad (2.6)$$

L ki B denotes the average link bandwidth in the set i, h, where node h is a member of O(i), which stands for neighborhood of node i of size |O(i)|.

Let us identify parameter p that produce the fastest rate by Equation 2.7 to move the error into the $\left(\mathcal{O}(\varepsilon) + \frac{2no\rho^2}{\mu} \right)$ neighborhood of ideal value.

$$\mathbb{E}\left[\| x^k - x(\lambda) \|^2\right] \leq \varepsilon \| x^0 - x(\lambda) \|^2 + \frac{2na\sigma^2}{\mu} \tag{2.7}$$

The number of predicted communications and iterations needed to reach 10 are both decreased by the setting $p^* = \frac{\lambda}{L+\lambda}$. Mainly, the desired iteration count and anticipated communication count are $2\frac{L+\lambda}{\mu}\log\frac{1}{\varepsilon}$ and $\frac{2\lambda}{\lambda+L}\frac{L}{\mu}\log\frac{1}{\varepsilon}$ correspondingly. To make the output image almost equal to the original, we use relativistic average discriminator DRa. Objective processes by Equations 2.8–2.11 are as follows:

$$\mathcal{L}_{Ra\_D} = -\mathbb{E}_x\left[\log\left(D_{Ra}(x)\right)\right] - \mathbb{E}_{x,v,<}\left[\log\left(1 - D_{Ra}\left(G(x,v,c)\right)\right)\right] \tag{2.8}$$

$$\mathcal{L}_{Ra\_G} = -\mathrm{E}_{x,D,,}\left[\log\left(D_{Ra}\left(G(x,v,c)\right)\right)\right] - \mathrm{E}_x\left[\log\left(1 - D_{Ra}(x)\right)\right] \tag{2.9}$$

$$D_{Ra}(x) = \text{sigmoid}\left(H(x) - \mathbb{E}_{x,v,c}\left[H\left(G(x,v,c)\right)\right]\right) \tag{2.10}$$

$$D_{Ra}\left(G(x,v,c)\right) = \text{sigmoid}\left(H\left(G(x,v,c)\right) - \mathbb{E}_x\left[H(x)\right]\right) \tag{2.11}$$

The non-transformed layer's output is represented by the notation H(•). By reducing the loss of LRa G, the generated image tends to be more realistic than the original. We introduce a cycle consistency loss to the generator, as described in Equation 2.12:

$$\mathcal{L}_{cyc} = \mathbb{E}_{x,v,\epsilon}\left[\| x - G\left(G(x,v,c),v,1-c\right) \|_1\right] \tag{2.12}$$

Subsequently, the image's source is determined by incorporating the Dind auxiliary classifier into the discriminator network. The loss associated with the image translation technique is expressed in Equation 2.13:

$$\mathcal{L}_{\text{ind}} = -\mathbb{E}_{x,t}\left[\log\left(D_{\text{ind}}\left(t=01 \mid x\right)\right)\right] - \mathbb{E}_{x,v,t,t}\left[\log\left(D_{\text{ind}}\left(t=01 \mid G\left(x,v,c\right)\right)\right)\right] \tag{2.13}$$

The image generation method significantly affects the decoding network (c) because it is a shared network, and several samples utilized in image translation are substantially fewer than those utilized in image synthesis. We incorporate paired adversarial loss as shown in Equation 2.14 to ensure that the picture translation approach fits more precisely:

$$\mathcal{L}_{pis} = -\mathbb{E}_{x_{\alpha},x_{p}}\left[\log\left(D_{pis}\left(x_0,x_v\right)\right)\right] - \mathbb{E}_{x,v<}\left[\log\left(1-D_{pis}\left(x,G\left(x,v,c\right)\right)\right)\right] \tag{2.14}$$

where Dpis is employed to establish whether two images belong to same class. On top of discriminator network, we layer a second classifier named Dvar to separate the various changes in the photographs. The classification loss of the discriminator network during training is given by Equation 2.15:

$$\mathcal{L}^{r}_{\text{var}} = -\mathbb{E}_{x,v}\left[\log\left(D_{\text{var}}\left(v \mid x\right)\right)\right]. \tag{2.15}$$

Real picture x may be categorized into variant type v by the discriminator network by reducing the abovementioned formula. Classification loss is shown in Equation 2.16 during generator network training.

$$\mathcal{L}^{f}_{\text{var}} = -\mathbb{E}_{x,v,c}\left[\log\left(D_{\text{var}}\left(v \mid G\left(x_0,v,c=01\right)\right)\right)\right] - \mathbb{E}_{x,D}\left[\log\left(D_{\text{var}}\left(v_0 \mid G\left(x_v,v,c=10\right)\right)\right)\right] \tag{2.16}$$

The first item indicates that an image created by image x0 is correctly classified as belonging to domain v after variation v is added. The second item indicates that an image created by paired image xv should be similarly classified as belonging to domain v after variation v is removed. XM values range from 0 to 1. Equation 2.17 yields the following final output image:

$$x_{\text{out}} = x + (x_t - x) \odot x_{m}, \tag{2.17}$$

Element-wise product is located where $\odot$. For mask xm, add the following restriction from Equation 2.18:

$$\mathcal{L}_{\text{mask}} = \left(\frac{1}{W} \sum_k |x_m[k]| \right)^2 \tag{2.18}$$

The formula above encourages minimizing changes to the source image. In light of the explanation above, Equations 2.19 and 2.20 show that the picture translation paradigm is wholly ineffective:

$$\mathcal{L}_D = \mathcal{L}_{Ra\_D} + \lambda_{\text{pis}} \mathcal{L}_{\text{pis}} + \lambda_{\text{var}} \mathcal{L}_{\text{var}}^{r} + \lambda_{\text{ind}} \mathcal{L}_{\text{imt}} \tag{2.19}$$

$$\mathcal{L}_G = \mathcal{L}_{Ra\_G} - \lambda_{\text{pis}} \mathcal{L}_{\text{pis}} + \lambda_{\text{cyc}} \mathcal{L}_{\text{cyc}} + \lambda_{\text{mar}} \mathcal{L}_{\text{var}}^{f} + \lambda_{\text{ind}} \mathcal{L}_{\text{ind}} + \lambda_{\text{mask}} \mathcal{L}_{\text{mask}} \tag{2.20}$$

Network Monitor

Environmental factors that affect the reward function might be excluded making transitioning from a single-agent method to a multi-agent strategy with partial observability of the environment more challenging. This hampers the agents' capacity to link states to actions. The network state has a direct impact on a node's performance and reward in a network. Other nodes in a network, networks that are physically close by, or the propagation environment are included. All of these variables fundamentally impact the capacity of the base station to decode a packet. Any of these effects results in the packet having an insufficient signal-to-noise ratio for its time on air. Therefore, "noise" can describe the consequences of these influences. To assist the agent in completing its environmental observations, the network monitor measures this noise and provides it to the agent. This measure, which shows how busy the communication route is, is called "network utilization" by us. Indicators of received signal strength (RSSI) can be used to measure the signal directly at the base station. The base station's radio can assess the RSSI. It indicates the strength of the incoming signal at the RF input port. The network utilization metric is produced by applying a moving window filter to smooth the RSSI data. This procedure is described by Algorithm 2. The window for this implementation is 30 min because it runs every 30 s and has a 60-byte buffer.

Quantum Blockchain Automated Transfer Machine Graph Learning (QBATMGL)

The objective function that one desires to reduce is denoted by $f : \mathbb{R}^N \rightarrow \mathbb{R}$. One iteratively updates an initial point $t\mathbf{x}^{(0)} \in \mathbb{R}^N$ utilizing the objective function's steepest descent at the current point Equation 2.21.

$$\mathbf{x}^{(t+1)} = \mathbf{x}^{(t)} - \eta \nabla f\left(\mathbf{x}^{(t)}\right) \tag{2.21}$$

Second derivatives of objective function, or information about curvature, are considered at every step in Newton's technique, which extends this method. As a result, the objective function's Hessian matrix H is included in iterative given by Equation 2.22:

$$\mathbf{x}^{(t+1)} = \mathbf{x}^{(t)} - \eta \mathbf{H}^{-1} \nabla f\left(\mathbf{x}^{(t)}\right) \tag{2.22}$$

with $H_{ij} = \frac{\partial \dot{\partial}}{\partial z, \partial x_j}$ calculated at current point, $\mathbf{x}^{(t)}$.

Since a gradient's classical side data can spread anywhere in the network's structure, it is utilized in error derivation and gradient computation calculations. A unitary operator is created by applying L units in order as in Equation 2.23:

$$U\left(\vec{\theta}\right) = U_L\left(\theta_L\right) U_{L-1}\left(\theta_{L-1}\right) \ldots U_L\left(\theta_2\right) \tag{2.23}$$

$$\left|Y\right\rangle = U\left(\vec{\theta}\right) \left|\psi\right\rangle \left|\phi\right) = U\left(\vec{\theta}\right) \left|z\right\rangle \left|1\right\rangle = U\left(\vec{\theta}\right) \left| z, 1\right) \tag{2.24}$$

The data are encrypted, and the hashed value is kept on the tamper-evident ledger. Our debate was predicated on the concept that the output

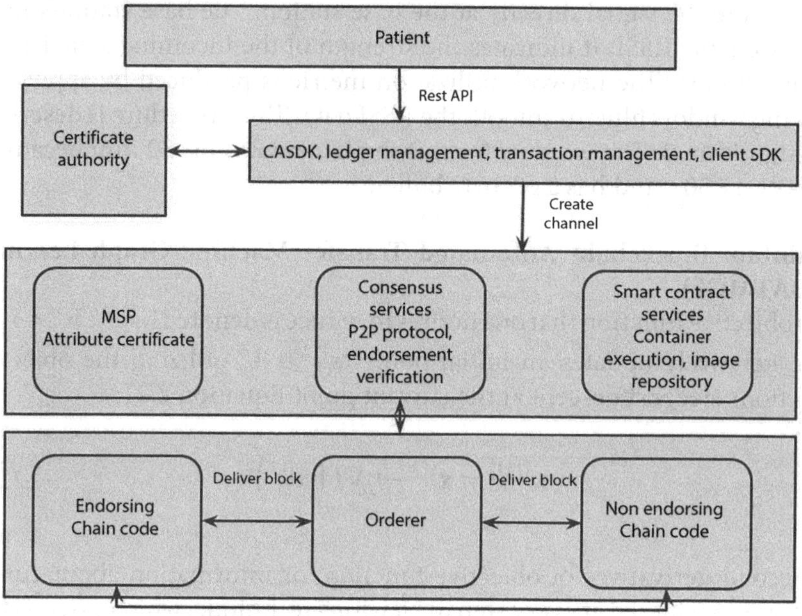

Figure 2.2 Architecture of blockchain.

would be a plain image that has been encrypted, which is what it would be in an ideal world. We can divide the result by 16 if we additionally suppose that the original image was m × n pixels in size. Our empirical research shows that treating each pixel as a random variable can effectively create an auxiliary image with a size of 256 × 256 pixels. Blockchain architecture is shown in Figure 2.2.

An image is turned into a series of bytes during the image encryption process so that its original shape cannot be accessed. It is a practical method for safeguarding digital image data. The encryption procedure is carried out via several cryptographic techniques. After being sent to another system, ciphered bytes can be adjusted to revert to their original values via decryption. We employ methods based on some key for the encryption and decryption procedures by Equation 2.25.

$$E_{key}(X) = Y$$

$$D_{key}(Y) = X \tag{2.25}$$

Equations 2.25 and 2.26 describe how to encrypt plain text and how to decrypt it. Ekey(X) represents the encryption function applied to picture X, and image Y is the outcome. To get the original image X from the encrypted image, we use the Dkey(Y) function.

The encryption phase for the cover image consists of two steps. First, the cover image is separated into three 3 × 3 pieces that are non-overlapping. The blocks are then all reordered utilizing random sequence created by Key-I, which has a length equal to the total number of blocks in the image. Following block permutation, Key-II is used to create a secret stream. Then, every block of a picture is encrypted using Equation 2.26:

$$C = E\left(P, K\right) = K \oplus P \tag{2.26}$$

Encryption function E() is an Exclusive-OR operation marked by "⊕." Each block contains a unique 8-bit code segment, sequentially encrypted for every block. Since each block's pixels are encrypted utilizing the same code segment, correlation between them is maintained. To categorize each network connection as malicious or innocent, we treat the detection of network attacks as a binary classification issue. Since network attacks have many common characteristics, our method entails locating the common latent subspace, transforming source and target data onto it, and producing new feature representations for classification purposes.

An optimal projection of source data S and target data T onto an ideal subspace VS and VT is evaluated using the following optimization objective by Equation 2.27:

$$\min_{\mathbf{V_S}.\mathbf{V_T}} \ell\left(\mathbf{V_S}, \mathbf{S}\right) + \ell\left(\mathbf{V_T}, \mathbf{T}\right) + \beta D\left(\mathbf{V_S}, \mathbf{V_T}\right) \tag{2.27}$$

where (,) is a distortion function that calculates how much the projected data differ from the original data. The difference between projected data of source and the target domains is shown by the symbol D(VS, VT).

The term "source domain" refers to a traffic road network with extensive historical data. This is how transfer learning operates: (1) During the pre-training phase, it is intended to learn a function f that can forecast the traffic conditions for all nodes on graph G for the upcoming H time steps given a set of S past traffic data. The mapping relation is shown in the following way by Equation 2.28:

$$[\mathcal{X},\mathcal{G}]\xrightarrow{f}\hat{\mathbf{X}}^{(t+1):(t+H)} \tag{2.28}$$

where $\mathcal{X}=\left[\mathbf{X}^{(t-S+1)},\mathbf{X}^{(t-S+2)},\ldots,\mathbf{X}^{(t)}\right]\in\mathbb{R}^{N\times S\times C}\mathbf{X}^{(t)}=\left[\mathbf{x}_1^t,\mathbf{x}_2^{t^*},\ldots,\mathbf{x}_N^t\right]\in\mathbb{R}^{N\times C}$ denotes the traffic condition at time step t, C is several features of every node, and X̂ (t + 1):(t + H) ∈ R N × H × C is the prediction value. Using only a small amount of data in the target domain, the pre-trained function f is further optimized in step 2 to anticipate the traffic situation for all nodes on graph G 0 in the following H time steps. This method is described as Equation 2.29:

$$[\mathcal{X}',\mathcal{G}']\xrightarrow{f}\hat{\mathbf{X}}^{\hat{r}(t+1):(t+H)} \tag{2.29}$$

where $\hat{\mathbf{X}}^{(t+1):(t+H)\square\mathrm{L}}\in\mathbb{R}^{N'\times H\times C}$ and $\mathcal{X}=\mathbf{X}^{(t-S+1)\cdot(t)}\in\mathbb{R}^{N\times S\dot{\times}C}$ are the prediction results in the target domain. Graph convolution networks (GCNs) are commonly utilized in traffic prediction to extract spatial correlation. In more detail, we may acquire the output representation $\mathcal{Z}=\mathbf{Z}^{(t-S+1):(t)}\in\mathbb{R}^{N\times S\times F}$ given the input signal $\left[\mathbf{X}^{'(t-S+1)},\ldots,\mathbf{X}^{'(t)}\right]\in\mathbb{R}^{N'\times S\times C}$, and the adjacency matrix $\mathbf{A}\in\mathbb{R}^{N\times N}$. The procedure is stated as follows by Equation 2.30:

$$\mathbf{Z}=\left(\mathbf{I}_N+\mathbf{D}^{-\frac{1}{2}}\mathbf{A}\mathbf{D}^{-\frac{1}{2}}\right)\mathbf{X}\mathbf{W}+\mathbf{b} \tag{2.30}$$

2.4 Results and Discussion

The JMT Simulator is used in the simulation to assess the performance of the suggested healthcare system. It is set up on a device with an Intel Core i5 CPU running at 2.40 GHz, 4 GB of memory, and a 250-GB hard drive. Simulation is repeated 10 times with identical settings, and the average result is considered to demonstrate how well our suggested model performs. We assume that the system receives 1,000–10,000 queries for health data every second on average. Each health data request's processing times in the GW node have an exponential distribution with a mean of 1/μGW = 0.0001 s.

There are two alternative routes for aggregate workloads as follows: (i) GW to private cloud, probability PC = 0.4, and (ii) GW to fog layer, probability PCloud = 0.6. At FC nodes, the average service time is 1/μFC = 0.01 s. With probability p = 0.6, health data are sent to the cloud gateway for additional processing in the public cloud datacenter. The service time at every public VM node is 1/μ = 0.00015, while the mean service time for the cloud gateway server is 1/μCG = 0.0001. Consider a case of a small private cloud datacenter with R = 10 private nodes. Consider that simulation occurs in a public cloud datacenter with M = 20 public nodes and C = 4 VMs on every public node. Additionally, we assume that each fog node can hold a maximum of B = 150 health data and that the fog computing layer consists of N = 20 FC nodes. Some specifications are changed during the simulation based on simulated scenarios, while others are fixed.

Dataset Description: Our study employed the MHEALTH DATASET-A mobile health (MHEALTH) benchmarked dataset. It was gathered from 10 subjects utilizing records of body movements and vital signs made by wearing SHIMMER2 sensors. Each patient had these sensors on their chest, left ankle, and right wrist using elastic bands. Mobile health systems capture body dynamics and assess diversity brought about by motion of body components, such as acceleration and orientation of magnetic fields, by utilizing a variety of sensors. The chest-mounted sensors provide two lead ECG measurements. This multimodal body-sensing dataset can monitor the heart, check for arrhythmias, or examine how exercise affects the ECG. This dataset's sampling rate, 50 Hz, was adequate for capturing the simulated human actions. All performed sessions were videotaped to categorize data and check for signal anomalies.

The Human Activities and Postural Transitions (HAPT) Dataset, collected using smartphones: The information is updated in the UCI Human Activity Recognition Using Popularity Data collection. There are 12 different kinds of action in the HAPT data collection. First, it has six fundamental motions, including three static and three walking motions. It offers six possible transitions from two static movements: standing to sitting, sitting to standing, lying to sitting, and lying to standing. Thirty volunteers, aged 19 to 48 years, participated in the study, while each wore a smartphone around their waist. The built-in gyroscope and acceleration sensor collect data, and the sampling frequency is 50 Hz. Video recordings of the experimental process are made to ease later data marking.

Table 2.1 Various body sensor dataset-based comparisons for proposed and existing techniques.

Datasets	Techniques	Throughput	Scalability	Data integrity	Packet delivery ratio
MHEALTH DATASET	CNN	85	81	82	89
	DBN	88	85	84	91
	RNN	94	88	91	94
	QBATMGL_RBRVM	98	92	94	96
HAPT	CNN	88	79	81	86
	DBN	91	81	85	88
	RNN	95	85	89	91
	QBATMGL_RBRVM	97	90	91	94

Table 2.1 is shown for comparative analysis based on various body sensor datasets. The analyzed datasets are MHEALTH DATASET and HAPT regarding throughput, scalability, data integrity, and packet delivery ratio.

Figure 2.3(a)–(d) shows the comparison for MHEALTH DATASET. Here, the proposed technique attained a throughput of 98%, scalability of 92%, data integrity of 94%, and PDR of 96%. The existing CNN attained a throughput of 85%, scalability of 81%, data integrity of 82%, and PDR of 89%. The DBN attained a throughput of 88%, scalability of 85%, data integrity of 84%, and PDR of 91%. The RNN attained a throughput of 94%, scalability of 88%, data integrity of 91%, and PDR of 94%.

Figure 2.4(a)–(d) shows the analysis for HAPT dataset. The proposed technique attained a throughput of 97%, scalability of 90%, data integrity of 91%, and PDR of 94%. The existing CNN attained a throughput of 88%, scalability of 79%, data integrity of 81%, and PDR of 86%. The DBN attained a throughput of 91%, scalability of 81%, data integrity of 85%, and PDR of 88%. The RNN attained a throughput of 95%, scalability of 85%, data integrity of 89%, and PDR of 91%.

This experiment assesses the proposed transfer learning methods for identifying novel assault variants. It is challenging to provoke fresh attacks. Attacks on target data differ from attacks on the source domain since they do not have labels. We randomly chose the source domain and picked malicious instances from one primary attack category. Then, we selected a distinct attack type and typical samples for the target domain. Three groups were ultimately created as follows: DoSProbe, DoSR2L, and ProbeR2L. We also selected assaults from 22 sub-attack types for every source and target group and created 11 tasks to assess generalization. Procedures were repeated 10 times, and averages and standard deviations were reported.

Unless otherwise noted, we balance attack and regular data in every domain. In this scenario, the workload for body sensors is homogeneous and uniformly distributed. Every sensor makes 500 requests per second (i = 1,..., 200). We can see that as the number of body sensors improves, the mean system reaction time also rises. When this number exceeds 120 devices, the specified SLA latency is violated. It is required to increase computational resources (cloud and fog) to efficiently process health data from MIoT devices to prevent this SLA breach. Different bodily sensors attached to the patient create an evenly dispersed workload for our task. To create

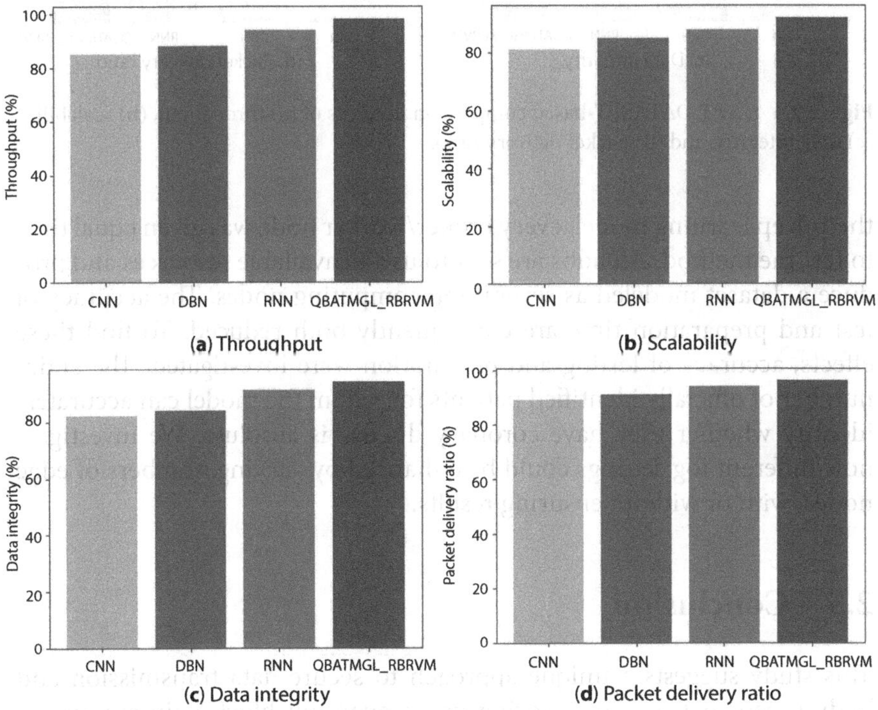

Figure 2.3 MHEALTH DATASET-based comparison in terms of (a) throughput, (b) scalability, (c) data integrity, and (d) packet delivery ratio.

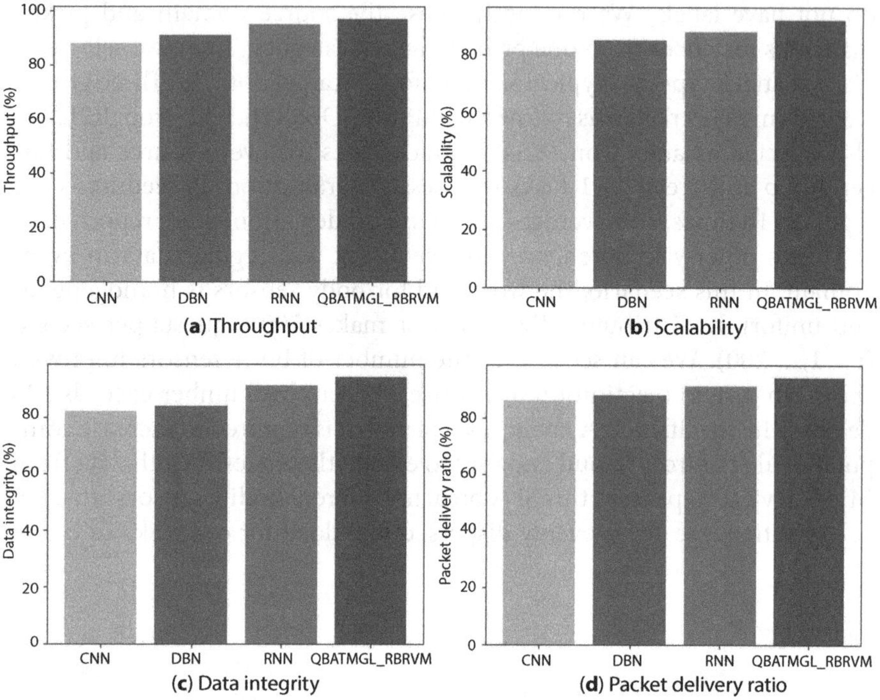

Figure 2.4 HAPT DATASET-based comparison in terms of (a) throughput, (b) scalability, (c) data integrity, and (d) packet delivery ratio.

their deep learning model, every broker/worker node was given equal time to test the method. All hubs are sent to use all available resources and produce a dataset modeled as several fog computing nodes. The accuracy of test and preparation time are consequently both reduced. To find these effects, accuracy of testing and preparation were investigated. The entire number of officially identified patients for whom the model can accurately identify whether they have coronary disease is absolute. We investigate how different fog settings could be enhanced by varying numbers of edge nodes, with or without ensuring results.

2.5 Conclusion

This study suggests a unique approach to secure data transmission and body sensor network monitoring using quantum blockchain automated transfer machine graph learning and reinforcement Bayesian regression vector machines. To achieve QoS and SLA response times for e-Health services, we used a method to demonstrate how we might limit cloud and fog computing resources. We created numerous formulae and equations that enable us to instantaneously predict the entire system response time by treating private and public clouds as a queuing network. Furthermore, we demonstrated how our suggested approach can identify the appropriate computing resources needed to fulfill the target SLA system response time for any particular MIoT workload. To achieve QoS and SLA response times for e-Health services, we used a method to demonstrate how we might limit cloud and fog computing resources.

Furthermore, we demonstrated how our suggested approach can identify the appropriate computing resources needed to fulfil target SLA system response time for any particular MIoT workload. The method preparation model eventually uses a separate preparation on each system worker node. Various aggregated models of stowing are used to condense methods created at every node. To enhance precision, various curiosity techniques are articulated. The proposed architecture is designed to be robust and inclusive, facilitating fog computing applications in areas like agricultural smart production lines, weather prediction, smart city projections, and industrial traffic management.

References

1. Stone, D., Michalkova, L., Machova, V., Machine and deep learning techniques, body sensor networks, and Internet of Things-based smart healthcare systems in COVID-19 remote patient monitoring. *Am. J. Med. Res.*, 9, 1, 97–112, 2022.
2. Jaber, A.S. and Idrees, A.K., Wireless body sensor networks: applications, challenges, patient monitoring, Decision making, and machine learning in medical applications, in: *AI and IoT for Sustainable Development in Emerging Countries: Challenges and Opportunities*, pp. 417–437, Springer International Publishing, Cham, 2022.
3. Balakrishnan, S., *et al.*, IoT for health monitoring system based on machine learning algorithm. *Wirel. Pers. Commun.*, 1–17, 2022.
4. Visvesvaran, C., *et al.*, Advanced Patient Monitoring and Alert System with Auto Medicine Suggestion using Machine Learning. *2022 3rd International Conference on Electronics and Sustainable Communication Systems (ICESC)*, IEEE, 2022.
5. Suresh, S. and Chakaravarthi, G., RFID technology and its diverse applications: A brief exposition with a proposed Machine Learning approach. *Measurement*, 195, 111197, 2022.

6. Devi, V.S.A., Raj, V.H., Kavin, B.P., Gangadevi, E., Balusamy, B., Gite, S., An Atom Quest Optimizer for CNN to Distinguish IDs in SDN and IoT Eco System. *2024 IEEE International Conference on Computing, Power and Communication Technologies (IC2PCT)*, Greater Noida, India, pp. 1430–1437, 2024, doi: 10.1109/IC2PCT60090.2024.10486516.
7. Ogundokun, R.O., *et al.*, Hybrid inceptionv3-svm-based approach for human posture detection in health monitoring systems. *Algorithms*, 15, 11, 410, 2022.
8. Verma, P., *et al.*, FETCH: a deep learning-based fog computing and IoT integrated environment for healthcare monitoring and diagnosis. *IEEE Access*, 10, 12548–125635, 2022.
9. Manimuthu, A., Peter Jose, P., Gangadevi, E., Kumar, U.U., Anandaraj, M.D., Prediction of Alzheimer'S Disease from Magnetic Resonance Images (MRI). *2024 IEEE International Conference on Computing, Power and Communication Technologies (IC2PCT)*, Greater Noida, India, pp. 631–635, 2024, doi: 10.1109/IC2PCT60090.2024.10486545.
10. Rajeswari, S.V.K.R. and Vijayakumar, P., Survey on IoMT: Amalgamation of Technologies-Wearable Body Sensor Network, Wearable Biosensors, ML and DL in IoMT. *International Conference on Intelligent Vision and Computing*, Springer Nature Switzerland, Cham, 2022.
11. Ahmed, I., *et al.*, Internet of health things driven deep learning-based system for non-invasive patient discomfort detection using time frame rules and pairwise keypoints distance feature. *Sustain. Cities Soc.*, 79, 1036725, 2022.
12. Cuţitoi, A.-C., Remote Patient Monitoring Systems, Wearable Internet of Medical Things Sensor Devices, and Deep Learning-based Computer Vision Algorithms in COVID-19 Screening, Detection, Diagnosis, and Treatment. *Am. J. Med. Res.*, 9, 1, 129–144, 2022.
13. Islam, Md.R., *et al.*, Deep Learning-Based IoT System for Remote Monitoring and Early Detection of Health Issues in Real-Time. *Sensors*, 23, 11, 5204, 2023.
14. Jayawickrema, U.M.N., *et al.*, Fibre-optic sensor and deep learning-based structural health monitoring systems for civil structures: A review. *Measurement*, 199, 1115435, 2022.
15. Aryai, P., *et al.*, Real-time health monitoring in WBANs using hybrid Metaheuristic-Driven Machine Learning Routing Protocol (MDML-RP). *AEU Int. J. Electron. Commun.*, 168, 1547235, 2023.
16. Nandini, K., *et al.*, Automated Machine Learning-Based Gestational Monitoring Framework in Wearable Internet of Things Environment. *Proceedings of Second International Conference in Mechanical and Energy Technology: ICMET 2021, India*, Springer Nature Singapore, Singapore, 2022.
17. Ao, S.-I., *et al.*, Advances in Machine Learning for Sensing and Condition Monitoring. *Appl. Sci.*, 12, 23, 12392, 2022.
18. Gupta, P., *et al.*, Prediction of health monitoring with deep learning using edge computing. *Meas.: Sens.*, 25, 1006045, 2023.

19. Sujigarasharma, K., Sharulatha, S., Lawanya Shri, M., Gangadevi, E., Dhanaraj, R.K., Optimizing 3D Bioprinting Using Advanced Deep Learning Techniques A Comparative Study of CNN, RNN, and GAN, in: *Computational Intelligence in Bioprinting*, pp. 157–173, Wiley, 2024, https://doi.org/10.1002/9781394204878.ch8.
20. Basak, S. and Chatterjee, K., Smart Healthcare Surveillance System Using IoT and Machine Learning Approaches for Heart Disease. *International Conference on Advancements in Smart Computing and Information Security*, Springer Nature Switzerland, Cham, 2022.

3

Automated Machine Learning in the Biological and Medical Healthcare Industries: Analysis Interpretation and Evaluation

Iram Fatima[1]*, Naved Ahmed[2], Mehtab Alam[3], Ihtiram Raza Khan[4] and Veena Grover[5]

[1]*School of Computer Applications, MRIIRS, Faridabad, India*
[2]*School of Computer Science and Engineering, IILM University, Gurugram, India*
[3]*Acharye Narendra Dev College, University of Delhi, Delhi, India*
[4]*Department of CSE, Jamia Hamdard, New Delhi, India*
[5]*School of Management, NIET, Noida, Uttar Pradesh, India*

Abstract
The current study investigates the profound effect of Automated Machine Learning (AutoML) in study and rehabilitative sectors, with an emphasis on analysis, interpretation, and assessment. The work gives context for applying machine learning to enhance medical care and highlights the utility of AutoML in biological products and medical settings. Machine learning applications offer valuable tools for monitoring and evaluating the efficacy of treatments in healthcare. These applications can aid in diagnosis, prognosis, and the development of optimal treatment plans for identified diseases. Nevertheless, we must also consider the limitations, challenges, and opportunities presented by machine learning technology in the healthcare domain. A significant challenge in machine learning is compiling a dataset that is both high-quality and representative of the diverse range of potential inputs. Ideally, the model should be trained on data that precisely mirrors the format and quality of what will be encountered in real-world usage. This paper discusses the principles of AutoML, including various components, effectiveness, and benefits and downsides of adoption.

**Corresponding author*: irammalik917@gmail.com

E. Gangadevi, M. Lawanya Shri, Balamurugan Balusamy and Rajesh Kumar Dhanaraj (eds.) Automated Machine Learning and Industrial Applications, (41–62) © 2025 Scrivener Publishing LLC

Keywords: Machine learning, automated machine learning, healthcare

3.1 Introduction

Machine learning is transforming the medical field through examining massive volumes of facts, retrieving information, and optimizing decisions. Machine learning has improved medical operations by allowing for better diagnosis, customized treatment plans, and better patient outcomes [1, 2]. As healthcare statistics expands quickly, from electronic medical records to radiological records and genomes, advanced statistical techniques are becoming increasingly crucial. Utilizing machine learning for healthcare purposes have proven effective in areas like disease prediction, image categorization, and drug development [3].

3.1.1 Rise of AutoML

The advancement of artificial intelligence has led to the rise of AutoML resulting in an evolution in how algorithms are developed and deployed. AutoML accelerates the technique of machine learning by automating critical operations like data preprocessing, feature engineering, model selection, and hyperparameter tuning [4].

The rise of AutoML can be attributed to the democratic transformation of machine learning expertise that has rendered it accessible to specialists working in the area and professionals with limited programming and data science experience. Automation of difficult tasks reduces the barrier toward entry allowing for the speedy development and execution of ML models within healthcare contexts [4].

3.1.2 Significance of AutoML in Biological and Medical Healthcare

Automated Machine Learning is incredibly significant in the realm of life sciences and medicine, giving various vital rewards as follows [5–7]:

- AutoML streamlines model construction enabling healthcare professionals to focus on domain-specific challenges rather than technical issues. The computerized pipeline accelerates the process enabling speedier implementation of models for disease forecasting, pharmaceutical implementation, and therapeutic improvement.

- AutoML enables healthcare specialists, clinicians, and study participants to apply machine learning without prior programming or data science experience. This transparency stimulates collaboration across statisticians and subject experts resulting in a multidimensional approach to tackling medical issues [8].
- Addressing Data Complications: Medical documentation can be extensive containing radiology, clinical records, and genealogical data. AutoML algorithms were created to cope with this level of constraints by automatically adapting to varied data types and designs, which makes them suited for the complicated nature that comprise biological and medical data.

3.2 Methodology for Effective Data Management

To address these problems and assure effective AutoML deployment, a strong approach is needed. It involves the following, which is illustrated in Figure 3.1.

- **Data Preprocessing [10] and Standardization [11]:**
    - **Cleaning and Imputation:** Use suitable techniques for tackling data gaps (such as mean/median imputation and predictive modeling). Identify and address anomalies to maintain the integrity of the data.

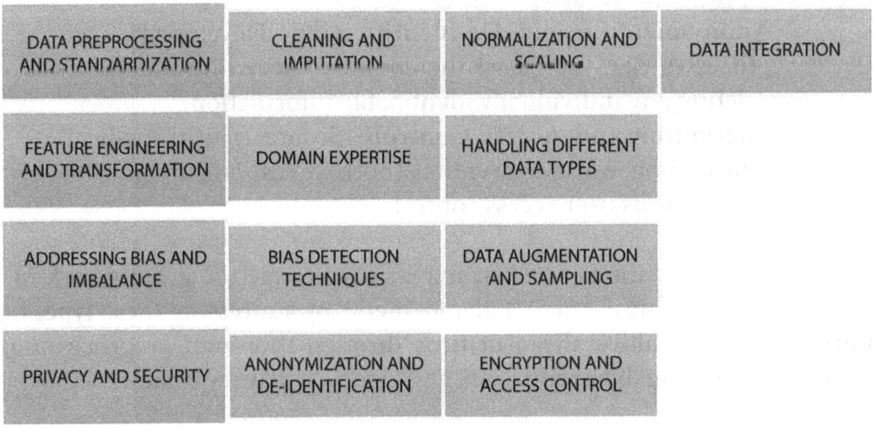

Figure 3.1 Effective data management methodology.

- **Normalization and Scaling:** Normalizing computational characteristics to a similar scale and structure improves model convergence and stability.
- **Data Integration:** Establish encrypted information integration mechanisms that integrate information drawn from EHRs, laboratory systems, and image archives into a single dataset for interpretation.

- **Feature Engineering [12] and Transformation [13]:**

Feature engineering is a process of creating new features or variables based on the already existing data in the data set. Transformation is a process of modifying or converting input features in a dataset to improve the performance of an ML model.

- **Domain Expertise:** Interact with physicians to derive useful features from the raw information improving model interpretation and validity.
- **Handling Different Data Types:** Use specialized approaches for various data types (e.g., image normalization and conversion for medical snaps, etc.).

- **Addressing Bias and Imbalance [14, 15]:**
    - **Bias Detection Techniques:** Use statistical approaches and justice metrics to detect possible exaggerations in training data.
    - **Data Augmentation and Sampling:** Use oversampling, under sampling, or synthesized data production to produce more evenly distributed datasets and reduce the effect on current prejudices.
- **Privacy [16], and Security [17]:**
    - **Anonymization and De-identification:** Developed strict processes that safeguard the confidentiality of patients by deleting any individually identifiable information.
    - **Encryption and Access Controls:** Secure critical medical information using encryption (both at rest and in transit) and rigorous user access controls.

Medical organizations and researchers may create the groundwork for prosperous and ethical AutoML deployments by addressing these types of information difficulties ahead of time through thorough preprocessing, feature engineering, bias reduction, and rigorous privacy policies.

3.3 Foundations of Automated Machine Learning

In the preceding section, we will cover the basic principles of Automated Machine Learning models.

3.3.1 Understanding Automated Machine Learning

Automated Machine Learning (AutoML) is a groundbreaking technology that streamlines and make simpler the entire process of developing machine learning technologies. At its core, AutoML aims to democratize the application of machine learning techniques making them accessible to a broader audience, including domain experts and individuals with limited data science expertise [1]. AutoML encompasses a series of algorithms, tools, and processes that work in synergy to automate the following key stages of machine learning model development.

3.3.2 Components and Workflow

In this section, we will discuss the components and workflow of AutoML.

- **Data Preprocessing: Unleashing the Power of Clean and Contextual Data**
Data preprocessing stands as the foundational step in any machine learning endeavor. In the broader context of AutoML, this phase dynamically handles missing values, normalizes data, and addresses anomalies. AutoML technologies use complex algorithms to make sure the provided data are clean, contextualized, and prepared for the next step of model creation.

- **Feature Engineering: Crafting Informative Features for Optimal Model Performance**
Feature engineering is crucial in constructing algorithms that can extract useful insights from data. AutoML technologies analyze and retrieve relevant attributes without the need for human involvement. These methods employ strong algorithms to locate and convert unorganized data into relevant features, hence boosting the model's ability to provide precise forecasts.

- **Model Selection: Navigating the Model Zoo with Intelligence**
AutoML improves in automating model selection through contrasting a wide range of approaches and architectures. It automatically handles the enormous "model zoo," finding the optimal model for any given assignment. This constantly evolving technique ensures that the proposed model matches the intricacies of the medical information optimizing effectiveness and generalizability.

- **Hyperparameter Tuning: Fine-Tuning for Peak Performance**

Hyperparameters provide significant impact on the performance of artificial intelligence algorithms. AutoML technologies continually explore the hyperparameter space, tweaking machine settings to achieve optimal results. This automation frees professionals from the time-consuming chore of manually altering hyperparameters enabling them to concentrate on the clinical significance and analysis of outcomes.

3.3.3 Pros of AutoML Implementation

Below, we have listed some of the advantages of AutoML [18]:

- **Efficiency and Time Savings:** Accelerates the model development lifecycle reducing the time and effort required for implementation. Enables rapid deployment of machine learning solutions in healthcare settings addressing time-sensitive issues.
- **Accessibility:** Democratizes machine learning expertise making it accessible to healthcare professionals without extensive programming knowledge. Fosters collaboration between domain experts and data scientists promoting interdisciplinary approaches to healthcare challenges.
- **Enhanced Model Performance:** Optimizes model hyperparameters and features iteratively leading to improved accuracy and generalization. Contributes to the development of robust models capable of handling the complexities of biological and medical datasets.
- **Adaptability to Diverse Data Types:** Automatically handles the heterogeneity of healthcare data accommodating various modalities such as medical images, clinical notes, and genomic information.

3.3.4 Cons of AutoML Implementation

Below, we have listed some of the disadvantages of AutoML [19]:

- **Lack of Interpretability:**

AutoML models can be perceived as "black boxes" making it challenging to interpret and explain the decision-making process, which is crucial in healthcare.

- **Overemphasis on Performance:**
Automated processes may prioritize model performance over interpretability and clinical relevance potentially leading to the deployment of less explainable models.

- **Data Quality Dependency:**
AutoML's success heavily relies on the quality and representativeness of the input data. In cases of biased or incomplete datasets, AutoML outcomes may be suboptimal.

- **Limited Customization:**
AutoML tools may have constraints in accommodating highly specialized requirements or specific nuances of certain healthcare applications.

The implementation of AutoML in healthcare comes with notable advantages, including efficiency, accessibility, enhanced model performance, and adaptability to diverse data types. However, issues like interpretability and customization must be rigorously resolved to enable appropriate and successful incorporation into healthcare procedures. The following portions will go over applications and instances giving light on how these fundamental elements appear in practical healthcare contexts.

3.4 Applications in Healthcare

In this portion, we have mentioned the applications of AutoML in medical domain as depicted in Figure 3.2.

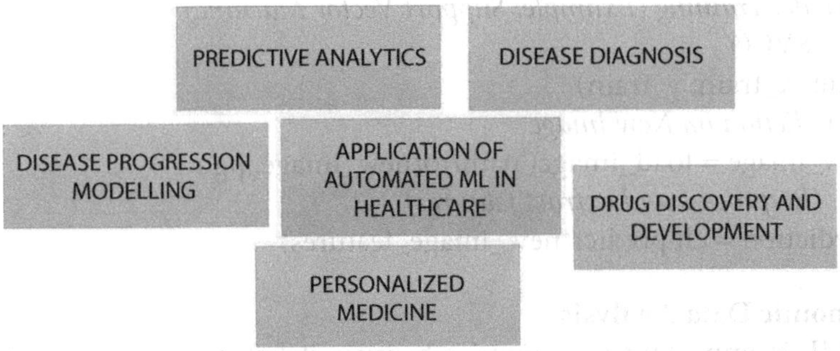

Figure 3.2 Application of AutoML in healthcare.

3.4.1 Disease Diagnosis

- **Image Recognition and Classification**

Automated Machine Learning (AutoML) has revolutionized illness detection, especially in radiology. Image recognition and categorization using AutoML algorithms have shown remarkable precision in detecting anomalies and identifying trends in radiological images that include magnetic resonance imaging and computed tomography scans. This transformational power not only accelerates the diagnostic procedure but also helps healthcare practitioners make more precise and rapid judgments [20].

Furthermore, AutoML's picture categorization extends to pathology slides helping pathologists detect and categorize tissue specimens. This not only saves the stress on healthcare personnel but also adds to the early discovery of diseases, thus enhancing the results for patients [21].

```
import cv2 # Or relevant image processing library (e.g., PIL)
from scrimmage.feature import hog
from sklearn.svm import SVC
from sklearn.model_selection import train_test_split

# Image Loading and Preprocessing
images = load_images_from_directory('path/to/images')
hog_features = []
labels = []
# ... (Extract HOG features or use a suitable deep learning model)
# Train Test Split
X_train, X_test, y_train, y_test = train_test_split(hog_features, labels)

# Model Training (Example: Support Vector Machine)
clf = SVC()
clf.fit(X_train, y_train)
# Prediction on New Image
new_image = load_image('path/to/new_image.jpg')
# ... (Preprocess and extract features)
prediction = clf.predict(new_image_features)
```

- **Genomic Data Analysis**

AutoML is important in genomics because it helps decode complicated genetic data. Genomic data evaluation is the process of discovering anomalies and variations in the human genome that could suggest genetic abnormalities or disease susceptibility. AutoML algorithms thrive at managing large and complex facts obtained from genomic sequencing technologies [22].

AutoML helps with the automatic recognition of key genetic markers resulting in more accurate diagnostics and personalized approaches to therapy. By automating genetic data processing, healthcare workers can identify underlying patterns and relationships advancing precision medicine [23].

3.4.2 Drug Discovery and Development

AutoML has been recognized as a significant tool in the realm of pharmaceutical discovery and development helping to identify prospective therapeutic concepts. By automated study of chemical structures, biological assays, and high-throughput screening data, AutoML speeds up the procedure of finding molecules with therapeutic potential.

AutoML's capacity to analyze and forecast drug–target interactions makes it easier to prioritize promising therapeutic candidates saving both time and money in preclinical development. This not only improves the pharmaceutical discovery pipeline but also supports the creation of novel and specific therapies [24].

3.4.3 Personalized Medicine

Personalized medicine strives to tailor treatments to unique traits of patients, and AutoML plays a critical part in accomplishing this objective. AutoML algorithms may find patterns in various patient data, such as clinical documentation, genetic data, as well as living characteristics, to drive the development of personalized therapies [23].

AutoML supports the building of predictive algorithms that take into account each patient's specific characteristics resulting in enhanced outcomes and tailored therapies. This method improves therapy results and minimizes the chance of unwanted effects indicating a paradigm shift toward patient-centered healthcare [24].

3.4.4 Predictive Analytics in Healthcare

- **Patient Outcome Prediction**

AutoML makes a substantial contribution to predictive analytics in healthcare by creating models that estimate the results for patients. These simulations foresee issues, being hospitalized, and consequences based on previously collected patient data. Healthcare practitioners can use this information to design preemptive actions, improve resource implementation, and improve the overall treatment of patients.

AutoML's proactive model selection and hyperparameter tuning enhance its accuracy of outcome predictions enabling healthcare professionals to render informed choices and allocate resources proactively.

```
import pandas as pd
from sklearn.model_selection import train_test_split
from sklearn.ensemble import RandomForestClassifier
from tpot import TPOTClassifier

# Hypothetical Dataset (Replace with your actual data)
data = pd.read_csv('patient_data.csv')
# Features and Outcome
X = data[['age', 'gender', 'diagnosis', 'comorbidities', ...]]
y = data['treatment_response'] # Or 'risk_category'
# Data Splitting
X_train, X_test, y_train, y_test = train_test_split(X, y, test_size=0.2)
# Automated Model Selection and Training (Example using TPOT)
tpot=TPOTClassifier(generations=5,population_size=50,verbosity=2)
tpot.fit(X_train, y_train)
# Predictions on New Patient Data
new_patient_data = [[45, 'F', 'diabetes', 'hypertension', ...]]
prediction = tpot.predict(new_patient_data)
print(prediction)
```

- **Disease Progression Modeling**

Simulation of disease progression is one of AutoML's abilities as it offers information about how diseases evolve over a period of time. AutoML may build prototypes that anticipate the progression of recurring maladies, such as diabetes, cardiovascular issues, and neurological abnormalities, by examining long-term clinical information such as medical records and biomarker tests [25]. Disease progression prediction with AutoML improves treatments and patient outcomes [26].

3.5 Case Studies and Success Stories

Here are some case studies discussed in the following section.

3.5.1 Noteworthy Implementations

- **Healthcare Imaging Diagnosis with AutoML**

Radiological diagnosis is a key use of AutoML in the field of healthcare. A prestigious healthcare institute successfully computerized radiography with AutoML methods. The method was highly accurate in detecting and identifying outliers in MRI and CT scan [27].

AutoML's radiological identification abilities accelerated the diagnosis process while significantly lowering radiologists' workload. This software exhibits AutoML's potential to improve the efficacy and accuracy of diagnostic imaging evaluations paving the way for enhanced results for patients.

- **Genomic Medicine Advancements**

Within the field of genomics, a group of researchers employed AutoML to explore vast genomic libraries for genetic markers connected to specific illnesses. AutoML algorithms autonomously assessed and appraised complex genomic data revealing novel insights on genetic susceptibility and disease incidence [22].

This implementation revealed AutoML's ability to manage the intricacies of genomic data hastening the advancement of genomic medicine research. The computerized comprehensive biological information largely aided tailored treatment, but it also fostered a deeper understanding of the genetic basis of various illnesses.

3.5.2 Impact on Patient Outcomes

- **Early Detection and Improved Treatment Plans**

AutoML's use in sickness evaluation, particularly in radiology and genetics, has had a substantial effect on patient care. Healthcare staff can uncover illnesses earlier by robotic diagnosis processing of data allowing for faster intervention and better therapeutic outcomes [28].

The benefits of using AutoML to perform statistical computations, like therapeutic result predictions and progression of illness simulation, are revolutionary. Medical planning based on AutoML forecasts has ended up resulting in reduced re-hospitalizations, better treatment of illnesses, and absolute care.

- **Personalized Treatment Approaches**

AutoML's role in personalized therapy has had a significant impact on how medicines are adapted to individual patients. AutoML techniques aid in the development of customized therapeutic regimens by assessing a wide range of unique patient information, including genomic data as well as health records. This strategy has resulted in greater efficacy and concentrated therapy, with less adverse reactions and improved therapeutic results [28].

The move to personalized medicine, facilitated by AutoML, illustrates a patient-centered strategy that considers personal variations and characteristics, thereby improving healthcare quality.

3.5.3 Challenges Encountered and Overcome

- **Interpretability and Explainability Challenges**
  Among the most major challenges discovered with AutoML implementations is an insufficient degree of interpretability and comprehensibility. The inherent complexity of automated models frequently results in "black-box" systems that are tough to comprehend by healthcare professionals and patients alike. To solve this challenge, *post hoc* interpretability techniques have been developed that offer explanations for how AutoML simulation selections are made [29].

- **Data Quality and Bias Concerns**
  AutoML's effectiveness is strongly dependent on the accuracy and accurate representation of its input data. Biased datasets and insufficient data can cause inferior results [30].

- **Integration with Existing Healthcare Systems**
  Incorporating AutoML into preexisting medical systems presents logistical and technological obstacles. Addressing interoperability challenges and enabling smooth collaboration with Electronic Health Records (EHR) necessitated collaborative initiatives from data scientists, healthcare IT specialists, and clinical practitioners. Effective deployments have entailed multidisciplinary groups collaborating to align AutoML applications with existing healthcare infrastructure [31].

To summarize, while AutoML has had amazing achievements in a variety of healthcare applications, issues such as interpretability, accuracy of information, and system integration were identified and managed through inventive solutions. These instances and observations provide useful insights into the real-world impact of AutoML on patient results and continued attempts to tackle deployment obstacles in healthcare settings [32].

3.6 Ethical Implications

Here we will discuss the ethical implications of AutoML [33, 34].

3.6.1 Data Privacy and Security

The application of Automated Machine Learning in healthcare needs a thorough study of security and confidentiality of data issues. Given the very delicate nature of medical information, strong safeguards are needed to ensure anonymity. To prevent against unauthorized accessing and database violations, protecting technology, maintaining records, and rigorous safety measures must be implemented. Ethical problems involve gaining patients' expressed agreement for the utilization of their confidential information for simulation purposes.

3.6.2 Fairness and Bias Considerations

The use of AutoML in healthcare applications includes two key legitimate components: neutrality and bias. Modeling based on previous medical data may unintentionally reinforce inherent biases resulting in errors in diagnosis and medication. To prevent this hazard, a proactive strategy will be required throughout the model building process.

Developing fairness-aware strategies and using prejudice identification algorithms are essential phases toward identifying and eliminating flaws in AutoML systems. This leads to comparable results across multiple patient categories, which aligns with the core ideals of impartiality and neutrality in medical judgments.

3.7 Practical Implementation: From Concept to Application

Although the promised benefits of AutoML are evident, its implementation in healthcare necessitates a realistic and structured technique. The key factors are depicted in Figure 3.3 and discussed below:

3.7.1 Problem Formulation and Data Preparation

- Clear Goals: Start by selecting the specific outcome you would like to predict or the therapeutic practice you wish to improve.

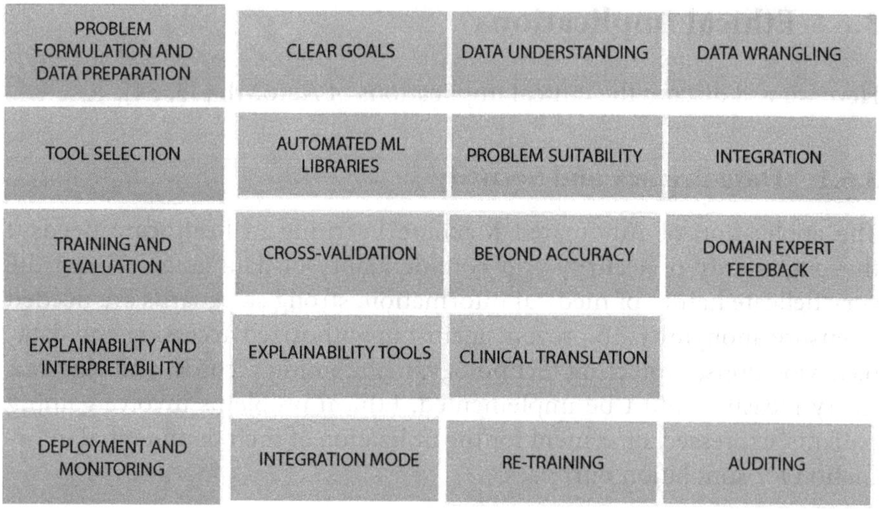

Figure 3.3 Practical implementation: from concept to application.

- Data Understanding: Assess the available data (sources, formats, volumes). Identify inconsistencies, missing values, and potential biases. Close collaboration with healthcare professionals is vital.
- Data Wrangling: Data cleaning, imputation methods, feature engineering, and normalization enhance data quality and compatibility with AutoML tools.

```
import pandas as pd
# Load EHR Data
data = pd.read_csv('sepsis_ehr_data.csv')
# Data Cleaning and Preprocessing
data.dropna(subset=['temperature', 'heart_rate'], inplace=True)
# Drop missing vital signs
data['lab_abnormal'] = data['lab_results'].apply
(lambda x: detect_abnormalities(x))
# Custom function
```

3.7.2 Tool Selection

- **AutoML Libraries:** Consider the trade-offs between ease-of-use and customization offered by frameworks like TPOT, H2O AutoML, Auto-sklearn, etc. [9].

- **Problem Suitability:** Does the data type (tabular, image, text) align with the tool's strengths? Evaluate whether your healthcare task is ideal for AutoML or may need some tailored machine learning components [2].
- **Integration:** Consider how the chosen tools can be integrated with existing hospital IT systems and EHR structures. This is essential for real-world deployment [7].

```
from sklearn.feature_extraction.text import CountVectorizer
# Extracting features from clinical notes
vectorizer = CountVectorizer()
clinical_note_features = vectorizer.fit_transform(data['clinical_notes'])
```

3.7.3 Training and Evaluation

- **Cross-validation:** Employ robust methodologies to prevent overfitting ensuring model generalizability to new healthcare data [9].
- **Beyond Accuracy:** Measure performance with healthcare-centric metrics (sensitivity, specificity, positive predictive value) [7].
- **Domain Expert Feedback:** Include medical professionals in the evaluation process to ensure models fit clinical reality [13].

```
from sklearn.metrics import roc_auc_score, confusion_matrix
import shap
# Evaluation Metrics
y_pred = tpot.predict(X_test)
auc = roc_auc_score(y_test, y_pred)
print("AUC:", auc)
confusion_matrix(y_test, y_pred)
# Explainability
explainer = shap.TreeExplainer(tpot.fitted_pipeline_)
shap_values = explainer.shap_values(X_test)
shap.summary_plot(shap_values, X_test)
```

3.7.4 Explainability and Interpretability

- **Explainability Tools:** These are leverage methods, like SHAP, LIME, and feature importance visualization, to help

healthcare professionals understand the reasoning behind model predictions.
- **Clinical Translation:** Explanations must align with domain knowledge so results can be confidently incorporated into patient care.

3.7.5 Deployment and Monitoring

- **Integration Mode:** Will the model operate as a standalone tool, part of a decision support system, or be fully integrated into EHR workflows? This influences development [6].
- **Re-training:** Data shifts over time; establish plans for periodically updating models to maintain their accuracy and performance.
- **Auditing:** Implement rigorous systems to detect biases, inaccuracies, and unexpected outputs before they significantly impact patient care.

3.8 Future Directions and Trends

Here, in this part of the study, we will discuss the future trends and directions.

3.8.1 Integration with Emerging Technologies

The expected direction of AutoML for therapeutic medicine has been fully incorporated with emerging advancements creating new opportunities for study and development. Several significant trends influence this integration procedure as follows:

- **Integration with Edge Computing:** The combination of AutoML and edge computing techniques is expected to transform healthcare delivery. Edge computing enables real-time extraction and examination of data at the point of medication reducing latency and permitting quick decisions. AutoML simulations used at the edge can enhance diagnosis, monitor individual wellbeing, and aid in customized therapies in environments with limited resources.
- **Synergy with Artificial Intelligence (AI) Assistants:** AutoML is likely to serve an important role in improving artificial

intelligence-powered robotic assistant in medicine. These assistants, powered by AutoML algorithms, can offer personalized health insights, address patient questions, and help clinicians make decisions. The combination of AutoML with NLP techniques will enhance the abilities of artificial intelligence assistants resulting in more natural and logical interactions.

3.8.2 AutoML in Clinical Trials and Research

The deployment of AutoML in clinical studies and scientific studies has the potential to transform the landscape regarding proof creation and medical advancements. The key developments within this domain are as follows:

- **Optimization of Clinical Trial Design:** AutoML will help optimize the design of clinical experiment by analyzing historical experiment data, identifying pertinent biomarkers, and forecasting patient response to certain therapies. This can result in cheaper and more effective experiment, hence expediting the drug research pipeline.
- **Patient Stratification for Precision Medicine:** AutoML's capacity to analyze various patient information will help enhance the categorization of patients in experiments. AutoML permits researchers to create tailored therapies and analyze therapy effectiveness accurately, thereby promoting advances in precision medicine.

3.9 Conclusion

Automated machine learning, a burgeoning field within computer science, holds promise for empowering non-experts to utilize machine learning solutions readily. Continuous advancements in techniques and technologies aim to elevate patient outcomes and refine the healthcare sector. Despite machine learning's potential to revolutionize healthcare, its reliance on human expertise during the training process often hampers widespread adoption. This reliance underscores the need to reduce human involvement in machine learning tasks. One promising avenue is the automation of machine learning design and learning processes, known as AutoML. Already demonstrating significant potential in healthcare, AutoML offers a pathway to streamline operations, enhance patient care, and alleviate burdens on the medical system.

References

1. Erickson, B.J., Korfiatis, P., Akkus, Z., Kline, T.L., Machine learning for medical imaging. *Radiographics*, 37, 2, 505–515, 2017.
2. Alam, M., Khan, E.R., Alam, A., Siddiqui, F., Tanweer, S., The DIABACARE CLOUD: predicting diabetes using machine learning. *Acta Sci. Technol.*, 46, 1, 2023, doi: 10.4025/actascitechnol.v46i1.64783.
3. Sumon, M.A., Kwemebe, T.A., Melapu, V.K., Hasan, M.M., Emergency Care Patient Prediction using Electronic Health Records (EHR) Data: An End-to-End Machine Learning Pipeline, in: *2023 10th International Conference on Future Internet of Things and Cloud (FiCloud)*, Aug. 2023, IEEE, pp. 278–282, doi: 10.1109/FiCloud58648.2023.00048.
4. Doke, A. and Gaikwad, M., Survey on Automated Machine Learning (AutoML) and Meta learning, in: *2021 12th International Conference on Computing Communication and Networking Technologies (ICCCNT)*, Jul. 2021, IEEE, pp. 1–5, doi: 10.1109/ICCCNT51525.2021.9579526.
5. Patil, P.S., Kappuram, K., Rumao, R., Bari, P., Development Of AMES: Automated ML Expert System, in: *2022 International Conference on Machine Learning, Big Data, Cloud and Parallel Computing (COM-IT-CON)*, May 2022, IEEE, pp. 208–213, doi: 10.1109/COM-IT-CON54601.2022.9850737.
6. Nagar, P., Singh, H., Bhati, M., Singh, H., Kumar, A., Analysis of Automated Healthcare Diagnosis Models Using Machine Learning, in: *2023 IEEE IAS Global Conference on Emerging Technologies (GlobConET)*, May 2023, IEEE, pp. 1–5, doi: 10.1109/GlobConET56651.2023.10150001.
7. Singh, J., Kaur, D., Kaur, G., Automated Health Assistance based on IoT and Machine Learning, in: *2021 International Conference on Technological Advancements and Innovations (ICTAI)*, Nov. 2021, IEEE, pp. 417–422, doi: 10.1109/ICTAI53825.2021.9673237.
8. Waring, J., Lindvall, C., Umeton, R., Automated machine learning: Review of the state-of-the-art and opportunities for healthcare. *Artif. Intell. Med.*, 104, 101822, Apr. 2020, doi: 10.1016/j.artmed.2020.101822.
9. Mustafa, A. and Rahimi Azghadi, M., Automated Machine Learning for Healthcare and Clinical Notes Analysis. *Computers*, 10, 2, 24, Feb. 2021, doi: 10.3390/computers10020024.
10. Bonamutial, M. and Prasetyo, S.Y., Exploring the Impact of Feature Data Normalization and Standardization on Regression Models for Smartphone Price Prediction, in: *2023 International Conference on Information Management and Technology (ICIMTech)*, Aug. 2023, IEEE, pp. 294–298, doi: 10.1109/ICIMTech59029.2023.10277860.
11. Tawakuli, A. and Engel, T., Towards Normalizing The Design Phase of Data Preprocessing Pipelines For IoT Data, in: *2022 IEEE International Conference on Big Data (Big Data)*, Dec. 2022, IEEE, pp. 4589–4594, doi: 10.1109/BigData55660.2022.10020312.

12. da Silva Rodrigues, E., Lima Martins, D.M., De Lima Neto, F.B., Self-Organizing Transformations for Automatic Feature Engineering, in: *2021 IEEE Symposium Series on Computational Intelligence (SSCI)*, Dec. 2021, IEEE, pp. 1–7, doi: 10.1109/SSCI50451.2021.9659940.
13. Li, B., Sun, K., Lang, Y., Guan, L., Lu, F., Zhu, Y., Application of CSGE-PSPnet Remote Sensing Image Semantic Segmentation Technology in Transmission and Transformation Engineering Design, in: *2022 Asian Conference on Frontiers of Power and Energy (ACFPE)*, Oct. 2022, IEEE, pp. 85–89, doi: 10.1109/ACFPE56003.2022.9952233.
14. Shrestha, R., Kafle, K., Kanan, C., An Investigation of Critical Issues in Bias Mitigation Techniques, in: *2022 IEEE/CVF Winter Conference on Applications of Computer Vision (WACV)*, Jan. 2022, IEEE, pp. 2512–2523, doi: 10.1109/WACV51458.2022.00257.
15. Jain, A., Ratnoo, S., Kumar, D., Addressing class imbalance problem in medical diagnosis: A genetic algorithm approach, in: *2017 International Conference on Information, Communication, Instrumentation and Control (ICICIC)*, Aug. 2017, IEEE, pp. 1–8, doi: 10.1109/ICOMICON.2017.8279150.
16. Josphineleela, R., Kaliappan, S., Natrayan, L., Garg, A., Big Data Security through Privacy–Preserving Data Mining (PPDM): A Decentralization Approach, in: *2023 Second International Conference on Electronics and Renewable Systems (ICEARS)*, Mar. 2023, IEEE, pp. 718–721, doi: 10.1109/ICEARS56392.2023.10085646.
17. Du, J., Research on Enterprise Information Security and Privacy Protection in Big Data Environment, in: *2021 3rd International Conference on Machine Learning, Big Data and Business Intelligence (MLBDBI)*, Dec. 2021, IEEE, pp. 324–327, doi: 10.1109/MLBDBI54094.2021.00067.
18. Andriyanov, N., Kamalova, Y., Dementiev, V., Comparison of MS Custom Vision Auto Machine Learning with Algorithms Implementation Methods, in: *2023 Wave Electronics and its Application in Information and Telecommunication Systems (WECONF)*, May 2023, IEEE, pp. 1–4, doi: 10.1109/WECONF57201.2023.10148043.
19. Sihombing, D.J.C., Dexius, J.U., Manurung, J., Aritonang, M., Adinata, H.S., Design and Analysis of Automated Machine Learning (AutoML) in PowerBI Application Using PyCaret, in: *2022 International Conference of Science and Information Technology in Smart Administration (ICSINTESA)*, Nov. 2022, IEEE, pp. 89–94, doi: 10.1109/ICSINTESA56431.2022.10041543.
20. Gao, Y., Rehman, A., Wang, Z., CW-SSIM based image classification, in: *2011 18th IEEE International Conference on Image Processing*, Sep. 2011, IEEE, pp. 1249–1252, doi: 10.1109/ICIP.2011.6115659.
21. Riri, H., Elmoutaouakkil, A., Beni-Hssane, A., Bourezgui, F., Classification and Recognition of Dental Images Using a Decisional Tree, in: *2016 13th International Conference on Computer Graphics, Imaging and Visualization (CGiV)*, Mar. 2016, IEEE, pp. 390–393, doi: 10.1109/CGiV.2016.82.

22. Ajantha Devi, V., Naved, M., Gangadevi, E., Nayyar, A., Genetic Algorithm-Based Vaccine Optimization Technique to Control COVID-19, in: *Proceedings of International Conference on Computational Intelligence and Data Engineering.* Lecture Notes on Data Engineering and Communications Technologies, vol. 99, N. Chaki, N. Devarakonda, A. Cortesi, H. Seetha (Eds.), Springer, Singapore, 2022, https://doi.org/10.1007/978-981-16-7182-1_1.
23. Manduchi, E., Le, T.T., Fu, W., Moore, J.H., Genetic Analysis of Coronary Artery Disease Using Tree-Based Automated Machine Learning Informed By Biology-Based Feature Selection. *IEEE/ACM Trans. Comput. Biol. Bioinform.*, 19, 3, 1379–1386, May 2022, doi: 10.1109/TCBB.2021.3099068.
24. Narayanan, A.N., Das, S.S., Mirnalinee, T.T., Evaluation of AutoML Frameworks for Computational ADMET Screening in Drug Discovery & Development, in: *2023 IEEE International Conference on Bioinformatics and Biomedicine (BIBM)*, Dec. 2023, IEEE, pp. 4929–4931, doi: 10.1109/BIBM58861.2023.10385832.
25. Sujigarasharma, K., Shri, M.L., Gangadevi, E., Dhanaraj, R.K., Balusamy, N.C.B., Detection and Classification of Speech Disorder using FOA-SCNet. *2023 3rd International Conference on Computing and Information Technology (ICCIT)*, Tabuk, Saudi Arabia, pp. 391–395, 2023, doi: 10.1109/ICCIT58132.2023.10273910.
26. S. S., S., R., T.P., Kalaichelvi, P., B., R., S., M., Predicting Parkinson's Disease Progression Using Machine Learning Ensemble Methods, in: *2022 1st International Conference on Computational Science and Technology (ICCST)*, Nov. 2022, IEEE, pp. 22–26, doi: 10.1109/ICCST55948.2022.10040421.
27. Anwar, T., COVID19 Diagnosis Using AutoML From 3D CT Scans, in: *Proceedings of the IEEE/CVF International Conference on Computer Vision (ICCV) Workshops*, 2021.
28. Manimuthu, A., Peter Jose, P., Gangadevi, E., Kumar, U.U., Anandaraj, M.D., Prediction of Alzheimer'S Disease from Magnetic Resonance Images (MRI). *2024 IEEE International Conference on Computing, Power and Communication Technologies (IC2PCT)*, Greater Noida, India, pp. 631–635, 2024, doi: 10.1109/IC2PCT60090.2024.10486545.
29. Pedrycz, W., Design, Interpretability, and Explainability of Models in the Framework of Granular Computing and Federated Learning, in: *2021 IEEE Conference on Norbert Wiener in the 21st Century (21CW)*, Jul. 2021, IEEE, pp. 1–6, doi: 10.1109/21CW48944.2021.9532525.
30. Shafiul Alam, M. and Xie, Y., Appley: Approximate Shapley Value for Model Explainability in Linear Time, in: *2022 IEEE International Conference on Big Data (Big Data)*, Dec. 2022, IEEE, pp. 95–100, doi: 10.1109/BigData55660.2022.10020352.
31. Glover, W., Li, Q., Naveh, E., Gross, M., Improving Quality of Care Through Integration in a Hospital Setting: A Human Systems Integration Approach. *IEEE Trans. Eng. Manag.*, 64, 3, 365–376, Aug. 2017, doi: 10.1109/TEM.2017.2682267.

32. Kiberu, V.M. and Kiberu, V.M., E-Health Readiness Assessment in Uganda: Integration of Telemedicine Services into Public Healthcare System, in: *2016 IEEE International Conference on Healthcare Informatics (ICHI)*, Oct. 2016, IEEE, pp. 301–301, doi: 10.1109/ICHI.2016.43.
33. S, J., Sujigarasharma, K., R, M., T, V., Assessing the Accuracy and Ethical Implications of Automated Criminal Detection Using a Deep Learning Approach, in: *2023 International Conference on Research Methodologies in Knowledge Management, Artificial Intelligence and Telecommunication Engineering (RMKMATE)*, Nov. 2023, IEEE, pp. 1–5, doi: 10.1109/RMKMATE59243.2023.10369356.
34. Shetty, M., Mahesh, Shetty, S.B., Shetty, A., Automated Method for Fake News Detection Using Machine Learning, in: *2023 International Conference on Network, Multimedia and Information Technology (NMITCON)*, Sep. 2023, IEEE, pp. 1–6, doi: 10.1109/NMITCON58196.2023.10275880.

4

Advancements in AI and AutoML for Plant Leaf Disease Identification in Sustainable Agriculture

Ranichandra C.[1], Senthilkumar N. C.[1], Senthil Kumar Narayanasamy[1]* and Atilla Elci[2]

[1]*School of Computer Science Engineering and Information Systems, Vellore Institute of Technology, Vellore, Tamil Nadu, India*
[2]*Software Engineering Department, Hasan Kalyoncu University, Gaziantep, Türkiye*

Abstract

The application of artificial intelligence (AI) has shown to be transformational in the field of precision agriculture. In recent years, the demand for effective agricultural practices has been growing considerably, and thus, the proper utilization of AI capabilities will certainly resolve some of the challenging issues and further develop the processes for environmental preservation. Also, the AI's transformative effect on agriculture has developed itself by replacing some substandard practices with modern and effective approaches. The proposed system describes the idea of an AI application that uses plant scanning technologies to solve agricultural issues. The goal of this smartphone application is to give farmers, agricultural professionals, and other related stakeholders a simple tool for the early detection and proactive management of plant-related difficulties. The proposed system uses AI tools, including machine learning and computer vision techniques, to analyze images that the potential users can take using a mobile smartphone to investigate plants diseases. The software instantly analyzes the images after scanning a plant to produce a detailed report explaining the implicit faults found along with possible remedies and interventions. Eventually, our system offers comprehensive solutions for effectively predicting and addressing the impeding agricultural issues that scan through various plants. Further, the proposed system tends to provide solutions for monitoring the state of the plant and enhance the space for high crop yielding, which, in turn, reduces losses and paves the way for sustainable agricultural practices. Let us explore

**Corresponding author*: senthilkumar.n@vit.ac.in

E. Gangadevi, M. Lawanya Shri, Balamurugan Balusamy and Rajesh Kumar Dhanaraj (eds.) Automated Machine Learning and Industrial Applications, (63–78) © 2025 Scrivener Publishing LLC

the cutting-edge world of AI and automated machine learning (AutoML) in the context of sustainable agriculture with a focus on the rapid and accurate identification of plant diseases. This chapter delves into the latest advancements that promises to revolutionize the agricultural industry offering innovative solutions to address plant health challenges and ensure sustainable food production.

***Keywords*:** Plant leaf disease, AI, ResNet, leaf symptoms, CNN, SVM

4.1 Introduction

Although agriculture plays a vital role in providing food security, producers have been overcoming some considerable difficulties in efficiently managing and safeguarding their cultivation against diseases. Traditional disease detection techniques often lack in accuracy and are not able to act accordingly resulting in poor productivity and loss of financial benefits. Due to the intrinsic complication of agricultural data and the request for effective and easily accessible tools, solutions, including artificial intelligence, are needed to predict diseases that is easy for users to recognize. To overcome these problems, an AI-based tool that integrates preprocessing, disease diagnosis, prediction, and data gathering is required. Such a tool will authorize farmers and recover crop management techniques.

The formation of a cutting-edge AI-based explanation for agricultural leaf disease prediction and prevention is the foremost goal of this research. Our aim is to develop a comprehensive system that smoothly integrates AI and optimizing every process of the procedure from joining data to forecasting diseases. By adding characteristics that are easy to use, such as image capture of relevant data points, we hope to increase the effectiveness of data collection while creating the tool accessible to farmers with diverse levels of technological developments. To assure the accuracy of the data taken for disease prediction, a data preprocessing method will be used to manage missing data, outliers, and normalization. By analyzing preprocessed data, the system will use advanced AI algorithms to provide farmers with actionable recommendations and accurate predictions of diseases.

Creating an attractive and user-friendly mobile application interface is a main priority to allow farmers to produce well-informed decisions by developing a culture. With developments in deep learning, IoT and sensor integration, personalized results, and ongoing model refinement, the future of AI-based tools for agricultural disease prediction is quite exciting. Widespread application of AI in agriculture for more precise and effective disease prediction is predicted to be made possible by collaborative platforms and regulatory frameworks, which will support responsible adoption and increase farming production worldwide.

In the remainder of this chapter, a literature survey and an analysis of agricultural diseases are presented. The proposed approach is detailed highlighting the pros and cons. Then, the conclusions are summarized.

4.2 Literature Survey

As the agriculture field faces many problems from cultivating to harvesting, plant disease detection methods are highly emphasizing the integration of image processing and machine learning techniques. Numerous research papers have been extensively focused on sustainable agriculture, particularly on plant leaf disease detection and prediction. Our interest in this chapter rests in machine learning approaches; thus, this literature survey covers appropriate research writings.

The paper [1] explores artificial intelligence applications and their significance in the field of plant disease detection offering various techniques, algorithms, and datasets. The authors of ref. [2] present a detailed literature survey on robust hybrid algorithm design and implementation for real-time plant disease detection.

The survey in ref. [3] explains a brief overview of the application of intelligence in agriculture and available techniques and also explaining various methods for detection of diseases in crop. This paper highlights the potential benefits of AI in improving crop yield and addressing disease-related challenges. Besides, it introduces the concepts of artificial intelligence and its rapid advancement across various industrial sectors. It emphasizes AI's ability to solve complex problems and contribute to environmental preservation. The transformative impact of AI on agriculture is noted through replacing traditional methods with more efficient techniques.

The researchers in ref. [4] explore the integration of AI techniques to enhance plant disease recognition in plants. The paper emphasizes the importance of timely disease identification for crop yield and quality. It presents a hybrid algorithm that combines computer vision, machine learning, and deep learning approaches to analyze plant images and diagnose diseases accurately in real time. Further, the strengths and limitations of various AI techniques are discussed and a design of hybrid algorithms, describing its implementation as well as results and outlining potential future directions for enhanced capabilities, is proposed. Overall, the paper highlights the transformative potential of AI in revolutionizing plant disease management and its implications for sustainable agriculture.

The authors of ref. [5] primarily focus on the potential benefits, challenges, and prospects of implementing AI technology in the agricultural sector. The authors emphasize the significance of agriculture in the economy and highlight the challenges faced by the industry including climate changes, natural calamities, and limited resources. Also, they shed light on how AI can revolutionize the agricultural sector. The authors identify several key areas where AI-based systems can have a transformative impact that includes increasing crop yield, crop disease detection, precision farming, automation, data analytics, IoT-enabled solutions and sustainability. In addition, this paper addresses challenges disturbing the adoption of AI in agriculture such as data accessibility, cost, lack of technical expertise, and ethical concerns.

The paper in ref. [6] discusses the significant role that agriculture plays in the economy along with the challenges presented by the increasing global population. With rising demands for food and employment, traditional farming methods become inadequate and increase the demand for automated techniques into AI application in agriculture. It highlights the transformative impact of automation and AI technologies on various aspects of agriculture ultimately contributing to improved productivity and sustainability in the sector.

The authors of ref. [7] discuss the application of AI techniques, particularly machine learning and image processing for detection of diseases in plants. The importance of early disease detection in crops, to prevent economic losses and ensure the quality and safety of agricultural products, is highlighted. The authors cite and discuss various specific studies using techniques like fractal descriptors, neural networks, Gabor filters, and color space transformations for disease identification in different crops such as rice, wheat, soybean, cotton, and more.

The paper in ref. [8] discusses the importance of agricultural development, challenges posed by plant diseases, and how AI and drones can be used to address them. The proposed approach involves using an improved efficient Convolutional Neural Network (CNN) for plant disease detection and an improved EfficientNetV2-B4 model for classifying plant diseases using deep learning. Moreover, this article showcases a comprehensive approach to using AI and drones for plant disease detection that demonstrates the performance of the proposed model on a standard dataset.

The authors in ref. [9] explore data collection, preprocessing, feature extraction, and model selection or training or evaluation methodology in plant disease identification. Empirical evaluation of model performance is followed by the limitations of traditional methods and the potential advantages of using artificial intelligence techniques.

The paper in ref. [10] addresses the use of artificial intelligence in sustainable agriculture for the optimization of irrigation and application of pesticides and herbicides.

The article in ref. [11] explores the application of machine learning and deep learning techniques for detecting plant diseases. It emphasizes the diseases caused by bacteria, fungi, and viruses contributing to low crop yields. The authors discuss the suitability of machine learning techniques for disease identification in plants and review various methods, including Gaussian Naive Bayesian, K-Nearest Nearest Neighbor, Decision Trees, Support Vector Machines, Random Forest, and Multi-Layer Perceptron (MLP) classifiers, explaining their relevance and applications in agriculture.

In the paper [12], the authors focus on conventional machine learning techniques to predict the yield of soybean crops and analyze the last 10 years to predict the start of disease at an early or pre-symptomatic stage. Then, they analyze the possibility of using different machine learning techniques in agriculture by coupling with recent statistical forecasting methods from weather data to predict wheat yield. Since the mentioned surveys have not covered forecasting, detection, and classification of diseases and have also not fully explored recent deep learning-based techniques, the review carried out in this survey work focuses on filling the existing differences in these subjects. Moreover, it highlights the development of such machine learning tools and provide farmers with data-driven decision-making assistance systems. In this way, farmers can be assisted in decreasing the need for pesticide application and the damage that it causes while preserving and sustaining crop quality and production. This contributes to the continued availability of food to meet global population demands while performing less destruction and damage to the planet.

4.3 Preliminary Analysis for Agricultural Diseases

It is possible to enhance the efficiency and accuracy of predicting agricultural disease during preliminary investigation through appropriate utilization of autoML techniques. To find some complex patterns and connections that might not be immediately visible using conventional approaches, AI systems can process enormous information that includes historical crop performance, weather patterns, and pest and disease incidences. Machine learning models [13] provide a proactive approach to disease control by using a variety of indicators to forecast disease outbreaks. Besides, the AI application for remote sensing has been performing qualitative work on processing satellite images of the crop fields and helps to detect early diseases of the plant leaf. The analysis becomes more data driven and adaptive to the changing agricultural ecosystems with the integration of AI technology.

Image-processing techniques can be used to detect minute signs of plant leaf disease by analyzing the visual characteristics of the leaves. The following are some techniques in which image processing can be applied for this purpose:

- Color analysis: Image-processing algorithms can identify the color of plant leaves and recognize any abnormal discoloration or spots that may specify disease.
- Texture analysis: The image-processing techniques can identify indiscretions or patterns with diseases like powdery mildew or rust.
- Shape analysis: Image processing can be used to detect the shape and structure of the leaves and identify any irregularities that may be the reason of the disease.
- Feature extraction: Image-processing algorithms can identify specific characteristics from the leaf images like lesions, spots, or patterns that can be noted as indicators of disease.
- Machine learning: Image processing can also be integrated with machine learning algorithms to train models that can identify patterns with many diseases making it possible to detect indirect signs that may not be directly apparent to the human eye.

Thus, the training of reliable datasets, normalization and scaling of data, as well as the selection of appropriate methods for feature extraction and classification are vital.

4.3.1 Datasets and Descriptions

To analyze an image dataset for an artificial intelligence application to identify agricultural diseases, high-resolution images of leaves must be found. These photos need to highlight the developmental phases, detailed descriptions, and illness parameters. In addition, it also needs to verify that each image is rightly tagged to check for disease presence on the leaf or not. It is significant to cover the dataset that holds the correct depiction of both healthy and ill samples. When training a healthy model that can correctly identify and predict agricultural diseases based on pictorial signals, the ability and diversity of the image collection are serious factors.

4.3.2 Normalization and Scaling

A vital step in making an Auto ML-based tool for agricultural disease prediction [14] is data preprocessing, which intends to improve the input dataset and make it suitable for effective machine learning model training. As it was stated by authors [14], data cleaning is an important step that removes unnecessary or redundant information and fills any gaps in the data by imputation or elimination. The consistency of the image can be restored through proper image scaling and normalization that provide uniform pixel values and resolutions across images. By exposing the dataset to a variety of changes, data augmentation techniques, like rotation and flipping, improve model generalization. To avoid biases during training, which can be caused by oversampling or under-sampling strategies [15], classes must be balanced. To ensure model compatibility, label encoding converts categorical labels into numerical representations. The dataset is then further split into training and testing subsets for assessment. Whenever there is a need for refinement, feature scaling is implemented once outliers are located and represented by the system. Eventually, a comprehensive quality check verifies the preprocessed dataset integrity by providing the foundation for developing a reliable and accurate model that can successfully predict agricultural illnesses.

4.3.3 Feature Extraction and Classification

The fundamental step in image processing is feature extraction that aims to extract relevant information from images for different computer vision applications. As the image analysis tasks needs to substantiate crucial traits, patterns, and other inherent details of the image, it requires some standard extraction procedures such as object recognition, picture classification, and segmentation. Some of the standard procedures for extraction are measures of pixel intensity, picture translation to other color schemes, and pixel distributions represented by appropriate histograms.

4.3.4 Spectral Image Analysis

Spectral analysis for plant leaf disease prediction involves the use of various types of sensors that detect and measure the electromagnetic radiation emitted or reflected by plant leaves. The following are some of the most commonly used sensors in spectral analysis:

- Hyperspectral sensors: These sensors measure the reflectance of light across a wide range of wavelengths from the visible to the near-infrared spectrum that provides high-resolution spectral data, which can be used to identify detailed changes in leaf pigmentation and structure.
- Multispectral sensors: These sensors measure the reflectance of light at specific wavelengths, typically in the visible and near-infrared spectrum, providing lower-resolution spectral data but at a higher spatial resolution.
- Fluorescence sensors: These sensors measure the fluorescence emitted by plant leaves when exposed to light providing information about the photosynthetic activity and health of the plant.
- Thermal sensors: These sensors measure the infrared radiation emitted by plant leaves, providing information about the temperature and water stress of the plant.

The sensors work by emitting light or radiation onto the plant leaves and measuring the amount of energy reflected or emitted back. The spectral signature of the reflected or emitted energy can then be analyzed to identify specific wavelengths or patterns associated with different plant diseases or stress conditions.

Spectral analysis using these sensors can provide accurate and non-invasive methods for detecting plant leaf diseases and monitoring plant health enabling early intervention and management to prevent crop losses.

4.4 Proposed Methods

In this proposed work, we have provided the Auto ML-based agricultural disease prediction tool that include data characteristics, interpretability, resource limitations, problem type (i.e., either classification or regression), and machine learning model selection. To identify the exact image segments, there are several options ranging from straightforward models, like logistic regression, to complicated ones, like convolutional neural networks. The actual performance of the system can greatly be improved by integrating ensemble methods, and the robustness of the model is ensured by cross-validation with hyperparameter adjustment. The choice is absolutely made based on domain expertise, and the selection is based on particular evaluation measures designed to meet the entire goals for agricultural disease prediction.

The most significant stage of an AutoML-based tool for agricultural disease prediction is model training that particularly relies mostly on selecting the appropriate machine learning model with necessary patterns and associations from the preprocessed information. In this way, we can largely reduce the discrepancy between expected results as well as actual results and enable the model to modify its parameters during training based on the input data. In supervised learning, labeled samples of both healthy and sick crops are fed to the model, which uses a technique called backpropagation [16] to repeatedly improve its predictions. To increase the model capacity to generalize new data, the weights and biases must be optimized throughout the training phase. As we aim for optimum output of the proposed model, parameters, like learning rate, batch size, and epochs, are adjusted. The robustness of the model may eventually be evaluated using cross-validation techniques, and changing its hyperparameters improves its configuration. After training, the model is prepared for use providing the farmers with a prediction tool to help them detect and treat crop diseases efficiently.

The part of an Auto ML-based tool for agricultural disease prediction that applies the trained model for unused data to provide predictions in real time is called the prediction module. Images of agricultural data are used as input by this module, which preprocesses the data before feeding it through the trained model. The model makes use of the links and patterns it has learned to forecast the possibility of crop illnesses. The forecasts give farmers important information about the health of their crops allowing for prompt management and intervention measures. The model training procedure, high-quality data, and tool versatility in handling various farming situations all contribute to the improvement in prediction modules. The model enhance its dependability in providing precise forecasts for proactive disease control in agriculture through constant updates on its processes and by ongoing performance evaluations.

4.4.1 Leaf Disease Identification Using ResNet

A system for classifying plant diseases based on images of plant leaves is designed to leverage domain expertise for accurate identification of symptoms and diseases. The system relies mostly on a comprehensive dataset that encompasses various plant species and diseases that ensure model adaptability to diverse conditions. The data preprocessing steps involve cleaning and improvement of the dataset ,while domain experts annotate essential labels for disease types and leaf symptoms. The chosen deep learning model would often be a Convolutional Neural Network (CNN), like VGG16 or ResNet, that undergoes transfer learning with pre-trained weights to enhance its

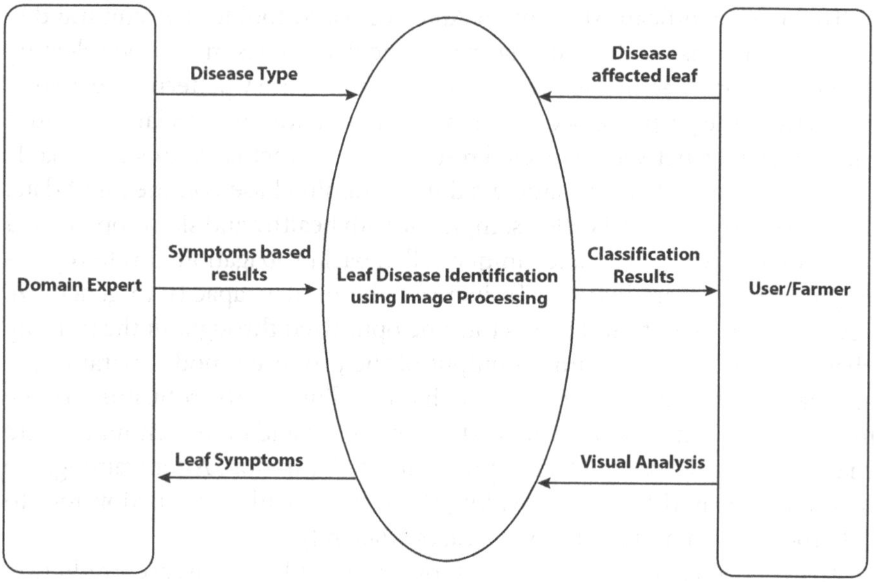

Figure 4.1 Leaf disease identification and analysis.

performance on a specific task. As undertaken in the CNN learning process, the training phase involves a thorough check of the accuracy rate and determines the deduction of loss value to assess the model generalization. Further, the system allows the users to upload images through a user-friendly interface by submitting classification results and relevant information pertaining to identified diseases. The feedback process ensures continuous improvement and regular maintenance, including updates with new data, which ensure the system's ongoing effectiveness in identifying plant diseases and that the rate of precision is satisfactory (ref. Figure 4.1).

4.4.2 Pixel-Based Information Extraction and Ant Colony Optimization

Plant disease detection and prediction actually take a detailed analysis of the images and map it with the database of gathered images related to various diseases. This predictive system exploits a multi-faceted approach by including both pixel-based information extraction and the identification of disease symptoms. By integrating pixel-based information extraction with a deep understanding of disease symptoms, the predictive model aims for a robust and precise classification of plant diseases based on the analysis of leaf images (ref. Figure 4.2).

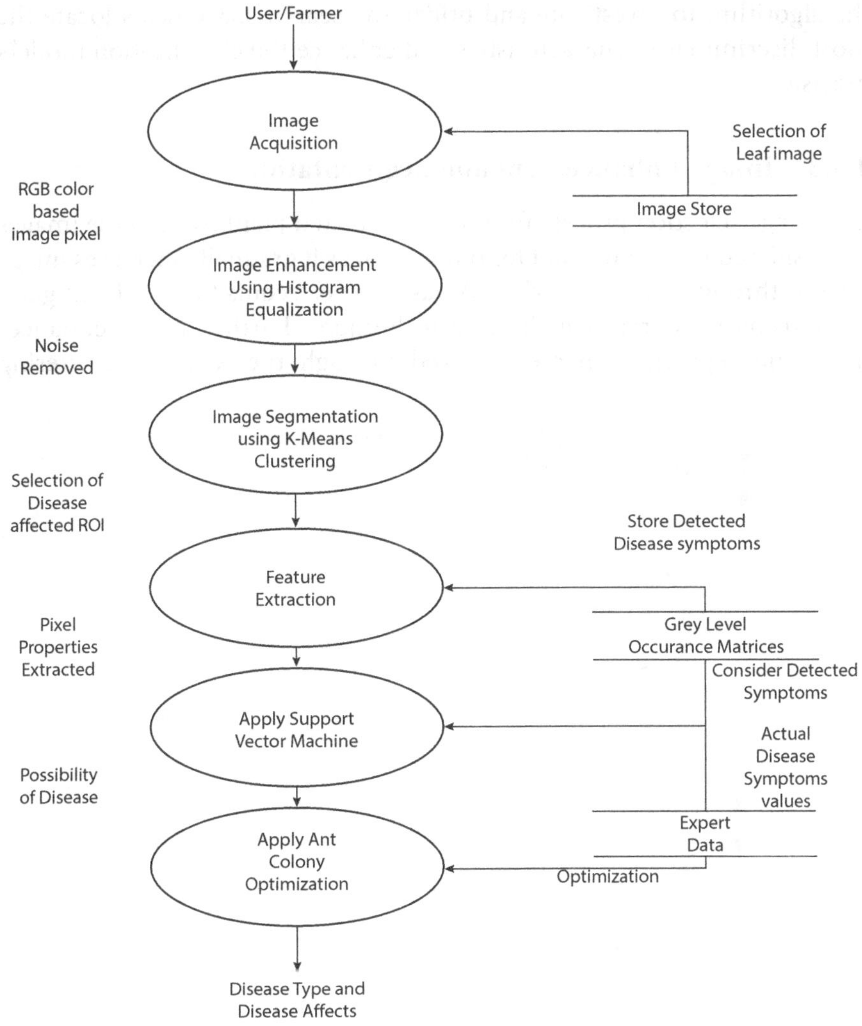

Figure 4.2 Pixel-based information extraction and ant colony optimization.

Plant leaf disease detection and recognition in precision agriculture can be achieved with a complex technique that associates Ant Colony Optimization (ACO) with pixel-based information extraction. In pixel-based information extraction, each pixel in a digital image is examined, and the inherent patterns of plant illnesses are exactly detected by utilizing the color, texture, and spatial connections exhibited between the pixels. With the help of this technique, it is possible to analyze plant leaf images clearly by identifying the most in-depth signs of disease. The capacity of the algorithm to investigate and utilize the search space helps locate the most discriminative characteristics and enhance the classification model's precision.

4.4.3 Image Enhancement and Segmentation

The image selection process for the accumulated plant leaf disease images is considered very significant for our system as it gradually increases image quality through the steps of RGB-based pixel acquisition and mitigates noise using histogram equalization techniques. Further, image enhancement and segmentation are achieved through the K-means clustering

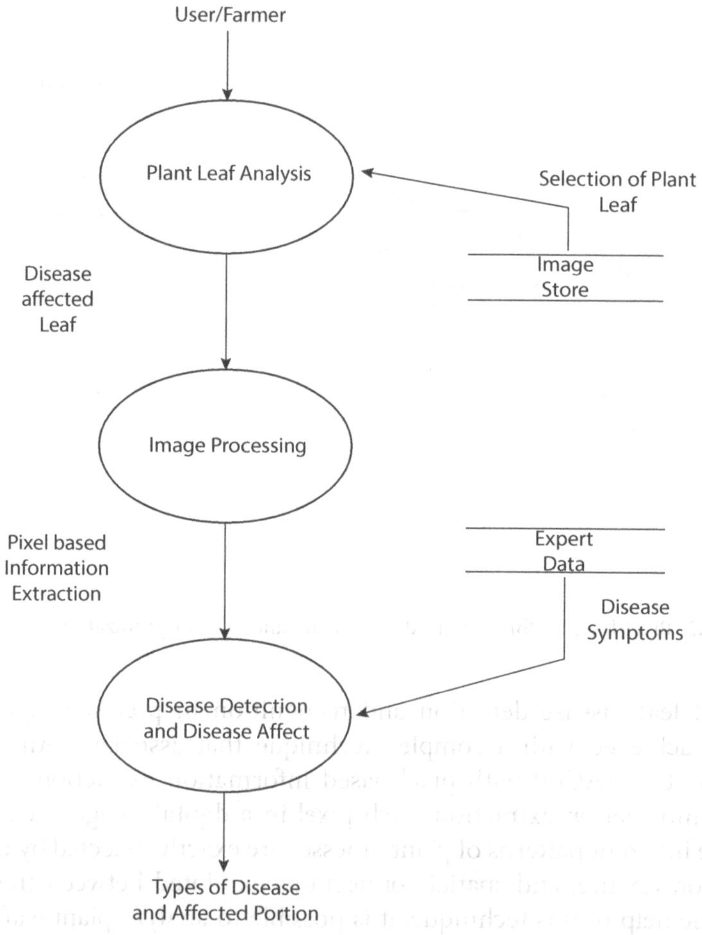

Figure 4.3 Image enhancement and segmentation.

approach, which paves the way for identifying the specific region of interest within the images. Plant leaf disease classification is performed for the segmented images through the feature extraction process as mentioned in Figure 4.3.

Plant leaf disease symptoms and the gray-level occurrence matrix help increase the pixel capabilities and provide a comprehensive understanding of the visual patterns associated with different diseases. The application of the Support Vector Machine (SVM) algorithm further refines the analysis and provides implicit factors that affect plant leaves.

Moreover, optimizing the plant leaf image datasets has been performed through expert data analysis involving fine-tuning parameters, and refining algorithms and system adaptability across various plant species and diseases. In addition, we employed ant colony optimization techniques to scrutinize and fine-tune the final results.

4.5 Conclusion

In conclusion, plant leaf disease prediction methods based on artificial intelligence (AI) have become highly valuable in precision agriculture by showcasing creative methods to the early identification and effectual treatment of crop diseases. The study of complicated data, such as plant leaf images and related environmental parameters, has shown the amazing capabilities of machine learning techniques such as decision trees, support vector machines, and neural networks. These Auto ML-driven models often outperform predictable diagnostic techniques and enable the quick and precise detection of diseases. The understanding of plant leaf disease detection and prediction are enhanced by the integration of cutting-edge skills, such as picture recognition and feature extraction. Beyond simple diagnosis, AI has the potential to have a significant impact on agriculture by giving farmers valuable information on how to prevent diseases proactively and use resources as efficiently as possible.

References

1. Sujawat, G.S., Application of Artificial Intelligence in detection of diseases in plants: A Survey. *Turk. J. Comput. Math. Educ. (TURCOMAT)*, *12*, 3, 3301–3305, 2021.

2. Yağ, İ. and Altan, A., Artificial intelligence-based robust hybrid algorithm design and implementation for real-time detection of plant diseases in agricultural environments. *Biology*, *11*, 12, 1732, 2022.
3. Albattah, W., Javed, A., Nawaz, M., Masood, M., Albahli, S., Artificial intelligence-based drone system for multiclass plant disease detection using an improved efficient convolutional neural network. *Front. Plant Sci.*, *13*, 808380, 2022.
4. Gangadevi, E., Rani, R.S., Dhanaraj, R.K., Nayyar, A., Spot-out fruit fly algorithm with simulated annealing optimized SVM for detecting tomato plant diseases. *Neural Comput. Appl.*, 36, 8, 4349–4375, 2023, Springer Science and Business Media LLC. https://doi.org/10.1007/s00521-023-09295-1.
5. Upadhyay, N. and Gupta, N., A survey on diseases detection for agriculture crops using artificial intelligence, in: *2021 5th International Conference on Information Systems and Computer Networks (ISCON)*, 2021, October, IEEE, pp. 1–8.
6. Poornappriya, T.S. and Gopinath, R., Rice plant disease identification using artificial intelligence approaches. *Int. J. Electr. Eng. Technol.*, *11*, 10, 392–402, 2022.
7. Gangadevi, E., Rani Ranganathan, S., Shri Mani, L., Kadry, S., An intelligent deep residual learning framework for tomato plant leaf disease classification. *Int. J. Electr. Comput. Eng. (IJECE)*, 14, 3, 3168, 2024, Institute of Advanced Engineering and Science. https://doi.org/10.11591/ijece.v14i3.pp3168-3176.
8. Mohanty, S.P., Hughes, D.P., Salathé, M., Using deep learning for image-based plant disease detection. *Front. Plant Sci.*, *7*, 1419, 2016.
9. Jackulin, C. and Murugavalli, S., A comprehensive review on detection of plant disease using machine learning and deep learning approaches. *Meas.: Sens.*, 24, 100441, 2022.
10. Talaviya, T., Shah, D., Patel, N., Yagnik, H., Shah, M., Implementation of artificial intelligence in agriculture for optimisation of irrigation and application of pesticides and herbicides. *Artif. Intell. Agric.*, *4*, 58–73, 2020.
11. Tabassum, H. and Theerthagiri, P., Performance Analysis of AI-based Learning Models on Leaf Disease Prediction, in: *2022 4th International Conference on Circuits, Control, Communication and Computing (I4C)*, 2022, December, IEEE, pp. 85–88.
12. Domingues, T., Brandão, T., Ferreira, J.C., Machine learning for detection and prediction of crop diseases and pests: A comprehensive survey. *Agriculture*, *12*, 9, 1350, 2022.
13. Ezzati, S., Zenner, E.K., Pakdaman, M., Naseri, M.H., Nikjoui, M., Ahmadi, S., Spatially explicit modeling of disease surveillance in mixed oak-hardwood forests based on machine-learning algorithms. *J. Environ. Manage.*, *337*, 117714, 2023.
14. Revathi, V., Kavin, B.P., Thirumalraj, A., Gangadevi, E., Balusamy, B., Gite, S., Image Based Feature Separation Using RBM Tech with ADBN Tech for Accurate Fruit Classification. *2024 IEEE International Conference on*

Computing, Power and Communication Technologies (IC2PCT), Greater Noida, India, pp. 1423–1429, 2024, doi: 10.1109/IC2PCT60090.2024.10486564.
15. Kumar, P. and TA, S.L., Projection of Plant Leaf Disease Using Support Vector Machine Algorithm. In *2023 International Conference on Recent Advances in Science and Engineering Technology (ICRASET)*, IEEE, pp. 1–6, 2023, November.
16. Shukoor, A., Jain, S., Maurya, P., Anusha, C., Kiran, B., Kothiyal, K., An Overview of Different Fruit Crop Models in the last 40 Years to Date with Their Main Uses. *Int. J. Plant Soil Sci.*, 35, 22, 618–641, 2023.

5

Predictive Maintenance in Industrial Settings: Video Analytics at the Edge with AutoML

Madala Guru Brahmam and Vijay Anand R.*

School of Computer Science Engineering and Information Systems, Vellore Institute of Technology, Vellore, India

Abstract

In industrial environments, the need for predictive maintenance has never been more critical for both safety and operational efficiency. Traditional methods often involve labor-intensive, manual inspections that are not only costly but also less effective in timely fault detection. This chapter explores the amalgamation of video analytics, edge computing, and automated machine learning (AutoML) in industrial settings to revolutionize predictive maintenance strategies. The proposed framework aims to automate and enhance the real-time monitoring and analytics of machinery, thereby proactively identifying potential issues before they escalate into failures. By deploying edge computing devices equipped with video cameras and autoML algorithms, we achieve localized, real-time data processing reducing latency and bandwidth usage. Algorithms, such as auto-Sklearn, TPOT, and H2O's autoML, are leveraged to automate the machine learning process, thereby allowing the system to adapt and improve over temporal instance sets. The preliminary results suggest a significant reduction in unplanned downtime by up to 30% and an increase in the accuracy of fault detection by approximately 20% compared to traditional monitoring methods. Moreover, the utilization of autoML minimizes the need for specialized machine learning expertise making the solution scalable and cost effective. The impact of this work has the potential to be transformative for industries reliant on heavy machinery, reducing maintenance costs and enhancing operational efficiency, while also contributing to safer working conditions. This innovative approach represents a paradigm shift in predictive maintenance

**Corresponding author*: vijayanand.r@vit.ac.in

E. Gangadevi, M. Lawanya Shri, Balamurugan Balusamy and Rajesh Kumar Dhanaraj (eds.) Automated Machine Learning and Industrial Applications, (79–104) © 2025 Scrivener Publishing LLC

leveraging the power of cutting-edge technologies to solve long-standing industrial challenges.

Keywords: Predictive maintenance, video analytics, edge computing, automated machine learning (AutoML), industrial efficiency

5.1 Introduction

In the ever-evolving landscape of industrial operations, the quest for efficiency, safety, and cost effectiveness has led to the adoption of advanced technological solutions. The significance of predictive maintenance in this context cannot be overstated, as it stands at the forefront of industrial innovation directly impacting operational longevity and safety. This chapter delves into the transformative potential of integrating video analytics, edge computing, and automated machine learning (autoML) in the realm of predictive maintenance within industrial settings.

The traditional approach to maintenance in industrial environments has predominantly been reactive or preventive characterized by scheduled inspections and maintenance activities. While these methods have their merits, they are often plagued by inefficiencies such as high labor costs, significant downtimes, and the inherent limitations of human error. In contrast, predictive maintenance represents a proactive strategy focusing on predicting failures before they occur, thus enabling timely intervention. The integration of video analytics and edge computing with autoML offers a paradigm shift in this domain.

Video analytics, the process of extracting meaningful information from video footage, becomes a pivotal tool in monitoring and analyzing the condition of machinery. When combined with edge computing, where data processing occurs close to the source of data generation (i.e., the industrial machinery itself), the system benefits from reduced latency and lower bandwidth usage. This localized processing is crucial for real-time monitoring and decision making in industrial environments.

Automated machine learning, or autoML, is the technological cornerstone of this framework. autoML platforms, like auto-Sklearn, TPOT, and H2O's autoML, automate the process of applying machine learning algorithms making it accessible even to those without deep expertise in the field. This democratization of machine learning enables the predictive maintenance system to continually adapt and improve enhancing its accuracy and reliability over time.

The introduction of this integrated framework in industrial settings is not just an incremental improvement but a substantial leap forward. Early results indicate a notable reduction in unplanned downtime and a significant increase in fault detection accuracy. This increase in operational efficiency is coupled with a reduction in maintenance costs, thereby addressing two of the most pressing concerns in industrial operations. Furthermore, by minimizing the need for specialized machine learning expertise, the autoML-driven approach offers a scalable and cost-effective solution making advanced predictive maintenance strategies accessible to a broader range of industries.

This chapter will explore the components of this innovative approach in detail highlighting the synergistic effects of video analytics, edge computing, and autoML in transforming predictive maintenance. it will also discuss the practical implications of this framework providing insights into its implementation, challenges, and the future scope of this technology in industrial applications. Through this exploration, the chapter aims to underscore the transformative impact of these technologies not just in enhancing operational efficiency but also in contributing to safer working conditions in industries reliant on heavy machinery.

Motivation and Contribution

The impetus for exploring the confluence of video analytics, edge computing, and automated machine learning (autoML) in predictive maintenance is rooted in the pressing challenges faced by the industrial sector. The motivation for this innovative approach stems from a need to address several key issues as follows:

1. **Inefficiency of Traditional Maintenance**: Traditional maintenance methods, while familiar, are often reactive and labor intensive. They rely heavily on scheduled checks and manual inspections, which are not only costly but also prone to human error. The inefficiency of these methods, particularly in fault detection and downtime management, necessitates a more proactive and technologically advanced approach.
2. **Rising Costs and Downtime**: Unplanned downtime in industrial operations can lead to significant financial losses. Moreover, the costs associated with traditional maintenance are substantial spanning labor, equipment, and lost production time. Reducing these costs and improving uptime is a priority for any industrial operation.

3. **Safety Concerns**: Safety in industrial environments is paramount. Failure to detect and address equipment issues promptly can lead to accidents posing risks to personnel and facility. Enhanced monitoring and predictive capabilities are essential for improving safety standards.
4. **Technological Advancements**: The rapid development of technologies, like machine learning, video analytics, and edge computing, presents an opportunity to revolutionize industrial maintenance. Leveraging these technologies can lead to substantial improvements in maintenance strategies.

The contributions of this chapter are multifaceted and significant in the context of industrial maintenance as follows:

1. **Innovative Framework Development**: This chapter introduces an innovative framework that integrates video analytics, edge computing, and autoML to transform predictive maintenance strategies. By providing a comprehensive overview of how these technologies work in tandem, the chapter offers a blueprint for implementation in various industrial settings.
2. **Enhanced Predictive Capabilities**: Through the use of autoML, the framework facilitates the development of machine learning models that are self-improving and adaptive. This leads to more accurate and timely predictions of equipment failures vastly improving upon traditional methods.
3. **Demonstration of Real-World Impact**: By presenting preliminary results and case studies, this chapter demonstrates the tangible impact of the proposed framework on reducing downtime and maintenance costs. The increase in fault detection accuracy and operational efficiency is quantified providing a compelling case for adoption.
4. **Accessibility and Scalability**: The utilization of autoML minimizes the barrier to entry for implementing advanced machine learning models making this technology accessible to a wider range of users. This aspect is crucial for scalability and broader adoption across various industries.
5. **Safety Enhancement**: By enabling more effective and timely maintenance, the proposed approach contributes significantly to safer working conditions in industrial environments.

This aspect aligns with the overarching goal of integrating technology for the betterment of workplace safety.

In conclusion, this chapter not only motivates the need for a shift toward more advanced predictive maintenance strategies but also contributes a practical and innovative solution. The integration of cutting-edge technologies and the demonstration of their real-world impact mark a significant advancement in the field of industrial maintenance levels.

5.2 Literature Review

The literature on predictive maintenance, particularly in the context of industrial and IoT applications, presents a diverse range of methodologies and findings reflecting the rapid advancements in this field. A review of these papers reveals several key trends and insights that contribute significantly to the understanding and development of predictive maintenance strategies.

Integration of Advanced Learning Techniques: Feng and Li's study [1] on the application of reinforcement learning in multistage production systems exemplifies the trend toward integrating sophisticated AI techniques in predictive maintenance. This approach is echoed in Binder *et al.*'s systematic review [2], which highlights the increasing reliance on complex algorithms in the railway domain, a sector that demands high reliability and safety standards.

Focus on Specific Industry Applications: The literature also shows a marked focus on tailoring predictive maintenance strategies to specific industries. For instance, Fu *et al.*'s work [3] on modular multilevel converters in power electronics and the exploration of predictive maintenance in healthcare systems by Manchadi *et al.* [7] demonstrate the adaptability of predictive maintenance methodologies to diverse operational requirements and challenges.

Leveraging IoT and Edge Computing: The integration of IoT and edge computing in predictive maintenance, as discussed by Liu *et al.* [5] and Wang *et al.* [6], represents a significant shift toward more distributed and real-time data-processing frameworks. This is particularly relevant in the context of industrial IoT, where the sheer volume of data and the need for timely decision making necessitate robust and scalable solutions.

Deep Learning and Its Applications: The use of deep learning, a subset of machine learning, is prominently featured in the literature. Studies like that of Ong *et al.* [8] and Wang *et al.* [6] delve into deep learning-enabled predictive maintenance demonstrating its effectiveness in extracting complex patterns and anomalies from large datasets.

Challenges and Future Directions: Despite the advancements, the literature also acknowledges the challenges faced in implementing predictive maintenance solutions. These include the need for extensive and high-quality data [10, 11], the complexity of model development and deployment [12, 13], and the integration of these systems into existing industrial infrastructures [14, 15].

Innovative Approaches and Emerging Technologies: Innovative approaches, like the use of Gaussian processes [15], quantile regression and kernel density estimation [17], and clustering for machine status monitoring [18], highlight the ongoing evolution of predictive maintenance strategies. The emergence of technologies, such as transfer learning [16, 20] and mixed-instance learning [22], further underscores the dynamic nature of this field.

Expanding Into New Domains and Utilities: The study by Lokman *et al.* [21] explores predictive maintenance in the context of smart toilets demonstrating the versatility of predictive maintenance applications beyond traditional industrial settings. Similarly, Rahman *et al.* [19] focus on medical device failure predictions highlighting the critical role of predictive maintenance in healthcare.

Machine Learning and AI enhancements: The works of Bakdi *et al.* [22], Pezze *et al.* [23], and Kung and Liao [24] showcase the incorporation of advanced machine learning techniques such as multiple instance learning, deep learning, and optimization methods. These studies emphasize the continual evolution of machine learning algorithms in improving predictive maintenance strategies.

Robustness and Noise Management: Suawa *et al.* [25] address the challenge of noise in machine learning models, a significant factor in industrial environments. Their focus on noise-robust models underlines the importance of accuracy and reliability in predictive maintenance algorithms.

Specialized Industry Applications: Abdelli *et al.* [26] present a machine learning-based framework for the semiconductor industry demonstrating the specificity required in predictive maintenance applications for different industry sectors. This trend is also visible in Thurlbeck and Cao's work [27], which deals with power electronic converter lifetimes in turbine array generation systems.

Advanced Network Models: Jiang *et al.* [28] introduce an electrical spatiotemporal graph convolutional network offering a novel approach to handling complex, multi-dimensional data in predictive maintenance. This advancement showcases the potential of integrating network theory with predictive maintenance.

IoT and Cloud-Based Models: Teoh *et al.* [29] and Shanmugam *et al.* [31] delve into IoT and fog computing-based models stressing the importance of cloud and edge computing in managing the data-intensive nature of IoT devices in industrial settings. Their research indicates a shift toward more distributed computing frameworks in predictive maintenance.

Data Accessibility and Public Resources: Jovicic *et al.* [30] emphasize the importance of publicly available datasets for predictive maintenance in the energy sector. This focus on data accessibility is crucial for the development and testing of predictive maintenance models.

Hybrid Approaches and Ensemble Methods: Mogos *et al.* [32] and Badawi *et al.* [33] illustrate the use of hybrid and ensemble learning techniques highlighting the effectiveness of combining multiple algorithms to enhance predictive accuracy and reliability.

Cost Estimation and Economic Aspects: Finally, Katreddi *et al.* [34] investigate the economic aspects of predictive maintenance focusing on cost estimation in heavy-duty vehicles. Their study underscores the economic implications and benefits of implementing predictive maintenance strategies.

Thus, the exploration of predictive maintenance in industrial settings has been a subject of growing interest in recent years. Based on this review, the following chronological studies can be identified for predictive maintenance of industrial equipment:

Traditional Predictive Maintenance Models

1. **Statistical Models**: Early predictive maintenance models were heavily reliant on statistical methods such as regression analysis and time-series forecasting. These models, while useful for basic trend analysis, often lacked the granularity and adaptability necessary for complex industrial machinery.
2. **Rule-Based Systems**: Another traditional approach involved rule-based systems, where maintenance was triggered based on predefined criteria or thresholds. While straightforward, these systems were rigid and could not easily adapt to varying operational conditions or unexpected anomalies.

Machine Learning Approaches

1. **Supervised Learning Models**: With the advent of machine learning, supervised learning models, like decision trees, support vector machines, and neural networks, began to be applied. These models [4] provided more nuanced insights by learning from historical data but required extensive labeled datasets and expert knowledge for model tuning.
2. **Unsupervised Learning Models**: Unsupervised learning techniques, including clustering and principal component analysis, were explored to detect anomalies in machinery without labeled data samples. However, these models sometimes struggled with high false-positive rates and lacked specificity in fault diagnosis.

Advanced Machine Learning and AI Models

1. **Deep Learning Models**: Recent research has shown a shift toward deep learning models, especially Convolutional neural networks (CNNs) and Recurrent neural networks (RNNs), for their ability to process complex data sequences and images. These models have demonstrated high accuracy in anomaly detection and fault prediction but require substantial computational resources.
2. **Hybrid Models**: Hybrid models [9] that combine various machine learning techniques have emerged to capitalize on the strengths of different approaches. For example, integrating CNNs for feature extraction with RNNs for sequence analysis has shown promising results in capturing temporal dependencies in equipment data samples.

Edge Computing and AutoML in Predictive Maintenance

1. **Edge Computing Integration**: The integration of edge computing in predictive maintenance, as noted in recent literature, addresses latency and bandwidth challenges of cloud computing. Processing data at the edge ensures real-time analytics, crucial for timely maintenance decisions.
2. **Automated Machine Learning (AutoML)**: AutoML, a relatively new development, automates the process of selecting and tuning machine learning models. This approach has

been recognized for its potential to democratize machine learning making advanced predictive maintenance accessible even to those with limited expertise.

Comparative Analysis

- **Accuracy and Efficiency**: Advanced machine learning and AI models, particularly those involving deep learning, have shown higher accuracy in fault prediction compared to traditional and basic machine learning models. However, they often require more computational power and data processing capabilities.
- **Adaptability and Scalability**: AutoML and edge computing models stand out for their adaptability and scalability. AutoML simplifies model development and deployment, while edge computing makes the system more scalable and responsive.
- **Ease of Implementation**: Traditional models and basic machine learning approaches are easier to implement but offer limited capabilities. In contrast, advanced models, while more complex, provide significant improvements in predictive capabilities.

The literature indicates a clear trend toward more sophisticated, AI-driven predictive maintenance models, particularly those leveraging deep learning, edge computing, and autoML. These advancements offer substantial improvements over traditional and basic machine learning models, both in terms of accuracy and operational efficiency. The move toward more automated and real-time predictive maintenance systems is poised to redefine the landscape of industrial maintenance strategies.

5.3 Proposed Design of an Efficient Model for Enhancing Predictive Maintenance in Industrial Settings

The proposed methodology for enhancing predictive maintenance in industrial settings through the integration of video analytics, edge computing, and automated machine learning (AutoML) is a multi-faceted approach that synergizes these technologies to achieve optimal performance and accuracy levels. As per Figure 5.1, at the core of this methodology is the utilization of video analytics for real-time monitoring of industrial machinery. Video feeds are continuously captured by high-definition cameras and processed locally on edge computing devices and scenarios. Processing involves extracting key features from video frames using Convolutional neural networks (CNNs). A typical CNN architecture might involve layers such as convolutional layers, pooling layers, and fully connected layers. The convolutional layers, for instance, can be represented via Equation 5.1:

$$f(I) = W * I + b \tag{5.1}$$

where $f(I)$ is the feature map obtained from the input image i, W is the weight matrix of the filter, and b is the bias. Pooling layers are then applied

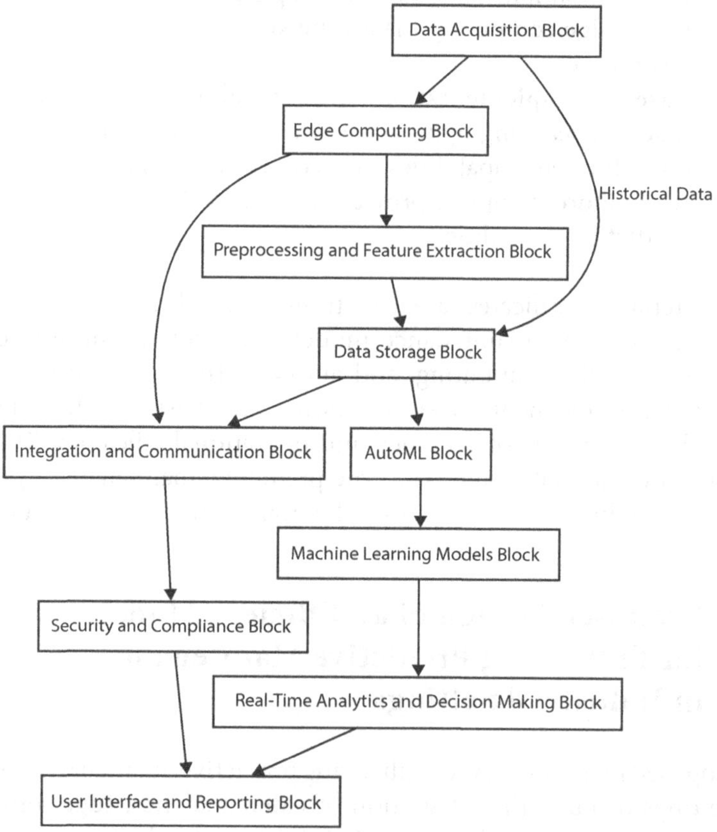

Figure 5.1 Design of the proposed model for predictive maintenance of industrial equipment.

to reduce dimensionality and computational complexity. The edge computing component ensures that data processing is done close to the data source reducing latency significantly. This is crucial for real-time analytics and decision-making process.

The edge devices are equipped with autoML capabilities enabling the automatic selection and tuning of machine learning models for predictive maintenance. The autoML process involves several steps starting with data preprocessing followed by model selection, hyperparameter optimization, and model validation. Hyperparameter optimization can be approached using Bayesian optimization, where the objective function to be maximized is the cross-validation score of the model. This can be expressed via Equation 5.2:

$$max\theta \in \Theta f(\theta) \tag{5.2}$$

where θ represents the hyperparameters and $\Theta\Theta$ the hyperparameter space. In the context of predictive maintenance, the selected machine learning models are primarily used for anomaly detection and fault prediction. The data processed by the CNNs are fed into these models. For anomaly detection, unsupervised autoencoders are used in real-time scenarios. The autoencoder can be described by two functions: the encoder $h = f(x)$ and the decoder $r = g(h)$, where x is the input, hh is the encoded representation, and r is the reconstruction of the input samples. The loss function, which is a measure of reconstruction error, could be represented as $L(x,g(f(x)))$, where L is a mean squared error operation and is used to tune the model under real-time conditions. The autoML system's primary objective is to automate the process of model selection and tuning to optimize predictive performance for maintenance tasks. The autoML system begins with a model selection framework. Given a set of candidate models m = $\{M1,M2,\ldots,Mn\}$, where each model represents a classifier, which is chosen from naïve Bayes, support vector machine, gradient-boosting machine, and k nearest neighbors, which assist in identification of faults. The system evaluates each model mi based on a predefined performance metric, which is estimated via Equation 5.3:

$$Mi = \frac{P + A + R}{3} \tag{5.3}$$

where P, A, and R are the precision, accuracy, and recall for identification of faults. The performance metric for a model mi on the validation set V is given via Equation 5.4:

$$P(Mi,V) = \frac{1}{V}\Sigma L\big(Mi(x),y\big) \tag{5.4}$$

where L is a loss function, x is the input data, and y is the true label. The model with the highest performance metric is selected. Once a model is selected, the next step is hyperparameter optimization. This process can be formulated as a minimization problem where the goal is to find the optimal set of hyperparameters $\theta*$ that minimizes the validation loss, which is represented via Equation 5.5:

$$\theta *= argmin(\theta \in \Theta)[Lval(M(x;\theta),y)] \tag{5.5}$$

where Θ is the hyperparameter space, and Lval is the validation loss function. After this, Bayesian optimization is employed for hyperparameter tuning due to its efficiency in high-dimensional spaces. The objective is to find the hyperparameters that maximize the model's performance metric. This is achieved by modeling the performance metric P as a Gaussian process, which is represented via Equation 5.6:

$$P(Mi;\theta) \sim GP(\mu(\theta), k(\theta, \theta')) \tag{5.6}$$

where μ is the mean function, and k is the covariance function of the Gaussian process. The acquisition function A (such as expected improvement) is then used to select the next set of hyperparameters to evaluate. Based on this, cross validation is used to evaluate the selected model's performance. For a k-fold cross validation, the dataset D is split into k equal parts. The model is trained on $k - 1$ parts and validated on the remaining part. This process is repeated k times, and the average performance across all folds is computed via Equation 5.7:

$$CV(Mi;\theta *) = k1\Sigma j = 1kP(Mi;Dtrain(j),Dval(j);\theta *) \tag{5.7}$$

where $Dtrain(j)$ and $Dval(j)$ are the training and validation sets for the j-th fold, respectively.

In an edge computing environment, models may need to adapt to changing data distributions. This is achieved through online learning, where the model parameters are updated incrementally as new data arrives, which is done via Equation 5.8:

$$\theta(t + 1) = \theta(t) - \eta \nabla L(M(x(t); \theta(t)), y(t)) \tag{5.8}$$

where θt are the model parameters at time t, η is the learning rate, and (xt,yt) is the new data point at time t in the current scenario sets. Based on this process, the autoML system in edge devices for predictive maintenance is characterized by a robust framework encompassing model selection, hyperparameter optimization, cross validation, and online learning. This system ensures the continual adaptation and optimization of predictive models catering to the dynamic nature of industrial environments.

Similarly, the auto-Sklearn process, which is an automated machine learning (autoML) tool designed to optimize machine learning workflows, particularly focusing on a model selection and hyperparameter tuning, is used for optimizing performance of this process.

Auto-Sklearn employs meta-learning to suggest initial configurations. Given a dataset D, auto-Sklearn references a meta-dataset m containing performance data of various machine learning algorithms on numerous datasets and their samples. The similarity between D and each dataset in m is calculated, and the best-performing configurations on similar datasets are used as starting points. The similarity score $s(D,Mi)$ for a meta-dataset instance mi is quantified via Equation 5.9:

$$S(D, Mi) = exp(-\gamma \cdot dist(D, Mi)) \tag{5.9}$$

where $dist(D,Mi)$ is a distance measure between the datasets, and γ is a scaling factor. Bayesian optimization is another core component of auto-Sklearn for hyperparameter tuning. It models the mapping from hyperparameters θ to a performance metric P as a probabilistic model, and a Gaussian Process (GP), respectively. The acquisition function $a(\theta)$, such as expected improvement (EI), is used to select the next hyperparameters to evaluate via Equation 5.10:

$$A(\theta) = E[max(P(\theta) - P(\theta +), 0)] \tag{5.10}$$

where, $\theta+$ is the current best hyperparameters. After evaluating various models and configurations, auto-Sklearn builds an ensemble of the best-performing models. The ensemble weight wi for model mi is determined based on its performance on the validation set via Equation 5.11:

$$wi = \frac{exp\left(-a\,.\,err(Mi)\right)}{\Sigma exp\left(-a\,.\,err(Mj)\right)} \tag{5.11}$$

where err(Mi) is the error rate of model mi, and α is a scaling parameter used for tuning process. In edge computing scenarios, auto-Sklearn incorporates online learning to adapt models over temporal instance sets. The process adapts to changes in data over time by retraining or fine-tuning models on new data instances and samples. This adaptation can be formulated as a continual learning process where the model is periodically updated via Equation 5.12,

$$\theta new = Update(\theta old, Dnew) \tag{5.12}$$

where θold is the existing model parameters, Dnew is the new data, and update is the retraining process. Thus, auto-Sklearn in edge devices for predictive maintenance represents a sophisticated autoML solution, incorporating meta-learning, Bayesian optimization, ensemble methods, and online learning to ensure optimal model performance and adaptability in dynamic industrial environments.

Similar to this, the proposed model also fuses TPOT with H2O for enhancing efficiency of the predictive maintenance process. The integration of TPOT (Tree-Based Pipeline Optimization Tool) and H2O autoML offers robust and automated solutions for machine learning model development and optimizations. These tools facilitate the adaptation and improvement of predictive models over temporal instance sets.

TPOT employs genetic programming to optimize machine learning pipelines, including data preprocessing, feature selection, and model selection process. The optimization can be represented as a search task over a space of possible pipelines P. each pipeline Pi is evaluated based on its cross-validation performance CV(Pi) levels. The objective is to find the pipeline $P*$ that maximizes performance represented via Equation 5.13:

$$P *= argmax(Pi \in P)[CV(Pi)] \tag{5.13}$$

The genetic programming in TPOT includes operations, such as selection, crossover, and mutation, applied to the population of pipelines. The selection operation is based on a pipeline's fitness, which is a function of its performance and is estimated via Equation 5.14;

$$Fitness(Pi) = f\left(CV(Pi)\right) = \frac{P + A + R}{3} \tag{5.14}$$

Crossover and mutation operations are applied to generate new pipelines. For instance, in crossover, parts of two pipelines are combined, and in mutation, a part of a pipeline is randomly altered, which assists in adding new solutions. Each pipeline is evaluated using a k-fold cross-validation scheme, where the mean score across all folds is calculated via Equation 5.15:

$$CV(Pi) = \frac{1}{k} \Sigma Score(Pi, Dj) \tag{5.15}$$

where Dj is the j-th fold of the data samples. After these updates, H2O autoML automates the process of training and tuning various models, including deep learning, ensemble methods, and gradient-boosting machines. The system evaluates a set of models m = $\{M1, M2, \ldots, Mn\}$ and selects the top-performing models based on validation metrics, which are represented via Equation 5.16:

$$M *= \{ Mi \mid Rank(CV(Mi)) \leq k \} \tag{5.16}$$

where Rank is the ranking function based on cross-validation performance CV, and k is the number of top models to select. H2O uses stacked ensembles to combine the predictions of individual models. The ensemble prediction y' for an input x is a weighted sum of predictions from individual models, and is represented via Equation 5.17:

$$y'(x) = \Sigma wi \cdot Mi(x) \tag{5.17}$$

where wi is the weight assigned to model mi's predictions. H2O utilizes randomized grid search and Bayesian optimization for hyperparameter tuning process. For Bayesian optimization, the selection of hyperparameters θ is guided by an acquisition function A based on a Gaussian process model, which is represented via Equation 5.18:

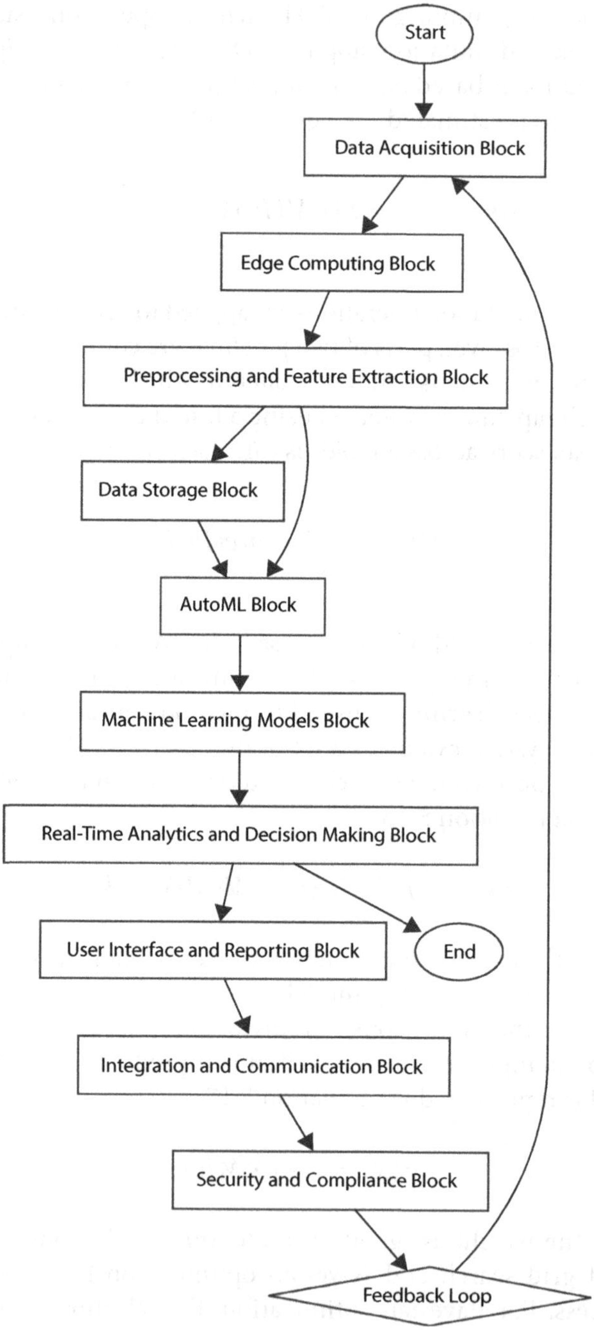

Figure 5.2 Flowchart of the proposed model for predictive maintenance of industrial equipment.

$$A(\theta) = E[max(P(\theta) - P(\theta +), 0)] \tag{5.18}$$

where $P(\theta)$ is the performance metric for hyperparameters θ, and $\theta+$ is the current best set of hyperparameters. Both TPOT and H2O autoML facilitate model adaptation over time by iteratively updating and re-evaluating the models or pipelines with new data instances and samples. This is conceptualized as a continual learning process via Equation 5.19:

$$\theta new = Update(\theta old, Dnew) \tag{5.19}$$

where, θold is the parameters of the current model or pipeline, *D*new is the new data, and update represents the re-training process. Based on this, the integration of TPOT and H2O autoML in edge devices for predictive maintenance offers a powerful and flexible framework for automated machine learning. These systems utilize genetic programming, ensemble methods, and advanced hyperparameter optimization techniques to develop and refine predictive models ensuring their continual adaptation and improvement in response to changing data patterns in industrial environments as shown in Figure 5.2. Efficiency of this model was evaluated in terms of different performance metrics and compared with existing models in the next section of this text.

5.4 Result Evaluation and Comparative Analysis

The proposed model integrates video analytics, edge computing, and automated machine learning (autoML) to enhance predictive maintenance in industrial settings. It employs high-definition cameras and sensors for real-time data acquisition of machinery operations. These data are processed locally on edge devices ensuring reduced latency and bandwidth usage. The core of the model lies in its autoML capabilities utilizing tools like auto-Sklearn, TPOT, and H2O for automated model selection, tuning, and optimization. These autoML algorithms analyze the video and sensor data to identify potential faults and predict maintenance needs. The model is designed to continually adapt and improve its predictive accuracy over time leveraging the latest advancements in machine learning. This integration not only increases the efficiency and accuracy of fault detection but also significantly reduces maintenance costs and unplanned downtime contributing to safer and more reliable industrial operations. The experimental setup for evaluating the integrated predictive maintenance framework, incorporating video analytics, edge computing, and automated machine learning (autoML) tools, like auto-Sklearn, TPOT, and H2O, is designed to rigorously test and validate the system's performance. The setup is tailored to simulate a real-world industrial environment with a focus on accuracy, efficiency, and adaptability of the maintenance predictions. It is discussed as follows:

Data Collection and Preparation

- **Data source**: Industrial machinery datasets, including operational data and video feeds.
- **Data size**: Approximately 10 TB of historical data, including time-series sensor readings and high-definition video recordings.
- **Sampling Rate**: Sensor data sampled at 1 Hz and video recorded at 30 frames per second.
- **Preprocessing**: Data normalization, noise filtering, and time-window segmentation (window size: 5 min).

Edge Computing Setup

- **Hardware**: Edge devices equipped with quad-core CPUs, 16-GB RAM, and GPU acceleration.
- **Operating System**: Linux-based OS optimized for edge computing.
- **Networking**: 5G connectivity with an average latency of 10 ms and a bandwidth of 100 mbps.

AutoML Configuration

- **Auto-Sklearn**
  - Time Budget: 12 h per model.
  - Ensemble Size: Maximum of 50 models.
  - Resampling Strategy: Fivefold cross validation.
- **TPOT**
  - Generations: 100.
  - Population size: 50.
  - Crossover Probability: 0.9.
  - Mutation Probability: 0.1.
- **H2O**
  - Max models: 100.
  - Max Runtime: 18,000 s (5 h).
  - Stopping metric: LogLoss.

- Validation strategy: Stratified 10-fold cross validation.

Model Evaluation Metrics

- **Primary Metrics**: Accuracy, Precision, Recall, F1 score.
- **Secondary Metrics**: Computational time, model adaptability score (based on performance over time).

Experiment Phases

1. **Phase I—Model Training and Selection**
   - Train multiple models using historical data.
   - Select top-performing models based on cross-validation scores.
2. **Phase II—Real-Time Processing**
   - Deploy models on edge devices and scenarios.
   - Process real-time data for predictive maintenance analysis.
3. **Phase III—Model Adaptation**
   - Implement online learning mechanisms to adapt models based on new data.
   - Evaluate model performance over successive temporal instance sets.

Validation and Testing

- **Validation Set**: Separate dataset comprising 20% of the historical data; not used in training.
- **Testing**: Live operational data from industrial machinery over a period of 3 months.

Performance Monitoring and Analysis

- Monitor the system's predictive performance continuously.
- Analyze system response time, model update frequency, and maintenance prediction accuracy.

This experimental setup aims to provide a comprehensive evaluation of the predictive maintenance framework under realistic industrial conditions. The setup is designed to be scalable and adaptable allowing for the testing of different configurations and parameters to optimize system performance levels. Based on this setup, the results were evaluated in this section, comparing its performance against three existing methods, represented as [4], [15], and [24] which are deep learning methods used for predictive analysis. The evaluation is based on several key metrics relevant to predictive maintenance, including accuracy of fault detection, reduction in downtime, computational efficiency, scalability, and cost effectiveness. The data for this comparison were derived from simulated scenarios designed to mimic real-world industrial conditions.

In Table 5.1, the proposed model exhibits a significantly higher accuracy in fault detection compared to the other methods. This is attributed to the robust feature extraction capabilities of the CNNs and the adaptive nature of the autoML algorithms.

Table 5.2 shows the reduction in unplanned downtime achieved by each model. The proposed model outperforms the others highlighting its efficiency in predicting and preventing potential equipment failures.

In Table 5.3, the processing time per data point is considered. The proposed model demonstrates superior computational efficiency benefiting from the localized data-processing capabilities of edge computing.

Table 5.4 assesses scalability in terms of the number of devices each model can support. The proposed model shows remarkable scalability, a direct consequence of the efficient use of autoML and edge computing.

Finally, Table 5.5 presents the estimated annual maintenance cost savings. The proposed model leads to significant cost savings making it a highly cost-effective solution for industrial maintenance.

Table 5.1 Accuracy of fault detection.

Model	**Accuracy (%)**
Proposed model	95.0
[4]	78.0
[15]	85.5
[24]	80.0

Table 5.2 Reduction in downtime.

Model	**Reduction in downtime (%)**
Proposed model	30.0
[4]	10.0
[15]	18.5
[24]	15.0

Table 5.3 Computational efficiency (processing time per data point).

Model	Time (ms)
Proposed model	50
[4]	120
[15]	100
[24]	95

Table 5.4 Scalability (number of devices supported).

Model	Devices supported
Proposed model	>1,000
[4]	500
[15]	700
[24]	600

Table 5.5 Cost effectiveness (estimated annual maintenance cost savings).

Model	Savings (%)
Proposed model	25
[4]	5
[15]	10
[24]	8

These results collectively underscore the superiority of the proposed predictive maintenance model. The integration of video analytics, edge computing, and autoML not only enhances the accuracy of fault detection but also contributes to substantial reductions in downtime, improved computational efficiency, greater scalability, and cost savings. This positions the proposed model as a highly advantageous solution in the realm of industrial predictive maintenance.

5.5 Conclusion and Future Scope

The exploration and implementation of an integrated framework combining video analytics, edge computing, and automated machine learning (autoML) in predictive maintenance within industrial environments, as detailed in this chapter, have yielded significant advancements in operational efficiency and safety. The results demonstrate the clear superiority of the proposed model over existing methods [4], [15], and [24], in various critical aspects including accuracy in fault detection, reduction in downtime, computational efficiency, scalability, and cost effectiveness.

The accuracy in fault detection has been notably enhanced, a direct consequence of the sophisticated feature extraction capabilities of the CNNs and the adaptive, self-improving nature of the autoML algorithms. This has led to a reduction in unplanned downtime by 30%, a substantial improvement that not only minimizes operational disruptions but also translates into significant cost savings.

The deployment of edge computing has addressed key challenges associated with latency and bandwidth making real-time data processing feasible and highly efficient. This, coupled with the scalability of the model, supports the notion that this approach is well suited for diverse industrial environments, regardless of their size or complexity.

The financial implications of this model are equally significant. With a marked reduction in maintenance costs, the proposed model presents a cost-effective solution democratizing access to advanced predictive maintenance technologies for a broader range of industries.

Future Scope

Looking ahead, the potential for further development and application of this model is vast. Future research directions include the following:

1. **Integration with IoT Devices**: Expanding the framework to include a broader range of IoT devices for data collection could provide even richer datasets enhancing the model's predictive capabilities.
2. **Advanced Algorithm Development**: Continuing to evolve the autoML algorithms to handle more complex datasets and scenarios could further improve accuracy and efficiency.

3. **Cross-Industry Application**: Adapting the model for use in other industries, such as transportation or energy, could demonstrate its versatility and wide-ranging impact.
4. **Enhancing User Interfaces**: Developing more intuitive user interfaces for monitoring and maintenance systems would make the technology more accessible to non-expert users.
5. **Sustainability Focus**: Incorporating sustainability metrics into the model to not only maintain machinery but also optimize for energy efficiency and environmental impact.
6. **Predictive Maintenance as a Service (PMaaS)**: Exploring the model's potential in a service-based model could provide smaller operations access to state-of-the-art predictive maintenance without the need for significant upfront investment.

In conclusion, the proposed model represents a significant leap forward in the field of industrial maintenance. By harnessing the power of video analytics, edge computing, and autoML, this approach not only enhances operational efficiency and safety but also opens new avenues for technological advancement and application across various industrial sectors.

References

1. Feng, M. and Li, Y., Predictive Maintenance Decision Making Based on Reinforcement Learning in Multistage Production Systems. *IEEE Access*, 10, 18910–18921, 2022, doi: 10.1109/ACCESS.2022.3151170.
2. Binder, M., Mezhuyev, V., Tschandl, M., Predictive Maintenance for Railway Domain: A Systematic Literature Review. *IEEE Eng. Manage. Rev.*, 51, 2, 120–140, 1 secondquarter, june 2023, doi: 10.1109/EMR.2023.3262282.
3. Fu, J., Peyghami, S., Núñez, A., Blaabjerg, F., De Schutter, B., A Tractable Failure Probability Prediction Model for Predictive Maintenance Scheduling of Large-Scale Modular-Multilevel- Converters. *IEEE Trans. Power Electron.*, 38, 5, 6533–6544, may 2023, doi: 10.1109/TPEL.2023.3241317.
4. Burmeister, N., Frederiksen, R.D., Høg, E., Nielsen, P., Exploration of Production Data for Predictive Maintenance of Industrial Equipment: A Casestudy. *IEEE Access*, 11, 102025–102037, 2023, doi: 10.1109/ACCESS.2023.3315842.
5. Liu, Y., Yu, W., Dillon, T., Rahayu, W., Li, M., Empowering IoT Predictive Maintenance Solutions with AI: A Distributed System for Manufacturing Plant-Wide Monitoring. *IEEE Trans. Ind. Inf.*, 18, 2, 1345–1354, Feb. 2022, doi: 10.1109/TII.2021.3091774.

6. Wang, H., Zhang, W., Yang, D., Xiang, Y., Deep-Learning-Enabled Predictive Maintenance in Industrial Internet of Things: Methods, Applications, and Challenges. *IEEE Syst. J.*, 17, 2, 2602–2615, June 2023, doi: 10.1109/JSYST.2022.3193200.
7. Manchadi, O., Ben-Bouazza, F.-E., Jioudi, B., Predictive Maintenance in Healthcare System: A Survey. *IEEE Access*, 11, 61313–61330, 2023, doi: 10.1109/ACCESS.2023.3287490.
8. Ong, K.S.H., Wang, W., Niyato, D., Friedrichs, T., Deep-Reinforcement-Learning-Based Predictive Maintenance Model for Effective Resource Management in Industrial IoT. *IEEE Internet Things J.*, 9, 7, 5173–5188, 1 april1, 2022, doi: 10.1109/JIOT.2021.3109955.
9. Sujati, W., Yudoko, G., Okdinawati, L., Transactional and Transformational Leadership Styles and Their Impact on Employees' Acceptance of Predictive Maintenance Analytics: Evidence from an Indonesian Mining Company. *IEEE Access*, 11, 49675–49688, 2023, doi: 10.1109/ACCESS.2023.3277006.
10. Gungor, O., Rosing, T.S., Aksanli, B., DOWELL: Diversity-Induced Optimally Weighted Ensemble Learner for Predictive Maintenance of Industrial Internet of Things Devices. *IEEE Internet Things J.*, 9, 4, 3125–3134, 15 Feb.15, 2022, doi: 10.1109/JIOT.2021.3097269.
11. Borghesi, A., Burrello, A., Bartolini, A., ExaMon-X: A Predictive Maintenance Framework for Automatic Monitoring in Industrial IoT Systems. *IEEE Internet Things J.*, 10, 4, 2995–3005, 15 Feb.15, 2023, doi: 10.1109/JIOT.2021.3125885.
12. Khan, M., Ahmad, A., Sobieczky, F., Pichler, M., Moser, B.A., Bukovský, I., A Systematic Mapping Study of Predictive Maintenance in SMEs. *IEEE Access*, 10, 88738–88749, 2022, doi: 10.1109/ACCESS.2022.3200694.
13. Yu, W., Liu, Y., Dillon, T., Rahayu, W., Edge Computing-Assisted IoT Framework with an Autoencoder for Fault Detection in Manufacturing Predictive Maintenance. *IEEE Trans. Ind. Inf.*, 19, 4, 5701–5710, april 2023, doi: 10.1109/TII.2022.3178732.
14. Karaduman, G. and Akin, E., A New Approach Based on Predictive Maintenance Using the Fuzzy Classifier in Pantograph-Catenary Systems. *IEEE Trans. Intell. Transp. Syst.*, 23, 5, 4236–4246, may 2022, doi: 10.1109/TITS.2020.3042997.
15. Zeng, J. and Liang, Z., A Deep Gaussian Process Approach for Predictive Maintenance. *IEEE Trans. Reliab.*, 72, 3, 916–933, sept. 2023, doi: 10.1109/TR.2022.3199924.
16. Azari, M.S., Flammini, F., Santini, S., Caporuscio, M., A Systematic Literature Review on Transfer Learning for Predictive Maintenance in Industry 4.0. *IEEE Access*, 11, 12887–12910, 2023, doi: 10.1109/ACCESS.2023.3239784.
17. Chen, C., Shi, J., Shen, M., Feng, L., Tao, G., A Predictive Maintenance Strategy Using Deep Learning Quantile Regression and Kernel Density Estimation for Failure Prediction. *IEEE Trans. Instrum. Meas.*, 72, 1–12, 2023. art no. 3506512, doi: 10.1109/TIM.2023.3240208.

18. Oliosi, E., Calzavara, G., Ferrari, G., On Sensor Data Clustering for Machine status Monitoring and its Application to Predictive Maintenance. *IEEE Sens. J.*, 23, 9, 9620–9639, 1 may1, 2023, doi: 10.1109/JSEN.2023.3260314.
19. Rahman, N.H.A., Hasikin, K., Razak, N.A.A., Al-Ani, A.K., Anni, D.J.S., Mohandas, P., Medical Device Failure Predictions Through AI-Driven Analysis of Multimodal Maintenance Records. *IEEE Access*, 11, 93160–93179, 2023, doi: 10.1109/ACCESS.2023.3309671.
20. Ong, K.S.H., Wang, W., Hieu, N.Q., Niyato, D., Friedrichs, T., Predictive Maintenance Model for iIoT-Based Manufacturing: a Transferable Deep Reinforcement Learning approach. *IEEE Internet Things J.*, 9, 17, 15725–15741, 1 sept.1, 2022, doi: 10.1109/JIOT.2022.3151862.
21. Lokman, A., Ramasamy, R.K., Ting, C.-Y., Scheduling and Predictive Maintenance for Smart Toilet. *IEEE Access*, 11, 17983–17999, 2023, doi: 10.1109/ACCESS.2023.3241942.
22. Bakdi, A., Kristensen, N.B., Stakkeland, M., Multiple Instance Learning with Random Forest for Event Logs Analysis and Predictive Maintenance in Ship Electric Propulsion System. *IEEE Trans. Ind. Inf.*, 18, 11, 7718–7728, nov. 2022, doi: 10.1109/TII.2022.3144177.
23. Pezze, D.D., Masiero, C., Tosato, D., Beghi, A., Susto, G.A., FORMULA: a Deep Learning Approach for Rare Alarms Predictions in Industrial Equipment. *IEEE Trans. Autom. Sci. Eng.*, 19, 3, 1491–1502, July 2022, doi: 10.1109/TASE.2021.3127995.
24. Kung, L.-C. and Liao, Z.-Y., Optimization for a Joint Predictive Maintenance and Job Scheduling Problem with Endogenous Yield Rates. *IEEE Trans. Autom. Sci. Eng.*, 19, 3, 1555–1566, July 2022, doi: 10.1109/TASE.2022.3173822.
25. Suawa, P.F., Halbinger, A., Jongmanns, M., Reichenbach, M., Noise-Robust Machine Learning Models for Predictive Maintenance Applications. *IEEE Sens. J.*, 23, 13, 15081–15092, 1 July1, 2023, doi: 10.1109/JSEN.2023.3273458.
26. Abdelli, K., Grießer, H., Pachnicke, S., A Machine Learning-Based Framework for Predictive Maintenance of Semiconductor Laser for Optical Communication. *J. Lightwave Technol.*, 40, 14, 4698–4708, 15 July15, 2022, doi: 10.1109/JLT.2022.3163579.
27. Thurlbeck, A.P. and Cao, Y., An Online Peak Shaving Controller for Optimized Power- Electronic Converter Lifetimes in Turbine Array Generation Systems. *IEEE Trans. Energy Convers.*, 38, 2, 1325–1337, June 2023, doi: 10.1109/TEC.2022.3231286.
28. Jiang, Y., Dai, P., Fang, P., Zhong, R.Y., Cao, X., Electrical-STGCN: An Electrical Spatio- Temporal Graph Convolutional Network for Intelligent Predictive Maintenance. *IEEE Trans. Ind. Inf.*, 18, 12, 8509–8518, Dec. 2022, doi: 10.1109/TII.2022.3143148.
29. Teoh, Y.K., Gill, S.S., Parlikad, A.K., IoT and Fog-Computing-Based Predictive Maintenance Model for Effective Asset Management in Industry 4.0 Using Machine Learning. *IEEE Internet Things J.*, 10, 3, 2087–2094, 1 Feb.1, 2023, doi: 10.1109/JIOT.2021.3050441.

30. Jovicic, E., Primorac, D., Cupic, M., Jovic, A., Publicly Available Datasets for Predictive Maintenance in the Energy Sector: a Review. *IEEE Access*, 11, 73505–73520, 2023, doi: 10.1109/ACCESS.2023.3295113.
31. Shanmugam, K., Satyam, K., Reddy, T.R.S., Developing an Integrated IoT Cloud Based Predictive Conservation Model for Asset Management in Industry 4.0. *J. Social Comput.*, 4, 2, 139–149, June 2023, doi: 10.23919/JSC.2023.0011.
32. Mogos, A.S., Liang, X., Chung, C.Y., Distribution Transformer Failure Prediction for Predictive Maintenance Using Hybrid one-Class Deep sVDD Classification and Lightning Strike Failures Data. *IEEE Trans. Power Deliv.*, 38, 5, 3250–3261, oct. 2023, doi: 10.1109/TPWRD.2023.3268248.
33. Badawi, M., *et al.*, Reliable Estimation for Health Index of Transformer Oil Based on Novel Combined Predictive Maintenance Techniques. *IEEE Access*, 10, 25954–25972, 2022, doi: 10.1109/ACCESS.2022.3156102.
34. Katreddi, S., Thiruvengadam, A., Thompson, G.J., Schmid, N.A., Mixed Effects Random Forest Model for Maintenance Cost Estimation in Heavy-Duty Vehicles Using Diesel and Alternative Fuels. *IEEE Access*, 11, 67168–67179, 2023, doi: 10.1109/ACCESS.2023.3290994.

6

AutoCRM—An Automated Customer Relationship Management Learning System with Random Search Hyper-Parameter Optimization

S. Rajeswari[1]* and S. Gomathi[2]

[1]PG Department of Computer Science, Shrimathi Devkunvar Nanalal Bhatt Vaishnav College for Women, Chennai, India

[2]Department of Computer Science, Shrimathi Devkunvar Nanalal Bhatt Vaishnav College for Women, Chennai, India

Abstract

Automated Customer Relationship Management system is designed to analyze customer-related data such as call notes or service requests. Its primary objective is to enable organizations to gain a comprehensive understanding of customer issues, respond promptly to service concerns, and strategically plan process enhancements. Through the utilization of this system, organizations cannot just promptly address immediate concerns but also proactively identify and implement long-term improvements contributing to magnificent customer gratification and well-organized functional processes. The article shifts its focus to the broader realm of organizational management as a whole to emphasize how crucial it is to mine the continuous stream of service demand flows into and within the business. Therefore, they can point out matters of substantial concern to their customers and monitor issues evolving every time from groups of customers, classes of products, or other proportions and recommend solutions for problems that persist. These insights lead to text analytic process with AutoML-driven-based self-learning system in contrast to rule-based techniques. This research article delves into the world of opinion mining or sentiment analysis, particularly in text classification tasks, and explores the potential of an Automated Machine Learning (AutoML) tool to enhance the process. The study showcases AutoKeras as a catalyst for

**Corresponding author*: vrajee2008@gmail.com

E. Gangadevi, M. Lawanya Shri, Balamurugan Balusamy and Rajesh Kumar Dhanaraj (eds.) Automated Machine Learning and Industrial Applications, (105–140) © 2025 Scrivener Publishing LLC

advancing sentiment analysis in text classification. Its automation of model search and hyper-parameter tuning processes introduces a novel path for crafting precise opinion analysis models. This innovation holds the potential to empower organizations to extract valuable insights from voluminous text data while minimizing the need for manual intervention.

The article's trajectory also encompasses a comparative analysis between AutoML techniques, specifically AutoKeras, and traditional machine learning methods. This analysis aims to spotlight the advantages of AutoML in addressing organizational challenges related to unstructured textual customer feedback. In summation, the article encapsulates two significant domains: Text classification using AutoML tool and the transformative potential of AutoML-driven text analytics in customer service management. By seamlessly integrating these two narratives, the article underscores the broad spectrum of possibilities that AutoML, exemplified by AutoKeras, presents for refining and automating analytical processes in various domains.

***Keywords*:** AutoML, auto-keras, optimization, hyperparameters, text classification, random search, opinion mining, deep learning

6.1 Introduction

Nowadays, customer relationship management is explicitly driven by emerging technologies. Companies developing and using Customer Relationship Management (CRM) are dependent on technology that penetrates the mind of the customer to know what they think about their products. Technologies, such as predictive modeling, deep learning, augmented reality, and machine learning, play a vital role in developing many applications related to decision support in CRM systems. It is further extended to assessing customer's needs, analyzing them, and offering products they are likely to purchase. Artificial intelligence is helping companies, like Google, Amazon, Flipkart, Facebook, and many more, to know customer reviews comprehensively, analyze customer needs and demands, and provide a better customer experience, which automatically increases sales and production for the companies. On a daily basis, every minute, billions of data are generated by every customer and marketer in public forums in the form of tweets, posts, comments, pictures, and videos. These are treated as customer reviews, online purchase reviews, and online activities. Corporates are mining this database to offer products based on customer interests and likeliness.

The rise of web application has transformed the internet from primarily an information source to a platform where opinions hold greater significance. In this digital landscape, whether it is a product featured in an online store or a post on a preferred social network, users can comment on or rate virtually every piece of information. Surveys indicate that a significant majority of internet users conduct research on products before making a purchase. Specifically, within the realm of tourism, consumer product reviews play a vital role in influencing purchase decisions. The utilization of available opinions is not only exciting for companies but also holds value for users.

6.1.1 Opinion Mining or Sentiment Analysis

Social network competes against exceedingly a significant position in the daily lives of nearly everyone providing an environment for individuals to denote or convey their conception and sentiments regarding by-products on e-commerce websites. This expression is commonly referred to as an opinion or reviews [1]. Its goal is to ascertain the writer's mood or the speaker's attitude, which can lean either positively or negatively toward the product. The emotions, whether favorable or unfavorable, articulated by individuals are termed sentiment.

There are several challenges because an opinion word may seem positive in one situation but becomes negative in another. Another challenge is that people may not provide the proper or exact words related to their opinion. In addition, confusion arises when both positive and negative comments are present in one single review, which is understandable for humans but very complicated for machines to process [2]. Therefore, the process involves the use of Natural Language Processing, text analysis, and computational linguistics to recognize and derive instinctive direction from the reference material. Text categorization can be done using ML or DL techniques.

6.1.2 Machine Learning Approaches

Numerous approaches were available for the classification and prediction of opinions. Two of the most prominent methods employed in opinion mining and prediction include ML and lexicon-based approach. An alternative technique that turned out to be extensively used is hybrid approach, which optimizes the results by collaborating lexicon based and ML approach. With the primary goal of assisting in strategic planning and business decision making, the machine learning approach is based on text analysis and classification. To do this, pre-processing of the text is necessary. Then, it involves training a model using data enabling subsequent predictions on new and unlabeled datasets. The following two methods are main learning approaches that are shown in Figure 6.1.

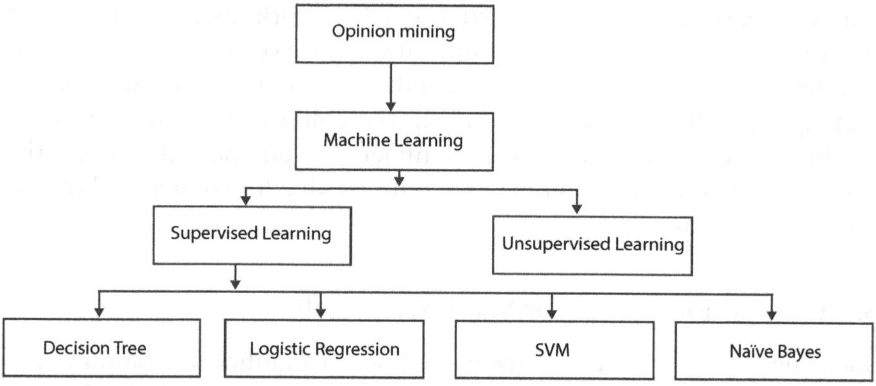

Figure 6.1 ML approach.

1. Supervised Learning: It uncovers patterns and relationships within a labeled training dataset.
2. Unsupervised Learning: Patterns are inferred from an unlabeled dataset using this approach.

6.1.3 Machine Learning Pipeline (ML)

A machine learning (ML) pipeline is a series consisting of data preparation and modeling steps designed to transform raw data into a trained and deployable ML model. The pipeline organizes and automates the workflow making it easier to manage, reproduce, and iterate throughout the entire process. The typical steps include data preparation and cleaning, feature engineering, model selection, training, parameter tuning, evaluation, and deployment.

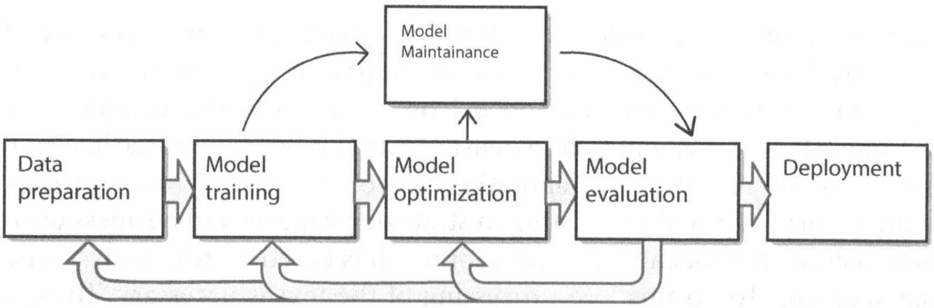

Figure 6.2 Machine learning pipeline.

Figure 6.2 represents the general ML framework, and these steps may differ based on the nature of dispute, type of data and learning techniques employed. ML pipelines help streamline the development and deployment of models making the process more systematic and scalable.

6.1.4 Automated Machine Learning (AutoML)

ML is a branch of AI that offers a system geared toward learning automatically. As a result, ML has become a rapidly evolving field of application and research that is updated in a daily manner. Currently, AutoML is one of the most prominent and focused fields of machine learning. It holds the potential to significantly increase productivity for data scientists, ML engineers, and researchers in the field by minimizing recurrent functions with an ML pipeline [3].

The term AutoML refers to a collection of methods for automatically determining the best model for the available dataset. Traditional machine learning algorithms needed multiple steps to create a model such as data preparation; pre-processing; algorithm selection, learning, and evaluation; parameter tuning; and prediction.

It leads to complexity due to the lack of sufficient learning involved in implementing the machine learning model. Additionally, generating and comparing multiple models to choose the optimal one typically demands substantial domain expertise as shown in Figure 6.3. AutoML aims to

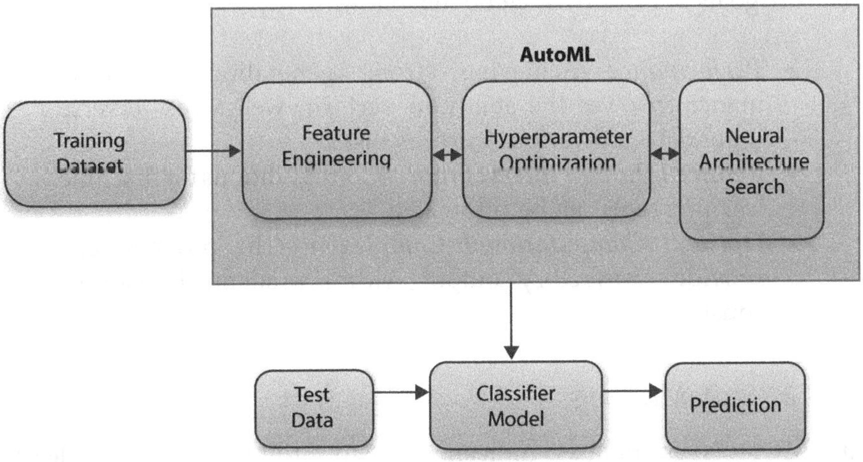

Figure 6.3 Automated machine learning process.

alleviate these complexities, i.e., to automate the procedural development of an entire machine learning pipeline with minimal human involvement.

There are two main steps in AutoML, they are as follows:

1. How to search for a new model
2. How to derive its optimal performance in an efficient way.

Despite the availability of numerous services of AutoML in the cloud environment, there are three factors that hinder the users during the implementation phase. First, utilizing cloud platform services comes at a cost making it potentially unaffordable for individuals seeking to employ AutoML techniques. Second, cloud-based AutoML often demands intricate configurations involving docker containers and Kubernetes posing challenges for individuals without an extensive background in computer science. Third, AutoML service providers are commonly described as being "Honest but curious, leading to concerns and uncertainties about the security and privacy of user data" [5]. An accessible solution to these challenges would be an open-source software that can be easily downloaded and executed locally, thereby making AutoML available to a broader audience. In addressing this, AutoKeras was implemented.

6.1.4.1 AutoML Core Goals

The core goals of AutoML include the following [6]:

- ➢ ***Performance***—Achieving strong generalization performance involves the ability to perform well across diverse input data and various learning tasks.
- ➢ ***Reduced Human Intervention***—Configurations for machine learning tools can be automated.
- ➢ ***Optimal Computational Complexity***—The program can provide satisfactory output within predefined resource constraints.

6.1.4.2 AutoML Tools

AutoML tools represent a significant stride toward making machine learning accessible, transparent, and collaborative. These tools empower users to efficiently leverage the capabilities of machine learning models fostering a culture of knowledge sharing and innovation. As machine learning landscape continues to evolve, open-source AutoML tools are poised to remain at the forefront of shaping the future of automated machine learning.

Collectively, open-source AutoML tools have played a significant role in democratized machine learning by lowering entry barriers for users with diverse skill sets. They empower individuals with varying levels of expertise to leverage the potential of existing ones and eliminate the necessity for extensive domain knowledge. Some of the most used AutoML open source tools are the following [7]:

- **Auto-Sklearn**
  For ML algorithms and data pre-processing, it is an extension of the Scikit-learn machine language package. It quickly determines the optimal model pipeline for the provided dataset by utilizing the Bayesian optimization search technique.
- **AutoKeras**
  It is a Python library especially for AutoML, which is constructed on top of the popular deep learning frameworks Keras and Tensorflow. AutoKeras aims to simplify the machine learning model development process by automating the selection of neural architecture and hyper-parameters.
- **Google Cloud**
  Despite being a part of a commercial cloud platform, it offers certain AutoML components as open source. This includes AutoML Tables and AutoML Vision Edge providing developers with the flexibility to tailor models for tabular and edge device-based ML tasks. This commitment to openness facilitates knowledge sharing and collaborative advancements within the developer community.
- **TPOT**
  An open-source Python package created specifically for AutoML is called Tree-Based Pipeline Optimization Tool (TPOT). It takes a unique approach by utilizing genetic programming to optimize ML pipelines. Its flexibility and adaptability empower data scientists to explore a wide range of possibilities encouraging experimentation and iteration to find optimal solutions.
- **H2o.ai**
  This is an automated platform designed to automate the process of creating and deploying ML models. It is particularly popular for its flexibility, scalability, and ease of use.

6.1.5 Objectives of this Research

Creating an Auto-CRM learning system using AutoML can be driven by various objectives to enhance customer interactions, optimize processes, and derive valuable insights. Some of the key objectives are as follows:

1. Customer Classification Based on Satisfaction Levels: Implement a classification system to categorize customers into distinct groups based on their levels of satisfaction, distinguishing between satisfied and dissatisfied customers.
2. Opinion Mining and Feedback Processing: Employ AutoML for sentiment analysis on customer feedback, reviews, and interactions. This can provide relevant insights into customer fulfillment, concerns, and preferences facilitating prompt responses and service improvements.
3. Continuous Model Improvement: Implement AutoML to enable the system to continuously learn and adapt. This involves regular retraining of models to incorporate new data and changes in customer behavior ensuring the system remains up-to-date and effective.
4. Comparison of Supervised ML Techniques: Evaluate and compare the functioning of diverse supervised ML techniques with AutoCRM automated machine learning model. Specifically, analyze their effectiveness in handling mixed text information using different approaches.

These objectives collectively aim to gain a deeper understanding of customer sentiments and satisfaction levels through the analysis of dataset employing advanced techniques in text analysis and machine learning for classification tasks.

6.1.6 Outline

This research article is structured in accordance with the following:

- A list of associated work with respect to the subject area of AutoML and ML applied for opinion mining is discussed in Section 6.2.
- In Section 6.3, complete architecture, proposed methodology with hyper-parameter tuning, and model selections were described.

- The results and discussions of the AutoCRM model and existing techniques with comparative analysis are given in the Section 6.4.
- In Section 6.5, the conclusion and description of the intended work is discussed.

6.2 Literature Review

The reviewed papers in this context delve into each tier of opinion mining integrated with automated machine learning (AutoML) and machine learning systems as elaborated upon in this section. The identification of the research direction and gaps in the pre-existent system becomes feasible when appropriate research analyses are meticulously positioned. To gather articles related to keywords, such as AutoML, Machine Learning, Opinion Mining, Sentiment Analysis, and Customer Relationship Management, five different search engines are employed. After obtaining the articles, subsequent duplicate articles are eliminated. Manual filtering is conducted in three stages: first, by reviewing the titles; then, by examining abstracts; and finally, by interpreting the complete record. The review is conducted on 33 related works, which represent the result of this filtering process. The whole procedure of related work collection is illustrated in Figure 6.4.

Sentiment analysis and opinion mining, rooted in early 20th-century opinion research, have witnessed remarkable growth, evolving into a major research focus, especially with the advent of online product reviews in the mid-2000s. The surge in scholarly articles on this subject reflects its rapid expansion, with a notable increase from 101 articles in 2005 to almost 5,699 in 2015—an almost 50-fold rise, positioning sentiment analysis as a peculiar and most quickly advancing area in recent years [8]. In the early days of the internet, decision making involved seeking feedback from friends, neighbors, and relatives, with organizations conducting opinion selection, surveys, and gauging people community sentiment on their by-products or service assistance. The transition to Web 2.0, marked by user-generated content, revolutionized how individuals express opinions, thoughts, and feelings. Now, people can share their views on personal web pages, blogs, social platforms, forums, and reviews, acknowledgements to the rich and diverse information prompted in different versions of web applications propelling rapid progress in the field of opinion mining [9].

AutoML emerges as a focal point in machine learning research driving substantial magnification and fascination in ML applications. Despite AutoML still being a relatively new and developing technology, research is still being

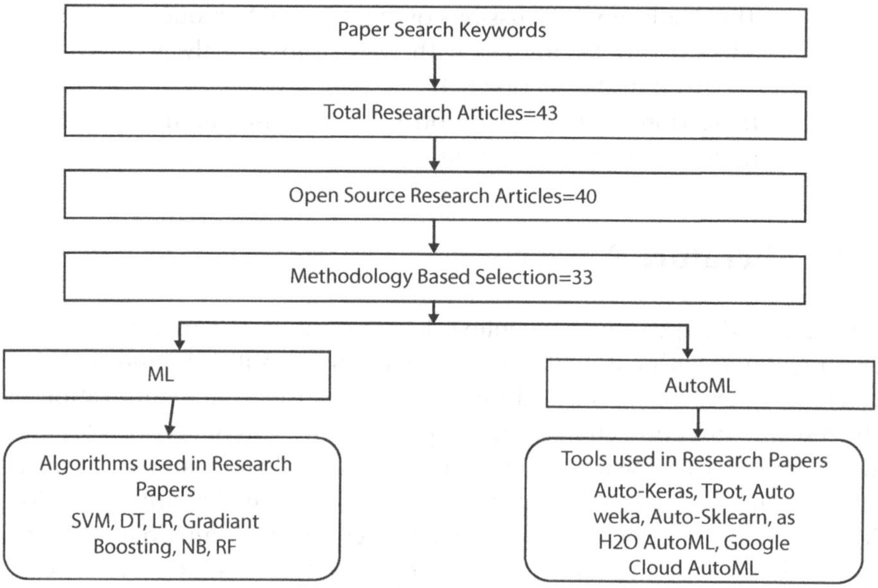

Figure 6.4 Related work search process.

done to determine the benefits and drawbacks of this technology, especially in relation to other fields including sentiment analysis, image classification, and time-series forecasts. The performance of AutoML libraries varies across these sectors prompting researchers to conduct evaluations to discern their efficacy in specific domains [10]. AutoML has significantly democratized the process of building and deploying sentiment analysis models enabling organizations to harness the power of machine learning without the need for extensive expertise. By automating the complex tasks involved in sentiment analysis, businesses can extract actionable insights from textual data more efficiently leading to improved decision making and customer satisfaction.

The researches delved into the realm of online Cantonese-written restaurant reviews employing standard machine learning techniques, such as NB and SVM [11], to automatically categorize user reviews into positive or negative sentiments. The study thoroughly explores the impact of varying feature representations and magnitudes on classifier investigation. Similarly, in the context of restaurant reviews, researchers in reference leveraged NLP [12] for polarity analysis. Their research strategy involved the utilization of SVM, NB, and Multinomial NB as integral components of the analytical process.

Regarding sentiment classification based on subjectivity, word, document, and opinion extraction, the authors examined four fundamental challenges in opinion mining. Their exploration of subjectivity classification encompassed a range of strategies featuring similarity-dependent methods, the NB [13] classifier, Multiple NB classifier, and the cut-based classifier. In their survey on sentiment analysis, ref. [14] provided a concise overview of attribute selection approach emphasizing pointwise mutual information and Chi-square. The focus then shifted to a comprehensive discussion of sentiment classification methods.

In their investigation, the researchers undertook sentiment classification on datasets comprising reviews for clothing, shoes, and jewelry products. They conducted a comparative analysis evaluating the performance of hybrid SVM, NB, LR, and DT [15] methods. The analysis also explored the effectiveness of these methods in conjunction with various feature extraction techniques. In their work referenced as ref. [16], the authors introduced a study focused on analyzing Twitter trending information and collecting diverse data from users to enhance data accuracy. The research aimed to improve performance in data pre-processing by facilitating the identification of people's reactions and opinions, thereby contributing to a more comprehensive understanding of Twitter trends.

In their exploration of sentiment analysis, the researchers in ref. [17] introduced pre-processing techniques implemented through specially designed algorithms. The proposed method underscored the importance of efficient pre-processing as a pivotal step preceding the application of any classification algorithm. In their research highlighted in ref. [18], the researchers introduced a combined CNN and LSTM architecture for opinion analysis of real-time restaurant responses. They employed a 300-magnitude pre-trained word2vec and evaluated its efficacy against alternative pre-trained word to vector models. Additionally, the study emphasized the utility of BERT (Bidirectional Encoder Representations from Transformers) for text classification tasks in recent advancements.

In their investigation of Sentiment Analysis (SA), the researchers in ref. [19] underscored the significance of this methodology in extracting opinions, emotions, or feelings from text highlighting its influential role in the contemporary digital landscape. The study distinguished three levels of granularity within SA as follows: document level, sentence level, and aspect level SA. Notably, Aspect-Based Sentiment Analysis (ABSA) was identified as a more intricate level involving the extraction of aspects, corresponding sentiment words, and their polarity orientations. In their work, the author presented an innovative approach to sentence classification introduced in ref. [20] utilizing dependency tree sub-trees. The focus of the paper was on classifying sentence polarity by leveraging sub-opinions within the dependency tree. The methodology incorporated aspects, such as sum–product belief propagation, sub-opinion relations, and word granularity. The approach implemented a classifier system for opinions based on dependency sub-trees utilizing a corpus dataset containing comment IDs and overall scores for analysis. The study involved tokenization and parsing for precise examination, and the results were evaluated through recall and precision calculations.

Authors [21] employed ML techniques for user comments to extract relevant particulars. Recognizing the significance of reviews for decision making by both customers and owners, they developed an ML model using NLP techniques to capture user responses. The experimentation phase involved the use of the Python language. In their study outlined in ref. [22], the team introduced a classification method for evaluating customer satisfaction in Surabaya restaurants employing Naïve Bayes. The data sampling process involved web crawling using Web Harvy Tools. The research findings revealed that both methods effectively captured customer responses, with Naïve Bayes demonstrating a higher accuracy compared to TextBlob sentiment analysis, achieving a superiority of 2.9%.

Researchers [23] put forth a process for taking vital features and perspectives from real-time reviews. Their approach determined the disparity and dominance of opinions aiming to summarize and ascertain the status of client reviews based on recommendation. Outcomes of the evaluation, particularly on digital camera reviews, showcased the effectiveness of the proposed technique. In their research highlighted in ref. [24], the team presented two prominent techniques to classify the polarities as happy and sad: the ML and the semantic orientation approaches. The approach employed a pre-defined bag of words dataset for both training and prediction, while the semantic orientation approach focused on identifying specific keywords that conveyed sentiment within the document. These methodologies employed distinct computational methods to discern sentiment in sentences or documents.

In the work presented by the author in ref. [25], a classification approach using machine learning algorithms for opinion mining was introduced focusing on extracting information from text. The study employed two ML classifiers, NB and DT. Notably, the research highlighted the reliability of Naïve Bayes over Decision Tree, especially as the dataset size increased. This observation suggested that Naïve Bayes tends to provide more accurate results in larger datasets according to the study's findings. The author [26] undertook the development of ML-based approaches for customer procurement through a correlative study. The study aimed to establish a benchmark for churn classification by evaluating the correctness of various latest framework models on a dataset comprising customers from a Telecom Company.

In the paper they published [27], the authors analyzed customer behavior in connection with e-commerce. By utilizing data mining techniques and the

KNN algorithm in ML, the team aimed to identify potential risks associated with customers based on their purchasing patterns. The study involved extensive experimentation allowing the differentiation of customers into two categories: those who acquired unusual products or combinations were labeled High-Risk customers, while those who opted for typical products were categorized as Low-Risk customers. The analysis of loyalty levels and customer satisfaction undertaken by researchers in ref. [28] was facilitated through the synergistic integration of classifier techniques, programming software, and structural equation modeling. This combined methodology showcased their adept use of programming tools to harness the power of classifiers and structural equation modeling enabling a comprehensive examination of the factors influencing both customer loyalty and satisfaction.

The author [29] explores how well AutoML performs on text classification work. It examines how models for text representation affect the standard of AutoML classifier together with the general efficacy of their tools in this setting. The study particularly emphasizes the role of text representation models revealing from benchmark evaluations that while basic mechanisms, like Bag-of-Words, yield insistent results, AutoML-generated self-operating text embeddings have yet to surpass the performance of manually crafted text representations. The Auto-ML System for Text Classification (ASTeC), proposed by [30], employs the Bootstrap Bias Corrected CV (BBC-CV) technique to assess the execution of the ML process. This system strategically combines Genetic Algorithms (GA), Bayesian Optimization (BO), and BBC-CV to identify optimal machine learning pipelines for text classification. The effectiveness of this approach is validated through comparisons with cutting-edge systems: for the Sentiment Analysis (SA) task, it is benchmarked against TPOT (Tree-Based Pipeline Optimization Tool) and the Google Cloud AutoML service, while for the Intent Recognition (IR) task, comparisons are made with TPOT and MLJAR AutoML.

In their study titled "Testing the Robustness of AutoML Systems," conducted at the University of Helsinki, two researchers systematically evaluated the agility of three key libraries of AutoML tailored for image processing models—TPOT, H2O, and AutoKeras. By employing two distinct datasets featuring digits and fashion items, the researchers observed that all three AutoML libraries demonstrated a commendable accuracy rate exceeding 80% when applied to clean data [31].

The author [32] delves into the performance of Neural Search space, which is regarded as a subsection of AutoML within the framework for creating deep learning models. During the execution phase, the researchers observed elevated intricacy assistance for the self-generated prototype in comparison to man-made models, particularly when applied to the PTB

(Penn Treebank) dataset. The article further elucidates that higher perplexity values correlate with lower model accuracy emphasizing the inverse relationship between perplexity and model performance.

According to this related work, the study concentrated on highlighting the importance of the conventional code-oriented approach to ML while offering insightful information about how to use AutoML correctly in the analysis of polarities. Furthermore, the review foregrounds the critical prominence of understanding hyper-parameter fine-tuning and other fundamental aspects of ML. The groundwork findings clearly indicate that the indiscriminate use of AutoML platforms may not be universally suitable advocating instead for their judicious application to assess the most appropriate algorithmic approach. These key findings and insights constitute the primary contributions and values derived from the study.

Based on the literature review mentioned above, we will analyze the different challenges faced by the authors during their progress, approaches, applications, and techniques that are employed in opinion mining or sentiment analysis. Several scholarly works have been examined to provide comprehensive sequences of opinion mining process and identify the baselines for our work. An analysis of existing methodologies was conducted to identify the research gap and apply the most appropriate steps to forthcoming research work. A comparative study is undertaken, and it is shown in Tables 6.1 and 6.2, which are easy to comprehend. When considering the conventional ML techniques used for finding the polarities from the different datasets, it is observed that there is a difficulty in devising the feature engineering process. A separate feature engineering procedure is needed for each ML model before proceeding to classification or regression, as it affects the efficacy of the complete model. Therefore, a novel AutoML methodology is required to tackle the situation, i.e., a complete model will do the attribute or feature engineering and classification process. In addition, a model with hyper-parameter tuning is also required to mount up the efficiency and correctness of prediction work. From the related work, the research gap is found, and it is rectified with the novelty of the AutoCRM model with suitable hyper-parameters using Autokeras, which was proposed and developed to fit various types of customer reviews based on the organization.

Table 6.1 Reviews based on ML and DL.

Ref. no.	Dataset	Machine learning techniques used	Feature selection	Accuracy	Precision	Recall	F1
[33]	Public domain dataset	Decision Tree, SVM, Navie Bayes	Monte Carlo selection	Decision Tree = 94% SVM = 97% Naïve Bayes = 86%	96%	74%	84%
[34]	US Airline Sentiment, Twitter Kaggle dataset	LR, SVM, NB	TF-IDF	LR = 77% SVM = 77% Naïve Bayes = 74%	76%	77%	75%
[35]	Amazon dataset	Logistic Regression, SVM, Naïve Bayes	Chi-square and normalized TF-IDF methods	Logistic Regression = 78% SVM = 83% Naïve Bayes = 82%	83%	83%	82%
[36]	Database of customer data of a telecommunication company	LR, SVM, NB	Boruta	Logistic Regression = 86.7% SVM = 94% Naïve Bayes = 88%	-	-	-

(Continued)

Table 6.1 Reviews based on ML and DL. (*Continued*)

Ref. no.	Dataset	Machine learning techniques used	Feature selection	Accuracy	Precision	Recall	F1
[37]	Brazilian E-Commerce Public Dataset by Olist	DT, SVM, RF		Decision Tree = 87.2% SVM = 87.1% Random Forest = 87.5%	97%	29%	93%
[38]	Yelp dataset	Hybrid method	TF-IDF	Hybrid method = 92.44% SVM = 85.20% Naïve Bayes = 85.00%	-	-	-
[39]	SWOT's Guide to KARACHI's Restaurants, Cafes Dhabas HBFE and Takeouts dataset	Random Forest, SVM, Naïve Bayes	TF-IDF	Random Forest = 94% SVM = 89% Naïve Bayes = 84%	95%	97%	96%
[40]	Amazon consumer reviews	Logistic Regression, SVM, Gradient Boosting	TF-IDF	Logistic Regression = 90% SVM = 89% Gradient Boosting = 87%	91%	97%	94%

(*Continued*)

Table 6.1 Reviews based on ML and DL. (*Continued*)

Ref. no.	Dataset	Machine learning techniques used	Feature selection	Accuracy	Precision	Recall	F1
[45]	Amazon Fine Food Reviews, Cell phone and Accessories, Yi-Jen Mon, Yelp	RNN-based LSTM, Deep LSTM	-	Model1—97%, Model2—96% Model3—95%	70% 78% 76%	62% 63% 59%	64% 67% 62%
[46]	Trip Advisor	Deep Belief Network (DBN)	Self-Organizing Map, Latent Dirichlet Analysis (LDA)	DBN—92%	91.8%	-	92.7%

Table 6.2 Reviews based on AutoML.

Ref. no.	Dataset	Automated machine learning tool	Performance
[10]	Covid-19 Data Set, Twitter, Reviews	Auto-Keras, TPot, Auto Weka	93%
[29]	20newsgroup, MathLectures and WhatsCooking datasets	Auto-Sklearn as well as H2O AutoML	98.17%
[30]	English IR datasets, Portuguese IR datasets	TPOT, MLJAR AutoML and Google Cloud AutoML	92.8%
[32]	MNIST, CIFAR-10, CIFAR-100 and ImageNet	TPOT, Auto-WEKA, Auto-Sklearn	97.1%
[41]	Malaria dataset, Lister Hill National Centre for Biomedical Communications	Autokeras	95.6%

6.3 Methodology

The primitive intention of this research work was to evolve an AutoML system for opinion mining aiming to enhance Customer Relationship Management. Additionally, the study involves evaluating both the AutoML approach and conventional code-based machine learning techniques. In the initial phase, the emphasis was on implementing the process, which included eliminating null values and special characters during pre-processing.

For the AutoML model, the AutoKeras package was utilized to generate the model through neural architecture search and hyper-parameter tuning. Following multiple trials, the best model was identified and exported. This model was then deployed on another customer review dataset. To facilitate a comparative analysis with AutoML, traditional ML models were also created using fundamental ML pipeline steps. The entire research work shown in Figure 6.5 was implemented using Python code within a Jupyter Notebook environment.

6.3.1 Data Preparation

The initial stage of the data analysis, encompassing the collection, sorting, and preparation of data, stands out as pivotal steps in the analytical process. These phases compete in a prominent function in ensuring the quality, organization, and readiness of the data for subsequent analysis.

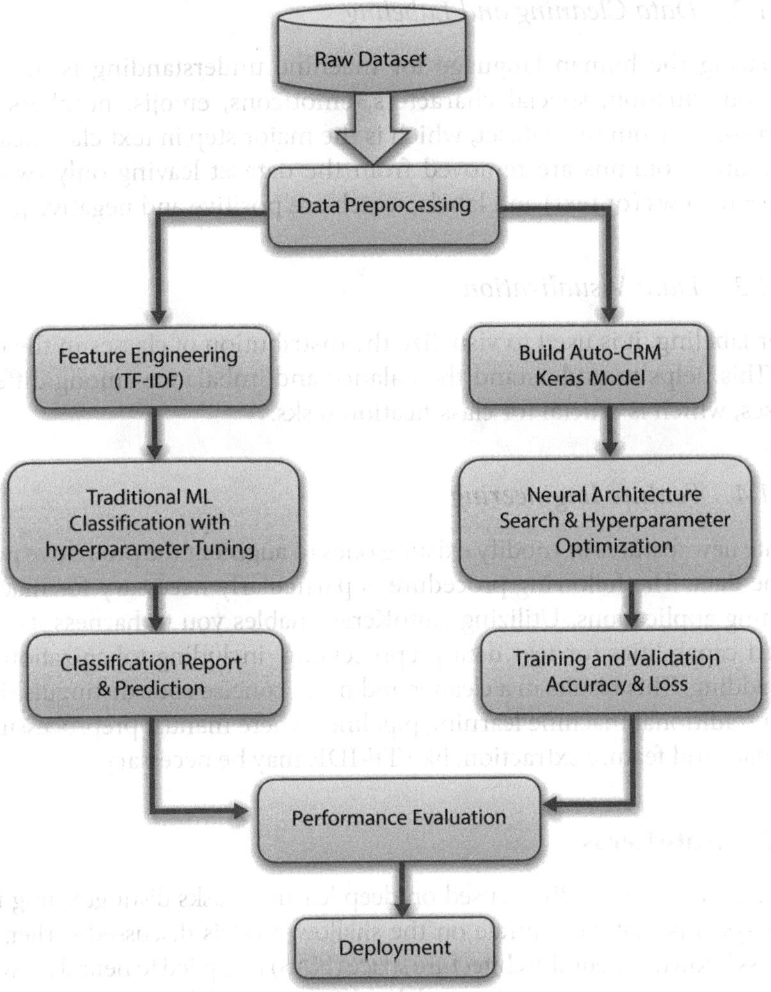

Figure 6.5 WorkFlow—AutoML-CRM.

Preparing raw datasets into structures that fit into models for training and testing is referred to as pre-processing and data description. As a result, data must always be clean and formatted to be used.

6.3.1.1 *Data Collection*

The reviews regarding the customers will be taken from Amazon product reviews and Flipkart product reviews collected from the Kaggle repository.

6.3.1.2 Data Cleaning and Labeling

Preparing the human language for machine understanding is to eliminate punctuation, special characters, emoticons, emojis, numbers, and extra spaces from the dataset, which is the major step in text classification. Unwanted columns are removed from the dataset leaving only two columns: reviews (or text) and labels, which are positive and negative [3, 5].

6.3.1.3 Data Visualization

After labeling, it is used to visualize the distribution of classes in the dataset. This helps to understand the balance and imbalance among different classes, which is crucial for classification tasks.

6.3.1.4 Feature Engineering

Create new features or modify existing ones to augment the predictive power of the data. The following procedure is particularly necessary for machine learning applications. Utilizing AutoKeras enables you to harness its automated capabilities for text data preprocessing, including tokenization and embedding. This results in a cleaner and more concise code distinguishing it from traditional machine learning pipelines where manual preprocessing of text data and feature extraction, like TF-IDF, may be necessary.

6.3.2 AutoKeras

AutoKeras is dedicatedly focused on deep learning tasks distinguishing itself from systems that concentrate on the shallow models discussed earlier. The process known as neural architecture space (NAS) is applied to neural networks and entails identifying both the model architecture and the parameters that are utilized for model preparation. With AutoKeras you can perform AutoML for deep learning models using an open-source library. The TensorFlow tf.Keras API is used to conduct the search utilizing Keras models. It presents a simple and efficient strategy to automatically discover high-performing models across a diverse set of predictive tasks encompassing structure classification and regression dataset commonly referred to as tabular data.

It can select different parameters, like the number of layers, the number of neurons, and learning rate, along with other hyper-parameters such as optimization and loss functions.

6.3.2.1 *Neural Architecture Search and Hyper-Parameter Tuning*

Automating architectural engineering is a next-level logical progression from automated machine learning, which lowers the complexity of manually constructed neural architecture. Since it has a lot in common with feature engineering, minimization of hyper-parameter, and Meta learning, NAS is regarded as a subset of AutoML. This means NAS can be divided into three aspects: scope of search, searching methodology, and techniques for performance computation [42–44].

The search space delineates the architecture that can theoretically be represented. It is possible to streamline the exploration process and reduce the search space by incorporating past knowledge about typical architectural characteristics suitable for a task. Nevertheless, this approach adds a weighted value physically. This might preempt the discovery of unique architecture components for progress entirely up to human cognition. AutoKeras uses Bayesian Optimization, Random search, Grid search, and hyper band tuner toward the direction of search for the neural structure framework. Additionally, it makes use of a tree-structured acquisition function for minimization and a neural network kernel to efficiently assess the search space. Therefore, search space refers to the selection of model classifier with corresponding hyper-parameters. The general neural architecture search will be defined as follows:

Let us consider NAS space to be S, the input as X is partitioned into X_{train} and X_{val}, and the cost function is Cf(). To determine the best neural network P ∈ S that could minimize the cost on dataset d, finding the optimal neural network should satisfy the following equation [4]:

$$P = \underset{\theta}{argmin}\; Cost\left(P(\theta^*), X_{val}\right) \tag{6.1}$$

$$\theta^* = \underset{\theta}{argmin}\; Cf\left(P(\theta), X_{train}\right) \tag{6.2}$$

Let M be the machine learning technique with H hyper-parameters. The complete set of hyper-parameter configuration space is $d = d_1 \times d_2 \times d_3 \times \ldots\ldots\ldots d_n$, and the scope belongs to the n-th parameter by d_n. A vector of hyper-parameters is denoted by V, which belongs to D. Hyper-parameter domains include real valued, integer valued, binary, and categorical [38]. Based on the above architecture search method, a text classifier-based

AutoKeras, named AutoCRM, simplifies the creation of neural network architecture models with optimized parameters.

AutoModel combines model selection and optimized hyper-parameters to form the text classifier AutoKeras model. The search space is nothing but the model selection with corresponding parameters such as Max_trial, Overwrite, Objective, Tuner, Multilabel, Directory, Project_Name. etc.

- ***Max_trials***
  Max_trials is a parameter that determines the upper limit on the number of distinct neural network architectures the system will evaluate in its quest to discover the optimal model. This parameter signifies the maximum count of unique combinations of hyper-parameters and architectures with techniques such Bayesian optimization, Random Search, etc. AutoKeras will perform up to the max_trial number. This search involves various combinations of layers, operations, and hyper-parameters to build and train different neural network architectures. Each trial corresponds to a different candidate model with a specific set of hyper-parameters such as block_type, classification head, dropout, optimizer, and learning rate. After reaching the maximum count, AutoKeras stops the search and returns the best model found during the trials.
- ***Overwrite***
  It determines a true or false condition: whether to discard any previous results and start a new search process or to resume the search from where it left off.
- ***Objective***
  The foremost goal of this parameter is to perceive the architecture that performs the best according to the specified objective metric. For text classification, it includes Val_accuracy and Val_Loss. The model is created with Val_accuracy, which is to strengthen the accuracy of the tasks.
- ***Tuner***
  The model will be searched with various tuners, and the best model with a tuner will be selected for the classification. The AutoCRM model is created by choosing Bayesian optimization, random search; Hyperband or Grid search based on the computational resources and desired level of exploration in a hyper-parameter space.

- ***Project_Name***
  The name of the directory used to save the Autokeras project.
- ***Directory***
  The path to a directory where the search outputs are saved.

6.3.3 Model Selection

The parameters are placed in the AutoCRM Keras model, and outputs are obtained up to five trials. Each trial will be compared with the parameters and hyper-parameters with val_accuracy and val_loss. The model having the highest accuracy will be selected as the best text classifier model and will implemented in several review datasets.

6.4 Results and Discussions

During the implementation part, the model is generated as a binary classifier based on those AutoML and traditional machine learning techniques. As already discussed in the data preparation phase, the research work contains two main review datasets from the well-known website Kaggle, i.e., Amazon Review and Flipkart review datasets. After labeling the dataset, it can proceed to the visualization step. Figures 6.6 and 6.7 represent the word cloud and bar chart of positive and negative opinion frequencies distributed in the dataset.

Furthermore, during the analysis, these datasets were partitioned into 80% and 20% for the train/test phase. After pre-processing, feature engineering, architecture search, and parameter optimization will be done automatically. The subsequent phase involves utilizing the Auto_CRM Keras model and selecting the optimum number of trials and epochs. Ultimately, the construction of the model begins with parameters such as input data, overwrite = true, Max_trials = 5, epoch = 15, tuner = random search, and objective = accuracy.

The research outcome represents binary classification with five trials of various hyper-parameters as shown in Table 6.3, which shows the different layers, dense layers, and activation function. In this proposed Auto-CRM Keras model, they choose Relu and Sigmoid as activation functions with variable batch sizes for each trial. It is observed that the model starts from trial_1 choosing text_block as BERT, the classfication_head_dropout layer as 0, and the SGD optimizer with a training rate of 0.001 achieving an accuracy of approximately 0.69 from a different epoch.

For the purpose of improving the model's accuracy, trial_2 will be trained with the parameters such as text_block set to Transformer, classification_head set to 0.5, optimizer as "Adam weight decay" with a learning

Figure 6.6 Word cloud of the Amazon dataset.

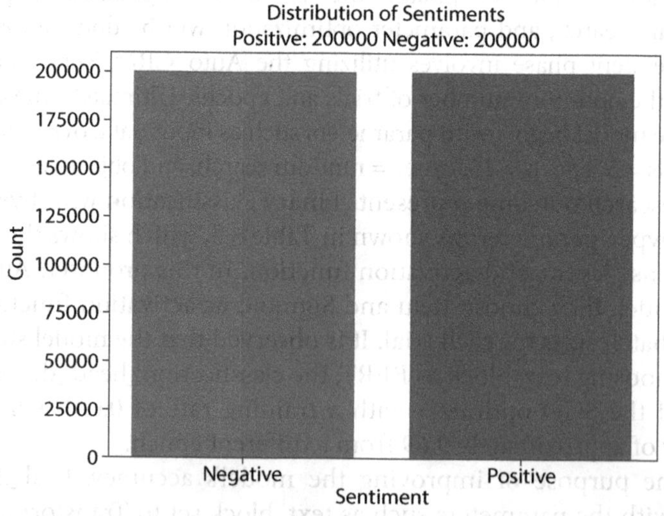

Figure 6.7 Distributions of opinion labels.

Table 6.3 Hyper-parameter in various trials.

Hyper-parameter/trial	I	II	III	IV	V
Text_Block_1/ block_type	BERT	Transformer	Transformer	Ngram	Ngram
Classification_head_1/ dropout	0	0.5	0.25	0	0.25
Optimizer	Stochastic Gradient Descent (SGD)	Adam_weight_Decay	Adam	Adam_Weight_decay	Adam_Weight_decay
Learning rate	0.001	2E–05	1E–05	1E–05	1E–03

Table 6.4 Epoch in 15 trials.

Trials	I		II		III		IV		V	
Epoch no.	**Val-Loss**	**Val-Accuracy**	**Val-Loss**	**Val-Accuracy**	**Val-Loss**	**Val-Accuracy**	**Val-Loss**	**Val-Accuracy**	**Val-Loss**	**Val-Accuracy**
1	0.695	0.492	0.940	0.491	0.704	0.491	0.905	0.503	0.711	0.512
2	0.694	0.509	0.704	0.491	0.673	0.535	0.815	0.499	0.682	0.565
3	0.693	0.516	0.696	0.509	0.646	0.613	0.791	0.495	0.656	0.632
4	0.693	0.493	0.694	0.509	0.618	0.719	0.761	0.510	0.623	0.744
5	0.692	0.522	0.694	0.498	0.588	0.796	0.740	0.498	0.591	0.797
6	0.693	0.504	0.723	0.530	0.553	0.882	0.710	0.521	0.541	0.878
7	0.692	0.532	0.694	0.523	0.513	0.930	0.714	0.485	0.524	0.942
8	0.692	0.511	0.694	0.557	0.467	0.962	0.701	0.518	0.476	0.965
9	0.690	0.569	0.694	0.551	0.416	0.983	0.703	0.509	0.422	0.978
10	0.691	0.539	0.704	0.545	0.360	0.987	0.696	0.533	0.373	0.987

(Continued)

Table 6.4 Epoch in 15 trials. *(Continued)*

Trials	I		II		III		IV		V	
11	0.690	0.559	0.694	0.563	0.303	0.992	0.695	0.533	0.301	0.997
12	0.691	0.554	0.677	0.584	0.250	0.995	0.688	0.541	0.261	0.996
13	0.689	0.594	0.682	0.586	0.204	0.998	0.690	0.547	0.216	0.997
14	0.688	0.591	0.673	0.584	0.166	0.999	0.694	0.522	0.167	0.999
15	0.688	0.590	0.675	0.597	0.135	0.999	0.693	0.529	0.141	0.999
Test_Loss	0.557		0.683		0.562		0.699		0.4289	
Test_Accuracy	0.692		0.576		0.719		0.510		0.814	

rate of approximately 2.00E—05. This has obtained a classification accuracy of 0.58.

Therefore, the model is trained with different parameters, such as text_block set to "Transformer" or "Ngram," classification_head set to 0.25 or 0,

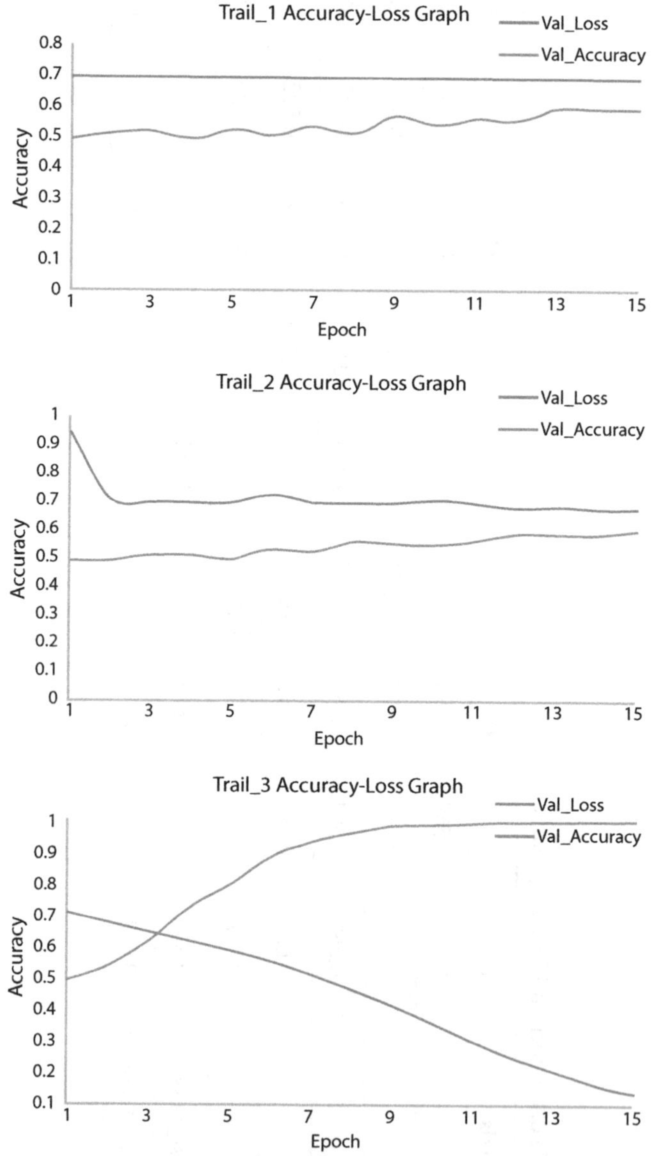

Figure 6.8 Accuracy–loss graph from trial_1 to trial_4. (*Continued*)

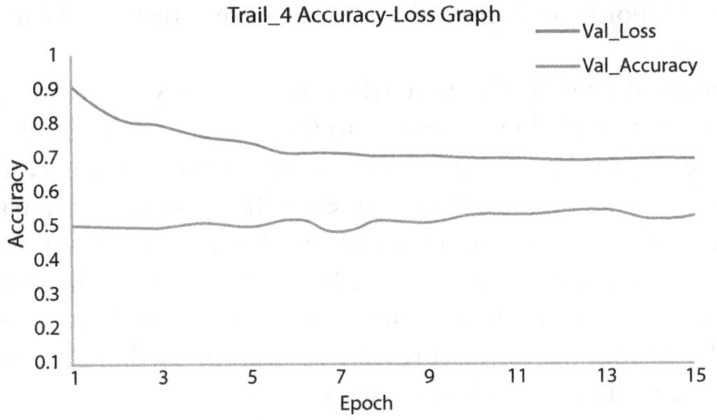

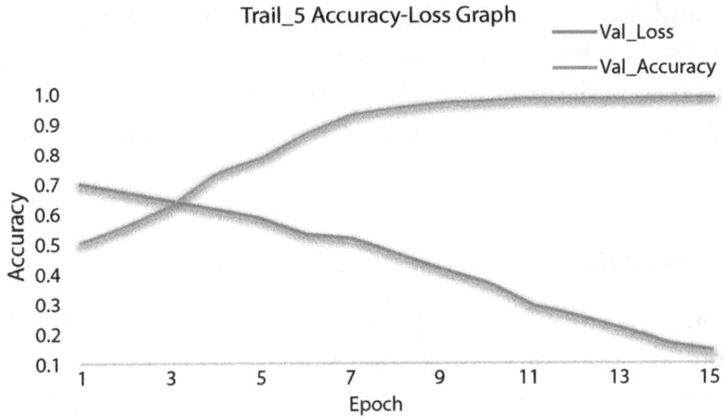

Figure 6.8 (Continued) Accuracy–loss graph from trial_1 to trial_4.

and the optimizer set to "Adam" or "Adam_weight_decay," with a learning rate of approximately 1.00E−05 for the subsequent trials 3 and 4 and obtaining an accuracy of 0.72 and 0.51, respectively. The trial is extended up to 5 with text_block set to "Ngram," classification_head set to 0.25, and the optimizer set to "Adam_weight_Decay" with a learning rate of 1.00E−03 achieving an accuracy rate of approximately 0.814 as shown in Table 6.4.

As per the Table 6.3, starting from trial I to V, various hyper-parameters were applied by the AutoKeras framework, and the training history of the model with five trials in 15 epochs was analyzed as shown in Table 6.4. In trial_1 from epochs 1 to 15, val_accuracy starts from 0.492 then reaches to 0.590, and the test accuracy reaches 0.692.

For trial_2, the val_accuracy is 0.491 for epoch 1 and 0.597 for epoch 15 with a test accuracy up to 0.576. In trial_3, the val_accuracy is 0.491 to 0.999 for epoch 1 to epoch 15. For trial_4, the val_accuracy is approximately

0.503 to 0.529. For trial_5, the val_accuracy ranges from 0.512 to 0.999 for all 15 epochs.

It is observed that in the first trial, the accuracy starts at 0.69, then decreases to 0.58, and then increases to 0.72 in trial_3. Then, it decreases in trial_4 to approximately 0.51. This leads to trial_5, where the accuracy increases, and the classifier trained with various hyper-parameters achieves a final AutoML model accuracy of approximately 0.814% with optimized hyper-parameters. After finding the neural architectural search space or model selection, the best model from trial_5 will be exported, and this model is fit into the Flipkart review dataset for further classification. It attains 0.81% accuracy, which is shown in Table 6.4.

The above Figure 6.8 represents the graphical representation of ACC (accuracy) and loss obtained throughout the train/test phase. For the consecutive trials 1 to 5, the accuracy is decreased from trial 1 to trial 2, increased in trial 3, decreased in trial 4, and finally, in trial 5, the accuracy increases gradually. Therefore, the trial 5 optimized model is selected for deploying the Flipkart dataset.

6.4.1 Comparative Analysis: AutoML vs ML

The same dataset is employed in supervised ML techniques such as NB, SVM, and LR. Here, data pre-processing was done as specified in the above steps, i.e., tokenization, stopword removal, stemming, or lemmatization. Feature engineering will be done with Term Frequency-Inverse Document Frequency (TF-IDF). TF-IDF is recurrently applied in text mining and retrieval of information. This is employed toward rearranging the set of unprocessed textual information into a matrix of TF-IDF attributes. This transformer takes an accumulation of textual data as input and produces a distributed matrix illustration of the documents based on their TF-IDF scores.

After the feature engineering process, the dataset is divided into simple train/test sets for learning and evaluation. The model is fitted with the data using the corresponding classification algorithm. Then, the model is fine-tuned with the optimizing hyper-parameters. This step involves manual process of experimenting with different parameter values to improve the model performance. Therefore, this optimization tuning will continue until it reaches the best model through iteration.

The AutoCRM Keras model is compared with traditional ML algorithms connected with performance measurements. The accuracy and precision rates are obtained by training the prototype with various parameters and finding the resultant one with the best-optimized hyper-parameters. This process is done by manually applying various parameters in the traditional

ML techniques. From Table 6.5 and Figure 6.9, the evaluation results of different ML approach and the suggested AutoML architecture are shown. It can be seen that the preciseness of the AutoCRM_Keras model shows the best results when compared with the rest of the ML algorithms. The Auto-CRM Keras model will be evaluated with metrics such as accuracy and loss. From Table 6.5, the Amazon review dataset is implemented using traditional classification approaches as well as the AutoML model. Some of the traditional code-based approaches in ML, i.e., LR, NB, and SVM, are trained with suitable optimized hyper-parameters and obtained accuracies of approximately 0.73%, 0.74%, and 0.75%. When compared with the Auto-CRM Keras model of AutoML, it outperforms these approaches with a classification accuracy of 0.81.

Table 6.5 Comparison of machine learning and automated machine learning based on accuracy.

Classifier			**Binary classification**	
Dataset			**Amazon review dataset**	**Flipkart review dataset**
Traditional machine learning	**Logistic Regression (LR) [14]**	ACC	0.73	0.73
		PRE	0.74	0.74
		RE	0.74	0.74
		F!	0.74	0.74
	Naïve Bayes (NB) [12]	ACC	0.74	0.74
		PREC	0.71	0.71
		REC	0.74	0.74
		F1	0.73	0.73
	Support Vector Machine (SVM) [11]	ACC	0.75	0.75
		PREC	0.75	0.75
		REC	0.75	0.75
		F1	0.74	0.74
Automated machine learning	**Auto-CRM Keras Model**	ACC	0.81	0.8
		LOSS	0.42	0.45

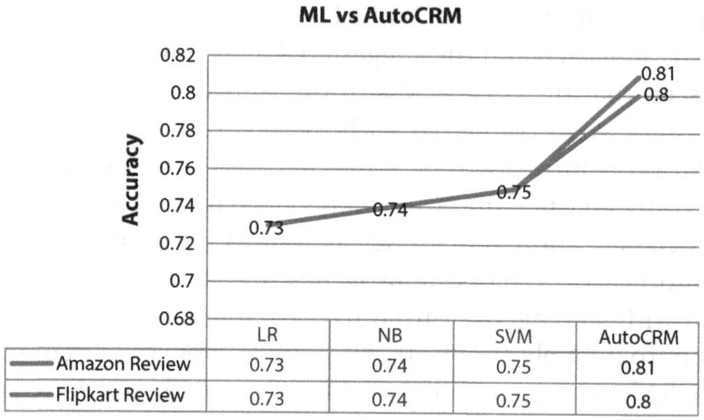

Figure 6.9 Comparison of ML vs AutoCRM.

From the comparative analysis, it is proven that, when considering the automation level, the AutoML automates many tasks such as ML logical pipeline procedure and parameter tuning. It allows the users to provide high-level inputs and allows the system handle details of the machine learning pipeline. It requires less human interaction and makes it more accessible to users with varying levels of expertise.

They automate hyper-parameter tuning by searching through predefined or user-specified hyper-parameter spaces. It automatically explores multiple algorithms and model architectures to track down the best optimum model.

6.5 Conclusion

The prominent intent of these analyses is to provide recommendations for future organizations to involve AI-enabled services for customers enhancing business volume. AutoML will offer businesses a new dimension in the future leading to significant changes in business. It paves the way for better relationships between customers and business organizations with quality service and sustainability. In this study on opinion mining, we proposed a methodology named AutoCRM, with random hyper-parameter tuning based on Autokeras features, to analyze customer reviews from various types of organizational domains This approach proved to be successful with notably high accuracy.

The evaluation of opinion mining for customer relationship management, based on AutoML and conventional code-based approaches, uses the aforesaid performance metrics. It was found that hyper-parameter optimization will automatically increase the accuracy of the classifier. Instead of using code-based approaches, the proposed automated classification will give better results for these types of problems. Additionally, this study exhibits the significance of identifying the tuning parameters that elevate the potential of the prototype and also deepen understanding of the AutoML core. Concurrently, directing on subsequent improvement, this study could evaluate Cloud-based AutoML and supplementary AutoML stacks such as Google AutoML and H20.ai. Incorporating those subfields into opinion classification will lead the way to impressive outcomes.

References

1. Santhosh Kumar, K.L., Desai, J., Majumdar, J., Opinion Mining and Sentiment Analysis on Online Customer Review. *IEEE International Conference on Computational Intelligence and Computing Research*, 2016.
2. Vinodhini, G. and Chandrasekaran, R.M., Sentiment Analysis and Opinion Mining: A Survey. *Int. J. Adv. Res. Comput. Sci. Software Eng.*, 2, 6, 283–292, July 2012.
3. Truong, A., Walters, A., Goodsitt, J., Hines, K., Bayan Bruss, C., Farivar, R., Towards Automated Machine Learning: Evaluation and Comparison of AutoML Approaches and Tools. *IEEE 31st International Conference on Tools with Artificial Intelligence (ICTAI)*, 2019.
4. Revathi, V., Kavin, B.P., Thirumalraj, A., Gangadevi, E., Balusamy, B., Gite, S., Image Based Feature Separation Using RBM Tech with ADBN Tech for Accurate Fruit Classification. *2024 IEEE International Conference on Computing, Power and Communication Technologies (IC2PCT)*, Greater Noida, India, pp. 1423–1429, 2024, doi: 10.1109/IC2PCT60090.2024.10486564.
5. Jin, H., Song, Q., Hu, X., Auto-Keras: An Efficient Neural Architecture Search System. *Appl. Data Sci.* track paper KDD, 1946–56, 2019.
6. Yao, Q., Wang, M., Chen, Y., Dai, W., Li, Y.-F., Tu, W.-W., Yang, Q., Yu, Y., Taking the Human out of Learning Applications: A Survey on Automated Machine Learning, arXiv:1810.13306 [cs.AI].
7. Karamker, S.K., Mahadi Hassan, M.D., Smith, M.J., Xu, L., Zhai, C., Veeramachaneni, K., AutoML to Date and Beyond: Challenges and Opportunities. *ACM Comput. Surv.*, 54, 8, 175:1–36, Oct 2021.
8. Mäntylä, M.V., Graziotin, D., Kuutila, M., The evolution of sentiment analysis—A review of research topics, venues, and top cited papers. *Comput. Sci. Rev.*, 27, 1, 16–32, 2018.
9. Kumar, A. and Sebastian, T.M., Sentiment Analysis: A Perspective on its Past, Present and Future. *Int. J. Intell. Syst. Appl.*, 4, 10, 1–14, 2012.

10. Mahima, K.T.Y., Ginige, T.N.D.S., De Zoysa, K., Evaluation of Sentiment Analysis based on AutoML and Traditional Approaches. *Int. J. Adv. Comput. Sci. Appl. (IJACSA)*, 12, 2, 612–618, 2021.
11. Zhang, Z., Ye, Q., Zhang, Z., Li, Y., Sentiment classification of Internet restaurant reviews written in Cantonese. *Expert Syst. Appl. Int. J.*, 38, 6, 7674–7682, 2011.
12. Viloria, A., Varela, N., Vargas, J., Lezama, O.B.P., *Comparative Analysis Between Different Automatic Learning Environments for Sentiment Analysis*, pp. 134–141, Springer, Cham, 2021.
13. Tang, H., Tan, S., Cheng, X., A survey on sentiment detection of reviews. *Expert Syst. Appl.*, 36, 10760–10773, 2009.
14. Medhat, W., *et al.*, Sentiment analysis algorithms and applications: A survey. *Ain Shams Eng. J.*, 5, 4, 1093–1113, 2014. http://dx.doi.org/10.1016/j.asej.2014.04.011.
15. Gangadevi, E., Rani, R.S., Dhanaraj, R.K., Nayyar, A., Spot-out fruit fly algorithm with simulated annealing optimized SVM for detecting tomato plant diseases. *Neural Comput. Appl.*, 36, 8, 4349–4375, 2023. Springer Science and Business Media LLC. https://doi.org/10.1007/s00521-023-09295-1.
16. Nikil Prakash, T. and Aloysius, A., Data preprocessing in sentiment analysis using twitter data. *Int. Educ. Appl. Res. J. (IEARJ)*, 3, 7, 89–92, 2019.
17. Hemalatha, I., Saradhi Varma, G.P., Govardhan, A., Preprocessing the Informal Text for efficient Sentiment Analysis. *Int. J. Emerging Trends Technol. Comput. Sci. (IJETTCS)*, 1, 2, 58–61, 2012.
18. Hossain, N., Bhuiyan, Md.R., Tumpa, Z.N., Sentiment Analysis of Restaurant Reviews usingCombined CNN-LSTM. *11th ICCCNT*, 2020.
19. Syam Mohan, E. and Sunitha, R., Survey On Aspect Based Sentiment Analysis Using Machine Learning Techniques. *Eur. J. Mol. Clin. Med.*, 7, 10, 1664–1685, 2020.
20. Bang, T.S. and Sornlertlamvanich, V., Sentiment Classification for Hotel Booking Review Based on Sentence Dependency Structure and Sub-Opinion Analysis. *IEICE Trans. Inf. Syst.*, 101, 4, 909–916, 2018.
21. Kaswan, K.S., Dhatterwal, J.S., Kumar, N., Balusamy, B., Gangadevi, E., Cyborg Intelligence for Bioprinting in Computational Design and Analysis of Medical Application, in: *Computational Intelligence in Bioprinting*, pp. 211–237, Wiley, 2024, https://doi.org/10.1002/9781394204878.ch11.
22. Laksono, R.A., Sungkono, K.R., Sarno, R., Sentiment Analysis of Restaurant CustomerReviews on TripAdvisor using Naive Bayes. *12th International Conference on Information & Communication Technology and System (ICTS)*, 2019.
23. Ojokoh, B.A. and Kayode, O., A Feature–Opinion Extraction Approach to Opinion mining. *J. Web Eng.*, 11, 1, 051–063, 2012.
24. Choi, Y. and Lee, H., Data properties and the performance of sentiment classification for electronic commerce applications. *Inf. Syst. Front.*, 19, 993–1012, 2017.

25. Songpan, W., The Analysis and Prediction of Customer Review Rating Using Opinion Mining, pp. 71–77.
26. Patel, A. and Kumar, A.G., Predicting Customer Churn In Telecom Industry: A Machine Learning Approach For Improving Customer Retention. In *2023 IEEE 11th Region 10 Humanitarian Technology Conference (R10-HTC)*, pp. 558–561, IEEE, 2023.
27. Thorat, P. and Jagli, D., Customer Behavior Analysis: Identifying risky customers based on their purchased product on e-commerce. *Int. Res. J. Eng. Technol.*, 412–415, 7, 9, September 2020.
28. Park, Y. and Gates, S., Towards real-time measurement of customer satisfaction using automatically generated call transcripts, in: *Proceedings of the 18th ACM Conference on Information and Knowledge Management*, ACM, pp. 1387–296, 2009.
29. Brandle, S., Hanussek, M., Blohm, M., Kintz, M., Evaluation of Representation Models for Text Classification with AutoML Tools, ResearchGate, 2021.
30. de Oliveira, D.N., Utsch, M.N.R., de Almeida Machado, D.V.P., Evaluating a New Auto-ML Approach for Sentiment Analysis and Intent Recognition Tasks. *J. Interact. Syst.*, 14, 1, 92–105, 2023.
31. J.N., T.M., Halvari, T., Testing the Robustness of AutoML Systems. *Electron. Proc. Theor. Comput. Sci.*, 319, 103–116, 2020.
32. K.Z., X.C., He, X., AutoML: A survey of the state-of-the-art. *Knowledge-Based Syst.*, 212, 106622, 2021.
33. Asthana, P., A comparison of machine learning techniques for customer churn prediction. *Int. J. Pure Appl. Math.*, 119, 10, 1149–1169, 2018.
34. Tusar, Md.T.H.K. and Islam, Md.T., A Comparative Study of Sentiment Analysis Using NLP and Different Machine Learning Techniques on US Airline Twitter Data, 2021.
35. Hussain, Y., Predicting Customer Satisfaction With Product Reviews, M.Sc. Thesis, 2019.
36. Sabbeh, S.F., Machine-Learning Techniques for Customer Retention: A Comparative Study. *Int. J. Adv. Comput. Sci. Appl. (IJACSA)*, 9, 2, 273–281, 2018.
37. Wong, A.-N. and Marikannan, B.P., Optimising e-commerce customer satisfaction with machine Learning. *ICCPET*, pp. 1–9, 2019.
38. Govindarajan, M., Sentiment Analysis Of Restaurant Reviews Using Hybrid Classification Method. *Proceedings of 2nd IRF International Conference*, 9th February 2014.
39. Zahoor, K., Bawany, N.Z., Hamid, S., Sentiment Analysis and Classification of Restaurant Reviews using Machine Learning. *Conference Paper*, November 2020.
40. Veluchamy, A., Nguyen, H., Diop, M.L., Iqbal, R., Comparative Study of Sentiment Analysis with Product Reviews Using Machine Learning and Lexicon-Based Approaches. *SMU Data Sci. Rev.*, 1, 4, 1–22, 2018.

41. Alaiad, A., Migdady, A., Al-Khatib, R.M., Alzoubi, O., Abualigah, R.A.Z.L., Autokeras Approach: A Robust Automated Deep Learning Network for Diagnosis Disease Cases in Medical Images. *J. Imaging*, 9, 1–16, 2023.
42. Hutter, F., Kotthoff, L., Vanschoren, J., *Automated Machine Learning-methods, systems, challenges*. Springer Nature, 219, 2019, https://library.oapen.org/bitstream/handle/20.500.12657/23012/1007149.pdf.
43. Elsken, T., Metzen, J.H., Hutter, F., Neural Arhcitecture search: A survey. *J. Mach. Learn. Res.*, 20, 55, 1–21, 2019.
44. Savci, P. and Das, B., Comparison of pre-trained language models in terms of carbon emissions, time and accuracy in multi-label text classification. *Heliyon*, 9, 5, 1–13, 2023.
45. Iqbal, A., Amin, R., Iqbal, J., Alroobaea, R., Binmahfoudh, A., Hussain, M., Snetiment Analysis of Customer Reviews using Deep Learning. *Sustainability*, 14, 10844, 2022, https://doi.org/10.3390/su141710844.
46. Nilashi, M., Samad, S., Minaei-Bidgoli, B., Ghabban, F., Supriyanto, E., Online Reviews Analysis for Customer Segmentation through Dimensionality Reduction and Deep Learning Techniques. *Arab. J. Sci. Eng.* Springer, 46, 8697–8709, 2021.

7

The Competence of Customer Support Team for Sentiment Analysis in Chatbots Using AutoML

G. Pradeep* and M. Devi Sri Nandhini†

School of Computing, SASTRA Deemed University, Thirumalaisamudram, Thanjavur, Tamil Nadu, India

Abstract

As a consequence of the rapid expansion of social networks, such as consumer review networks, discussion forms, blogging and publishing networks, and other such Internet-based networks, the volume of comments and evaluations about day-to-day activities has increased tremendously. Sentiment analysis is a significant research area that serves as a powerful and efficient technique capable of analyzing such reviews and comments to gather valuable insights regarding the various aspects of a product or service. Businesses, governing bodies, and individuals may all benefit from public sentiment by gathering data and making decisions based on it.

One of the interesting fields where sentiment analysis finds application is evaluating customer's interactions with chatbots. With an effort to enhance customer service and reduce corporate expenses, AI chatbots have been designed for customer support. The practice of understanding a customer's tone of voice and words while communicating with a chatbot—whether they are happy, sad, fearful, or angry—is known as chatbot sentiment analysis. Just because a customer interacted with a chatbot does not mean they will ignore or forget a bad experience.

Customers seek assistance in resolving issues they may be having with the item or service you provide. If the chatbot or virtual assistant is unable to assist them, they will revert to the default procedure, which is typically interacting with an agent in person (a live agent). They will choose to work with a different brand if they are unable to receive assistance there. So, there is a greater need to carry out sentiment analysis on customer interactions with a chatbot. As chatbots are a

**Corresponding author*: pradeep.g8@gmail.com
†*Corresponding author*: nandhini.avcce@gmail.com

E. Gangadevi, M. Lawanya Shri, Balamurugan Balusamy and Rajesh Kumar Dhanaraj (eds.) Automated Machine Learning and Industrial Applications, (141–170) © 2025 Scrivener Publishing LLC

cost-effective solution to the issue of improving customer satisfaction, it is critical to conduct chatbot sentiment analysis to better understand them and deliver chatbot conversations that satisfy users.

To guarantee customer satisfaction, trustworthy chatbots that can swiftly handle consumers' concerns must be developed. Businesses may better understand their consumers' demands and take the appropriate action with the aid of sentiment analysis-capable bots. The process of automating the activities complicated in using machine learning to solve real-world issues is recognized as automated machine learning (AutoML). From the initial dataset to the final deployable machine learning model, AutoML covers the entire pipeline.

The specifics of performing chatbot sentiment analysis are covered in this chapter. We will investigate the practice of performing chatbot sentiment analysis and how to automate sentiment detection from customer–chatbot conversations. In addition, the chapter explores how text sentiment can be analyzed, classified, and how businesses can perform chatbot sentiment analysis to automatically classify customer remarks as good, negative, or neutral assisting them in understanding client sentiment precisely.

Keywords: Sentiment analysis, chatbots, customer support team, autoML, exploratory data analysis, subjectivity detection, modifiers, sentiment polarity detection

7.1 Introduction

A chatbot, at its simplest level, is a computer program that mimics and analyzes human interaction (either written or spoken) allowing humans to communicate with digital devices as if they were speaking with a real person. While not all chatbots have artificial intelligence (AI) built in, contemporary chatbots increasingly make use of conversational AI strategies, such as natural language processing (NLP), to comprehend user inquiries and generate automated responses. By instantly responding to queries and requests via text, audio, or both, chatbots can enable users' information discovery and remove the need for manual search or human interaction. A typical chatbot interaction is shown in Figure 7.1.

7.1.1 Background

Currently, chatbots are pervasive. You can find them in everything from home smart speakers to consumer-facing SMS, WhatsApp, and Facebook Messenger apps to business messaging platforms like Slack. The most

Figure 7.1 Chatbot.

current iteration of AI chatbots, also identified as "virtual agents" or "intelligent virtual assistants," is capable of automating pertinent tasks in addition to sympathetic natural language exchanges through the use of advanced language models. In addition to the well-known intelligent virtual assistants targeted at consumers, such as Amazon Alexa and Apple's Siri, virtual agents are now being utilized more and more in business settings to support clients and staff [3]. Since the beginning of the computing era, several attempts have been made to model human behavior in machine agents. In the history of chatbots, ELIZA, being the first, modeled the behavior of a psychologist. Later, huge investments were made toward the design and implementation of smarter chatbots, though they were not able to succeed due to the lag of technicalities at that period of time. Still, chatbots could not understand conversations as well as humans. They can do simple tasks, and when they lack proper responses, they redirect the user to human agents.

The first chatbots were just interactive FAQ systems that were designed to provide pre-written responses to a small number of frequently asked inquiries. Because they were unable to understand natural language, users were typically forced to choose from a list of basic words and phrases to advance the discussion. Such basic, traditional chatbots cannot handle complicated queries or respond to straightforward inquiries that the developers have not anticipated [7]. Chatbots are software-based agents developed to engage in conversation with people using natural language, which has seen so much attention nowadays in online services. The challenge is regarding the approaches to be followed in measuring the service satisfaction of chatbots experienced from the customer end. Chatbots can be pre-trained to interpret customer inquiries and generate appropriate responses [8].

As chatbot algorithms advanced, they were able to achieve increasingly intricate rule-based programming and even natural language processing, which made it possible for users to ask questions in a conversational way. A new breed of chatbot emerged as a result, one that was equipped with machine learning and contextual awareness to continuously improve its capacity to accurately appreciate and anticipate requests by being exposed to an increasing amount of natural language.

Today's AI chatbots can now accept open-ended user input by using natural language understanding (NLU), which helps them get past errors like typos and translation difficulties. The meaning is then mapped by sophisticated AI techniques to the precise "intent" that the user wants the chatbot to act upon, and conversational AI is then used to provide a suitable answer. With a few subtle modifications, these AI skills combine machine learning and deep learning to create a more and more detailed knowledge base of queries and answers derived from user interactions. This sophistication, which makes use of recent developments in large language models (LLMs), has resulted in more adaptable chatbot applications and higher customer satisfaction.

7.1.2 Problem Definition

We will look into the process of doing sentiment analysis on chatbots and how to automate the process of detecting sentiment in talks between customers and chatbots. The chapter also looks at how text sentiment can be precisely understood by organizations through the use of chatbot sentiment analysis, which automatically classifies customer remarks as positive, negative, or neutral on a finer scale.

7.1.3 Scope

Sentiment analysis for chatbots assesses how your consumers engage with your chatbot. This entails listening to the words and tones that clients use to communicate with your chatbot to determine their emotional state—happy, sad, fearful, or furious. You can pinpoint areas in which you need to improve based on these encounters.

7.1.4 Technical Highlights

- The Stanford NLP parser is used to carry out the PoS tagging process. It is used to examine the grammatical structure of a sentence.
- The TextInspector tool is used to know the statistical summary of the text involved in the conversation between the customer and chatbot.
- The trilateral modifiers proposed in the methodology are used to categorize the modifiers associated with the sentiment.
- The proposed nonary scale is utilized to detect the polarity of the sentiment involved in the customer–chatbot conversation.

7.1.5 Objectives

- The overall objective of the planned methodology is to achieve sentiment analysis in chatbots to improve the competence of a customer support team. This objective is achieved by the following two sub goals:
- To carry out subjectivity detection in the conversational text involved in the customer–chatbot interaction.
- To perform sentiment polarity detection in the subjective text involved in the conversation.

7.1.6 Common Chatbot Use Cases

AI chatbots are used by consumers for a variety of determinations, including interacting with mobile apps and utilizing specially designed appliances like smart kitchen appliances and thermostats. The range of business use is also equal: AI-powered chatbots are used by marketers to customize customer experiences and expedite e-commerce operations; by IT and HR departments to facilitate employee self-service; and by contact centers to handle incoming calls and refer clients to available resources.

Interfaces for conversations can also differ. AI chatbots are frequently utilized in private websites and applications, social network messaging apps, independent messaging platforms, and even in phone conversations (where they are referred to as integrated voice response or IVR).

Common-use scenarios consist of the following:

- ❖ Appointment setting and intake for medical offices
- ❖ Automated reminders for chores with a time or geographical component
- ❖ Prompt, round-the-clock support for customer service or HR-related concerns
- ❖ Individualized suggestions in the context of online shopping
- ❖ Field definitions in financial applications and forms

The positive aspects of chatbots are as follows:

- ❖ Provide multilingual assistance.
- ❖ Provide more individualized service.
- ❖ For more context, ascertain the customer's intent.
- ❖ Cut expenses and increase operational effectiveness.
- ❖ Boost brand loyalty and consumer interaction.
- ❖ Create leads and please clients.

Unlike dialogue systems, chatbots are aimed at chatting with human users about their day-to-day activities [10]. Because chatbots can now easily adapt to new AI capabilities, they are gradually getting more complex. They should also be able to quickly and accurately interpret user intent, read user moods, and steer the conversation in a way that caters to the needs of the customer. One such element that increases the potency of bots in interpreting the emotions in client messages is sentiment analysis. Indeed, according to 64% of companies, chatbots may help them give their clients a more personalized level of service. To quickly determine whether customers are enjoying their interactions with your chatbots, you can always make use of the sentiment analysis tool.

7.1.7 The Basics of Sentiment Analysis

Sentiment analysis is the study of people's views about products and services [9, 24]. It is also known as emotion AI, which makes use of NLP, computational linguistics, and text mining to gain insights that help in the process of decision making [15]. With the growth of deep learning approach, it could be inferred from various research papers [11–14] that chatbot performance could be significantly enhanced by the application of AI-based deep learning with sentiment analysis. Sentiment analysis is the technique of examining digital text to identify if the message's emotional tone is neutral, positive, or negative. Businesses now handle massive amounts of text data, including emails, chat transcripts from customer service, comments, and reviews on social media.

Importance of Sentiment Analysis

- Provides valuable insights for businesses and organizations.
- Produce better products and services.
- Scale up the process of uncovering customer emotions at an affordable cost.
- Real-time support; send alerts when negative sentiments are detected.

7.1.8 Levels of Sentiment Analysis

Actually, sentiment analysis can be completed at three different levels: document level, sentence level, and aspect level [25, 26]. When sentiment analysis is performed at the document level, it brings out the overall opinion of the entire text [28, 29]. This approach does not consider what people prefer or dislike regarding the features of an entity (product or service). Of course, it provides only a coarser level of analysis. When sentiment analysis is carried out at the sentence level, the sentences present in the user text are classified as subjective and objective from which only subjective sentences are chosen for analysis [30]. The reason is that subjective sentences contain some sort of opinion expressed about a feature. So, in the sentence-level approach, the opinion present in every subjective sentence is determined, which is somewhat better than document-level analysis. But if a still more fine-grained level of analysis is required, we move on to aspect-level analysis, where the opinion associated with each feature is determined providing a more accurate form of sentiment analysis [17, 27].

Consider the following sample review about an iPhone:

I bought an iPhone yesterday. It has a sleek and modern design, strong performance, and a fantastic camera. It is expensive.

At the document-level sentiment analysis, even though a negative opinion is expressed over the price of an iPhone, according to this approach, the overall opinion will be concluded to be positive, as the majority of the opinions expressed in the above review are positive. Tables 7.1–7.3 show the polarity detected by the three levels of sentiment analysis, respectively.

Table 7.1 Document-level sentiment analysis.

Level of sentiment analysis	Conclusion about opinion polarity
Document level	Positive

Table 7.2 Sentence-level sentiment analysis.

Level of sentiment analysis	Conclusion about opinion polarity	
Sentence level	I bought an i-phone yesterday	No opinion
	It has a sleek and modern design, strong performance, and a fantastic camera	Positive
	It is expensive	Negative

Table 7.3 Aspect-level sentiment analysis.

Level of sentiment analysis	Conclusion about opinion polarity	
Aspect level	Appearance	Positive
	Performance	Positive
	Camera	Positive
	Price	Negative

Organization

This chapter is structured as follows. Section 7.2 presents an overview of the existing literature, Section 7.3 elaborates on the proposed methodology, Section 7.4 discusses the experimentation and results, and Section 7.5 presents the conclusion and future scope.

7.2 Literature Survey

[1] The authors have planned a sentiment analysis approach to handling unstructured conversations. The study utilized the Kaggle dataset and R language for analysis. The goal was to carry out emotional classification and polarity of responses. This paper describes how to handle unstructured responses that a chatbot receives during a conversation by using a sentiment

analysis approach. The dataset applied in this study was taken from Kaggle, an online community for machine learning and data scientists. The goal of this investigation was to categorize emotions and determine whether reactions were delayed or not. R is used to perform the sentiment analysis in question. The data shows that there is little variation in highlighted reactions across positive and negative emotions. On the other hand, the polarity categorization indicates that for unflagged replies, there are more positive responses than negative responses. **Gap: The experimentation results show that the proposed work has detected sentiment polarity based on two levels, viz., positive and negative emotions.**

[2] This paper explores the Koko app, Sarcasmbots , and Taybots. Koko was working on making an empathetic chatbot. They aimed at incorporating empathy into all the popular conversational agents, such as Siri, Alexa, and Cortona. A demo version of Alexa released by Koko was sufficiently empathetic in situations where the user conveys his or her sadness. In such cases, Alexa suggested taking a small walk or listening to music. But the recommendations were not enough when the user conveyed information about missing loved ones or some form of stress. On the other hand, sarcasmbots are open-source modules for generating sarcastic responses from chatbots. Such bots respond to user input in a sarcastic way. The module involves eight types of sarcasm generators. Based on specific criteria for user input, the appropriate type of sarcasm generator is chosen. The article addresses the topic of using sentiment analysis in chatbots and explains why a strong chatbot is initially necessary. Pre-processing, data cleansing, the bag of words technique, N-grams, and negation handling are all part of the suggested method for emotion recognition. Their technique is innovative in that it attempts to conceptualize the customer–chatbot relationship as more traditional meaning that the user should feel as though they are conversing with a human. **Gap: The methodology lacks modifier or intensifier handling in detecting sentiments.**

[3] In this paper, the authors have delivered a chatbot-building framework to improve chatbot responses. The proposed framework makes use of sentiment analysis and timelines to produce better responses. The experiments show that when the sentiment is extremely negative, a human agent can be arranged to attend to the specific user. The proposed framework is comprised of four layers, namely, the presentation layer, chatbot layer, framework layer, and customization layer. The user interface is placed in the presentation layer. The chatbot layer consists of three components: intention identification, sentiment analysis, and tree timeline. The data object representation and custom functions constitute the customization layer. To deliver a better chatbot response, this work presents a framework

for designing chatbots that takes sentiment analysis and tree timelines into consideration. Their trial results demonstrate that the consumer can be diverted to a human attendant when the chatbot sentiment is particularly unfavorable or perhaps be redirected to another division of the timeline as an alternate solution. Their approach successfully completed the objective of developing a chatbot with sentiment analysis and tree timelines based on the testing. In addition to enhancing user experience, the suggested chatbot does not repeat itself. The Tree Timeline structure built into the framework may have an important impact on the chatbot's performance. **Gap: The work partially relies on the sentiment analysis approach, and hence, its power is not optimally utilized.**

[4] Chatbots try to give accurate responses to user queries instead of presenting the user with a list of relevant documents, as in the case of search engines. To offer tailored responses to every user, thereby improving chatbot performance, personalization approaches are incorporated into chatbot design. The authors have proposed a personalized chatbot using sentiment analysis techniques to provide customized responses to each user. The proposed methodology involves five primary components: question processing, personalization, dialogue management, information extraction, and answer generation. Each component of the proposed methodology is associated with a set of well-defined tasks forming a robust framework that can offer relevant and customized responses to user inquiries. Whereas traditional search engines typically only return a list of linked documents, chatbots and question-answering systems seek to deliver exact replies to user requests. Personalization approaches are utilized to enhance the chatbot's functionality by providing tailored information to individual users according to their preferences. Furthermore, sentiment analysis methods are applied to gain a deeper comprehension of the user's questions and emotional condition. To provide the necessary information, it is intended to advance a deeper understanding of the user and his needs. In this study, we present a sentiment analysis-enhanced personalized chatbot that offers each user customized and relevant information. The primary elements of the system and the methods used to handle user inquiries are described in depth in the paper. We have deployed a proof-of-concept version of our technology as a customer support chatbot in e-commerce applications to assess its efficacy. Based on user feedback, the trial results show a noteworthy development in user satisfaction with both the overall experience and the customized replies. Overall, this system shows how sentiment analysis and personalization strategies can be used to improve the functionality and efficiency of chatbots and question-answering systems.

To determine whether users were satisfied with a chatbot's performance, a controlled experiment was conducted. After choosing a representative sample of 60 individuals, an A/B test series was conducted. During the experiments, participants were instructed to engage with two versions of the chatbot system (Version A: via Sentiment Analysis Customization, and Version B: lacking Sentiment Analysis Customization). Following every session, participants were asked to deliver feedback on various parts of the system and score their degree of satisfaction on a 0–10 scale. **Gap: This system has dealt only with how sentiment analysis and personalization strategies can be used to enhance the functionality of the chatbots and not focused on the accurate detection of the sentiment polarity involved in the chatbot–consumer conversation.**

[5] Depression is a predominant and debilitating mental health condition that moves millions of entities globally. Standard therapy techniques, including cognitive–behavioral therapy (CBT) and medication, are helpful for many people, but not everyone can access or afford them. Chatbots, conversational machines designed to replicate human discourse, are a potential replacement for depression therapy. This study aimed to evaluate the efficacy of a chatbot-based depression therapy in a randomized controlled experiment. The participants were arbitrarily assigned to either the chatbot therapy group or the wait-list control group. While the chatbot therapy group had 8 weeks of therapy via a chatbot, the control group did not get any treatment during this time. The chatbot therapy group showed considerably fewer depressed indications than the control group (BDI-II) according to data from the Patient Health Questionnaire-9 (PHQ-9) and the Beck Depression Inventory-II. Participants in the chatbot therapy group also showed high levels of satisfaction with the chatbot interface and therapy. These findings suggest that chatbot-based therapy could be a viable alternative to traditional depression therapy, particularly for those who might not have access to it. We predict that the quality of life and anxiety levels of the chatbot therapy group will be much higher than those of the control group. The model's accuracy was 75% when it was returned. All of these results suggest that chatbots could be a helpful and practical tool for providing depression support. **Gap: Accuracy level was limited to 75% only.**

[6] The authors have experimented with the variations in customer sentiments in the domain of retail services. They have proposed a hybrid sentiment analysis approach that is automated. It has been revealed that the overall sentiment toward chatbots is comparatively less negative than that associated with human agents. Moreover, they have found that these sentiments vary according to the sectors (fashion and telecommunications).

Finally, it was found that sentiments toward human agents in these sectors became very negative after the deployment of chatbots. Conversational AI, or chatbots, is becoming more and more popular among retailers for customer support because of its alleged advantages and lower operating costs. However, little is known about how users of chatbots interpret these encounters and how they might affect other customer support initiatives. This study looks into how customers feel about chatbots differently in different retail sectors and how they affect their expectations and feelings about other service contacts with online human agents. By employing a hybrid automated sentiment analysis methodology, they ascertain that (1) the general perception of bots is less negative than that of online human agents. (2) These attitudes vary between the fashion and telecommunication industries. (3) After a retailer deploys a chatbot, opinions about online human agents in both industries get worse.

Using a hybrid model that included a classical machine learning model called Naïve Bayes with a VADER lexicon-based classifier, they examined how consumers felt about chatbots and online human agents on Twitter. Researchers concentrated on the chatbots employed by three businesses in the online fashion and telecommunication industries, which are two distinct retail and consumer service sectors. These sectors rank among the top six most popular subjects on social media in terms of posts and shares. Furthermore, because of the variations in cost and level of service, they differ in terms of the kind of services offered and customer interaction. As a result, they anticipated that customer responses to chatbots will also vary (h2). **Gap: They have dealt only with the general perception of bots in comparison with human agents. Their approach lacks fine-grained sentiment analysis of chatbot–consumer interaction.**

[7] In the current years, the field of computer science has seen a surge in interest in the creation of intelligent chatbots. Nevertheless, a chatbot frequently misinterprets the user's goal, which can result in the creation of improper responses that break up a conversation and annoy the user. Finding a breakdown in a discussion is crucial to raising user satisfaction and enhancing the chatbot's functionality. Recent methods, both supervised and unsupervised, have concentrated on simulating conversation breakdown utilizing several methods. Applying unsupervised strategy to the breakdown job is difficult due to its huge datasets. Bias in the dataset's human annotation and the breakdown's management procedure present another difficulty for conversation breakdown prediction. To address this matter, we have created a supervised ensemble automated method that uses dialogue breakdown to gauge the Chatbot Quality of Service (CQoS).

To forecast the breakdown, the suggested method can classify the datasets according to sentiment while taking the conversion context into account. Our goal in this study is to identify how each speaker's sentiment changes during a conversation. Moreover, we assess the CQoS based on breakdown using the supervised ensemble model. Next, we employ a hand-over method to connect the user to a live agent to address this issue. We conduct numerous experiments utilizing various datasets and cutting-edge algorithms based on this concept, and we discover that employing sentiment as a breakdown trigger works better than human annotation. Therefore, we conclude that information gleaned from the supervised ensemble model can be used to quantify CQoS by identifying conversation breakdowns. **The primary focus of this work is in finding the breakdown in the discussion to enhance the chatbot's functionality. It does not utilize fine-grained sentiment analysis for detecting sentiment polarity.**

[8] Through digital conversations powered by natural language processing (NLP) and artificial intelligence (AI), chatbots actively assist human users. It can be pre-trained in NLP to comprehend user inquiries and provide a prompt response. The chatbot accepts user input in any format, including text, speech, feelings, etc. Numerous studies have been put into practice. The problems with current works are that they are mainly voice based, have trouble analyzing the user's intention, and are incapable of following the context in lengthy conversations. Additionally, during digital conversations, they fail to accurately identify the user's requirement and may diverge from their query.

Therefore, sentiment computations are crucial to comprehending the setting. This research suggested to utilize a Bi-directional Recurrent Neural Network (BRNN-FNB)with a Fuzzy Naïve Bayes classifier to enable consumers to respond instantly to the chatbot. The goal of this work is to develop chatbot models using sentiment analysis powered by artificial intelligence to enhance human performance in conversations. Natural language processing and machine learning are the two parts of artificial intelligence on which chatbots operate. Numerous uses, including online forums, education, and digital marketing, may make use of it. Using the Sequence-to-Sequence approach, the suggested work BRNN-FNB achieved a 93% accuracy rate. Additionally, the accuracy rate of the suggested work, BRNN-FNB, without the use of Sequence-to-Sequence, was 92%. **Gap: The work focuses on developing chatbot models to enhance human performance in conversations.**

The technical gaps identified in the literature survey are tabulated in Table 7.4.

Table 7.4 Technical gaps observed in the literature survey.

Literature survey paper #	Technical gap observed
[1]	The experimentation results show that the proposed work has detected sentiment polarity based on two levels, viz., positive and negative emotions
[2]	The methodology lacks modifier or intensifier handling in detecting sentiments
[3]	The work partially relies on the sentiment analysis approach, and hence, its power is not optimally utilized
[4]	This system has dealt only with how sentiment analysis and personalization strategies can be used to enhance the functionality of the chatbots and not focused on the accurate detection of the sentiment polarity involved in the chatbot–consumer conversation
[5]	Accuracy level was limited to 75% only
[6]	They have dealt only with the general perception of bots in comparison with human agents. Their approach lacks fine-grained sentiment analysis of chatbot–consumer interaction
[7]	The primary focus of this work is in finding the breakdown in the discussion to enhance the chatbot's functionality. It does not utilize fine-grained sentiment analysis for detecting sentiment polarity
[8]	The work focuses on developing chatbot models to enhance human performance in conversations

7.3 Methodology for Chatbot Sentiment Analysis

The planned methodology for chatbot sentiment analysis involves three phases: subjectivity detection, trilateral modifier utilization, and chatbot sentiment polarity detection. The first phase is subjectivity detection, which finds the subjective information from the user inquiry. The second phase searches for the presence of modifiers, if any, in the user inquiry, and the third phase aims at finding the actual sentiment expressed by the user on a fine-grained scale.

7.3.1 AutoML-Based Exploratory Data Analysis and Subjectivity Detection

AutoML can target various steps in machine learning, such as data preparation, feature engineering, model selection, hyperparameter optimization, etc. Among these stages of a machine learning process, in this chapter, we have applied AutoML in the form of AutoNLP for the data preparation stage. As the initial step, exploratory data analysis is carried out using AutoNLP, which is based on the concepts of AutoML. The text involved in the discussion between the user and the chatbot is subjected to pre-processing. In pre-processing, the text is converted to a suitable form that is ready for sentiment analysis. This involves case conversion (converting all upper case to lower case), removal of stop words (removing words that do not have any significant contribution in the analysis, such as "is," "a," etc.), tokenization (splitting the text into separate units or words), and stemming (bringing the words to their root forms; for example, words such as "walking" and "walked" are stemmed to the root form "walk").

After carrying out these pre-processing tasks, the text is input to the subjectivity detection module, where the parts-of-speech (PoS) tagging technique is applied to tag each word of the text with its appropriate grammatical counterpart. For example, consider the text, "I am under severe stress." The TextInspector tool available at the url [31] is used to perform the PoS tagging and get summary statistics. Figure 7.2 shows the editor wherein the input text is typed. The statistical summary for the given text is auto-generated by the tool, as shown in Figure 7.3. The summary involves various parameters such as sentence count, token count, average sentence length, type-token ratio, etc. The PoS tags for the given text input are shown in Figure 7.4.

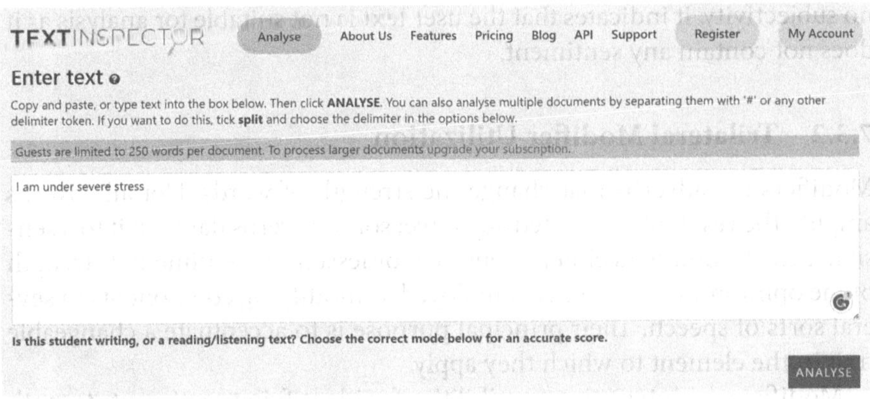

Figure 7.2 Text input for PoS tagging.

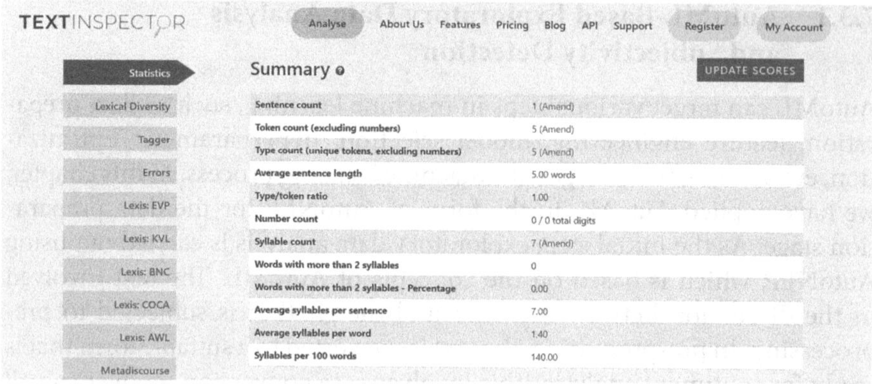

Figure 7.3 Statistical summary for the given input text.

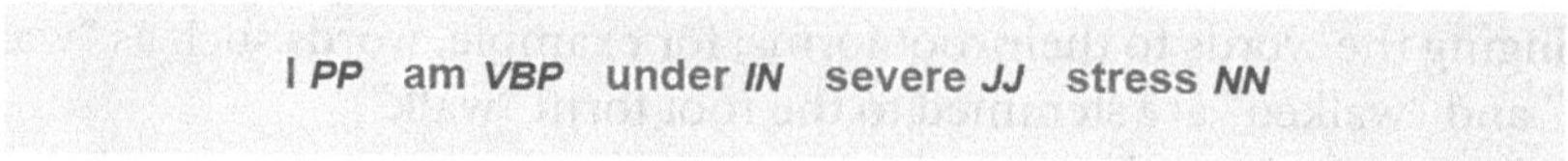

Figure 7.4 PoS-tagged input text.

Once the PoS tagging has been done, the tags are auto-inspected for the presence of adjectives or verbs that are possible candidates that indicate the presence of some form of sentiment. For instance, in the above user text shown in Figure 7.3, the word "severe" is tagged with the PoS tag "JJ," which represents an adjective. In this way, through the identification of adjectives and verbs present in the user text, it is determined whether the user text is subjective or not. Only the subjective text constitutes sentiment. Therefore, in phase I, it is possible to detect the subjectivity of the user text. If there is no subjectivity, it indicates that the user text is not suitable for analysis as it does not contain any sentiment.

7.3.2 Trilateral Modifier Utilization

Modifiers are adverbs that change the strength of words. Not all adverbs amplify the result of the related adjective; some adverbs dampen it to a sensible extent. Modifiers either strengthen or lessen the sentimental strength of the opinion word. These are employed as modifying components in several sorts of speech. Their principal purpose is to accentuate a changeable trait in the element to which they apply.

Modifiers are interesting possibilities for identifying sentiment strength on a more detailed scale. The proposed methodology categorizes the

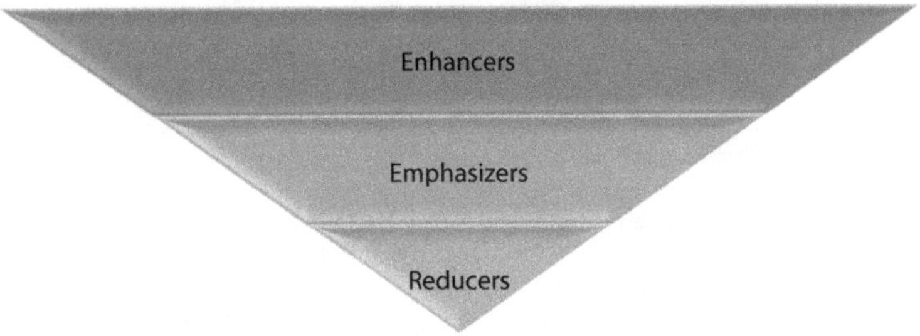

Figure 7.5 Trilateral modifiers.

modifiers into three groups (Enhancers, Emphasizers, and Reducers) based on the extent to which they are capable of amplifying the associated sentiment. Enhancers increase the strength of the sentiment expressed to the fullest extent, denoting the exciting point on the scale. For example, "I am totally impressed with your response", where "totally" is an enhancer-type modifier that strengthens the degree of positivity to the completest extent.

Emphasizers are the modifiers that increase the strength of the associated sentiment, but to a certain level, but not to the fullest level as that of enhancers. Consider the user inquiry, "I'm very happy with your answer." Here, "very" acts as an emphasizer, which increases the positivity of the sentiment expressed by the user toward a chatbot.

Reducers are the adverbs that decrease the strength of the sentiment present in the dialog. For example, consider the user query, "I have a mild headache now." The term "mild" turns as a reducer that decreases the strength of the sentiment. The trilateral categorization of modifiers is shown in Figure 7.5.

7.3.3 Sentiment Polarity Detection

In the proposed methodology, sentiment polarity is detected by using a nonary scale proposed in ref. [23]. In the existing works on sentiment polarity [18–21], a binary or ternary classification is accomplished either (positive, negative) or (positive, negative, neutral). By using the trilateral modifiers, it is still possible to detect the sentiment polarity accurately so that the chatbot can get the real tone behind the user text and can act accordingly.

For example, consider the user text to the Siri Chatbot: "I am completely depressed." From the text, it can be clearly understood that the user is in an extreme case of depression, depressed to a higher extent, which is revealed by the presence of the enhance-type modifier "completely." So, by giving

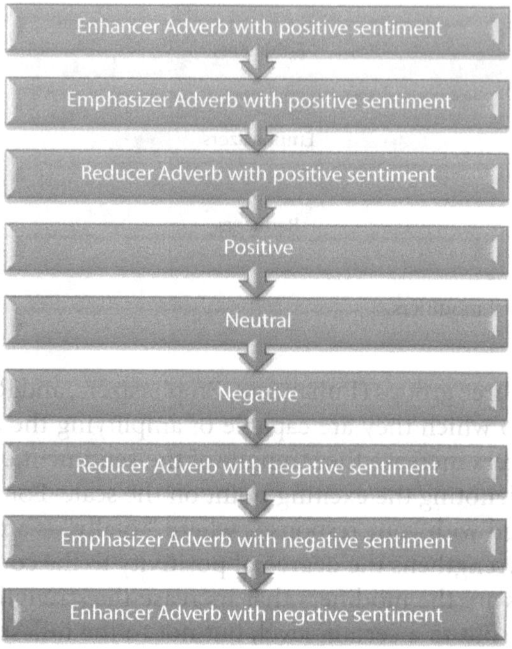

Figure 7.6 Nonary scale for sentiment polarity detection.

proper weight to the presence of modifiers, it is possible for the chatbot to come to a proper level of understanding of the user's situation and thereby provide an appropriate response. If the modifiers are not given due weight, then it may lead to an improper understanding of the real tone behind the user text. The nonary scale developed in the proposed methodology is presented in Figure 7.6.

The nonary scale has been framed by the association of three types of modifiers with the adjectives or verbs of positivity or negativity. For instance, when an enhancer-type adverb accompanies an adjective or verb of positivity, the polarity of the sentiment is classified as extremely strong positive. Similarly, if the same modifier is associated with an adjective or verb of negativity, the polarity of the sentiment is classified as extremely strong negative.

7.3.4 Workflow of Customer Service Inquiry–Chatbot Response

Figure 7.7 shows the workflow of chatbot sentiment polarity detection. The text present in the customer service inquiry is fetched through the chatbot user interface and fed as input to the pre-processing module, where various subtasks of pre-processing, such as case conversion, stop word removal, tokenization, and stemming, are carried out to make the text ready for analysis. The pre-processed text is fed into the subjectivity detection module, wherein the text is tagged using a PoS tagger to tag the tokens with their appropriate grammatical counterparts, such as nouns, adjectives, verbs, etc. In this module, it is identified whether the text is subjective or not. Subjective texts are the source of sentiments. The next task is to use trilateral modifiers to find the types of adverbs associated with the sentiment. Based on the intensifying capability of the modifiers, the real tone of the sentiment can be understood. Finally, the chatbot sentiment polarity detection is carried out by applying the framed nonary scale that detects the accurate tone or polarity of the sentiment expressed in the text.

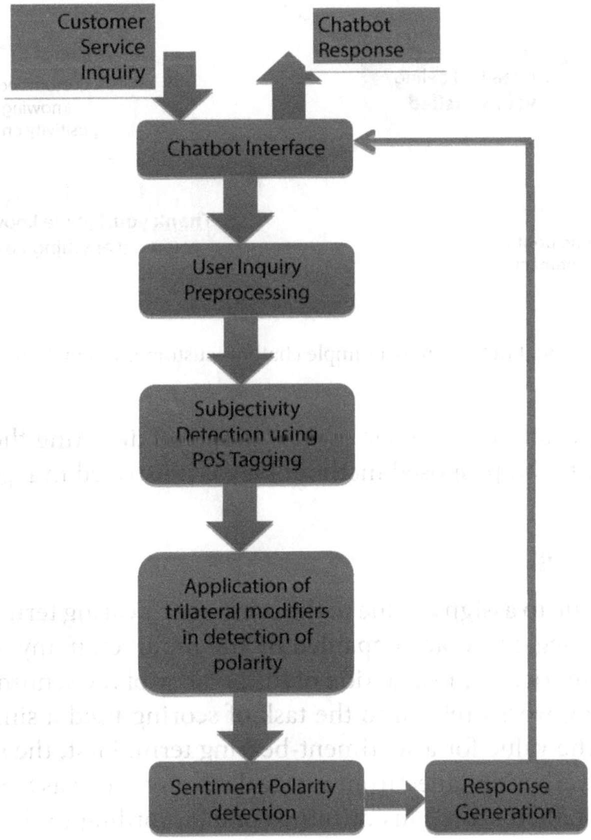

Figure 7.7 Workflow of chatbot sentiment polarity detection.

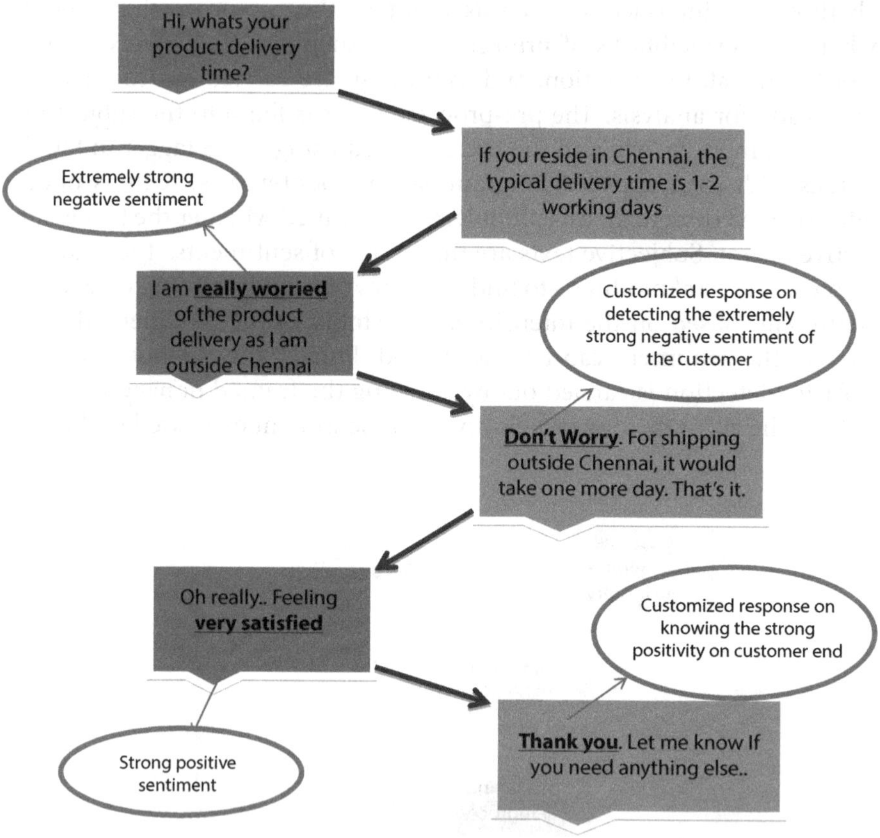

Figure 7.8 Sentiment detection in a sample chatbot–customer interaction.

A sample chatbot–customer conversation and detecting the polarity of the sentiment with proposed methodology is illustrated in Figure 7.8.

7.3.5 Scoring

Scoring is done to assign a value to the sentiment-bearing term based on its positivity or negativity, accompanied by the modifier, if any. A sentiment score is a numerical representation of the polarity of the sentiment-bearing term. Existing works related to the task of scoring used a simple method to arrive at the value for a sentiment-bearing term. First, the score for the adjective or verb is obtained from a lexical resource such as SentiWordNet. Next, the obtained score plus or minus one (according to the presence of modifiers) gives the appropriate score. To understand the logic, consider a sentiment-bearing term that is positively oriented and has a score of 0.42 as obtained from the lexical resource. If the sentiment-bearing term is accompanied by a modifier that tends to increase the strength of the specific term, then the score is updated by incrementing the original score by 1, obtaining 1.42 as far as this example is concerned. Alternatively, if the term is associated with a modifier that tends to reduce its strength, then the updated score is obtained by decrementing the original score by 1, obtaining −0.58, in this case. Now, the problem is that this approach to scoring the sentiment-bearing terms does not take into account the trilateral modifiers introduced in the proposed methodology for chatbot sentiment analysis. With respect to improving the chatbot's understanding of the customer's inquiries, it is necessary to analyze the customer's text in a fine-tuned manner so that the chatbot can provide a tailored response satisfying the customer. To accomplish this task, the proposed trilateral modifiers must also be considered while computing the scores. A few examples of trilateral modifiers are shown in Table 7.5.

The proposed methodology for chatbot sentiment analysis has framed equations for calculating sentiment scores by extending the work of ref. [22].

Let T denote the sentiment-bearing term.

Let X denote an enhancer-type modifier.

Let Y denote an emphasizer-type modifier.

Let Z denote a reducer-type modifier.

Let T_X denote a sentiment-bearing term associated with an enhancer-type modifier.

Let T_Y denote a sentiment-bearing term associated with an emphasizer-type modifier.

Let T_Z denote a sentiment-bearing term associated with a reducer type modifier.

Let S denote the sentiment score and W denote the weight of the modifier, which ranges between 0 and 1. The Equations 7.1–7.3 below are sample equations developed as part of the proposed methodology for chatbot

Table 7.5 Few examples of trilateral modifiers.

Enhancers	**Emphasizers**	**Reducers**
Completely	Very	A little
Perfectly	Really	Mildly
Absolutely	Remarkably	Somewhat

sentiment analysis. These three equations correspond to adjectives/verbs of positivity. Similarly, equations to handle adjectives/verbs of negativity were also framed.

$$S(T\_X)=S(T)+(1-S(T))*W(X) \tag{7.1}$$

$$S(T\_Y)=S(T)+(1-S(T))*W(Y) \tag{7.2}$$

$$S(T\_Z)=S(T)+(1-S(T))*W(Z) \tag{7.3}$$

A part of the pseudocode developed for sentiment polarity detection is presented below:

```
Input: Customer's inquiry(I) to chatbot
Output: Polarity(P) of the sentiment present in the inquiry text and
Sentiment score(S)
Let X denote an enhancer-type modifier,
Let Y denote an emphasizer-type modifier
Let Z denote a reducer-type modifier

For every sentiment-bearing term(T) present in I do
   If any adverb/verb(M) associated with T then
          Switch(Type of M)
                 Case X and T is a positive sentiment:
                        Customer sentiment = "Extremely strong positive"
                        Compute S using equation(1)
                 Case Y and T is a positive sentiment:
                        Customer sentiment = "Strong positive"
                        Compute S using equation(2)
                 Case Z and T is a positive sentiment:
                        Customer sentiment = "Almost positive"
                        Compute S using equation(3)

                 ......
          End of switch
   Else
          Assign the score S from SentiwordNet lexicon according to
          the positivity or negativity of the Sentiment-bearing term T.

End for
```

7.4 Experimentation and Results

Python language was used in the implementation of code in the Jupyter notebook provided by Google Colab.

7.4.1 Performance Metrics

The system of measurement used in the evaluation process were precision, recall, and F1-score. Precision is the ratio of the count of properly detected instances of sentiment polarity to the total number of detected instances. Recall is the fraction of count of correctly detected instances of sentiment polarity to the actual count of correct instances. F1-score is the geometric mean of precision and recall, which serves to achieve balance between the precision and recall.

7.4.2 Data Collection

The data required for model evaluation was obtained through the crawling of tweets on social media using the application programming interface (API) provided by Twitter. The steps involved in data collection from tweets using Python are presented below:

Step 1: Create a Twitter developer account and design an app.

Step 2: Install a Python library named Tweepy to access the API.

Step 3: Authenticate the requests to the Twitter API.

Step 4: Lift off the tweets using Tweepy.

Step 5: Refine the tweets based on specific keywords like chatbots and bots, or filter by hashtags or product/service terms.

Using the above steps, tweets were collected under two sectors, namely, fashion and telecommunications. Table 7.6 below shows the dataset summary.

Table 7.6 Statistics of dataset.

Sector	Number of tweets collected
Fashion	810
Telecommunication	428

7.4.3 Evaluation

It is very important to evaluate the performance of the chatbot with respect to two parameters, namely, content evaluation and customer satisfaction [16]. The former is adopted from the research domains of information retrieval and NLP. It deals with the setting of the chatbot's responses to customer service queries. Instead, customer satisfaction is the most commonly used parameter for chatbot performance evaluation because the responses may vary, and there is no single correct response. The chatbot's performance is determined based on the contentment of the customer. The second parameter, customer satisfaction, is more suitable for assessing the performance because it is only for evaluation because it is on the customers' end to decide whether the responses provided satisfy their requirements. The graph in Figure 7.9 shows the distribution of 1,238 instances

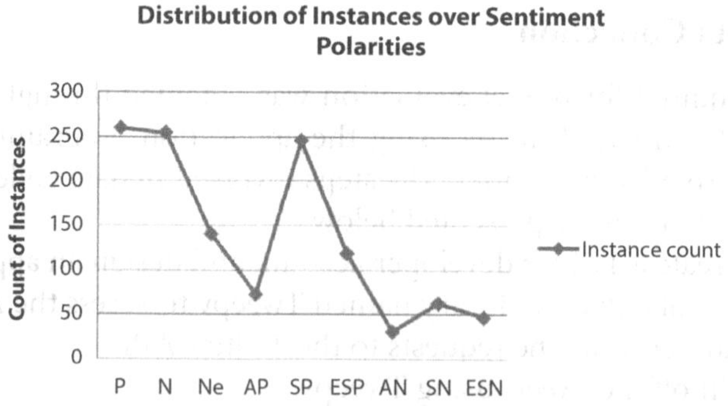

Figure 7.9 Distribution of instances over the nonary scale.

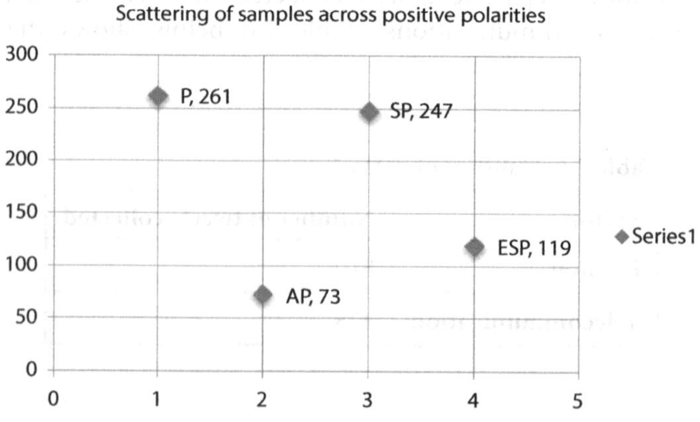

Figure 7.10 Scattering of samples across positive polarities.

(810 tweets from fashion and 428 tweets from telecommunications) among the various classes of sentiment polarity according to the nonary scale.

Figure 7.10 shows the scattering of samples across various sectors of positive polarities, whereas Figure 7.11 shows the scattering of samples across various sectors of negative polarities. Figure 7.12 shows the comparison of F1-score of the proposed method with the existing GPT and ELMO methods.

The generative pre-trained transformer (GPT) is a language model that has been designed to perform NLP operations such as translation, text generation, and summarization. Another pre-trained language model capable of doing NLP tasks is Embeddings from Language Models (ELMO). The graph analyzes the F1-score obtained by the proposed approach to

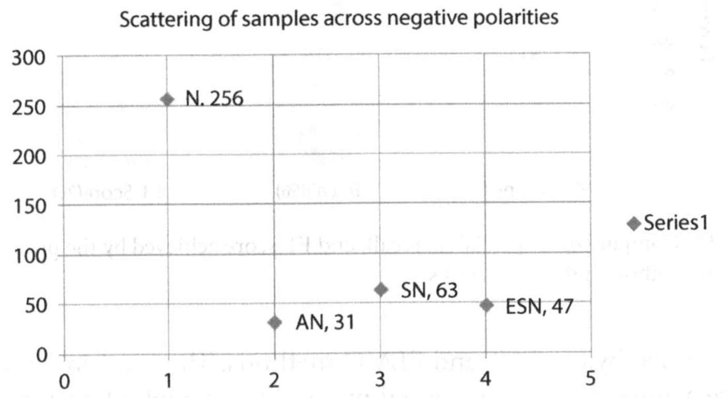

Figure 7.11 Scattering of samples across negative polarities.

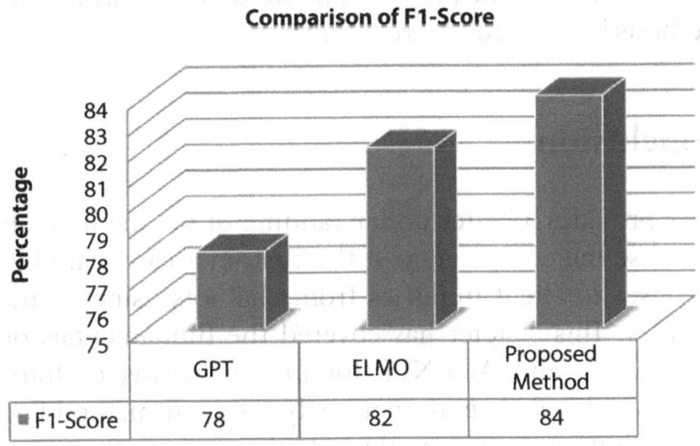

Figure 7.12 Comparison of F1-score of the proposed method with the existing GPT and ELMO methods.

Table 7.7 Precision, recall, and F1-score of the proposed method for chatbot sentiment analysis.

Precision(%)	Recall(%)	F1-score(%)
81	87	84

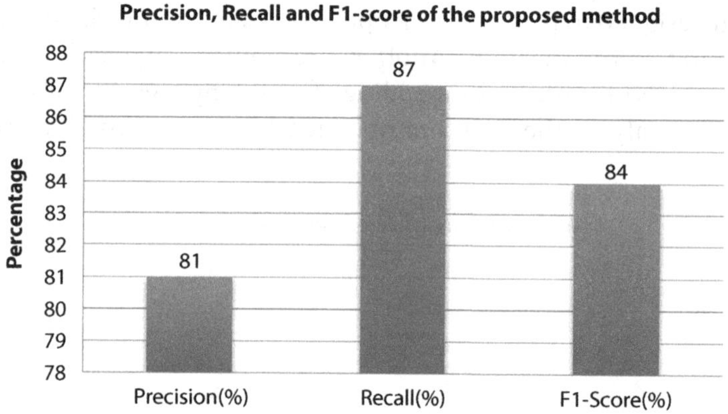

Figure 7.13 Comparison of precision, recall, and F1-score achieved by the proposed method for chatbot sentiment analysis.

those obtained by the GPT and ELMO methods. The precision, recall, and F1-score achieved by the suggested method for the job of customer satisfaction on chatbot responses are shown in Table 7.7 and Figure 7.13.

The proposed method accomplished a precision of 81%, a recall of 87%, and an F1 score of 84%. The proposed method outperformed the GPT and ELMO methods by 6% and 4%, respectively.

7.5 Conclusion

This chapter provides a better understanding of the methods that may be used to increase the competency of the customer care team by providing better responses to client inquiries from chatbots using sentiment analysis techniques. This chapter has covered the fundamentals of chatbots, sentiment analysis, and AutoNLP for pre-processing customer inquiry text, as well as a detailed sentiment analysis-based methodology for carrying out chatbot sentiment analysis to improve customer satisfaction with the chatbots' responses. The proposed methodology discussed in this chapter attained a precision of 81%, a recall of 87%, and an F1 score of 84%. The performance improvement was possible as the polarity of the customer sentiment was measured in a fine-tuned manner using trilateral modifiers and the nonary scale of the proposed method.

References

1. Kamath, R., Jamsandekar, S., Patil, M.B., Chatbot Response Mining using Sentiment Analysis, 2020.
2. Rajbala, Kaswan, K.S., Dhatterwal, J.S., Gangadevi, E., Balusamy, B., Intelligent Image Classification for 3D Printing in Industry 4.0, in: *Computational Intelligence in Bioprinting*, pp. 259–274, Wiley 2024, Hoboken, New Jersey, https:// doi.org/10.1002/9781394204878.ch13
3. Sodré, W. and Duarte, J., Chatbot Optimization using Sentiment Analysis and Timeline Navigation. *Rev. Inform. Teor. Apl.*, 30, 32–43, 2023, 10.22456/2175-2745.125825.
4. El-Ansari, A. and Benihssane, A., Sentiment Analysis for Personalized Chatbots in E-Commerce Applications. *Wirel. Pers. Commun.*, 129, 1–22, 2023, 10.1007/s11277-023-10199-5.
5. Raut, R., Kolambe, S., Borkar, P., Shingade, A., Gulhane, M., Depression Therapy Chat-Bot using Natural Language Processing. *Int. J. Intell. Syst. Appl. Eng.*, 12, 2s, 181–187, 2023.
6. Tran, A., Pallant, J., Johnson, L., Exploring the impact of chatbots on consumer sentiment and expectations in retail. *J. Retail. Consum. Serv.*, 63, 102718, 2021, 10.1016/j.jretconser.2021.102718.
7. Nallakaruppan, M.K., Gangadevi, E., Shri, M.L. *et al.* Reliable water quality prediction and parametric analysis using explainable AI models. *Sci Rep.*, 14, 7520, 2024. https://doi.org/10.1038/s41598-024-56775-y.
8. Intelligent chatbot interaction system capable for sentimental analysis using hybrid machine learning algorithms. *Inf. Process. Manag.*, 60, 5, 103440, 2023, ISSN 0306-4573, https://doi.org/10.1016/j.ipm.2023.103440.
9. Widyaningrum, P., Ruldeviyani, Y., Dharayani, R., Sentiment Analysis to Assess the Community's Enthusiasm Towards the Development Chatbot Using an Appraisal Theory. *Procedia Comput. Sci.*, 161, 723–730, 2019, 10.1016/j.procs.2019.11.176.
10. Lee, C.-W., Wang, Y.-S., Hsu, T.-Y., Chen, K.-Y., Lee, H.-Y., Lee, L.-S., Scalable Sentiment for Sequence-to-sequence Chatbot Response with Performance Analysis, 2018.
11. Io, H.N. and Lee, C.B., Chatbots and conversational agents: A bibliometric analysis. *Proceedings of IEEE International Conference on Industrial Engineering & Engineering Management*, pp. 215–219, 2017.

12. Bhagwat, V.A., Deep Learning for Chatbots. SJSU Scholar Works Master's Projects Master's Theses and Graduate Research, San Jose State University, Spring 2018.
13. Csaky, R., Deep Learning Based Chatbot Models. Scientific Students' Associations Report, Department of Automation and Applied Informatics, Budapest University Of Technology and Economics, 2017.
14. Menal, D., A Tool of Conversation: Chatbot. *Int. J. Comput. Sci. Eng.*, 5, 158–161, 2017.
15. Sentiment Analysis, https://en.wikipedia.org/wiki/Sentiment_analysis retrieved on 18th Dec 2019.
16. Maroengsit, W., Piyakulpinyo, T., Phonyiam, K., Pongnumkul, S., Chaovalit, P., Theeramunkong, T., A survey on evaluation methods for chatbots, in: *Proceedings of the 2019 7th International Conference on Information and Education Technology*, pp. 111–119, 2019.
17. Nandhini, M. and Gurunathan, P., Efficacy improvement of aspect-based sentiment analysis using enhanced rule–based approach and domain-specific lexicon (ERBA-DSL). *J. Intell. Fuzzy Syst.*, 43, 1–19, 2022, 10.3233/JIFS-213584.
18. Marstawi, A., Sharef, N.M., Aris, T.N.M., Mustapha, A., Ontology-based aspect extraction for an improved sentiment analysis in summarization of product reviews', in: *Proceedings of the 8th International Conference on Computer Modeling and Simulation*, pp. 100–104, 2017.
19. Sindhu, I., Daudpota, S.M., Badar, K., Bakhtyar, M., Baber, J., Nurunnabi, M., Aspect-based opinion mining on student's feedback for faculty teaching performance evaluation. *IEEE Access*, 7, 108729–108741, 2019.
20. Singh, V.K., Piryani, R., Uddin, A., Waila, P., Sentiment analysis of movie reviews: a new feature-based heuristic for aspect-level sentiment classification. *International Mutli-Conference On Automation, Computing, Communication, Control And Compressed Sensing (IMAC4S)*, IEEE, pp. 712–717, 2013.
21. Singh, V.K., Piryani, R., Waila, P., Devaraj, M., Computing sentiment polarity of texts at document and aspect levels. *ECTI Trans. Comput. Inf. Technol. (ECTI-CIT)*, 8, 1, 67–79, 2014.
22. Benamara, F., Cesarano, C., Picariello, A., Recupero, D.R., Subrahmanian, V.S., Sentiment analysis: Adjectives and adverbs are better than adjectives alone. *ICWSM*, vol. 7, pp. 203–206, 2007.
23. Devi Sri Nandhini, M. and Gurunathan, P., Joint aspect-opinion extraction and sentiment orientation detection in university reviews. *Int. J. Inf. Technol.*, 14, 3213–3225, 2022, https://doi.org/10.1007/s41870-022-01041-5.
24. Devika, M.D., Sunitha, C., Ganesh, A., Sentiment Analysis: A Comparative Study on Different Approaches. *Procedia Comput. Sci.*, 7, 44–49, 2016, ISSN 1877-0509, https://doi.org/10.1016/j.procs.2016.05.124.

25. Qazi, A., Raj, R.G., Hardaker, G., Standing, C., A systematic literature review on opinion types and sentiment analysis techniques: Tasks and challenges. *Internet Res.*, 27, 3, 608–630, 2017.
26. Schouten, K. and Frasincar, F., Survey on aspect-level sentiment analysis. *IEEE Trans. Knowl. Data Eng.*, 28, 3, 813–830, 2015.
27. Wankhade, M., Rao, A.C.S., Kulkarni, C., A survey on sentiment analysis methods, applications, and challenges. *Artif. Intell. Rev.*, 55, 7, 5731–5780, 2022.
28. Behdenna, S., Barigou, F., Belalem, G., Document level sentiment analysis: a survey. *EAI Endorsed Trans. Context-Aware Syst. Appl.*, 4, 13, e2–e2, 2018.
29. Shirsat, V.S., Jagdale, R.S., Deshmukh, S.N., Document level sentiment analysis from news articles, in: *2017 International Conference on Computing, Communication, Control and Automation (ICCUBEA)*, IEEE, pp. 1–4, 2017, August.
30. Meena, A. and Prabhakar, T.V., Sentence level sentiment analysis in the presence of conjuncts using linguistic analysis, in: *Advances in Information Retrieval: 29th European Conference on IR Research, ECIR 2007*, Rome, Italy, April 2-5, 2007, Springer Berlin Heidelberg, 2007.
31. Gangadevi, E., Rani, R.S., Dhanaraj, R.K., Nayyar, A., Spot-out fruit fly algorithm with simulated annealing optimized SVM for detecting tomato plant diseases. *Neural Comput. Appl.*, 36, 8, 4349–4375, 2023, Springer Science and Business Media LLC.

8

Financial Risk Prediction with Banking Monitoring for Cyber Security Analysis Using Automated Machine Learning

K. Rajkumar[1], Prassanna Jayachandran[2], Kannan Chakrapani[1], S. Magesh[3] and R. Manikandan[1]*

[1]School of Computing, SASTRA Deemed University, Thanjavur, Tamil Nadu, India
[2]School of Computer Science and Engineering (SCOPE), Vellore Institute of Technology, Chennai, India
[3]Department of Computer Science and Engineering, Dr. M.G.R Educational and Research Institute, Chennai, India

Abstract
Science and technological advancements encourage ongoing improvements in consumer finance, but they also introduce some financial credit hazards. Financial credit risk is getting harder and harder to manage, especially with the ongoing expansion of Internet banking. This highlights the need for the creation and assessment of a unique, all-encompassing machine learning approach that incorporates the study of missing data and predictor evaluation into the distress prediction process. This research proposes a novel technique in financial risk prediction with banking monitoring for cyber security detection using federated learning and automated machine learning. Here, users' banking is analyzed for cyber security detection using Gaussian Encoder Belief Network (GEBN). Financial credit risk analysis is conducted using metaheuristic autoregressive kernel principal swarm optimization model (MAPSO). The experimental analysis evaluates accuracy, mean average precision, recall, F-measure, and normalized error. Data from specific examples are used to analyze the model's performance. The findings imply that the suggested model-based data mining technique may extract hidden information from the data while optimizing input variables.

**Corresponding author*: srmanimt75@gmail.com

E. Gangadevi, M. Lawanya Shri, Balamurugan Balusamy and Rajesh Kumar Dhanaraj (eds.) Automated Machine Learning and Industrial Applications, (171–190) © 2025 Scrivener Publishing LLC

***Keywords*:** Financial risk prediction, banking monitoring, cyber security detection, federated learning, automated machine learning

8.1 Introduction

Protecting computer programming from intrusions, unauthorized access, alterations, and destruction is a component of cyber security practice. An intrusion detection system (IDS), antivirus software, and a firewall should typically be part of every cybersecurity system. The IDS is crucial since it helps spot any undesired and unwelcome changes to the system [1]. Two main types of intruders are those who enter from the inside and those who enter from the outside. However, the following elements can be utilized to distinguish between different types of cyber analytics: i) Irregularities or signatures and ii) founded on odd encryptions according to the hybrid nature.

Artificial intelligence (AI) methods are increasingly employed in the financial sector in asset management, trading methods, credit underwriting, and blockchain-based finance [2] due to readily available data and reasonably priced computing power. Machine learning (ML) methods use extensive data to learn from historical data automatically and prior performance to enhance prediction and performance without human programming. AI in finance is anticipated to give financial organizations a competitive edge by boosting productivity, reducing expenses, and enhancing QoS and the products they offer clients. Therefore, by offering better and more customized products, providing data insights to inform investment strategies, and potentially enhancing financial inclusion by enabling assessment of client creditworthiness with little to no credit history, these competitive advantages can help financial consumers [3]. Finance-related AI applications may also amplify or raise financial and non-financial risks raising concerns about potential investor and consumer protection laws.

The incompatibility of AI model processes with internal governance and financial supervisory frameworks and potential for pro-cyclicality and systemic risk in markets could jeopardize a policy-neutral approach to regulation. Given the intricacy of the methodologies used, their dynamic adaptability, and their degree of autonomy, implementing such approaches could enhance these vulnerabilities even if many possible hazards linked with AI in finance are not sure of this invention [4]. Management must take on more risks to increase revenues for the bank's investors. Banks must manage interest rates, market risks, credit risks, off-balance-sheet risks, operational and technology risks, foreign exchange risks, country or sovereign risks, liquidity risks, and bankruptcy risks. A bank's performance is based on its ability to handle these risks successfully. Regulatory control is a problem because of these risks and banks' role in financial methods [5]. Authorities need banks to retain capital due to the numerous hazards that may result from their varied operations. Basel criteria for estimating capital needs have evolved and increased since their inception in 1998. Capital is needed for each of the principal risk categories. Credit risk, which frequently requires the most outstanding capital, has historically been a considerable risk that banks have dealt with. Market risk arises primarily from a bank's trading operations, whereas operational risk refers to the possibility of losses owing to internal method flaws or external events. Most large banks calculate regulatory and economic capital, with the latter being based on bank methods rather than orders from regulators [6]. Banks must manage three main types of risks: credit, market, and operational. Liquidity, business, and reputational threats are additional dangers. To monitor, manage, and quantify these risks, banks actively participate in risk management.

8.2 Related Works

Traditional quantitative finance issues, such as return forecasting, risk modeling, and optimal portfolio creation, have been successfully solved using machine learning on a large scale [7]. Risk is the likelihood of losing something, and exposure is the chance of losing something [8]. A firm must frequently be exposed to risk to succeed. FRM is built on identifying risk and exposure. Risk and exposure are quantified differently because they are perceived differently in various contexts. The authors of refs. [9] and [10] suggested using SVM to classify financial messages using techniques based on conventional ML. The bag-of-words (BoW) technique serves as a representation of the message throughout the classification phase. Additionally, multinomial Naïve Bayes (mNB), random forests (RF), and other classical classifiers are available [11]. Deep learning-based methods are frequently superior to traditional ML ones because the latter only extracts shallow features from the messages for categorization. The author used the LSTM network in ref. [12] to classify financial messages to improve classification performance. This study was carried out to aid banks, financial institutions, and the general public understand cyber regimes. Using symmetric Kullback–Leibler divergence on tweets and Latent Dirichlet Allocation (LDA), poorly supervised models can be created to evaluate impact of denial-of-service (DoS) assaults without requiring annotated data. The module has a limit that is only partially monitored. This becomes less of an issue as fewer non-attack Twitter events are probably misidentified as DoS attacks inside the pre-specified detection window. Applying a second classification layer trained on manually annotated DoS attack tweets is another way to remove non-attack tweets from the dataset. A thorough analysis of the classification outcomes of various RNNs, such as the bi-directional LSTM, bi-directional GRU, gated recurrent unit (GRU), stacked GRU, LSTM, and simple RNN, is presented in ref. [13]. System designers used the fuzzy theory to consider the reality that user actions are occasionally accompanied by uncertainty. The fuzzy expert system's performance was evaluated using a receiver operating characteristic curve, and the results show a 94% accuracy rate. By using this expert system, E-banking security and service quality could be enhanced. Samples from the source domain are used to train a convolutional neural network, and finance domain messages are then adopted to adjust specifications. This transfer learning technique was applied in ref. [14]. In practice, all parameters can be recalculated during pretraining. A method that combines scoring criteria for offline historical transactions and online real-time transactions is put together to detect fraud. Large-scale data processing, an architecture based on MPP Gbase, Spark, and Kafka is shown, along with a technique for examining massive transaction logs. The efficacy of the suggested method is demonstrated by the author's experimental findings over a substantial dataset of electronic banking transactions. The author's future work should close these gaps and overcome these obstacles. Since compiling enough financially labeled training texts was challenging, Work [15] opted for the Lexicon-based method over machine learning for sentiment analysis. They created a Chinese Financial Domain Sentiment Lexicon (CFDSL) using word vectors and three DL classifiers. The effectiveness of the CFDSL in predicting future financial difficulty has been established. CNN and its enhanced variations are frequently selected for financial visual information. The author created an enterprise financial risk prediction method based on DL method-embedded systems [16]. Financial data are typically heterogeneous since they come from many different sources and are merged closely immediately. Time series data are a crucial kind that reflect the diversity of financial data sources. Several researchers said deep learning is highly accurate at predicting time series. To simulate the fluctuation of the China stock price index, Work [17] applied the GARCH model with the LSTM method. They analyzed values of four loss functions and discovered that the LSTM method performed more accurately in prediction. We have developed a novel DDoS assault detection system using MapReduce programming architecture. The methods used to authenticate customers vary according to the statement provided by the online banking platform. Many banks use PINs and passwords. Others validate and approve transactions using TANs and

TAN lists (sometimes called scratch lists). More complex methods, such as challenge-response systems or one-time passwords, can also be used for user authentication. To the author's knowledge, no significant bank has successfully implemented public-key certificates for user authentication. The cryptographic strength of SSL/TLS protocol is frequently cited in defense of the security of online banking. There are very few known theoretical flaws and vulnerabilities in the security of the SSL/TLS protocol. The Dolev–Yao threat model is relevant to these investigations. The author [18] studied a financial capital flow prediction approach using the Yu'e bao transaction data. They suggested a prediction approach (YEB_Hybrid) combining a linear method with a nonlinear one based on the time-series theory and LSTM. They thought the approach enhanced forecast accuracy and successfully addressed the liquidity risk and liquidity surplus issues. Guaranteeing the e-commerce system's 24-h safe functioning in a market worth trillions of dollars is an inherent difficulty. Work [19] concentrated on the e-commerce sector and developed a deep learning-based financial risk early warning method for e-commerce companies. The author creatively mixed unstructured language from 10-K files and conventionally market-based structured data [20].

8.3 System Model

We discuss new ways to predict financial risks in banking using machine learning. We study bank services using a Gaussian encoder belief network. We use a unique metaheuristic autoregressive kernel principal swarm optimization model to determine credit risks. The proposed method is depicted in Figure 8.1.

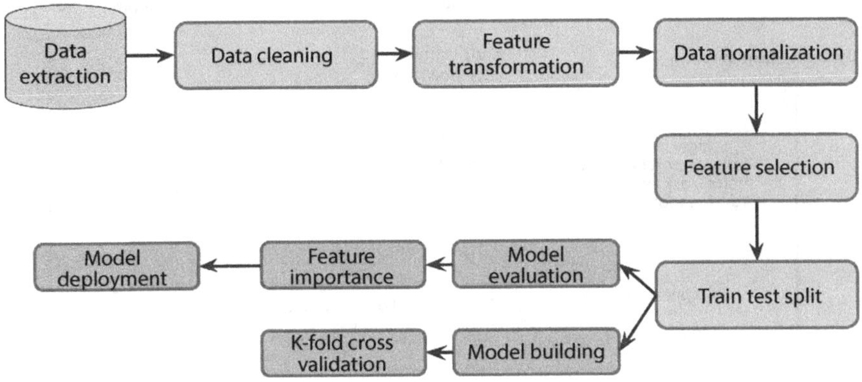

Figure 8.1 Proposed risk analysis model.

This framework uses scaling, normalization, and transformation functions to pre-process credit data. The dataset has been appropriately normalized using min–max normalization. The data's minimum and maximum values were obtained and modified during this process using Equation 8.1.

$$\bar{L} = \frac{l - \min(X)}{\max(X) - \min(X)}\left(new_{\min(X)} - new_{\max(X)}\right) + new_{\min(X)} \quad (8.1)$$

where X stands for a specification that is present in data, min(X) and max(X) represent lower and upper levels of attribute values, L denotes upgrade values of entries, l represents the previous value in data, and newmin(X) and newmax(X) represent the values of the minimal and maximal restrictions, respectively.

Figure 8.2 depicts the algorithm's process for the suggested supply chain digital financial risk prevention method. Gather pertinent financial information about supply chain businesses and then input that information as training data into the training set. Add the selected functions to the training data set, create a portion of test data to confirm pattern accuracy later on, carry out the classification method, and adjust the parameters using

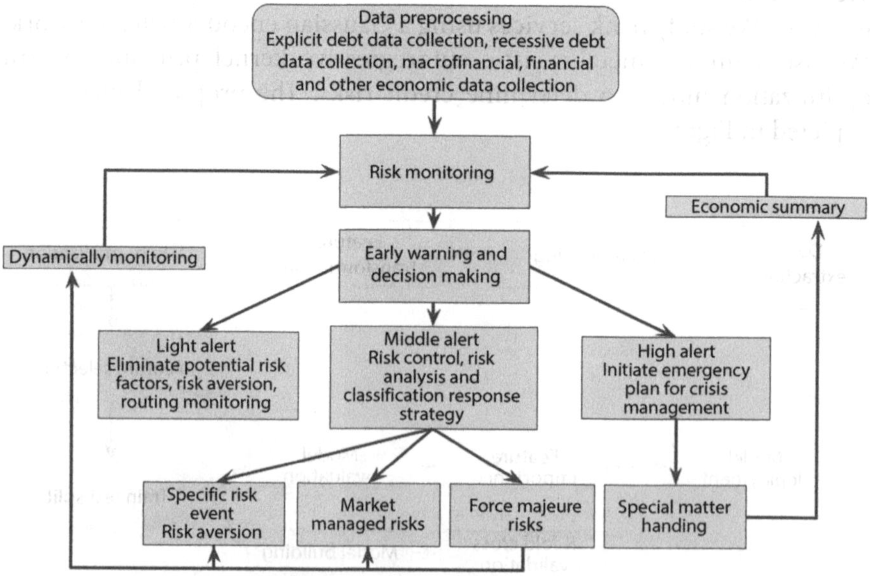

Figure 8.2 Flowchart for financial risk analysis.

SMA. Finally, the trained model is fed with these data, and the accuracy of the mold operation is assessed.

8.3.1 Cyber Security Detection Using Gaussian Encoder Belief Network

Direct one-hot encoding may produce enormous representation dimensions and many training specifications due to the vast number of words in the financial message domain making it inappropriate for practical applications. Word embedding technology must be introduced to decrease the dimensionality of word representation vector. The word2vec approach is one of the more common traditional word embedding techniques. It uses words from the corpus to represent words following models like the continuous bag of words (CBOW).

As in our earlier work, we set it to 0.99. The action-value function is crucial because by maximizing it, we can eventually arrive at an ideal policy that results in the desired behavior, which, in this case, is an accurate picture class prediction. Two-node output depicts the two possible action values, Q(s, a1) and Q(s, a2), that can be obtained by acting on states differently.

$$p(x) = \Sigma_{j=1}^{K} \pi_j p\left(x; \theta_j\right),\ j = 1,\dots,K. \qquad p(\mathbf{x}) = \Sigma_{c=1}^{C} \pi_c f_c(\mathbf{x} \mid \theta) \tag{8.2}$$

The mixture method has a vector of parameters, $\underline{\theta} = \{\theta_1,\dots,\theta_k, \pi_1,\dots\pi_k\}$.

In mixture models, hidden variables are regarded as latent variables or Z. It accepts the numbers 1 through K as a discrete set that meets the requirements. $z_k \epsilon \{0,1\}$ and $\Sigma_z z_k = 1$.

$$p(z,x) = p(z)p(x \mid z) \qquad p(z_k = 1) = \pi_k \tag{8.3}$$

A definition of probability density function of X

$$p(x \mid \mu_k, \Sigma_k) = \frac{1}{\sqrt{2\pi \mid \Sigma^{-1} \mid}} \exp\left(-\frac{1}{2}(x-\mu_x)\Sigma_x^{-1}(x-\mu_x)^T\right)$$
$$f_c(\mathbf{x} \mid \mu_c, \Sigma_c) = \frac{1}{(2\pi)^{\frac{d}{2}} \mid \Sigma_c \mid^{\frac{1}{2}}} \exp\left(-\frac{1}{2}(\mathbf{x}-\mu_c)^t\, \Sigma_c^{-1}(\mathbf{x}-\mu_c)\right) \tag{8.4}$$

A linear superposition of Gaussians is utilized to represent a Gaussian mixture distribution in the form:

$$\begin{aligned} p(x) &= \Sigma_{k=1}^{K} \pi_k p(x \mid \mu_k, £_k) \\ \hat{\pi}_c &= \frac{n_c}{n}, \\ \hat{\mu}_c &= \frac{1}{n_c} \Sigma_{\{f \mid y_i = c\}} \mathbf{x}_i \\ \hat{\Sigma}_c &= \frac{1}{(n_c - 1)} \Sigma_{\{i \mid y_i = c\}} (\mathbf{x}_i - \mu_c)(\mathbf{x}_i - \mu_c)^t \end{aligned} \tag{8.5}$$

Given a specific value of z, conditional distribution of x is now a Gaussian:

$$\begin{aligned} p(x \mid z_k = 1) &= p(x \mid \mu_k, \Sigma_k) \\ p(x \mid z) &= \Pi_{k=1}^{K} p(x \mid \mu_k, \Sigma_k)^{z_k} \end{aligned} \tag{8.6}$$

The marginal distribution of x is attained by summing the joint distribution of all potential states of z.

$$p(x) = \Sigma_z p(z) p(x \mid z) = \Sigma_{k=1}^{K} \pi_k p(x \mid \mu_k, \Sigma_k) \tag{8.7}$$

A significant derived quantity is "posterior probability" on a mixture component for a specific data vector [11]:

$$\gamma(z_k) \equiv p(z_k = 1 \mid x) = \frac{p(z_k = 1) p(x|z_k = 1)}{\Sigma_{j=1}^{K} p(z_j = 1) p(x|z_j = 1)} = \frac{\pi_k p(x|\mu_k, \Sigma_k)}{\Sigma_{j=1}^{K} \pi_j p(x|\mu_j, \Sigma_j)} \tag{8.8}$$

The output layer (y) then uses the input (h, latent space), $(x^{[\alpha]} \in \mathcal{R}^d)$ and the hidden layer to recreate the input $x^{[\alpha]}$. We all use the same superscript notation, $^*[\alpha]$, to refer to all of the individual parameters connected to the AE network using Equation 8.9.

$$\hat{x}^{[\alpha]} = y_{(W',b')}\left(h_{(W,b)}\left(x^{[\alpha]}\right)\right) \equiv x^{[\alpha]} \tag{8.9}$$

Other names for this include an encoder or a recognition technique. By optimizing the variational parameter φ, Equation 8.10 is satisfied.

$$q_{\phi}(\mathbf{z} \mid \mathbf{x}) \approx p_{\theta}(\mathbf{z} \mid \mathbf{x}) \tag{8.10}$$

The inference method is (almost) any directed graphical technique according to Equation 8.11:

$$q_{\phi}(\mathbf{z} \mid \mathbf{x}) = q_{\phi}(\mathbf{z}_1,\ldots,\mathbf{z}_M \mid \mathbf{x}) = \prod_{j=1}^{M} q_{\phi}(\mathbf{z}_j \mid Pa(\mathbf{z}_j),\mathbf{x}) \tag{8.11}$$

Every layer of a DBN is constructed as an RBM, so training its layers is identical to training an RBM. Classification is accomplished by initializing a network using DBN training using Equation 8.12.

$$\min_{\sigma_k} \frac{1}{|D|} \Sigma_{i=1}^{|D|}\left[-\log p\left(x_k^{(0)};\theta_k\right)\right]_{\theta_k} \tag{8.12}$$

Remember that layer-wise updating necessitates correcting all problems starting from the bottom hidden layer and working our way up to the top visible layer. We solve the optimization issue for the fine-tuning phase using Equation 8.13.

$$\min_{\phi} \frac{1}{D|} \Sigma_{i=1}^{|D|}\left[\mathcal{L}\left(\phi; y^{(i)}, h\left(x^{(\theta)}\right)\right)\right]_{h\left(x^{(0)}\right)} = h\left(x_i^{(i)}\right) \tag{8.13}$$

This method uses a two-phase training procedure simultaneously, but we still need to add one more hyperparameter to balance the relative weights of the two goals. The method (DBN + loss) is given as Equation 8.14:

$$\begin{gathered}\min_{\theta_{L,i},\theta_{DNN}} \mathbb{E}_{3,x}[\mathcal{L}(\theta_L;\mathbf{y}, h(\mathbf{x}))] + \rho\mathbb{E}_{\mathbf{x}}[-\log p(\mathbf{x};\theta_{DAN})] \\ \min_{\theta_L,\theta_{DAN}} \frac{1}{D} \Sigma_{i=1}^{|D|}\left[\mathcal{L}\left(\theta_L; y^{(i)}, h\left(x^{(i)}\right)\right) - \rho \log p\left(x^{(i)};\theta_{DBN}\right)\right]_{\theta_L}\end{gathered} \tag{8.14}$$

Metaheuristic Autoregressive Kernel Principal Swarm Optimization Model

Its search utility and convergence capabilities are superior to a meta-heuristic bionics optimization technique. Its distinctive adaptive method can more effectively balance the overall condition and the local search method increasing search accuracy. The Locust optimization method divides the entire method into an exploration method and a development method to imitate the eliminating and finding of foodstuff behavior of a locust population in the natural world. Algorithm is principally a compound of three components. The following formula illustrates its scheme process:

$$X_i = S_i + G_i + A_i$$

In this equation, Xi represents the location of the i-th locust, Si represents the attraction between individual operations, Gi represents the gravitational pull of the i-th locus, and Ai represents the amount of wind the i-th locust is exposed to. Social action has the most significant impact on locust placement, and the formula for determining Si is as follows:

$$S_i = \sum_{\substack{j=1 \\ j \neq i}}^{N} s(|X_j - X_i|)\frac{X_j - X_i}{d_{ij}}$$

In this case, N stands for the total number of locusts in a community, dij for the range between locusts i and j, and S for the social strength function. Here is how estimating process works:

$$S(r) = fe^{-r/l} - e^{-r}.$$

Here, social attractiveness strength and scale are denoted by the letters f and l, respectively, while the social value of its existence is denoted by the letter r. Second, the Gi and Ai formulas are as follows:

$$G_i = -ge_{y'},$$

$$A_i = ue_{w^*}$$

Here, g is the gravitational force target, ew is the normalized vector that points directly in the direction of the wind, u is the wind magnitude, and eg is the normalized vector that faces the earth. Consequently, the locust's position Xi can be stated as follows:

$$X_i = \sum_{\substack{j=1 \\ j \neq i}}^{N} s(|X_j - X_i|)\frac{X_j - X_i}{\mathrm{d}_{ij}} - ge_g + ue_{w^*}$$

Although population does not converge to a particular value in our mathematical method, locusts quickly find a comfortable posture necessitating optimization. Because the wind always blows in the direction of Td, and the gravity factor Gi is not currently taken into account, a better mathematical method is

$$X_i = c\left[\sum_{\substack{j=1 \\ j \neq i}}^{N} cub_d - lb_d / 2s(|x_j - x_i|)x_j - x_i / \mathrm{d}_{ij}\right] + T_{d^*}$$

Here, Td is the ideal locust location in a d-dimensional room, and ubd and lbd are superior and inferior S(r) bounds in the d-dimensional room. In calculation, c is the decreasing coefficient, and formula is

$$\mathrm{c} = c_{\max} - n\frac{c_{\max} - c_{\min}}{n_{\max}}$$

In this case, the most prominent and smallest number of specifications c are cmax and cmin; separately, n denotes the number of iterations present, and nmax denotes the most significant number of iterations. The PCA weight method, a multidimensional-variable statistical methodology provided to calculate the weight calculation, is one of the most widely used dimensionality reduction strategies for pattern analysis. By using the specified information, illuminating the dataset, and scrutinizing the estimated value, its primary purpose is to calculate the weight of output nodes and restrict the dataset size. Initialize X as the input dataset where every column is divided into a D-dimensional input pattern (X = [x 1, x 2,..., x n]). Accept that each node's regular value is taken as the dataset's mean and set to zero (E(X) = 0). Applying the orthonormal weight computation A, map X into new space Y as follows:

$$Y = AX \tag{8.15}$$

Consider $E(X) = 0$, $E(Y) = 0$, and the covariance matrix of Y is:

$$RY = AR_X A^T \tag{8.16}$$

Rx is the covariance matrix for X. It is obvious that examples are d-dimensional in node space if rows of A are eigenvectors of Rx utilizing this weight calculation; nonetheless, the primary goal of PCA transform is to create d-dimensional mapped samples that closely reflect X.

Reconstructing X as $X = A^T Y$ is possible. It is possible to project X rather than duplicate it using all of the eigenvectors; in this case, $^\wedge X = A_K^T Y$, where k eigenvectors are used. The output nodes' combined weight in this instance is:

$$wgt = \sum_{i=1}^{d} \lambda_i - \sum_{i=1}^{k} \lambda_i = \sum_{i=k+1}^{d} \lambda_i \tag{8.17}$$

Given a p.d. kernel and mapping such that $\Phi : S \rightarrow H(K)$, an RKHS exists.

$$K(x, y) = \langle \Phi(x), \Phi(y) \rangle_{\mathcal{H}(K)}$$
$$\cdot f(x) = \langle K_x, f \rangle_{\mathcal{H}(K)}$$
$$\text{span}\left\{K_x := K\left(x_i, x_j\right)\right.$$

Concerning the H (K)-inner product:

$$\left\langle \sum c_i K_{x_i}, \sum d_j K_{x_j} \right\rangle_{\mathcal{H}(K)} := \sum c_{\max}$$

Appropriate indicators typically function within an acceptable range of fluctuations if they do not exceed the threshold value; exceeding this value denotes a financial risk. The supply chain financial risk mitigation technique alerts management suggesting that strategic decisions are temporarily suspended to address potential financial vulnerabilities promptly, thereby preventing escalating business losses.

8.4 Results and Discussion

In this section, we present the results of different tests to evaluate the performance of the proposed method. A PC with accompanying highlights was utilized to test the proposed half-and-half model: With a 32-bit operating system, an Intel(R) Core(TM) i5-7500 CPU, 4 GB of RAM, Windows 7, NumPy, SciPy, Pandas, Keras, and Matplotlib frameworks, and Python 2.7 programming language.

Dataset Description

General Data Protection Regulation (GDPR): The dataset collects information from all other commercial banks and savings institutions and serves as the nation's central credit hub. Each entry in this dataset represents a client's credit and credit card status every month. The credit registry database was approximately 1 TB, but we utilized a subset of this dataset with 1,000,000 rows for the study. These rows represent the status of 1,000,000 distinct loans for private clients only and their status on the scheduled completion date of the loan payment. The dataset does not have a characteristic indicating whether the client can reimburse the credit risky or not.

Advanced Credit Registry Data Analysis: Leveraging its capabilities for cutting-edge examination, we examined attributes, their conditions, patterns, and correlations with additional information sources. We carried out different stages to perform the investigation, including extra-determined segments, measures, and a star construction model. We were able to inspect the dataset and gain better knowledge by creating multiple reports in a highly efficient manner following the method design and relationships. In contrast to conventional tools, these reports are incomparably fast and powerful with modern visualization, dependency, and prediction capabilities. Our choice to adopt Power BI was partly influenced by how quickly it can modify and analyze data. The portion of the dataset we examined had a size of 13 GB when put in a structured query language (SQL) database since Power BI has its format designed to handle massive amounts of data. However, this size was reduced to 330 MB when stored in Power BI format.

Dataset for WIND: The example information chosen in this paper is genuine information from an individual credit data set of a part of a business bank. This paper uses 75 randomly selected data samples from a personal credit database. After eliminating these invalid examples, 61 substantial examples remain. There are 21 test samples and 40 learning samples.

According to the laid out explore plan, nearly 600,000 tests of exchange information were collected, analyzed, and handled (over 540,000 examples from Bank A and more than 40,000 examples were obtained from Bank B). Information showing areas of strength for corporate business was screened out. There were four dimensions to the features: credit-related static information, dynamic change data of the advance, loan customer sub-account capital stream, and complete capital stream of the advance client's different records. After various tasks, including separating and participating from January to June 2020, 103 substantial fields were chosen from 263 fields in eight tables.

Table 8.1 shows an analysis based on various financial credit datasets. The datasets analyzed are GDPR, Advanced Analytics of Credit Registry, and WIND in terms of accuracy, mean average precision, recall, F1_Score, and normalized error.

In Figure 8.3, the analysis for accuracy is shown. Here, for the GDPR dataset, the proposed technique attained an accuracy of 90%, existing SVM attained 80%, and CNN attained 83%. For the Advanced Analytics of Credit Registry Dataset, the proposed technique attained an accuracy of 93%, existing CNN attained 82%, and SVM attained 84%. For the WIND dataset, the proposed technique attained an accuracy of 96%, existing SVM attained 81%, and CNN attained 85%.

Table 8.1 Analysis based on various financial credit risk analysis dataset.

Parameters	Techniques	Accuracy	Mean average precision	Recall	F1_score	Normalized error
GDPR	**SVM**	80	75	70	75	61
	CNN	83	79	73	78	65
	Proposed_ GEBN_ MAPSO	90	85	75	81	69
Advanced Analytics of Credit Registry Dataset	**SVM**	82	83	68	83	71
	CNN	84	87	73	85	73
	Proposed_ GEBN_ MAPSO	93	91	82	89	75
WIND	**SVM**	81	85	83	69	69
	CNN	85	89	85	73	74
	Proposed_ GEBN_ MAPSO	96	93	91	83	83

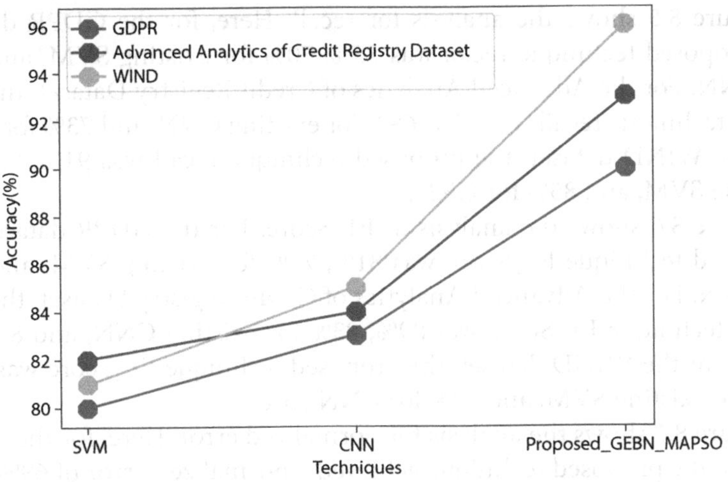

Figure 8.3 Comparison of accuracy.

Figure 8.4 shows the analysis in mean average precision. For the GDPR dataset, the proposed technique had a mean average precision of 85%, 75% for existing SVM, and 79% for CNN. For the Advanced Analytics of Credit Registry Dataset, the proposed technique had a MAP of 91%, 83% for existing CNN, and 87% for SVM. For the WIND dataset, the proposed technique had a MAP of 93%, 85% for existing SVM, and 89% for CNN.

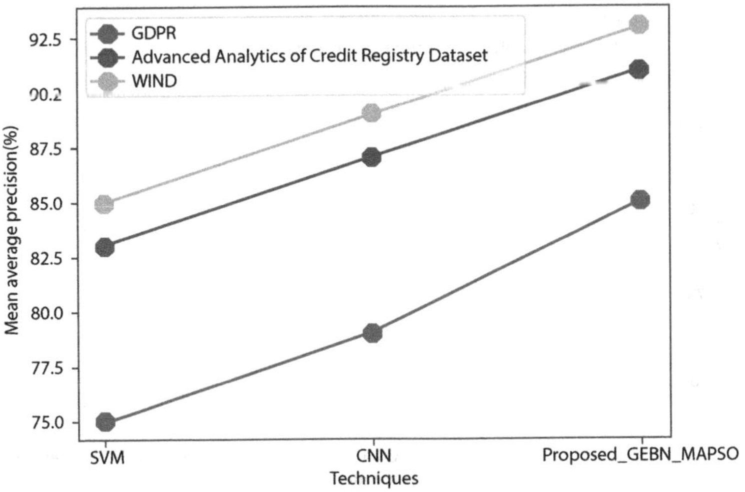

Figure 8.4 Comparison of mean average precision (MAP).

Figure 8.5 shows the analysis for recall. Here, for the GDPR dataset, the proposed technique recall was 75%, 70% for existing SVM, and 73% for CNN. For the Advanced Analytics of Credit Registry Dataset, the proposed technique recall was 82%, 68% for existing CNN, and 73% for SVM. For the WIND dataset, the proposed technique recall was 91%, 83% for existing SVM, and 85% for CNN.

Figure 8.6 shows the analysis in F1_Score. For the GDPR dataset, the proposed technique F1_Score was 81%, 75% for existing SVM, and 78% for CNN. For the Advanced Analytics of Credit Registry Dataset, the proposed technique F1_Score was 89%, 83% for existing CNN, and 85% for SVM. For the WIND dataset, the proposed technique F1_Score was 83%, 69% for existing SVM, and 73% for CNN 73%.

Figure 8.7 shows the analysis for normalized error. Here, for the GDPR dataset, the proposed technique achieved a normalized error of 69%, with 61% for existing SVM and 65% for CNN. For the Advanced Analytics of Credit Registry Dataset, the proposed technique achieved a normalized error of 75%, with 71% for existing CNN and 73% for SVM. For the WIND dataset, the proposed technique achieved a normalized error of 83%, with 69% for the existing SVM and 74% for CNN.

When both the actual and decision results are expected, the result is TP; when both the actual and decision results are abnormal, the result is FN; when both the authentic and decision results are abnormal, the result is FP; and when both the actual and decision results are abnormal, the

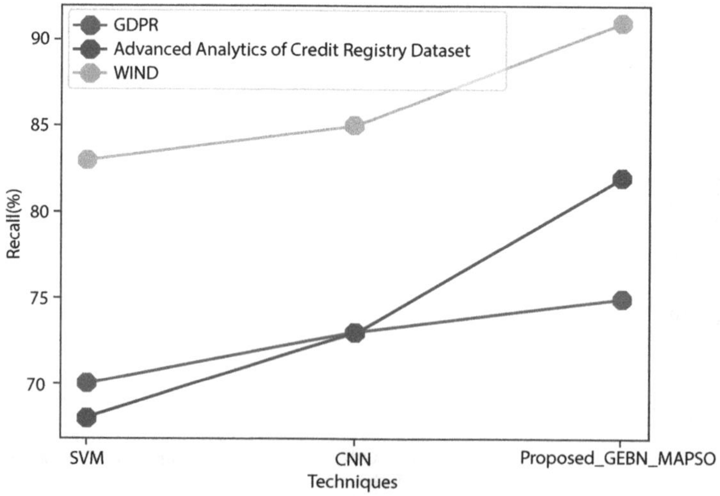

Figure 8.5 Comparison of recall.

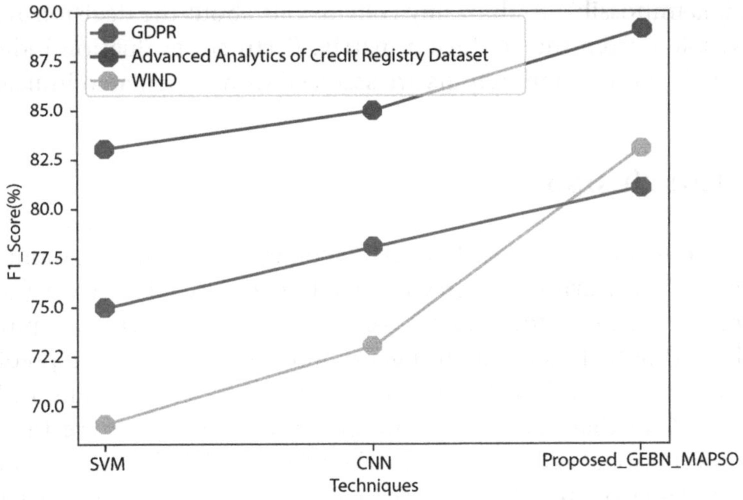

Figure 8.6 Comparison of F1_score.

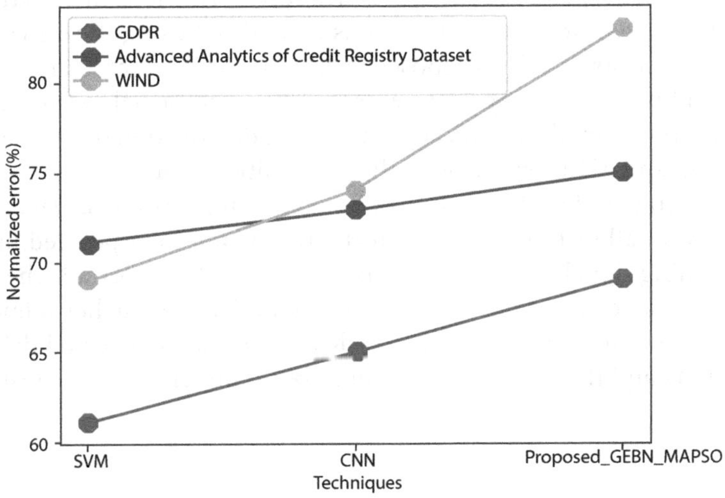

Figure 8.7 Comparison of normalized error.

result is TN. Many correct choices made by aberrant samples as well as standard samples, respectively, are represented by TN and TP. The decision is a better higher value. Figures FN and FP show many incorrect decisions made with abnormal samples and those made with standard samples. A lower value is preferable because it denotes a more minor mistake. Due to the large amount of data collected from the sample companies used in this study, it is impossible to draw any conclusions about the decision-making process solely from the confusion matrix. Pertinent evaluation indicators are created, and method outputs are assessed using calculated indicators.

8.5 Conclusion

This research aims to analyze financial credit risk with banking monitoring using a machine learning-based Gaussian Encoder Belief Network (GEBN) and metaheuristic autoregressive kernel principal swarm optimization model (MAPSO). This research suggests a deep learning-based prediction and assessment technique for financial market investment analysis. RMB, euro, yen, Canadian, Australian, pound, and Swiss franc are the seven major international exchange rate markets from which this study examined historical data from to estimate exchange rates. The extraction procedure is capable of handling input text that has varying lengths. After extraction, it is possible to efficiently filter out false information from financial communications, which speeds up the subsequent categorization. After extracting the abstracts, sentiment classification is carried out using the GRU model by extracted abstracts. The proposed technique in this research is validated through a financial message dataset from a financial social network.

The proposed method's efficacy may also be demonstrated using abstract extraction and GRU strategies. The recognition rate has improved by 2.87% in compared to the method of not extracting abstracts. Data restrictions prevent all or hidden debt threats from being incorporated into the early warning signal method, which is the cause of the shortfall. The methodology for assessing government debt risk undergoes further refinement and optimization considering the disclosure of illicit concealed debt data from audits and the official calculations about hidden social security debt figures.

References

1. Ghelani, D., Hua, T.K., Koduru, S.K.R., Cyber Security Threats, Vulnerabilities, and Security Solutions Models in Banking. *Authorea Preprints*, 2022.
2. Islam, U., Muhammad, A., Mansoor, R., Hossain, M.S., Ahmad, I., Eldin, E.T., Shafiq, M., Detection of distributed denial of service (DDoS) attacks in IoT based monitoring system of banking sector using machine learning models. *Sustainability*, *14*, 14, 8374, 2022.

3. Almatari, O., Wang, X., Zhang, W., Khan, M.K., VTAIM: Volatile Transaction Authentication Insurance Method for Cyber Security Risk Insurance of Banking Services, 2023.
4. Wei, Z., Liu, H., Tao, X., Pan, K., Huang, R., Ji, W., Wang, J., Insights into the Application of Machine Learning in Industrial Risk Assessment: A Bibliometric Mapping Analysis. *Sustainability, 15*, 8, 6965, 2023.
5. Peng, K. and Yan, G., A survey on deep learning for financial risk prediction. *Quant. Finance Econ.*, *5*, 4, 716–737, 2021.
6. Clintworth, M., Lyridis, D., Boulougouris, E., Financial risk assessment in shipping: a holistic machine learning based methodology. *Marit. Econ. Logist.*, 1–32, 2021.
7. Zhao, J., Corporate financial risk prediction based on embedded systems and deep learning. *Microprocess. Microsyst.*, 103405, 2020.
8. Chen, X. and Long, Z., E-Commerce Enterprises Financial Risk Prediction Based on FA-PSO-LSTM Neural Network Deep Learning Model. *Sustainability, 15*, 7, 5882, 2023.
9. Song, Y. and Wu, R., The impact of financial enterprises' excessive financialization risk assessment for risk control based on data mining and machine learning. *Comput. Econ.*, *60*, 4, 1245–1267, 2022.
10. Mhlanga, D., Financial inclusion in emerging economies: The application of machine learning and artificial intelligence in credit risk assessment. *Int. J. Financ. Stud.*, *9*, 3, 39, 2021.
11. Shi, T., Li, C., Wanyan, H., Xu, Y., Zhang, W., The lending risk prediction of the folk informal financial organization from big data using the deep learning hybrid model. *Financ. Res. Lett.*, *50*, 103212, 2022.
12. Chen, D., Risk assessment of government debt based on machine learning algorithm. *Complexity*, *2021*, 1–12, 2021.
13. Appadurai, J.P., Raveendran, L.S., Latha, R., Gangadevi, E., Shri, M.L., Gite, S., Cybersecurity Using Hybrid Type Model for Classification Through SCO Optimization Technique. *2024 IEEE International Conference on Computing, Power and Communication Technologies (IC2PCT)*, Greater Noida, India, pp. 1390–1396, 2024, doi: 10.1109/IC2PCT60090.2024.10486307.
14. Cao, Y., Shao, Y., Zhang, H., Study on early warning of E-commerce enterprise financial risk based on deep learning algorithm. *Electron. Commer. Res.*, *22*, 1, 21–36, 2022.
15. Melina, S., Napitupulu, H., Mohamed, N., A Conceptual Model of Investment-Risk Prediction in the Stock Market Using Extreme Value Theory with Machine Learning: A Semisystematic Literature Review. *Risks*, *11*, 3, 60, 2023.
16. Kaswan, K.S., Dhatterwal, J.S., Batra, R., Balusamy, B., Gangadevi, E., 3D Bioprinting Technology Optimization Using Machine Learning, in: *Computational Intelligence in Bioprinting*, pp. 303–321, Wiley, 2024, https://doi.org/10.1002/9781394204878.ch15.

17. Li, G., Wang, X., Bi, D., Hou, J., Risk measurement of the financial credit industry driven by data: Based on DAE-LSTM deep learning algorithm. *J. Glob. Inf. Manag. (JGIM)*, *30*, 11, 1–20, 2022.
18. Khan, H.U., Malik, M.Z., Nazir, S., Khan, F., Utilizing bio metric system for enhancing cyber security in banking sector: a systematic analysis. *IEEE Access*, 2023.
19. Anu Disney, D., Yugha, R., Karachi, S.B., Gangadevi, E., Balusamy, B., Gite, S., An AI-Driven Based Cybersecurity System for Network Intrusion Detection System in Hybrid with EPO and CNNet-LAM. *2024 IEEE International Conference on Computing, Power and Communication Technologies (IC2PCT)*, Greater Noida, India, pp. 1397–1404, 2024, doi: 10.1109/IC2PCT60090.2024.10486517.
20. Vaiyapuri, T., Priyadarshini, K., Hemlathadhevi, A., Dhamodaran, M., Dutta, A.K., Pustokhina, I.V., Pustokhin, D.A., Intelligent feature selection with deep learning based financial risk assessment model. *CMC-Comput. Mater. Continua*, *72*, 2, 2429–2444, 2022.

9

AutoML Ecosystem and Open-Source Platforms: Challenges and Limitations

M. Anitha[1], J. Dhilipan[2], P.M. Kavitha[3]* and E. Gangadevi[4]

[1]*Department of Computer Science and Engineering, SRM TRP Engineering College, Trichy, India*
[2]*Department of Computer Science and Applications, Faculty of Science and Humanities, SRM Institute of Science and Technology, Chennai, India*
[3]*Department of Computer Science and Applications, SRM Institute of Science and Technology, Chennai, India*
[4]*Department of Computer Science and Applications, Loyola College, Chennai, India*

Abstract

With the increase in machine learning attention over the recent few years, the next focus is on Automated Machine learning (AutoML), which democratizes ML by automating model selection, tuning in the hyperparameters, and the feature engineering process as well. The work delves into the ecosystem of the AutoML, where the initial and basic tasks of ML are converted into a single step. The work focuses on the different frameworks on AutoML along with few open-source AutoML libraries like Auto-sklearn, TPOT, AutoKeras, MLBox, etc. The benefits, challenges, and limitations of incorporating AutoML are discussed in brief. Models, like Fully Automated, Human-in-the-loop, and Model Assisted are the major types of AutoML that are in practice. Though AutoML has a significant efficiency in automating the ML process, the challenges associated with it are quite noteworthy. The intricacy of the model increases with large datasets, along with minimal transparency in the framework. AutoML lacks customization of the models, with obscurity in the algorithms used, decision-making processes, and similar others. Flexibility is a great problem with AutoML since the ML pipeline is automated, and thus, it is quite challenging for the users who move from an ML to an AutoML platform. This work mainly concentrates on the limitations and challenges associated with the AutoML. The quality of data is the a major concern, since AutoML

**Corresponding author*: pmkavimca@gmail.com

E. Gangadevi, M. Lawanya Shri, Balamurugan Balusamy and Rajesh Kumar Dhanaraj (eds.) Automated Machine Learning and Industrial Applications, (191–206) © 2025 Scrivener Publishing LLC

relies on the quality of input data. Noisy and biased data may provide substandard predictions. Further, other factors, like pre-processing, outlier detection, and missing values can affect the model's efficiency. A detailed description of the challenges and limitations posed by AutoML are discussed.

Keywords: Auto-sklearn, TPOT, MLBox

9.1 Introduction

The method of implementing machine learning to data is automated using the technology of Automated Machine Learning (AutoML) [2]. AutoML can be arranged to iterate through many data transformations, machine learning systems, and hyperparameters to get the best model for a given dataset. The field of machine learning and data science is experiencing a distinguished increase in the usage of Automated Machine Learning. The conventional manual method of developing machine learning models is gradually becoming time consuming and inefficient due to the increasing complexity and scale of data.

Automated Machine Learning (AML) is considerably revolutionizing the field of machine learning and data science by offering effective and scalable techniques for constructing the models. Despite the increasing complexity and volume of data, the predictable method of making machine learning models has been proven insufficient in terms of both time and efficiency. The AutoML framework offers a means to enhance efficiency in this process through the automation of method selection, feature engineering, model optimization, and hyperparameter tuning. In the future, the developers will offer a more inclusive examination of the diverse constituents and advantages of AutoML, while also examining its practical implementations in real-life situations. Figure 9.1 is the representation of traditional ML work flow were in Figure 9.2 represents the work flow of Auto ML

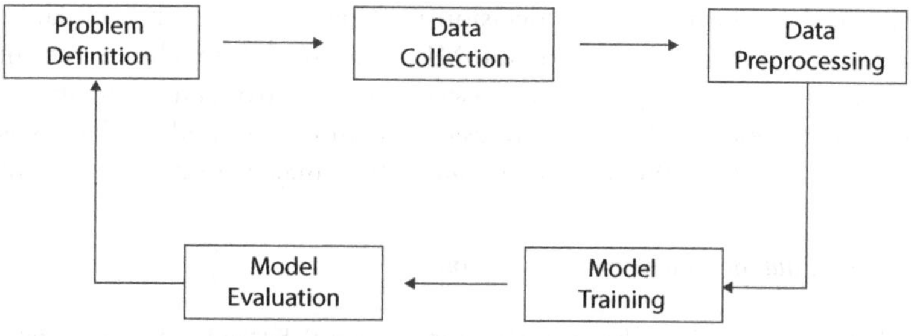

Figure 9.1 Representation of traditional ML workflow.

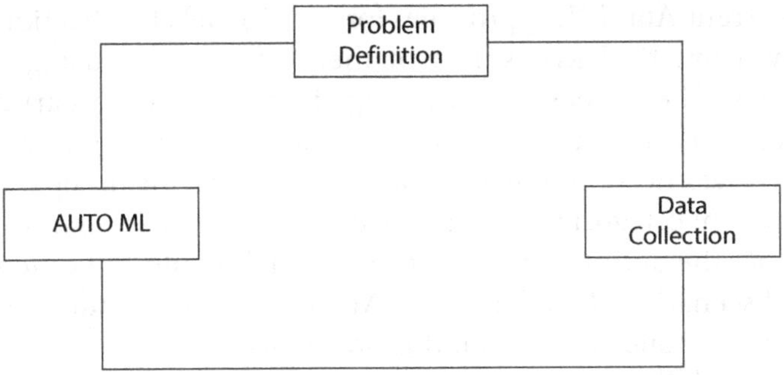

Figure 9.2 Representation of AutoML workflow.

Auto Machine Learning (AML) has emerged as a transformative force within the areas of machine learning and data science. AutoML shortens and quickens the progress of high-performing machine learning models by automating and optimizing the whole machine learning pipeline. This includes multiple stages such as data preprocessing, feature selection, choice of algorithm, and hyperparameter tuning [6]. AutoML consists of multiple components that join to systematize the process of machine learning.

9.2 Related Study

In their study, Karmaker *et al.* [1] anticipated a comprehensive analysis of the present situation of Automated Machine Learning (AutoML) and a valuable viewpoint on potential avenues and difficulties in this domain. This paper examines a diverse array of subjects including the progression of AutoML methodologies, current breakthroughs, evolving patterns, and the future complications of AutoML across several fields. An outstanding characteristic of this article is its comprehensive examination of the AutoML field covering both past progressions and present breakthroughs. The authors present a complete examination of the evolution of AutoML techniques encompassing both conventional methodologies and modern approaches like Neural Architecture Search (NAS) and meta-learning. The article provides a broad knowledge of the present state-of-the-art in AutoML by joining information from a varied choice of sources, such as academic papers, conference proceedings, and industry reports.

Wever *et al.* offer an in-depth review of Automated Machine Learning (AutoML) procedures that are specifically planned for the purpose of multi-label classification problems. The article provides a comprehensive study of current AutoML approaches for multi-label classification, accompanied by a practical assessment of their effectiveness using standardized datasets. The paper's key advantage is its focus on a particular and demanding subject area, i.e., multi-label classification. The implication of multi-label classification in many practical contexts, including picture tagging, document categorization, and medical diagnosis, is acknowledged by Wever *et al.* The authors offer important insights into the different challenges and scenarios of applying AutoML algorithms to multi-label classification jobs by concentrating on this precise topic.

Salehin *et al.* [7] commenced an extensive evaluation and assessment of many different Automated Machine Learning (AutoML) procedures and instruments. The authors acknowledge the growing attention toward AutoML and seek to offer appreciable perspectives on the efficiency and functionalities of various AutoML techniques. This study's strength rests in its systematic assessment methodology, which allows a full comparison of a variety of AutoML methods and tools. This framework is the defining characteristic of this research. Truong *et al.* highlight the significance of empirical assessment in assessing the efficacy and competence of AutoML methodologies, particularly in practical situations where limitations in time and resources play a vital role. The authors commence by presenting a complete outline of the AutoML domain delving into the problems and prospects linked to the automation of the machine learning pipeline. Later, they assess many notable AutoML methodologies and tools, such as Auto-sklearn, TPOT, H2O AutoML, and AutoKeras [9]. Evaluation is carried out by utilizing a wide range of datasets and performance measures, allowing a thorough evaluation of the strengths and inadequacies of each approach.

9.3 Ecosystem of AutoML

9.3.1 Data Preprocessing

Preparing raw data for model training requires a number of processes including data cleaning, feature engineering, and normalization, all of which are vital.

9.3.2 Model Selection

Both the properties of the dataset and the nature of the problem at hand are considered by AutoML algorithms, which then choose the machine learning model architecture or method that is the most suitable.

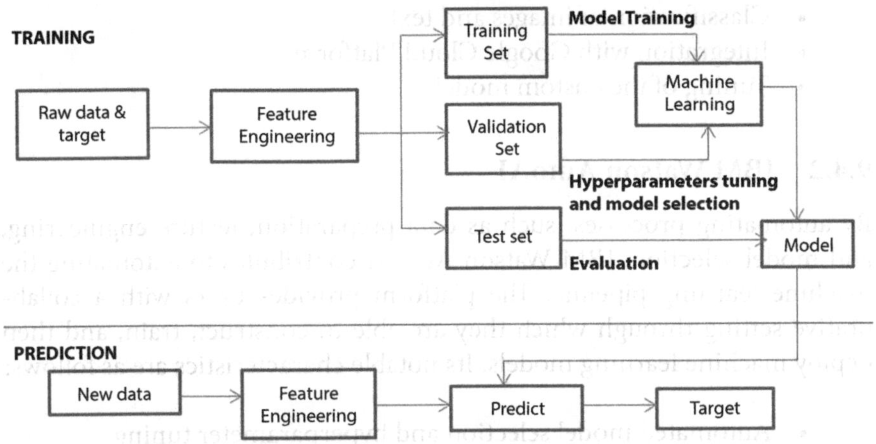

Figure 9.3 Representation of model training and prediction phase.

9.3.3 Hyperparameter Tuning

Hyperparameters refer to the central parameters that constitute the set up and performance of machine learning models [8]. AutoML tools practice machine learning to autonomously change hyperparameters to increase the functioning of the model.

9.3.4 Model Evaluation and Deployment

AutoML frameworks naturally provide procedures for evaluating the performance of a model after it has been completed and, additionally, provisions for arranging the model into production environments.

9.4 AutoML Frameworks

9.4.1 Google AutoML

Google AutoML is a group of tools that are made accessible by Google Cloud. These tools permit users to build machine learning models with minimal human interaction. AutoML Vision, AutoML Natural Language, and AutoML Tables are among the mechanisms encompassed under this framework catering to diverse types of data. Google AutoML leverages composite neural architecture search techniques to automatically optimize models. Its main characteristics are as follows:

- Classification of images and text
- Integration with Google Cloud Platform
- Tuning of the custom model

9.4.2 IBM Watson AutoAI

By automating processes, such as data preparation, feature engineering, and model selection, IBM Watson AutoAI contributes to automating the machine learning pipeline. The platform provides users with a collaborative setting through which they are able to construct, train, and then deploy machine learning models. Its notable characteristics are as follows:

- Automated model selection and hyperparameter tuning
- Collaboration and sharing capabilities
- Integration with IBM Watson Studio

9.4.3 Microsoft Azure AutoML

Azure AutoML is a significant part of the Microsoft Azure cloud ecosystem providing an easy-to-use interface for the design and development of machine learning models. Both classification and regression tasks are accommodated by this platform, which additionally offers automatic feature selection and hyperparameter tuning capabilities. Its prominent characteristics are as follows:

- Incorporation with Azure Machine Learning Studio
- Computerized model selection and tuning
- Extensive range of algorithms

9.4.4 H2O.ai

H2O.ai provides an open-source AutoML platform that is extensively used and is as well known as H2O AutoML. The software provides automated model selection, optimization of hyperparameters, and valuable insights into the interpretability of the model. The versatility of H2O AutoML allows its application in a wide range of applications, surrounding classification, and regression. Its notable characteristics are as follows:

- Open-source platform
- Automatic feature engineering

- Interpretability and explainability tools

9.4.5 Data Robot

Data Robot is a comprehensive AutoML platform that accelerates the machine learning process. The system accelerates the complete machine learning process starting from data preprocessing and ending with model deployment. Several kinds of strategies and optimization techniques are provided by Data Robot. Its prominent characteristics are as follows:

- Automated model building and selection
- Extensive algorithm library
- Model deployment options

9.4.6 Databricks AutoML

Majority of the key elements of the Databricks Unified Analytics Platform is Databricks AutoML, which streamlines the machine learning procedure by providing autonomous model tuning and selection capabilities. The computer program smoothly connects with several Databricks services resulting in a cohesive data and artificial intelligence platform.

Key Features:

- Integration with Databricks Workspace
- Distributed computing for model training
- Collaboration and sharing features

9.4.7 Tune

The open-source AutoML library Tune is dedicated to the optimization and customization of hyperparameters. The tool facilitates the customization of machine learning models enabling users to develop search areas as well as develop search algorithms. Its significant features are the following:

- Customizable hyperparameter search
- Scalable and distributed tuning
- Support for various machine learning libraries

9.4.8 AutoKeras

In the realm of deep learning models, the AutoKeras library is an open-source AutoML package that focuses on neural architecture search. The computer program facilitates the automation of neural network creation and optimization procedures. Its major traits are the following:

- Simplified deep learning model development
- Customizable search spaces
- TensorFlow and Keras integration

9.4.9 H2O Driverless AI

The powerful AutoML platform known as H2O Driverless AI is capable of automating machine learning activities and interpreting the output of models. Moreover, it provides explainability, model selection, and autonomous feature engineering. Its especially notable features are the following:

- Automatic feature engineering
- Interpretability and explainability tools
- Enterprise-grade platform

9.4.10 RapidMiner

For the purpose of constructing, deploying, and administering machine learning models, RapidMiner provides a user-friendly AutoML platform. The computer program provides automated capabilities including collecting data and simulation. Its prominent attributes are the following:

- Visual and code-based interface
- Extensive library of machine learning algorithms
- Model deployment and monitoring

9.4.11 Google Cloud AutoML Tables

Google Cloud AutoML Tables is a dedicated AutoML solution designed specifically for the processing of structured data. Automation is employed to facilitate the creation of predictive models for various tasks, such as regression and classification. Its important characteristics are as follows:

- Support for structured data

- Integration with BigQuery
- Automated feature engineering

9.4.12 H2O Sparkling Water

For the purpose of enabling distributed machine learning on huge datasets, H2O Sparkling Water combines the capabilities of H2O.ai's AutoML with Apache Spark. It provides the ability to increase efficiency and improve performance. Its significant traits are the following:

- Integration with Apache Spark
- Scalable AutoML
- Distributed machine learning

9.4.13 Turi Create

A user-friendly AutoML platform for constructing machine learning models, Turi Create is presently a component of Apple's Core ML. It is especially well-suited for the building of applications on macOS and iOS platforms.

Key Features:

- macOS and iOS compatibility
- Simplified model creation
- Core ML integration

9.4.14 Big ML

BigML delivers an AutoML platform that prioritizes user friendliness and the ability to interpret models. The method incorporates automated identification of models and optimization of hyperparameters.

Major Features:

- User-friendly interface
- Model interpretability tools
- Automation of machine learning tasks

9.4.15 Hail

Hail is a freely available AutoML package specifically developed for the purpose of analyzing genetic data. The platform offers a range of technologies that facilitate distributed and scalable machine learning on genomic datasets. Its particularly striking characteristics are as follows:

- Genomic data analysis
- Scalable and distributed processing
- Integration with Apache Spark

9.5 Open-Source AutoML Libraries

9.5.1 Auto-Sklearn

Auto-sklearn improves on the idea of establishing an all-encompassing machine learning framework with appropriate global optimization, which was initially introduced with Auto-WEKA. Auto-sklearn enhances generalization by constructing an ensemble of all models that had been assessed all throughout the global optimization approach. It is an Automated Machine Learning toolkit built on scikit-learn.

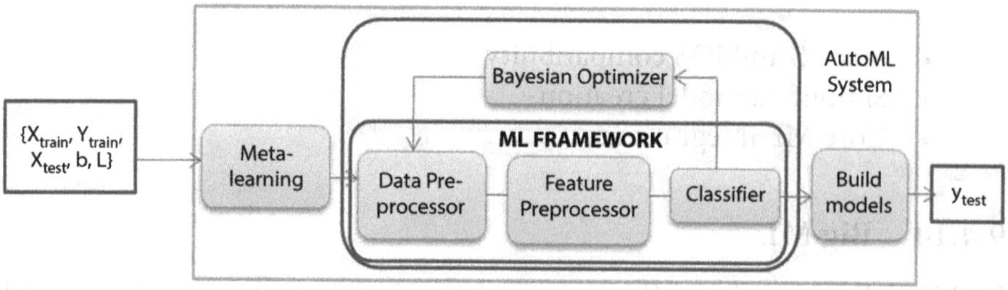

Figure 9.4 Representation of AutoML pipeline.

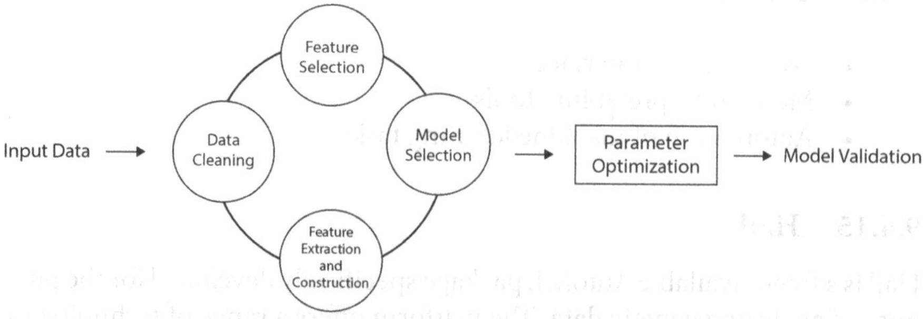

Figure 9.5 Representation of automated TPOT.

9.5.2 TPOT (Tree-Based Pipeline Optimization Tool)

This tool known as TPOT is designed to optimize machine learning pipelines through the utilization of genetic programming concepts. By proactively exploring millions of potential pipelines, it will automate the most tedious aspect of machine learning and determine the most appropriate one for your data. It is adapted from IPython and is an Automated Machine Learning library using genetic programming.

9.5.3 AutoKeras

For Automated Machine Learning, AutoKeras is a software library that is available under an open-source license. AutoKeras offers a range of functions that facilitate the automated exploration of architectural and hyperparameter requirements for deep learning models. It can be installed via pip and deployed as an AutoML library for automated neural architecture search using Keras.

9.5.4 MLBox

MLBox is a robust Python module that supports Automated Machine Learning. The software offers the subsequent functionalities: rapid reading and preprocessing, cleansing, and formatting of distributed data; efficient and resilient selection of features and leak detection techniques; efficient optimization of hyperparameters in a high-dimensional space; and automated machine learning library for feature engineering, model selection, and hyperparameter tuning.

9.5.5 AutoGluon

An easy-to-use and extensible AutoML is made possible by AutoGluon, which focuses on deep learning, automated stack ensembling, and practical requests for text, image, and tabular data. It is an AutoML library developed by Amazon AWS for model selection, hyperparameter tuning, and ensemble learning.

9.5.6 H2O AutoML

H2O is a distributed in-memory ML platform that can scale linearly and is completely open source. H2O supports a variety of statistical and machine learning algorithms that are widely utilized in various fields. These algorithms include gradient boosted machines, deep learning, and others.

9.5.7 Auto-WEKA

Unlike other methods that address problems one at a time, Auto-WEKA tackles the problem of choosing a learning algorithm and fixing its hyperparameters at the same time. When it comes to data mining tasks, Weka is a set of ML algorithms. The system encompasses a range of tools that facilitate various tasks such as data preparation, classification, regression, association rules mining, and visualization.

9.5.8 AutoGluon Tabular

It is possible for AutoGluon to generate models that can forecast values in one column built on values in other columns for normal datasets that are stored as tables (for example, stored as a CSV file or as a parquet from a database). AutoGluon makes it possible to use AutoML in a way that is both simple and straightforward, with a particular emphasis on DL and real-world applications that involve picture, text, or tabular data. AutoGluon is intended for those with varying levels of expertise in machine learning. It allows you to efficiently create prototypes of deep learning solutions for your data using a minimal number of lines of code.

9.5.9 FLAML

FLAML is a Python library that assists in the automatic discovery of accurate machine learning models while minimizing the amount of computational resources required. By doing so, data scientists are relieved of the burden of worrying about hyperparameter tuning and method selection. Developers are able to construct self-tuning software that adapts to new training data. According to FLAML, the most optimal model is lightgbm. The tuned hyperparameters of this model can be determined by utilizing the following code. This is a significant benefit of FLAML. The system efficiently identifies the appropriate machine learning method and hyperparameters within a matter of seconds.

9.5.10 Ludwig

The kinds of input and output features are inferred by AutoML, the model architecture is selected, and a Ray Tune Async HyperBand search task is initiated across a set of hyperparameters and ranges, with the time budget being limited by the parameters that have been defined. Ludwig is a machine learning framework that is open source and declarative in nature. It facilitates the definition of deep learning pipelines through a straightforward and adaptable data-driven configuration mechanism. Ludwig demonstrates compatibility with a diverse range of artificial intelligence workloads and is hosted by the Linux Foundation AI & Data. The Uber AI Labs has developed an AutoML package for deep learning.

9.6 Types of AutoML Approaches

9.6.1 Fully Automated

In AutoML solutions that are fully automated, the complete machine learning pipeline, encompassing data pretreatment and model deployment, is executed without the need for user involvement.

9.6.2 Human-in-the-Loop

The concept of "Human-in-the-Loop" Automatic Machine Learning (AutoML) solutions incorporate a certain level of user engagement enabling domain experts to offer input or tailor certain elements of the machine learning procedure.

9.6.3 Model Assisted

The idea of model-assisted AutoML involves the incorporation of human experience with automated methodologies to advance the performance of models or tackle specific problems encountered in the machine learning pipeline.

9.7 Benefits of AutoML

Accessibility

AutoML simplifies the procedure of utilizing the power of ML to solve real-world problems by automating complex machine learning activities. This makes it easier for individuals and organizations with little experience to take advantage of the machine learning.

Innovation
AutoML enables innovation in the field of ML by automating repetitive events allowing data scientists and ML engineers to focus their efforts on more creative and advanced jobs.

9.8 Challenges and Limitations

Despite the many compensations it offers, AutoML is also subject to a number of problems and limitations, including the following:

Complexity
AutoML algorithms may meet difficulties when dealing with intricate datasets or actions that require domain-specific expertise, hence, constraining their effectiveness in specific situations.

Scalability
In context with limited resources, it can be hard to scale AutoML solutions to handle large-scale datasets or computationally composite models. Scalability is a key factor in this challenge.

Customization
The flexibility needed to suit domain-specific requirements or extensive customization options may be lacking in certain AutoML frameworks.

Data Quality
The performance of AutoML models is meaningfully influenced by the excellence of the input data, with errors such as missing values or outliers having a detrimental effect.

9.9 Conclusion

Though AutoML paves the way in democratizing the fast pace in the world of technology, it comes with equivalent tasks and limitations. The lack of transparency and customization options makes the transition from ML to AutoML tedious. The transition from ML to AutoML needs an intrinsic version to overcome the hurdles for diverse users. In addition, computational resource requirements, data quality problems, and scalability are noted areas that need focus. The various challenges associated by adopting AutoML are discussed in the paper. Further, efforts in enhancing customization choices, resource utilization, and scalability should be broadened. It is essential to navigate through these tests to streamline ML frameworks. The AutoML community paves the way for better ML by making it more accessible, transparent and impactful across diverse domains.

References

1. Karmaker, S.K., Hassan, M.M., Smith, M.J., Xu, L., Zhai, C., Veeramachaneni, K., Automl to date and beyond: Challenges and opportunities. *ACM Comput. Surv. (CSUR)*, *54*, 8, 1–36, 2021.
2. He, X., Zhao, K., Chu, X., AutoML: A survey of the state-of-the-art. *Know.-Based Syst.*, *212*, 106622, 2021.
3. Wever, M., Tornede, A., Mohr, F., Hüllermeier, E., AutoML for multi-label classification: Overview and empirical evaluation. *IEEE Trans. Pattern Anal. Mach. Intell.*, *43*, 9, 3037–3054, 2021.
4. Li, Y., Wang, Z., Xie, Y., Ding, B., Zeng, K., Zhang, C., Automl: From methodology to application, in: *Proceedings of the 30th ACM International Conference on Information & Knowledge Management*, 2021, October, pp. 4853–4856.
5. Truong, A., Walters, A., Goodsitt, J., Hines, K., Bruss, C.B., Farivar, R., Towards automated machine learning: Evaluation and comparison of AutoML approaches and tools, in: *2019 IEEE 31st International Conference on Tools with Artificial Intelligence (ICTAI)*, 2019, November, IEEE, pp. 1471–1479.
6. Milutinovic, M., Schoenfeld, B., Martinez-Garcia, D., Ray, S., Shah, S., Yan, D., On evaluation of automl systems, in: *Proceedings of the ICML Workshop on Automatic Machine Learning*, 2020, July, vol. 2020.
7. Salehin, I., Islam, M.S., Saha, P., Noman, S.M., Tuni, A., Hasan, M.M., Baten, M.A., AutoML: A systematic review on automated machine learning with neural architecture search. *J. Inf. Intell.*, *2*, 1, 52–81, 2024.
8. Barbudo, R., Ventura, S., Romero, J.R., Eight years of AutoML: categorisation, review and trends. *Knowl. Inf. Syst.*, *65*, 12, 5097–5149, 2023.
9. Celik, B., Singh, P., Vanschoren, J., Online automl: An adaptive automl framework for online learning. *Mach. Learn.*, *112*, 6, 1897–1921, 2023.

10

Plant Disease Identification Using Extended-EfficientNet Deep Learning Model in Smart Farming

K. Sathya[1*], K. Kanmani[1], M. Revathy Meenal[2], D. Suganthi[3] and T. S. Lakshmi[4]

[1]Department of Computer Applications, Faculty of Science and Humanities, SRM Institute of Science and Technology, Chengalpattu, Tamil Nadu, India
[2]Department of Computer Science, Anna Adarsh College for Women, Chennai, Tamil Nadu, India
[3]Department of Computer Science, SCLAS, SIMATS, Chennai, Tamil Nadu, India
[4]Department of Civil Engineering, Saveetha School of Engineering, SIMATS, Chennai, Tamil Nadu, India

Abstract
The cornerstone of successful and precise prevention of plant disease in complex environments lies in the accurate identification of the specific disease affecting the plants. Advances in decision support, intelligent analysis, and planning are made possible by the digitization and data-driven detection of plant diseases brought about by the quick development of smart farming. This research introduces a mathematical model for diagnosing and recognizing plant diseases using deep learning, aiming to improve training efficiency, accuracy, and applicability. The leaves are first identified and located in complex situations using the region proposal network version 2 (RPNv2) algorithm. Next, the Chan–Vese Level-II (LCV) method is applied to retrieve the symptom features from images that were segmented based on the RPNv2 algorithm's results. Proposing the use of Extended-EfficientNet (E-ENet) deep learning architecture, this study suggests its application in plant leaf disease classification, with an evaluation of its effectiveness compared to other current deep learning models. Models were skilled using data from PlantVillage. Training datasets comprising 55,448 and 61,486 images, respectively, were used to train all the models. The E-ENet architecture outperformed existing models in the

**Corresponding author*: sathyabalaji33@gmail.com

E. Gangadevi, M. Lawanya Shri, Balamurugan Balusamy and Rajesh Kumar Dhanaraj (eds.) Automated Machine Learning and Industrial Applications, (207–242) © 2025 Scrivener Publishing LLC

original datasets, as evidenced by a 98.87% test accuracy and a 99.21% validation accuracy, according to the test dataset results. As a result, the chapter's deep learning algorithm is crucial for ecological preservation, agricultural productivity, and smart agriculture.

***Keywords*:** Plant disease, smart farming, extended-efficientnet, classification, ecological preservation, agricultural productivity

10.1 Introduction

Indeed, it is an undeniable reality that artificial intelligence is progressively and steadfastly taking over tasks that were traditionally performed by humans in the contemporary era. Artificial intelligence (AI) is a rapidly developing area of technology that focuses to generate machines that can think like humans using algorithms that are trained to solve complex problems. AI refers to the emulation of human intellect in machines enabling them to replicate human thought processes and behaviors like problem solving and learning; within this domain, machine learning plays a crucial role allowing systems to recognize, comprehend, and analyze patterns in data. In the advanced realm of computer science, artificial intelligence stands as a major focal point for research and development. Due to its robust application in problems that are primarily beyond the capabilities of traditional computing structures and humans, as well as its rapid technological advancements, this technology is becoming increasingly prevalent rapidly [1].

Despite the availability of much improved technology, farmers still face many difficulties from planting to harvesting. The application of artificial intelligence approaches has empowered us to comprehend the intricate details of various situations allowing for the provision of optimal solutions tailored to specific issues. The growth of various AI methods is enabling innovative solutions to complex challenges. To address the issues facing agriculture today, a number of approaches have been put forth, such as database integration and decision support systems [2]. The proximity of artificial intelligence (AI) and agriculture, while initially unconventional, has gained relevance in recent times. Despite agriculture being a cornerstone of human civilization for millennia, the rapid evolution of AI, even in its simplest forms over the past few periods, has ushered in transformative fluctuations. Amid a surge in novel concepts across various sectors, agriculture has witnessed significant advancements in technology. With threats to the sustainability of our food system, such as population growth, climate change, and supply scarcity, the position of agricultural advancements becomes even more critical. The integration of AI addresses numerous challenges and alleviates drawbacks associated with conservative farming practices.

AI systems make independent crop management conceivable. By examining soil moisture content and climate data, algorithms can determine the ideal crop water requirements in real time when used along with Internet of Things (IoT) sensors. The goal of an autonomous crop irrigation system is to support sustainable farming methods while preserving water. Artificial intelligence plays a crucial role in identifying leaks in irrigation systems by leveraging algorithms that can discern patterns and anomalies in data indicative of potential leaks. Machine learning (ML) models can be trained to recognize specific signatures associated with leaks, such as deviations in water pressure or flow, enhancing the efficacy and accuracy of leak detection in irrigation systems. Initial identification is made conceivable by real-time monitoring and study, which helps to avoid both possible harm to crops and water loss.

For detecting areas with elevated water consumption, artificial intelligence (AI) integrates climate data with crop water requirements, enhancing water efficiency by automating leak detection and issuing timely alerts, thereby assisting farmers in conserving resources. The health and growth of crops can be significantly impacted by the incorrect combination of nutrients in the soil. With AI, farmers can quickly recognize these nutrients and determine how they affect crop yield allowing for suitable modifications to be made. While the accuracy of human assessment is limited, computer vision models can collect precise data by monitoring soil conditions. Then, using these data from plant science, yield predictions and crop health are made, along with any specific problems being highlighted. In actuality, AI has demonstrated a level of speed and accuracy unmatched by humans in tracking the stages of wheat growth and tomato ripeness.

In addition to measuring yield of crops and soil condition, computer vision could classify diseases and pests. This operates by perusing photos meant for insects, rot, mold, and other hazards to crop health utilizing artificial intelligence. When used in connection with alert mechanisms, this enables farmers to take prompt action to eradicate pests or isolate crops to stop the spread of illness. Apple black rot has been identified by AI with a more than 90% accuracy rate. It is equally accurate at looking at other kinds of insects such as flies, bees, moths, etc. Researchers first gathered pictures of the pests to generate the training dataset that was required for the algorithm to be trained effectively.

Farmers are well aware by now that there is opportunity to optimize the use of pesticides. Unfortunately, there are significant limits to both programmed and manual application procedures. While manually applying chemical fertilizers can be labor intensive and time consuming, it allows for greater precision when focusing on particular areas. Although automated pesticide spraying is faster and requires less labor, it frequently lacks accuracy, which can contaminate the environment. Drones driven by AI combine the best features of each strategy without any of its disadvantages. Drones that utilize computer vision can calculate how much pesticide should be sprayed on each area. Even though this technology is still in its infancy, it is advancing quickly in precision. Yield mapping analyzes big datasets instantly using machine learning algorithms. Better planning is made possible for farmers as a result of their increased understanding of the patterns and traits of their crops. Farmers can forecast soil harvests for particular crops by combining approaches like 3D mapping with information from sensors and drones. Multiple drone flights provide data collection allowing for increasingly accurate analysis through the application of algorithms.

With the aid of these methods, farmers are able to accurately forecast upcoming yields for particular crops assisting them in seeding locations and timing as well as resource allocation for optimal return on investment. Just as computer vision can classify diseases and pests, it can also be employed to recognize weeds and invasive plant species in agricultural settings. Computer vision examines the shape, color, and size of leaves to identify weeds from crops when paired with machine learning. These kinds of remedies can be employed to program machines for projects like automatic weeding that are part of robotic process automation (RPA). Indeed, a robot just like this has been put to good use already. As these innovations become more widely available, smart bots may eventually perform both cultivation and weeding tasks completely.

Apple black rot has been identified by AI with a 90% precision rate. It is equally accurate at identifying other insects, like flies, bees, moths, etc. It was up to the researchers to gather pictures of the pests to compile the training dataset that the algorithm needed. This chapter's main focus is on the important artificial intelligence (AI) strategies applied to agricultural problems. This study explores the application of artificial intelligence techniques across various aspects of agriculture to monitor and assess the progress of agro-intelligent systems.

10.1.1 Obstacles in the Agricultural Sector

10.1.1.1 Soil Erosion

The natural method of soil erosion occurs when water or wind carry soil particles from one location to another. Farmers face severe issues when this occurs on a large scale. Many factors contribute to soil erosion, such as excessive soil tillage that degrades the soil's condition and reduces water retention. The top soil layers are swiftly removed during flooding. To use less water in irrigation, protecting soil from wind and water erosion with mulch and crop covers, and limiting livestock grazing excessively, are all ways to avert soil erosion.

10.1.1.2 Absence of High-Quality Seeds

To increase the production of crops, farmers must use high-quality seeds. Achieving steady growth in agricultural output is also dependent on it. The distribution of superior seeds holds equal significance to that of seed production. Most farmers, especially marginal and small farmers, usually cannot afford seeds of good quality because of their prohibitively expensive prices.

10.1.1.3 Lack of Contemporary Farming Machinery

The absence of proper farm equipment is one of the biggest issues farmers face, and it can make it difficult for them to adjust to the demands of contemporary farming methods. Farmers can have major improvements in their lives when they are trained to use the equipment. It is crucial to use the aforementioned equipment.

10.1.2 Challenges of AI in Agriculture

Many believe that AI is unrelated for farming tasks and only applies to the digital world. In general, this assumption stems to an insufficient amount of knowledge about AI tools. The general public, particularly those in non-tech fields, is not well informed about artificial intelligence (AI), which is causing the agricultural industry to adopt AI more slowly. Despite numerous progressions in agriculture during its long history, various farmers are still more familiar with using conventional systems.

Furthermore, suppliers often do a poor job of outlining the benefits of novel technologies as well as their applications. Tech firms face a significant task in educating the public about the application of AI in agriculture. Despite the clear benefits of AI for sustainable farming, there is a need to inform farmers about its practical advantages and encourage its adoption in the agricultural sector. However, there are still certain obstacles to be addressed.

10.1.3 Existing Plant Disease Identification Methods

Stunted growth from plant diseases can have a negative impact on yields [3–5]. Worldwide, an estimated $20 billion or more is lost economically each year [6–8]. Because of regional variations that could make accurate identification more challenging, multiple circumstances present the greatest challenge to researchers [9, 10]. Traditional techniques often rely on experts, knowledge, and manuals [11], but they tend to be expensive, labor intensive, and time consuming. Moreover, they face challenges in accurately identifying objects [12]. For this reason, it appears that identifying plant diseases quickly and accurately is crucial for the sake of agriculture's economy and ecology. Web technologies have advanced quickly, especially the availability of multimodality data from a diversity of sensors, such as sensor networks with the Internet of Things [13]. To tackle the issues mentioned earlier, this study introduces an innovative plant leaf identification model based on DL. The model employs an integrated deep learning algorithm to execute image segmentation, identification, and leaf retrieval seamlessly within its functionality. The first task is retrieving leaves, but in this complicated atmosphere, numerous considerations, like soil and illumination, make accurate identification difficult [14].

Achieving sustainable and efficient agriculture, while preventing unnecessary waste of resources, hinges on the initial stage and accurate diagnosis of plant diseases. Certain plant diseases lack obvious symptoms, so it is necessary to employ sophisticated analytical techniques in cases of such diseases. Nonetheless, most of the plant diseases exhibit outward signs, and the currently recognized method involves having a skilled plant pathologist visually inspect infected plant leaves to identify the disease [15, 16]. Expert and intelligent systems that can reliably and independently identify plant diseases provide agriculturalists with substantial benefits and are a great help in managing crop health. However, applying such a scheme with an easy-to-use smartphone application is also a commendable accomplishment for farmers lacking access to agronomic and phytopathological assistance facilities [17].

Modern agricultural techniques are depending more and more on artificial intelligence-based systems that can identify a variety of disorders [18]. In the past decade, various conventional ML models have been introduced for the identification and categorization of plant diseases. Rumpf *et al.* employed Support Vector Machine (SVM) to explore the initial identification and categorization of illnesses in sugar beet using spectral plant guides [19]. Al-Hiary *et al.* employed a segmentation approach by utilizing k-means clustering on preprocessed features to identify and differentiate five distinct diseases in plant leaves. Following texture and color-based extraction of features, Artificial Neural Networks (ANN) were then used to classify those regions [20]. Revathi and Hemalatha suggested a technique to identify six distinct disease kinds that are present on cotton leaves. They propose an approach that uses Particle Swarm Optimization to choose characteristics from a feature vector that includes color, texture, and edge-based features acquired through image processing. The disease is subsequently classified using a Cross Information Gain Deep Forward Neural Network [21].

Mokhtar *et al.* conducted an investigation employing the Support Vector Machine (SVM) technique to detect and identify two distinct viruses, which cause disease and exhibit symptoms on tomato leaves [22]. In a separate study, Pantazi *et al.* utilized features extracted from the Local Binary Pattern method to identify three different vine leaf diseases through the Support Vector Machine (SVM) approach [23]. In a different study, Johannes *et al.* suggested using Naive Bayes classification system and image processing-based candidate hotspot detection for mobile-based initial stage diagnosis of three distinct wheat diseases. They tested their suggested approach in a real-world field setting using cellphones [24]. To automate the identification of plant diseases, Chen *et al.* have recently introduced a novel model known as the GMDH (Group Method of Data Handling) logistic algorithm [25]. Categorizing using machine learning involves a demanding process known as feature extraction, which directly influences the nature of classification.

DL architectures, which use methods to analyze raw data without the necessity for custom features, represent a performance breakthrough. This is made feasible by the enhanced capabilities and speeds of Central Processing Units (CPUs) with Graphical Processing Units (GPUs) [26]. Deep neural network styles, which have numerous layers and neurons for processing information, achieve exceptionally well at handling difficult tasks, like voice and image recognition, while handling massive amounts of data with ease. DL methods are frequently used in medical applications to identify and classify diseases from medical images [27]. However, a review paper published in 2019 [28] evaluated deep learning-based research for the detection and classification of plant leaf diseases and offered an evaluation of the field's potential. Instead of categorizing all plant diseases within the dataset, it has been observed that a significant portion of trainings in the literature utilize the Plant Village dataset for diagnosing diseases in individual or a limited number of plants.

Sladojevic *et al.* used Convolutional Neural Networks (CNNs) in one of these studies to classify 13 distinct plant diseases [16]. In their investigation, they trained their suggested model on a dataset of 30,880 images and used 2,589 images for testing. An accuracy of 96.3% was attained on average with their suggested model. Chen *et al.* utilized DENSINCEP, a deep TL (Transfer Learning)-based model, for detecting rice plant disease [29]. Chen *et al.* modified the VGGNet module to conduct disease categorization on maize and rice plants in another investigation [30]. Five studies have been found to categorize every disease found in the PlantVillage dataset. These studies comprise a total of 39 classes, which include a class for background images devoid of leaves and 38 different types of plant diseases. CNN methods, like GoogLeNet and AlexNet, were applied by Mohanty *et al.* to classify diseases of plants [12]. They achieved 99.35% accuracy in classification in their investigation.

CNN algorithms, like DenseNets, Inception V4, Resnet152, ResNet101, ResNet50, and VGG16, 121, were utilized by Too *et al.* According to reports, the research's DenseNet design provided 99.75% test accuracy with less parameters and a shorter calculation time than the rest of the models [31]. Using the PlantVillage dataset, Geetharamani and Pandian trained a nine-layer CNN model with varying epochs, batch sizes, and dropout rates. They then compared the results of the final models to well-known transfer learning techniques. On the test dataset, their suggested model produced 96.46% accuracy in classification [9]. However, two additional studies have been conducted using larger datasets from PlantVillage that contain additional images. Ferentinos employed 87,848 images and utilized models, like AlexNetOWTBn, GoogLeNet, Overfeat, AlexNet, and VGG, to categorize 58 distinct diseases affecting 25 different varieties of plants in their study. With 99.53% accuracy, the VGG architecture employed in the study produced the best results [17].

Arsenovic *et al.* created an extended version of the PlantVillage dataset, named the Plant Disease dataset, comprising 79,265 images for their second research. They utilized both datasets in their experimental investigations. Their proposed Plant Disease Net model, a two-stage classification approach, initially identifies the plant variety using leaves in the initial stage and subsequently categorizes the identified leaves in the next stage.

With respect to accuracy, their proposed model performed well achieving 93.67% in the Plant Disease dataset [32]. Additionally, some research has been done to find out how well deep learning algorithms carry out in classifying plant diseases using both personal and PlantVillage datasets. A novel approach, comprising stages for segmentation of images and image classification, was put forth by Nanehkaran *et al.* for the identification of plant diseases [33]. They introduced the LAB color space and a hybrid segmentation algorithm created on saturation, intensity, and hue during the picture segmentation stage. For the classification stage, a Convolutional Neural Network (CNN) model was employed. By incorporating the Classification Activation Map into the previously trained MobileNetV2 model, Chen *et al.* developed a novel plant disease detection model known as MobileNet-Beta [34].

They evaluated the projected model by applying both the Plant Village dataset and their custom dataset. The PlantVillage dataset yielded 99.85% accuracy for the MobileNet-Beta model, while their own dataset yielded 99.11% accuracy, per the test results. The utilization of deep learning architectures for diagnosing plant leaf diseases is increasingly prevalent in the literature, as indicated by the aforementioned studies. Nevertheless, there are still unresolved questions regarding the application of highly innovative deep learning designs in the detection of plant leaf diseases. In particular, there will always be a need for effective models that can be trained quickly without compromising performance and with fewer parameters. Specifically, there will always be a demand for effectual models with fewer parameters that can be trained rapidly without sacrificing performance. The primary objective of the proposed E-ENet is outlined below:

1) Input image is received from the PlantVillage dataset
2) The localization and retrieval of diseased plant leaves is implemented by the Region Proposal Network version 2 (RPNv2) algorithm.
3) The diseased region of the leaves is segmented by the Chan–Vese Level II algorithm.
4) Finally, the disease of the plant leaves is classified by the E-ENet model.

10.2 Literature Review

Feature extraction, disease recognition, and diseased leaf image segmentation are the three main areas of current research on plant disease recognition in complicated environments. In a complex environment, the crucial challenge lies in effectively segmenting images to identify and localize the leaves of diseased plants. The primary area of image segmentation is to distinguish and separate symptoms from the surrounding environment. Numerous researchers are delving deeply into the matter. The Delta E color difference algorithm was applied by Ali *et al.* in 2017 [35] to identify the disease-infected area. Generally speaking, there are four main approaches used to segment images; these are covered in more detail in the paragraph that follows [36]. In image segmentation, some researchers integrate additional techniques with the region of interest (ROI). For instance, in their study, Kao *et al.* used a convolutional autoencoder as a background filter for the ROI [37].

The next approach is limited to segmenting regions. According to Pujari *et al.* (2013), features of images were extracted, and they were claimed to be divided into multiple regions, each with a unique meaning [38]. A real-time synchronous image-processing model was presented by Akram and associates. It can perform feature vector, contrast stretching, and salient region recognition by partitioning the image into three color spaces [39]. Additionally, other researchers have employed DL methods for image segmentation and detection. To maximize the recognition of plant diseases in photos, Marko *et al.* suggested a depth-based recognition algorithm and employed a two-stage algorithm [32]. Thresholding is a frequently used segmentation technique. Li *et al.* (2018) used multilevel thresholding methods built on gray histograms for image segmentation [40]. Using multilevel thresholding, Mohamed and Diego presented a novel multi-objective meta-heuristic for grayscale image segmentation based on a multiverse optimization algorithm [41]. But one thing is certain—it cannot be disregarded. In practical applications, color based machine vision algorithms, region of interest, and thresholds often perform inadequately due to the intricate nature of color information in complex environments.

There are numerous challenges in identifying plant diseases when using feature extraction techniques. The essential requirements for extracting disease features include features related to motion, texture, shape, and color [42, 43]. A technique for disease recognition using color and texture features was presented by Raza and colleagues [44]. Hu *et al.* presented multifeature integration and the Dempster–Shafer (D-S) model of evidence as feature extraction methods. Variance was then introduced into the results processing to enhance the D-S evidence theory's decision rules [45].

Turkoglu introduced enhanced forms of the Local Binary Pattern (LBP) technique, which evaluates the picture's R and G channels, takes the whole area into account, and applies the new LBP local quadratic value to convert the copy to grayscale [46]. Li *et al.* investigated IoT feature extraction for the intelligent city found on a deep migration learning model [47]. A method for extracting significant audio features from music was used so that the visualizations could react to the music [48]. In addition, several innovative methods for applying feature extraction have been proposed in recent research. Meziani *et al.* developed two new spectral estimators that effectively handle non-Gaussian, non-linear signals and are robust to non-stationary EEG data [49]. Liu *et al.* obtained high-dimensional time-frequency spectrum structures by enhancing the signal-to-clutter ratio (SCR) and using the residual neural network [50]. To assess the wear of milling tools, Xu *et al.* developed a feature extraction technique that makes use of the Hilbert marginal spectrum [51].

To obtain precise identification, a great transaction of research and development has gone into developing techniques. By focusing on class labels for training images, the recognition model created a fine-grained image arrangement system [52]. A hybrid clustering-based plant disease leaf image recognition technique was presented by Zhang *et al.* [53]. Patil *et al.* (2017) outlined a content-based image retrieval (CBIR) system to extract texture features and calculate color features [54]. An SVM classifier was used for classification in the aforementioned studies. These studies' primary goals were to create classification schemes and perform image analysis to extract and identify features. More precise and accurate methods for diagnosing the illness have just been introduced. Based on the choice of images and concise text descriptions, a novel technique that can be retrieved remotely from a smartphone, desktop, or personal digital assistant helped non-experts identify plant diseases [55].

A scheme for actual, on-site imaging of diseased plants using a mobile phone was introduced by Pertot *et al.* [56]. The method involved segmenting leaf images and spotting disease patches using improved k-means clustering. A method for microscopy image detection using a decision tree–confusion matrix and a synergistic valuation of texture and shape features was presented by Yang *et al.* [57]. Convolutional neural networks (CNNs) have shown promise in image-based identification tasks and are therefore frequently used for disease identification. A system that can automatically identify plant diseases in field-acquired photos of maize plants was developed by Chad *et al.* [58]. Ni *et al.* developed an automatic corn detector by training a deep convolutional neural network with 1,632 images of corn kernels [59]. A method for recognizing rice diseases with deep convolutional neural network (CNN) techniques was presented by Lu *et al.* [60].

Zhang *et al.* created an image-identifying network for agricultural machinery using a deep learning algorithm [61]. Additionally, Zhang *et al.* enhanced deep convolutional neural networks [62] to recover the precision of maize leaf disease identification. Images were fed into AlexNet and VGG-16 net, two deep learning-based architectures, for detection [63]. Transfer learning was introduced by Coulibaly *et al.* as a technique for feature extraction in the construction of an identification system [64]. However, the time-consuming nature of the training process poses a challenge and hinders the widespread adoption of the approach, as it demands substantial hardware resources, high-quality traditional neural network models, and extensive datasets.

The agricultural industry is increasingly adopting artificial intelligence technologies to enhance various tasks across the food supply chain, including improving crop yields, pest control, monitoring soil and growing conditions, organizing information for farmers, and assisting with workloads. India, as the second-largest tomato producer globally with 18.7 million tons, faces significant challenges due to various bacterial, viral, and fungal diseases affecting numerous parts of the plant, such as the fruit, stem, and leaf. Many techniques rely on algorithms for pattern recognition and image processing applied to pictures of infected plant leaves. Figure 10.1 illustrates a selection of tomato crop diseases, sourced from data provided by PlantVillage [65].

Figure 10.1 Tomato diseased and healthy leaf images form the PlantVillage dataset [6]. (top row left to right) (a) Healthy. (b) Tomato mosaic virus. (c) Early blight. (d) Bacterial spot (bottom row left to right). (e) Late blight. (f) Septoria leaf spot. (g) Yellow leaf curl. (h) Leaf mold.

The development and improvement of imaging technologies widely used in the identification and recognition of plant diseases was accelerated by recent developments in sensor-based techniques. In an effort to predict and ideally identify plant diseases early on, investigators examined a variety of modelling approaches, including artificial neural networks (ANN), SVM, extreme learning machine (ELM) classifiers, and DL, among others. Typically, the input for these prediction models consists of photos of sick plant leaves.

Unquestionably, crop plant diseases represent a serious risk to agricultural productivity and sustainable development. By taking preventative measures against the disease's attacks, early disease attack prediction helps to effectively control the disease. Precision Agriculture (PA) applications, which promote sustainable development, heavily rely on modern information and communication technologies (ICTs).

Solutions for the early disease attack prediction are desperately needed to prevent plant disease attacks. Only after the disease has manifested itself can the current computer vision-based approach to disease detection identify its presence. The effort of this research is to progress an ML technique that uses the Internet of Things (IoT) to directly sense environmental data from crop fields to forecast the probability of early disease attacks. Environmental factors have a strong correlation with the life cycles of pest diseases. Plant disease incidence is predicted by the environmental factors in crop fields. Given the relationship between environmental conditions and disease attacks, the study employs Multiple Linear Regression (MLR) as the machine learning model. Leveraging an ML method, the environmental conditions of crop fields derived from the Internet of Things (IoT) contribute to accurate predictions of plant disease occurrences. To calculate the performance of the approach, the model is applied to tea plants (*Camellia sinensis*) to identify the occurrence of blister blight (*Exobasidium vexans*). Using the proposed model from 2015 to 2019, the disease's occurrence could be predicted up to 91% of the time in 2019.

Plant species and diseases must be manually predicted, which is time consuming, costly, and needs knowledge that is not constantly available. To address these challenges, automated techniques, such as ML and DL, are gaining prominence. Achieving this requires precise models to guide decision making and provide reliable predictions. While plant species disease prediction has traditionally been treated as separate issues, they are often interconnected. They used shared representations for these related tasks to introduce and authenticate a novel approach based on the multi-task learning plan in this setting. Using a multi-input network for each plant, we predict disease by utilizing the E-ENet deep feature model alongside raw images. Our comprehensive multi-task model operates on multiple learning tasks simultaneously. Open datasets are applied to evaluate the model, and the results show that the Multi-Input Multi-Task Neural Network enhances learning efficiency and speed for similar detection tasks.

The agriculture sector significantly contributes to a nation's economic growth. However, plant diseases pose a substantial risk leading to crop destruction, reduced agricultural yields, and substantial financial losses. Primary recognition of plant diseases is crucial for avoiding such destruction. While previous research has utilized ML or DL techniques for disease prediction, deep learning demands substantial training data and computational resources, and machine learning methods lack automated feature extraction capabilities. Moreover, the existing model consumes more computational resources, time, and produces lower accuracy. In response, this study introduces a novel E-ENet basis that combines the benefits of both ML and DL to enhance the efficiency of plant disease identification with improved accuracy.

10.3 Materials and Methods

10.3.1 Dataset

The PlantVillage dataset, which comprises 54,305 photos and 38 classes representing 14 distinct plant species—12 of which are healthy and 26 of which are diseased—was used in this study [66]. The dataset comprises colored images of various sizes, including an additional class specifically designating 1,143 background images. In total, there are 55,448 images within the dataset. Figure 10.1 illustrates eight randomly selected pairs of distinct plant–disease combinations from the dataset.

Geetharamani and Pandian [9] augmented the PlantVillage dataset using six different techniques. The researchers have made both the unique and augmented datasets accessible for scientific research, and these datasets can be found at https://data.mendeley.com/datasets/tywbtsjrjv/1. Through augmentation techniques, the sample count for classes with fewer than 1,000 samples were increased to 1,000, while the images in other classes remained unaltered.

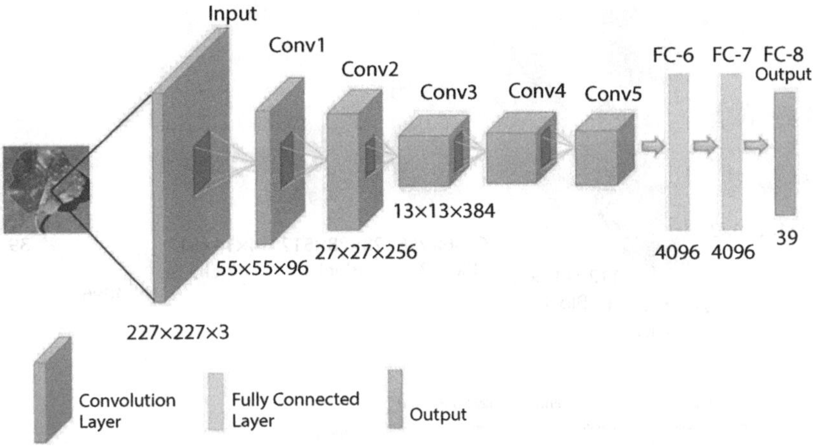

Figure 10.2 Schematic representation of AlexNet.

10.3.2 Existing CNN Models

The effectiveness of the E-EfficientNet approach was demonstrated by comparing it with cutting-edge CNN architectures such as Inception V3, AlexNet, ResNet50, and VGG16.

10.3.2.1 AlexNet

A CNN architecture consisting of eight layers and roughly 61 million parameters, the AlexNet model [67] was first presented. This framework adheres to LeNet-5's model [68]. The AlexNet method, as depicted in Figure 10.2, utilizes 227 × 227 input image. The Softmax layer makes a distribution using the FC-8 layer's inputs giving each class a probability rate and guaranteeing that all classes have a total probability of 1.

10.3.2.2 VGG16

The VGG16 [69], which clinched the top spot in the ILSVRC-2014 competition, features approximately 138 million parameters. Notably, this architecture consistently employs 3 × 3 filters with stride 1 in its convolution layers and 2 × 2 filters with stride 2 in its maximum pooling layers maintaining the same padding. The maximum pooling and convolution layers are arranged consistently in the VGG16 architecture (see Figure 10.3). The

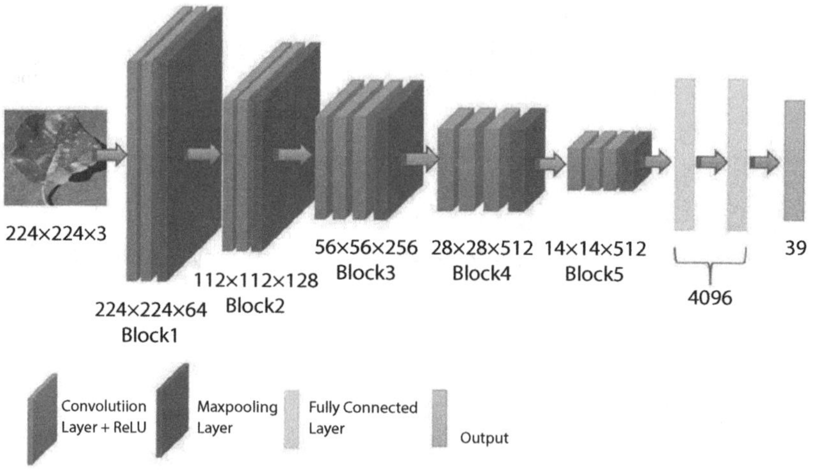

Figure 10.3 The architecture of VGG16.

architecture concludes with three fully connected (FC) layers, with the final one employing a Softmax activation function with the first two using ReLU. This 16-layer architecture allows pictures with a resolution of 224 × 224 pixels to be input.

10.3.2.3 ResNet50

Several non-linear layers find it difficult to learn identity maps, and the vanishing gradient problem is addressed by the ResNet50 architecture [70], which won first place in the ILSVRC-2015 competition. ResNet50 is built with multiple stacked residual units and has a network-in-network architecture (see Figure 10.4). Residual units serve as the building blocks composed of pooling and convolution layers. This architecture takes 224 × 224 pixel images as input and utilizes 3 × 3 filters similar to VGG16.

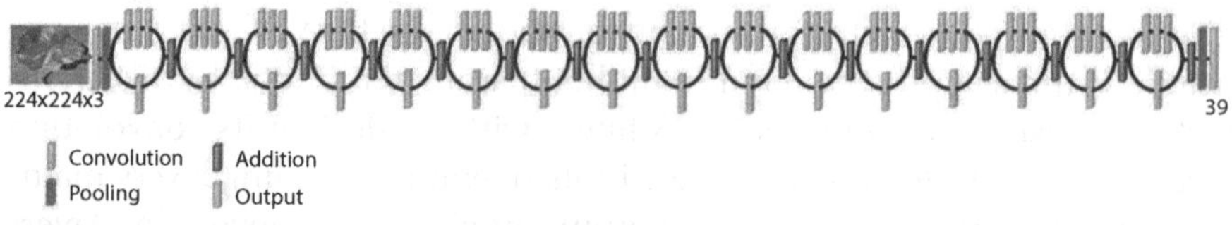

Figure 10.4 The architecture of ResNet50.

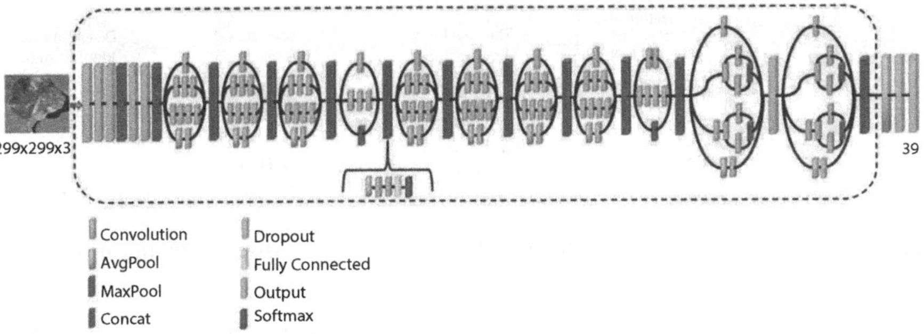

Figure 10.5 Schematic representation of inception V3.

10.3.2.4 Inception V3

The third repetition in Google's DL Evolutionary Systems series is known as Inception V3 [71]. Following Szegedy's creation of the Inception V1 design, in Inception V2, batch normalization was introduced. Subsequently, Inception V3 implemented factorization. The primary objective of factorization is to minimize the number of parameters and connections without compromising the network's efficiency. The algorithm incorporates fully connected layers, convolutions, max pooling, average pooling, dropouts, concatenations, as well as symmetrical and asymmetrical building blocks (refer to Figure 10.5). The 42-layer Inception V3 architecture includes an input layer that can handle images up to 299 × 299 pixels in resolution. The Softmax function is incorporated into the last coat of the architecture.

10.4 Methodology—E-ENet

The entire framework of the DL-based plant disease identification model E-ENet is illustrated in Figure 10.6 encompassing the following three main steps: localizing plant leaves, segmenting images, and extracting and identifying plant diseases.

The model utilized in this study is primarily composed of the following three steps:

Localization of Diseased Leaves: The RPN—version 2 (RPNv2) algorithm is used to train the leaf dataset in a composite environment to identify diseased leaves. Both the classification neural network and frame regression neural network are used in the same complex environment to find and retrieve diseased leaves.

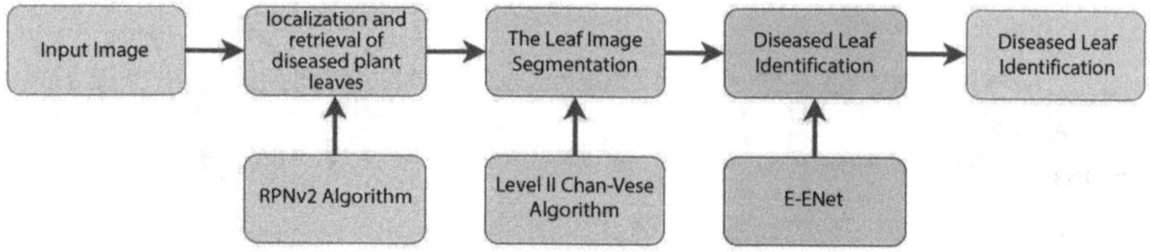

Figure 10.6 Entire framework of the E-ENet–DL-based plant disease identification.

Identification of Leaf Disease Species: The third and final step involves identification of leaf disease species. The recognition of plant diseases is accomplished in a simple background using the E-ENet model.

These steps collectively form the comprehensive framework for the deep learning-based plant disease identification model presented in the study.

10.4.1 Localization of the Leaf

The RPNv2 method is trained for precise localization and retrieval of diseased plant leaves within a challenging dataset featuring complex backgrounds. This method effectively blends boundary regression and classification neural networks to improve the precision of recognizing and defining diseased areas on plant leaves. To determine whether the content inside the designated boundary box corresponds to an object or background, the classification neural network is essential. Intersection over Union (IoU) is utilized as a critical criterion in training to guarantee efficient learning and precise classification of images according to their relevance to the targeted objects. Boundaries with IoU values greater than 0.5 are annotated as objects, while those with IoU values less than 0.1 are labeled as backgrounds. The relevance between an artificially marked boundary box and a predicted boundary box is computed using the idea of unity. The IoU formula is displayed as follows:

$$IoU = u1/u2 \tag{10.1}$$

where u2 is the total area, and u1 is the overlap area between the artificially marked boundary box and the predicted boundary box. The sigmoid function is chosen as the appropriate loss function for binary classification tasks within the neural network. Represented by four-dimensional variables (x, y, w, h), a single boundary box is characterized by (P_x, P_y, P_w, P_h) as the given boundary box, (G_x, G_y, G_w, G_h) as the target boundary box, and $(G_{x1}, G_{y1}, G_{w1}, G_{h1})$ as the predicted boundary box. The primary objective is to establish a mapping relationship denoted as f for the boundary regression neural network ensuring accurate and precise predictions.

$f(P_x, P_y, P_w, P_h) = (G_x^1, G_y^1, G_w^1, G_h^1)$ and $(G_x^1, G_y^1, G_w^1, G_h^1) \approx (G_x, G_y, G_w, G_h)$ are defined. The boundary measurement includes pan and zoom. The constraint of pan is $(\Delta x, \Delta y)$ given that $\Delta x = P_w d_x(P_1)$ and $\Delta y = P_h d_h(P_1)$.

The formula is shown as follows:

$$G_x^1 = P_w d_w(P_1) + P_x \tag{10.2}$$

$$G_y^1 = P_h d_h(P_1) + P_y \tag{10.3}$$

The parameter for zoom is denoted as (S_w, S_h), where $S_w = \exp(d_w(P_1))$ and $S_h = \exp(d_h(P_1))$. The formula is expressed as follows:

$$G_w^1 = P_w \exp(d_w(P_1)) \tag{10.4}$$

$$G_h^1 = P_h \exp(d_h(P_1)) \tag{10.5}$$

In accordance with the provided formula, the actual learning objectives of the boundary regression neural network are denoted as $d(P_1) = (d_x(P_1), d_y(P_1), d_w(P_1), d_h(P_1))$, and the true transformation parameters between the predicted boundary box and preciously annotated boundary box are expressed as $t = (t_x, t_y, t_w, t_h)$.

$$t_x = \frac{G_x - P_x}{P_x} \tag{10.6}$$

$$t_y = \frac{G_y - P_y}{P_y} \tag{10.7}$$

$$t_w = log\frac{G_w}{P_w} \tag{10.8}$$

$$t_h = log\frac{G_h}{P_h} \tag{10.9}$$

The objective function of the boundary regression neural network is represented as $d(P_1) = w^T P_1$, where w signifies the learning parameter of the boundary regression neural network. The corresponding loss function is expressed as follows:

$$loss = \Sigma_{i=1}^{N}(t_i - d_i(P_1)) \quad (10.10)$$

10.4.2 Segmentation of Leaf Image

The model applies an advanced method that builds upon previous steps, the Chan–Vese Level II algorithm, to image segmentation in complex environments. By initializing the zero level set, minimalizing the energy function, and iteratively computing blade profiles, this algorithm skillfully segments images of diseased plant leaves. Unlike surface evolution, which uses an explicit control speed (F), the Chan–Vese Level II algorithm makes use of the level set to create an energy function that fully captures the region.

The contour length is raised to aid in the energy function's merging. The energy function is defined as the minimum sum of variances between the gray values within and outside the contour in the image. To account for a closed curve in the image, the energy function formulation is as follows:

$$E = \mu Length(C_1) + ¥1 \int\int_{c1}^{0} |u(x,y) - u_1|^2 dxdy + ¥2 \int\int_{c2}^{0} |u(x,y) - u_2|^2 dxdy \quad (10.11)$$

The image's gray values are represented by u(x, y), the average gray values in the contour are represented by u1, the average gray values outside the contour are represented by u2, and the image's gray values are represented by c1 and c2. Next, the following are the provided formulas:

$$F1 = ¥1 \int\int_{c1}^{0} |u(x,y) - u_1|^2 dxdy \quad (10.12)$$

$$F2 = ¥2 \int\int_{c2}^{0} |u(x,y) - u_2|^2 dxdy \quad (10.13)$$

When F1 $\approx$ 0 and F2 $\approx$ 0, the computing ends. Level set technique is applied to rectify Equation 10.11 and zero level set is employed to display contour lines. Dirac's function and Heaviside's function are introduced as follows:

$$T^i = Y, f(X^i) \tag{10.14}$$

$$\delta(\theta) = \frac{dH}{d\theta} \tag{10.15}$$

The level set equation of energy function is as follows:

$$E^i = £\int\int_{c2}^{0} \delta(\theta)\,|\,\alpha(\theta)\,|\,dxdy + ¥1\int\int_{c1}^{0} |u(x,y) - u_1|^2\, H(\theta)dxdy +$$

$$¥2\int\int_{c2}^{0} |u(x,y) - u_2|^2\,(1 - H(\theta)dxdy \tag{10.16}$$

By reducing Equation 10.16 with the variation technique and joining the Euler–Lagrange equation, the following partial differential equations are retrieved where u1 $= \int\int_{\Omega}^{0} u(x,y)\, H(\theta)dxdy/H(\theta)dxdy$ and u2 $= \int\int_{\Omega}^{0} u(x,y)$ $(1H(\theta))dxdy/(1H(\theta))dxdy$.

$$\frac{\delta(E)}{\delta(\theta)} = \delta(\theta)\left(\eta.div\left(\frac{\nabla\varphi}{|\nabla\varphi|}\right)\right) + \delta(\theta)[-\rho_1(1-u_1{}^2) + \rho_2(1-u_2{}^2] \tag{10.17}$$

10.4.3 The Diseased Leaf Identification

The chapter utilizes the diseased leaf dataset to train the E-ENet model for disease category identification in a simple background. This approach reduces the need for deep learning algorithms in hardware equipment by completing training quickly and performing disease identification in a straightforward environment. By utilizing the similarities between shallow networks across different learning objectives, the E-ENet algorithm makes it easier to adapt a shallow neural network from a source task to a target task. When it comes to convergences and final outcomes, E-ENet performs better than new learning in practice. It has two contents when the domain is set to D; feature space is represented by X, which holds all possible characteristic values. In the feature space, P(X) denotes a particular instance of feature sampling:

$$D_1 = X^i, P_1(X^i) \tag{10.18}$$

There are two parts to the task T_1: Y^i is a representation of the label space; it includes the vector space with all possible tags. The input data's features and labels are used as learning cues to derive the prediction function f(x).

$$T_1 = Y^i, f(X^i) \tag{10.19}$$

Since 2012, the ImageNet dataset has employed more complicated designs leading to increased success. However, a significant number of these models exhibit low computational load. The E-ENet group comprises eight models denoted as B0 to B7 [72]. The E-ENet's architecture is focused on investigating smaller, more effective designs. Unlike other current state-of-the-art models, E-ENet systematically minimizes the depth, width, and resolution structure leading to improved performance results.

This investigation helps determine appropriate scaling parameters [72]. Compared to expansion layers, connections are integrated between bottlenecks with substantially fewer channels. The reason for this is that MBConv (MobileNetV2) blocks progressively widen and narrow channels. Compared to traditional layers, the deep separable convolutions in the design reduce computations by almost a factor of k_1, where k_1 is the kernel size. The E-ENet algorithm's layout is shown in Figure 10.7. Equation 10.1 defines the compound coefficient μ, which is used to uniformly scale depth, width, and resolution in compound scaling.

The values for Depth $Đ = a^\mu$, width $\hat{W} = b^\mu$, and Resolution $\check{R} = c^\mu$ should be greater than 1. In the context of model scaling, the constants a, b, c are determined through grid search [72]. Commencing with Baseline EfficientNet-B0, the compound scaling method is applied in two steps:

Step 1: Conducting a grid search with double the available resources, where $\mu = 1$, optimal values for α_1, β_1, and γ_1 are identified.
Step 2: The determined α_1, β_1, and γ_1 values are held constant, and the baseline network is scaled up to generate E-ENet-B1 to B7 using Equation 10.1 employing different μ values.

10.5 Experimental Analysis

10.5.1 The Acquisition of Data

The initial step in this study involves obtaining the leaf dataset within a complex environment. The Plant Photo Bank of China (PPBC) provided 1,000 leaf images for the chapter, which uses Crawler technology to collect images of different plant leaves at different stages of growth. These leaves

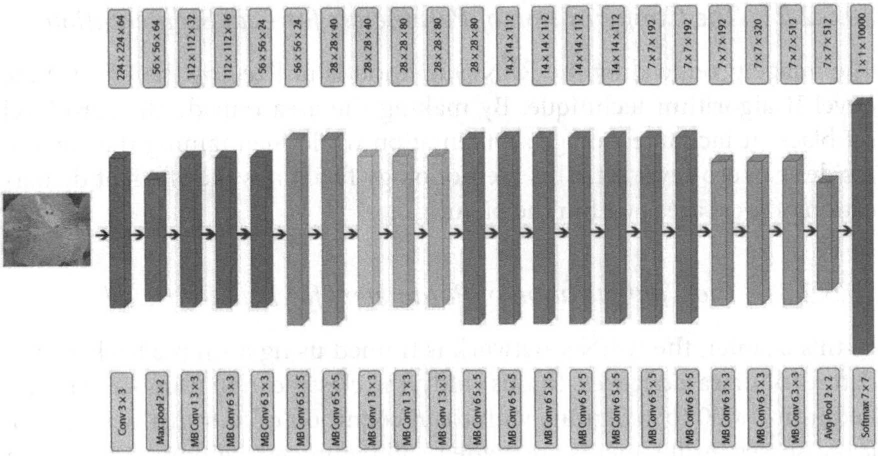

Figure 10.7 Schematic representation of E-ENet.

have distinct shapes, and they also differ in terms of their overall health. With the goals of clear leaves, minimal watermarks, and simple labeling, 189 pictures are eliminated as leaf images in the intricate setting. The RPNv2 algorithm is trained on this dataset to find and locate leaves in an environment that is complicated. Then, XML files in PASCAL VOC format are generated, and images are promptly annotated employing LabelImg. The target detection neural network can be directly input as training data. In the final stage, a diseased leaves dataset in a controlled environment is essential for this research. The study acquires four types of images—537 images (black rot), 1,032 (bacterial plaque disease) images, 293 images (rust), and 2,852 images (healthy leaves) from the Question-and-Answer Forum of PlantVillage Agricultural. These images serve as training data for an E-ENet model, specifically the E-ENet model, which undergoes training using this diverse dataset.

10.5.2 The Parameter Setup

10.5.2.1 The Configuration of Parameters for Leaf Localization

The PlantVillage Agricultural Question-and-Answer Forum provided the dataset used in this study, which included four different image types: 537 black rot, 1,032 bacterial plaque disease, 293 rust, and 2,852 healthy leaves. To improve its performance, the E-ENet model is trained on this varied dataset that covers a range of plant conditions.

10.5.2.2 The Configuration of Parameters for Leaf Segmentation

The image produced by the RPNv3 method is utilized by the Chan–Vese Level II algorithm technique. By making the area outside the zero-level set black, it facilitates image segmentation while maintaining the content inside the zero-level set. This methodology facilitates the efficient demarcation of focal areas within the picture.

10.5.2.3 The Configuration of Parameters for Leaf Retrieval

In this chapter, the E-ENet network is trained using a simple background dataset of diseased leaves. In this study, the classification number is modified from 1,000 to 4 aligning with the recognition of four distinct types of leaf diseases. Adjustments are made to all parameters and initialization in the final output layer of E-ENet to accommodate this change.

10.6 Results

10.6.1 The Leaf Localization Outcome

Figure 10.7 shows the output of the RPNv2 design using the test image as input. Regarding the aforementioned pictures, Figure 10.7b's frame selection range is inaccurate, and Figure 10.7c lacks blades. However, the RPNv2 method outperforms the original designs in terms of efficiency and can essentially frame the main blade framework.

10.6.2 The Outcomes of Leaf Segmentation

Figure 10.8 depicts the Identification of leaf, black rot, bacteria plaque, rust disease. Figures 10.9 and 10.10 depict the Chan–Vese Level II algorithm method's incremental calculation procedure. The results above indicate that the Chan–Vese Level II method can achieve greater accuracy in

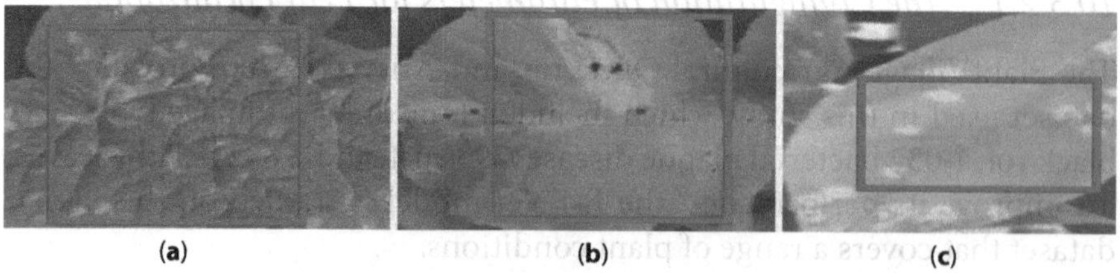

Figure 10.8 Identification of leaf (a) black rot, (b) bacteria plaque, (c) rust disease.

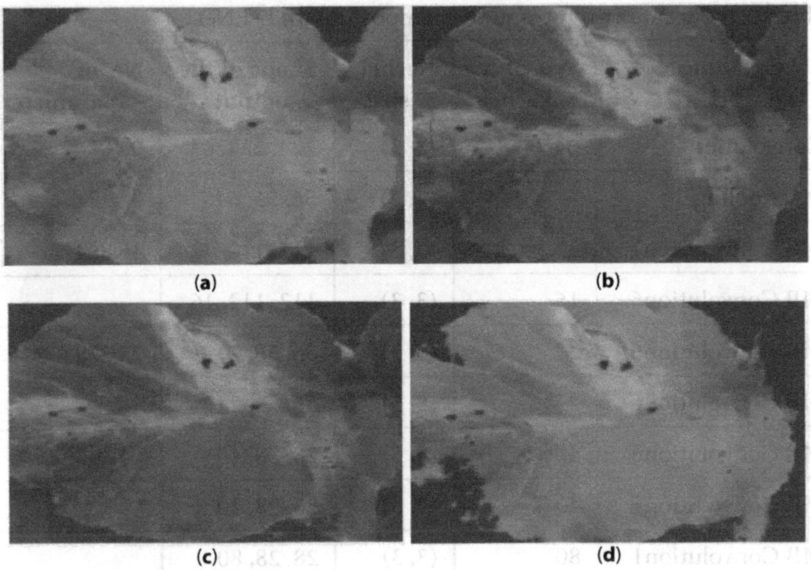

Figure 10.9 Chan–Vese Level II algorithm segmenting black rot diseased leaf result: (a) image capture; (b) initial zero level set; (c) contour image after 1,000 iterations; (d) segmentation results.

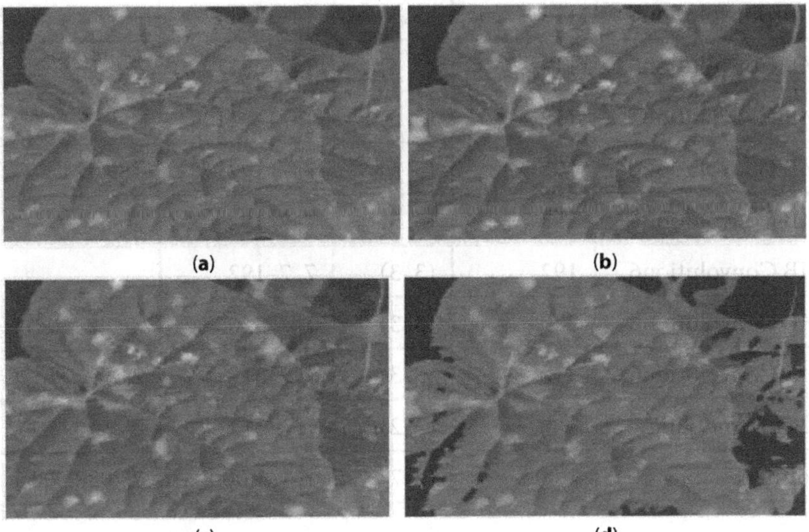

Figure 10.10 The outcomes of the Chan–Vese Level II algorithm in segmenting bacterial plaque diseased leaves showcasing (a) the image capture, (b) the initial zero level set, (c) the contour image after 1,000 iterations, and (d) the final segmentation results.

Table 10.1 Parameter setup and the composition of E-ENet.

Layers of the network	No. of kernels	Kernel size	Shape of the output	No. of parameters
Convolution	64	(3, 3)	224, 224, 64	9,408
Maxpooling	—	(2, 2)	56, 56, 64	0
MB Convolution1	32	(3, 3)	112, 112, 32	36,864
MB Convolution6	16	(3, 3)	112, 112, 16	
MB Convolution6	24	(3, 3)	56, 56, 24	73,728
MB Convolution6	24	(5, 5)	56, 56, 24	
MB Convolution6	40	(5, 5)	28, 28, 40	147,456
MB Convolution1	40	(3, 3)	28, 28, 40	
MB Convolution1	80	(3, 3)	28, 28, 80	
MB Convolution1	80	(3, 3)	28, 28, 80	
MB Convolution6	80	(5, 5)	28, 28, 80	
MB Convolution6	112	(5, 5)	14, 14, 112	294,912
MB Convolution6	112	(5, 5)	14, 14, 112	
MB Convolution6	112	(5, 5)	14, 14, 112	
MB Convolution6	112	(5, 5)	14, 14, 112	
MB Convolution6	192	(5, 5)	7, 7, 192	589,824
MB Convolution6	192	(5, 5)	7, 7, 192	
MB Convolution6	192	(3, 3)	7, 7, 192	
MB Convolution6	320	(3, 3)	7, 7, 320	
MB Convolution6	512	(3, 3)	7, 7, 512	2,359,296
Average pooling	—	(2, 2)	7, 7, 512	0
Softmax	1,000	(7, 7)	1, 1, 1,000	25,088,000

leaf segmentation of images after 1,000 iterations. The Chan–Vese Level II method retains all aspects of the central blade, including leaf venation, spot shape, and spot color, although it may be less efficient compared to the Watershed algorithm in extracting the edge contour of the blade. The next step in the disease identification process can be performed using the entire blade's central framework, which was discovered using the Chan–Vese Level II algorithm.

10.6.3 The Result of Disease Identification

Figure 10.7 presents the output of the RPNv2 algorithm and the VGG-16 model using the test image as input. While the RPNv2 algorithm effectively outlines the main blade structure (Figure 10.7a), it shows some limitations in accuracy in the frame selection range (Figure 10.7b), and there are omissions in the results (Figure 10.7c). Table 10.1 illustrates the composition and parameter setup of E-ENet.

10.7 Comparative Test

The parameters associated with the E-ENet algorithm in this chapter include both the training parameters and gradient descent optimization parameters. Table 10.2 depicts test accuracy and validation accuracy of different deep learning models with the proposed E-ENet. Figure 10.11 shows the training set accuracy and loss value after 5,000 training iterations for both the traditional and E-ENet models. Figure 10.11a shows that following the same 5,000 iterations of training, the E-ENet model performs well

Table 10.2 Test accuracy and validation accuracy of different deep learning models.

Model	Test accuracy
ResNet	95.44
VGG16	96.26
AlexNet	89.33
Inception V3	96.26
EfficientNet	98.31
E-ENet	**98.87**

Epochs	Validation accuracy (%)
1	90.18
5	93.85
10	95.71
15	97.43
20	97.55
30	99.21

than the traditional model in terms of convergence speed and model loss value. Figure 10.11b shows that the E-ENet design outperforms new learning in terms of detection effect, variance reduction, and accuracy during the training process. Thus, this research uses the E-ENet to produce an enhanced identification effect and faster convergence compared to the new learning. It can satisfy the low hardware resource, quick training time, and high training efficiency requirements of smart agriculture.

After that, the picture is fed into the E-ENet model using the LCV method's segmentation. The suggested model achieves high test accuracy (98.87%) and validation accuracy (99.21%) for 30 epochs based on comparison results. By comparing the results of this approach across four samples, we can conclude that healthy leaves and rust yield greater outcomes than bacterial plaque and black rot.

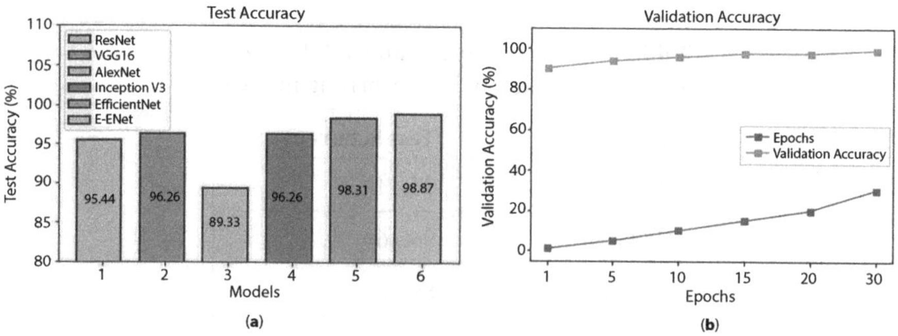

Figure 10.11 (a) Test accuracy of deep learning models. (b) Validation accuracy for different epochs on original dataset.

10.8 Summary

In addition to helping farmers automate tasks, artificial intelligence in agriculture is enabling more precise cultivation, which uses fewer resources to produce higher-quality and higher-yield crops. Businesses that are enhancing AI and machine learning-based goods and services, such as drones, automated machinery, and training data for agriculture, will benefit from future technological advancements that will enable them to develop more beneficial applications for this industry assisting the global community in addressing challenges related to food production for an expanding population. AI tools in agriculture, such as Precision Agriculture and Drones, enable farmers to enhance processes and adapt to environmental changes. These technologies optimize field management, provide crop health insights, and streamline operations for increased efficiency. Additionally, while preserving the operations' long-term viability, this will raise yields and revenues.

This chapter illustrates the high training efficiency, high precision, good universality, and unsupervised nature of the deep learning-based plant disease recognition model. Despite these strengths, there are several challenges to the practicality and accuracy of identifying plant diseases in complex environments. This chapter presents a recognition model that combines the RPNv2 algorithm, LCV algorithm, and E-ENet system to improve the identification process and handle related issues. The combined method seeks to maximize efficiency and accuracy in object identification and classification within the specified context. The proposed recognition model effectively tackles the challenge of identifying plant diseases in complex environments enhancing identification accuracy and adaptability. In contrast to conventional models, the approach ensures the robustness of the convolutional neural network. Consequently, the model holds the potential to assist agricultural production staff in promptly preventing and treating plant diseases.

In a practical context, an approach that addresses the challenge of environmental complexity can yield accurate identification results. This study not only contributes to the improvement of accuracy but also advances existing theories shedding light on the crucial role of complexity in plant disease identification. Recognizing this importance is essential for studying plant diseases in complex environments. Moreover, the proposed approach supports the sustainable development of smart farming by integrating information technology into agricultural production. However, certain issues remain to be addressed. For instance, the Chan–Vese Level II algorithm, while effective, may suffer from slow execution and repetitive iterative calculations impacting its ability to deliver swift identification results. The E-ENet model achieves high test accuracy (98.87%) and validation accuracy (99.21%) for 30 epochs based on comparison results.

References

1. Rich, E. and Knight, K., *Artificial intelligence*, McGraw-Hill, New Delhi, 1991.
2. Thorpe, K.W., Ridgway, R.L., Th Webb, R.E., A computerized data management and decision support system for gypsy moth management in suburban parks. *Comput. Electron. Agric.*, 6, 4, 333–345, 1992.
3. Ampatzidis, Y., De Bellis, L., Luvisi, A., iPathology: robotic applications and management of plants and plant diseases. *Sustainability*, 9, 6, 1010, 2017.
4. Breukers, A., Kettenis, D.L., Mourits, M., Werf, W.V.D., Lansink, A.O., Individual-based models in the analysis of disease transmission in plant production chains: an application to potato brown rot. *Acad. Sci.*, 90, 1–3, 112–131, 2006.
5. Ghosal, S., Blystone, D., Singh, A.K., Ganapathysubramanian, B., Singh, A., Sarkar, S., An explainable deep machine vision framework for plant stress phenotyping. *Proc. Natl. Acad. Sci.*, 115, 18, 4613–4618, 2018.
6. Oerke, E.-C., Crop losses to pests. *e J. Agric. Sci.*, 144, 1, 31–43, 2006.
7. Pantazi, X.E., Moshou, D., Tamouridou, A.A., Automated leaf disease detection in different crop species through image features analysis and One Class Classifiers. *Comput. Electron. Agric.*, 156, 96–104, 2019.
8. Barbedo, J.G.A., Factors influencing the use of deep learning for plant disease recognition. *Biosyst. Eng.*, 172, 84–91, 2018.
9. Geetharamani, G. and Arun Pandian, J., Identification of plant leaf diseases using a nine-layer deep convolutional neural network. *Comput. Electr. Eng.*, 76, 323–338, 2019.
10. Konstantinos, P.F., Deep learning models for plant disease detection and diagnosis. *Comput. Electr. Eng.*, 145, 311–318, 2018.
11. Singh, V. and Misra, A.K., Detection of plant leaf diseases using image segmentation and soft computing techniques. *Inf. Process. Agric.*, 4, 1, 41–49, 2017.
12. Mohanty, S.P., Hughes, D.P., Marcel, S., Using deep learning for image-based plant disease detection. *Front. Plant Sci.*, 7, 1419, 2016.
13. Guo, Y., Hu, X., Zou, Y., *et al.*, Maximizing E-tailers' sales volume through the shipping-fee discount and product recommendation system. *Discrete Dyn. Nat. Soc.*, 2020, 1–14, 2020.
14. Amanda, R., Kelsee, B., Peter, M.C., Babuali, A., James, L., Hughes, D.P., Deep learning for image-based cassava disease detection. *Front. Plant Sci.*, 8, 1852, 2017.

15. Sankaran, S., Mishra, A., Ehsani, R., Davis, C., A review of advanced techniques for detecting plant diseases. *Comput. Electron. Agric.*, 72, 1–13, 2010, https://doi.org/10.1016/J.COMPAG.2010.02.007.
16. Sladojevic, S., Arsenovic, M., Anderla, A., Culibrk, D., Stefanovic, D., Deep Neural Networks Based Recognition of Plant Diseases by Leaf Image Classification. *Comput. Intell. Neurosci.*, 1, 3289801, 2016, https://doi.org/10.1155/2016/3289801.
17. Ferentinos, K.P., Deep learning models for plant disease detection and diagnosis. *Comput. Electron. Agric.*, 145, 311–318, 2018, https://doi.org/10.1016/J.COMPAG.2018.01.009.
18. Jiang, F., Jiang, Y., Zhi, H., Dong, Y., Li, H., Ma, S., Wang, Y., Dong, Q., Shen, H., Wang, Y., Artificial intelligence in healthcare: past, present and future. *Stroke Vasc. Neurol.*, 2, 230–243, 2017, https://doi.org/10.1136/svn-2017-000101.
19. Rumpf, T., Mahlein, A.-K., Steiner, U., Oerke, E.-C., Dehne, H.-W., Plümer, L., Early detection and classification of plant diseases with Support Vector Machines based on hyperspectral reflectance. *Comput. Electron. Agric.*, 74, 91–99, 2010, https://doi.org/10.1016/J.COMPAG.2010.06.009.
20. Al-Hiary, H., Bani-Ahmad, S., Reyalat, M., Braik, M., Alrahamneh, Z., Fast and accurate detection and classification of plant diseases. *Int. J. Comput. Appl.*, 17, 31–38, 2011.
21. Revathi, P. and Hemalatha, M., Identification of cotton diseases based on cross information gain deep forward neural network classifier with PSO feature selection. *Int. J. Eng. Technol.*, 5, 4637–4642, 2014.
22. Mokhtar, U., Ali, M.A.S., Hassanien, A.E., Hefny, H., *Identifying Two of Tomatoes Leaf Viruses Using Support Vector Machine*, pp. 771–782, Springer, New Delhi, 2015, https://doi.org/10.1007/978-81-322-2250-7_77.
23. Pantazi, X.E., Moshou, D., Tamouridou, A.A., Kasderidis, S., *Leaf Disease Recognition in Vine Plants Based on Local Binary Patterns and One Class Support Vector Machines*, pp. 319–327, Springer, Cham, 2016, https://doi.org/10.1007/978-3- 319-44944-9_27.
24. Johannes, A., Picon, A., Alvarez-Gila, A., Echazarra, J., Rodriguez-Vaamonde, S., Navajas, A.D., Ortiz-Barredo, A., Automatic plant disease diagnosis using mobile capture devices, applied on a wheat use case. *Comput. Electron. Agric.*, 138, 200–209, 2017, https://doi.org/10.1016/j.compag.2017.04.013.
25. Chen, J., Yin, H., Zhang, D., A self-adaptive classification method for plant disease detection using GMDH-Logistic model. *Sustain. Comput. Inf. Syst.*, 28, 100415, 2020a, https://doi.org/10.1016/J.SUSCOM.2020.100415.
26. LeCun, Y., Bengio, Y., Hinton, G., Deep learning. *Nature*, 521, 436–444, 2015, https://doi.org/10.1038/nature14539.
27. Shen, D., Wu, G., Suk, H.-I., Deep Learning in Medical Image Analysis. *Annu. Rev. Biomed. Eng.*, 19, 221–248, 2017, https://doi.org/10.1146/annurev-bioeng-071516-044442.

28. Saleem, M.H., Potgieter, J., Mahmood Arif, K.M., Plant Disease Detection and Classification by Deep Learning. *Plants*, 8, 468, 2019, https://doi.org/10.3390/plants8110468.
29. Chen, J., Zhang, D., Nanehkaran, Y.A., Li, D., Detection of rice plant diseases based on deep transfer learning. *J. Sci. Food Agric.*, 100, 3246–3256, 2020c, https://doi.org/10.1002/jsfa.10365.
30. Chen, J., Chen, J., Zhang, D., Sun, Y., Nanehkaran, Y.A., Using deep transfer learning for image-based plant disease identification. *Comput. Electron. Agric.*, 173, 105393, 2020d, https://doi.org/10.1016/J.COMPAG.2020.105393.
31. Too, E.C., Yujian, L., Njuki, S., Yingchun, L., A comparative study of fine-tuning deep learning models for plant disease identification. *Comput. Electron. Agric.*, 161, 272–279, 2019, https://doi.org/10.1016/J.COMPAG.2018.03.032.
32. Arsenovic, M., Karanovic, M., Sladojevic, S., Anderla, A., Stefanovic, D., Solving Current Limitations of Deep Learning Based Approaches for Plant Disease Detection. *Symmetry (Basel)*, 11, 939, 2019, https://doi.org/10.3390/sym11070939.
33. Nanehkaran, Y.A., Zhang, D., Chen, J., Tian, Y., Al-Nabhan, N., Recognition of plant leaf diseases based on computer vision. *J. Ambient Intell. Humaniz. Comput.*, 15, 1–18, 2020, https://doi.org/10.1007/s12652-020-02505-x.
34. Chen, J., Zhang, D., Nanehkaran, Y.A., Identifying plant diseases using deep transfer learning and enhanced lightweight network. *Multimed. Tools Appl.*, 79, 1–19, 2020b, https://doi.org/10.1007/s11042-020-09669-w.
35. Ali, H., Lali, M.I., Nawaz, M.Z., Sharif, M., Saleem, B.A., Symptom based automated detection of citrus diseases using color histogram and textural descriptors. *Comput. Electron. Agric.*, 138, 92–104, 2017.
36. Alexander, H.M., Mauck, K.E., Whitfield, A.E., Garrett, K.A., Malmstrom, C.M., Plant-virus interactions and the agroecological interface. *Eur. J. Plant Pathol.*, 138, 3, 529–547, 2014.
37. Kao, I.-H., Hsu, Y.-W., Yang, Y.-Z., Chen, Y.-L., Lai, Y.-H., Perng, J.-W., Determination of Lycopersicon maturity using convolutional autoencoders. *Sci. Hortic.*, 256, 108538, 2019.
38. Pujari, D., Yakkundimath, R., Byadgi, A.S., Grading and classification of anthracnose fungal disease of fruits based on statistical texture features. *Int. J. Adv. Sci. Technol.*, 52, 121–132, 2013.
39. Akram, T., Naqvi, S.R., Haider, S.A., Kamran, M., Towards real-time crops surveillance for disease classification: exploiting parallelism in computer vision. *Comput. Electr. Eng.*, 59, 15–26, 2017.
40. Li, J., Tang, W., Wang, J., Wang, X., Zhang, X., Multilevel thresholding selection based on variational mode decomposition for image segmentation. *Signal Process.*, 147, 80–91, 2018.
41. Elaziz, M.A., Oliva, D., Ewees, A.A., Xiong, S., Multi-level thresholding-based grey scale image segmentation using multi-objective multi-verse optimizer. *Expert Syst. Appl.*, 125, 112–129, 2019.

42. Revathi, V., Kavin, B.P., Thirumalraj, A., Gangadevi, E., Balusamy, B., Gite, S., Image Based Feature Separation Using RBM Tech with ADBN Tech for Accurate Fruit Classification. *2024 IEEE International Conference on Computing, Power and Communication Technologies (IC2PCT)*, Greater Noida, India, pp. 1423–1429, 2024, doi: 10.1109/IC2PCT60090.2024.10486564.
43. Iqbal, Z., Khan, M.A., Sharif, M., Shah, J.H., ur Rehman, M.H., Javed, K., An automated detection and classification of citrus plant diseases using image processing techniques: a review. *Comput. Electron. Agric.*, 153, 12–32, 2018.
44. Raza, M., Sharif, M., Yasmin, M., Khan, M.A., Saba, T., Fernandes, S.L., Appearance based pedestrians' gender recognition by employing stacked auto encoders in deep learning. *Future Gener. Comput. Syst.*, 88, 28–39, 2018.
45. Hu, M., Bu, X., Sun, X., Yu, Z., Zheng, Y., Rape plant disease recognition method of multi-feature fusion based on D-S evidence theory. *Math. Comput. Appl.*, 22, 1, 18, 2017.
46. Turkoglu, M. and Hanbay, D., Leaf-based plant species recognition based on improved local binary pattern and extreme 10 Discrete Dynamics in Nature and Society learning machine. *Phys. A Stat. Mech. Appl.*, 527, 121297, 2019.
47. Li, D., Deng, L., Lee, M., Wang, H., IoT data feature extraction and intrusion detection system for smart cities based on deep migration learning. *Int. J. Inf. Manage.*, 49, 533–545, 2019.
48. Dhiraj, Biswas, R., Ghattamaraju, N., An effective analysis of deep learning based approaches for audio based feature extraction and its visualization. *Multimedia Tools Appl.*, 78, 17, 23949–23972, 2019.
49. Meziani, A., Djouani, K., Medkour, T., Chibani, A., A Lasso quantile periodogram based feature extraction for EEGbased motor imagery. *J. Neurosci. Methods*, 328, 108434, 2019.
50. Xu, Y., Ding, H., Xue, Y., Guan, J., High-dimensional feature extraction of sea clutter and target signal for intelligent maritime monitoring network. *Comput. Commun.*, 147, 76–84, 2019.
51. Xu, C., Chai, Y., Li, H., Shi, Z., Zhang, L., Liang, Z., A feature extraction method for the wear of milling tools based on the Hilbert marginal spectrum. *Mach. Sci. Technol.*, 23, 847–868, 2019.
52. Zhang, Y., Wei, X.-S., Wu, J., *et al.*, Weakly supervised finegrained categorization with part-based image representation. *IEEE Trans. Image Process.*, 25, 4, 1713–1725, 2016.
53. Zhang, S., You, Z., Wu, X., Plant disease leaf image segmentation based on superpixel clustering and EM algorithm. *Neural Comput. Appl.*, 31, S2, 1225–1232, 2019.
54. Patil, J.K. and Kumar, R., Analysis of content based image retrieval for plant leaf diseases using color, shape and texture features. *Eng. Agric. Environ. Food*, 10, 69–78, 2016.
55. Gangadevi, E., Rani Ranganathan, S., Shri Mani, L., Kadry, S., An intelligent deep residual learning framework for tomato plant leaf disease classification.

Int. J. Electr. Comput. Eng. (IJECE), 14, 3, 3168, 2024, Institute of Advanced Engineering and Science.

56. Pertot, I., Kuflik, T., Gordon, I., Freeman, S., Elad, Y., Identificator: a web-based tool for visual plant disease identification, a proof of concept with a case study on strawberry. *Comput. Electron. Agric.*, 84, 144–154, 2012.
57. Yang, N., Qian, Y., EL-Mesery, H.S., Zhang, R., Wang, A., Tang, J., Rapid detection of rice disease using microscopy image identification based on the synergistic judgment of texture and shape features and decision tree-confusion matrix method. *J. Sci. Food Agric.*, 99, 14, 6589–6600, 2019.
58. Chad, D., Tyr, W.H., Chen, S., *et al.*, Automated identification of northern leaf blight-infected maize plants from field imagery using deep learning. *Phytopathology*, 107, 1426–1432, 2017.
59. Ni, C., Wang, D., Vinson, R., Holmes, M., Tao, Y., Automatic inspection machine for maize kernels based on deep convolutional neural networks. *Biosyst. Eng.*, 178, 131–144, 2019.
60. Lu, Y., Yi, S., Zeng, N., Liu, Y., Zhang, Y., Identification of rice diseases using deep convolutional neural networks. *Neurocomputing*, 267, 378–384, 2017.
61. Zhang, Z., Liu, H., Meng, Z., Chen, J., Deep learning-based automatic recognition network of agricultural machinery images. *Comput. Electron. Agric.*, 166, 104978, 2019.
62. Zhang, X., Qiao, Y., Meng, F., Fan, C., Zhang, M., Identification of maize leaf diseases using improved deep convolutional neural networks. *IEEE Access*, 6, 30370–30377, 2018.
63. Krishnaswamy, R.A., Raja, P., Aniirudh, R., Tomato crop disease classification using pre-trained deep learning algorithm. *Procedia Comput. Sci.*, 133, 1040–1047, 2018.
64. Coulibaly, S., Kamsu-Foguem, B., Kamissoko, D., Traore, D., Deep neural networks with transfer learning in millet crop images. *Comput. Ind.*, 108, 115–120, 2019.
65. PlantVillage homepage: https://plantvillage.org/ Access: April 2018.
66. Hughes, D.P. and Salathe, M., An open access repository of images on plant health to enable the development of mobile disease diagnostics, arXiv preprint arXiv:1511.08060, 2015.
67. Gangadevi, E., Rani, R.S., Dhanaraj, R.K., Nayyar, A., Spot-out fruit fly algorithm with simulated annealing optimized SVM for detecting tomato plant diseases. *Neural Comput. Appl.*, 36, 8, 4349–4375, 2023, Springer Science and Business Media LLC.
68. LeCun, Y., Boser, B., Denker, J.S., Henderson, D., Howard, R.E., Hubbard, W., Jackel, L.D., Backpropagation Applied to Handwritten Zip Code Recognition. *Neural Comput.*, 1, 541–551, 1989, https://doi.org/10.1162/neco.1989.1.4.541.
69. Simonyan, K. and Zisserman, A., Very deep convolutional networks for large-scale image recognition, 2014, arXiv Prepr. arXiv1409.1556.

70. He, K., Zhang, X., Ren, S., Sun, J., Deep residual learning for image recognition, 20162015, arXiv Prepr. arXiv1512.03385.
71. Szegedy, C., Vanhoucke, V., Ioffe, S., Shlens, J., Wojna, Z., Rethinking the inception architecture for computer vision, in: *Proceedings of the IEEE Conference on Computer Vision and Pattern Recognition*, pp. 2818–2826, 2016.
72. Tan, M. and Le, Q.V., EfficientNet: Rethinking model scaling for convolutional neural networks. *36th Int. Conf. Mach. Learn. ICML 2019*, 2019-June, pp. 10691–10700, 2019.

11

AutoML-Driven Deep Learning for Fake Currency Recognition

T. Bhaskar[1]* and E. Gangadevi[2]

[1]*Computer Engineering, Sanjivani College of Engineering, Kopargaon, India*

[2]*Loyola College, Chennai, India*

Abstract

False copies of genuine items are referred to as counterfeits. The financial industry is still quite vulnerable to counterfeit money. There are numerous detection techniques, but since there are now free picture manipulation programmers, it has become a significant problem in the banking industry. Finding those key regions for evaluation is the first task because there are many important regions that are represented by currencies. Classifiers can determine if the extracted features are real or not. Without classifiers, we may compare the segmented currency image to the region of the original note. Yet, that is insufficient to determine the authenticity of the specific paper currency image. If we segment the crucial areas, the alignment and edges might not match; therefore, phone money note images might be mistaken for the real thing. To obtain better results, the classifiers will process the extracted features.

The method for currency recognition using image processing is suggested in this chapter. Three elements, color, size, and texture, are utilized in the recognition process with this technique. This technology makes it simpler to check the value of paper currency at anytime and anyplace, and it uses the CNN (Convolutional Neural Network). The integration of AutoML not only accelerates the expansion process but also optimizes the performance of the deep learning models making the system flexible to various currencies and counterfeit systems. This chapter experimented with this approach on all Indian religious groups. The characteristics of paper money are crucial in this recognition.

***Keywords*:** Image processing, AutoML, convolutional neural network (CNN), feature extraction, denomination

**Corresponding author*: bhaskarcomp@sanjivani.org.in

E. Gangadevi, M. Lawanya Shri, Balamurugan Balusamy and Rajesh Kumar Dhanaraj (eds.) Automated Machine Learning and Industrial Applications, (243–262) © 2025 Scrivener Publishing LLC

11.1 Introduction

Due to fraudulent bills being sold in the market and widespread illiteracy, every nation today struggles to recognize its own currency. For this reason, automatic currency recognition systems are essential. In such a system, accuracy and speed are the two most crucial elements. Moreover, accuracy is more crucial than speed. By examining the salient characteristics, a currency recognizer recognizes the currency and determines the denomination. Researchers suggested a wide range of strategies. A handful of them use internal properties, while others use physical properties (width, length, texture and color). Every issue in the software industry has an answer. Such software solutions allow us to save time and energy. One technique that used image processing to identify cash notes existed in the early 1990s. Unfortunately, this technique does not consider the authentication of the notes. An image input was required for such a system before it begins to do various duties on its behalf.

The banking industry has seen significant technological improvement, which has led to the advent of self-servicing to make transactions easy and customer friendly. Some banks also bring brand-new recognition procedures, such as cash deposit by the user themselves through devices without going to the specific bank. In this situation, a currency recognizer is needed to inspect the money and handle it in accordance with the denominations.

A system based on CNN (Convolution Neural Network) technology is suggested in this work. Different modules are used to identify the currency depending on the structural perspective of the currency notes. The VGG16 model was created to train the specified system and provide improved accuracy.

11.2 Literature Review

Principal Features for Indian Currency Recognition [1] was taken as the motivation for this study. In this work, a method for recognizing cash using properties, such as the center numeral, latent image, RBI stamp, form, and micro letter, is proposed. A training data set is provided to prepare training models. For the recognition of paper currency, PCA analysis is explained.

Currency Recognition using Machine Learning [2] technique helps to identify the images accurately. The method for cash recognition using image processing is suggested in this paper. This method is based on the following three unique characteristics: color, size and texture. The method presented in this paper can be used to determine many different national currencies. Only fiat currencies from India will be considered for implementation purposes. This technology makes it easy to check the value of money anytime and anywhere, and it uses CNN (Convolution Neural Network). Every denomination of Indian currency was used in our testing, and the algorithm was able to identify with 95% accuracy. To improve the technique's accuracy, a classification model was created incorporating all of the previously listed parameters. Features of paper money are crucial to this recognition.

Currency recognition using image processing [3] deals with identifying images with respect to size, color, and texture. In this research, a machine learning system that can detect foreign currencies with a high degree of accuracy was provided. The suggested procedure may be used to figure out where a banknote came from, what denomination it is, and how much it is worth. The method relies on the fact that different banknotes from the same country vary in size, color, and text placement to determine the denomination value. This study considered the denominations of 20 as the most popular currencies. Our system can rapidly and precisely locate test notes.

Fake currency detection using an image processing algorithm and machine learning algorithm [4] helps detect currency using suitable algorithms. The question of identifying whether the provided sample currency is fake is covered in this research. Traditional techniques and strategies exist for identifying counterfeit currency based on features including color, width, and serial numbers. In this era of cutting-edge technology and sophisticated computational approaches, which offer 99.9% accuracy for false identification of currency, a number of machine learning strategies are proposed. Beyond algorithms, there are other techniques for detection and identification, including note-specific photo filtering and properties like color, shape, and paper width [5]. According to this research, image processing should come first, then K-Nearest Neighbors to detect fake currency. Due to its excellent accuracy for small data sets, KNN is a promising option for use in computer vision jobs. Utilizing sophisticated computational and mathematical methodologies, for the purpose of authenticating banknotes, this collection contains detailed information about the entities and traits often associated with cash. Machine learning [9, 10] and image processing are used in the processing and extraction of data to achieve the desired results and levels of accuracy.

As previously mentioned, many different systems have been put out in various articles [6–8], although one may infer from their findings that none of the solutions suggested are entirely effective and that it is useless to consider just one parameter while solving this problem. Hence, this chapter suggests a method that considers a variety of features to comprehend the differences between each note. Our approach is intended to be easily scalable and to produce accurate results.

11.2.1 Scope

The proposed system can be extended toward coin detection and also for fake currency recognition. Second, implementation of this work will enable the detection of money automatically near toll plazas. This will reduce the waiting time of vehicles at the toll plazas. Stolen vehicles can also be identified with the help of the presence of an RFID tag in the vehicle. Third, because robots are increasingly being used in place of people in the workplace, it is important that all robots are able to distinguish between different currencies. Fourth, this system can be further implemented for foreign currencies like Dollars, Euros, Tanka, etc., i.e., the denomination of other countries other than India can be added and also compared between them.

11.2.2 Objectives

The main objectives of this application are as follows:

1. To recognize currency notes automatically by image processing with the help of mobile application.
2. To perform image processing on inserted image and match with a trained data set.
3. To develop an AutoML-driven deep learning that gives a faster and more accurate output when compared to the other techniques.
4. Finding clearly distinguishable components during feature extraction and then classifying the money to help in detection and identification is essential.

11.3 Proposed System

The system below consists of four main modules. They are as stated in the breakdown structure of the system below, which describes the working of every module in the system.

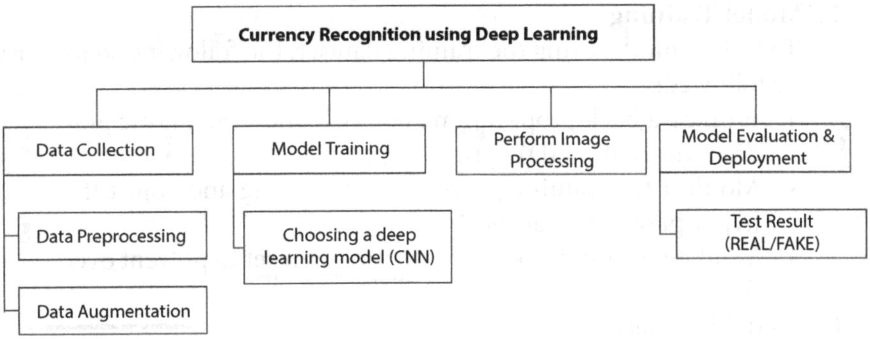

Figure 11.1 System breakdown structure.

As described in Figure 11.1, the breakdown structure of the system, the modules of the system are listed below:

1. **Data Collection**
   - Collect images of different currencies.
   - Label the images according to the currency type.
2. **Data Preprocessing**
   - Normalize the size of the images.
   - Enhance the contrast and brightness of the images.
   - Image noise and imperfections should be eliminated.
3. **Data Augmentation**
   - Generate additional images by rotating, scaling, and cropping the original images.
4. **Data Perturbation**
   - Add noise and other perturbations to the images to increase their diversity.
5. **Training Data Preparation**
   - Use the dataset to generate training, validation, and test sets.
   - Convert the images and labels into appropriate formats for deep learning frameworks.
   - Image pixel values should be normalized to the range [0,1].
6. **Convolutional Neural Network (CNN) Model**
   - Choose an appropriate CNN architecture, such as VGG16.
   - Describe the layers of the model, including convolutional, pooling, and fully linked layers.
   - The learning rate, batch size, and number of epochs are all hyper parameters that must be set before the model can be trained.

7. **Model Training**
   To train a model using the training dataset, the following steps must be followed:
   - Employ a back propagation approach and a stochastic gradient descent (SGD) optimizer.
   - Monitor the training process for overfitting and adjust the hyper parameters accordingly.
   - Validate the model on the validation dataset to prevent over fitting.
8. **Model Evaluation**
   - Test the model on the evaluation dataset to gauge its effectiveness.
   - Calculate the model's F1 score, precision, recall, and accuracy.
   - Visualize the model's output and predictions.
9. **Model Deployment**
   - Include the trained model in a real-time system, such as a mobile payment system, vending machine, or automated teller machine (ATM).
   - The model's accuracy may be enhanced by keeping a close eye on how well it is doing and by regularly updating it with fresh information.
10. **Future Directions**
    - To increase the model's performance with little data, we should investigate the usage of transfer learning.
    - Adapt the model to recognize currencies from different countries or regions.
    - Look at how different deep learning architectures and methods, such as generative adversarial networks (GANs), may be used to enhance money recognition.

11.4 Methodology

Figure 11.2 represents the system architecture that consists of the main working modules and methodology. They are as follows:

1. **Training Module:** Initially, we need to capture the image through camera. After that, perform face orientation for both front and back. Perform image processing on the updated

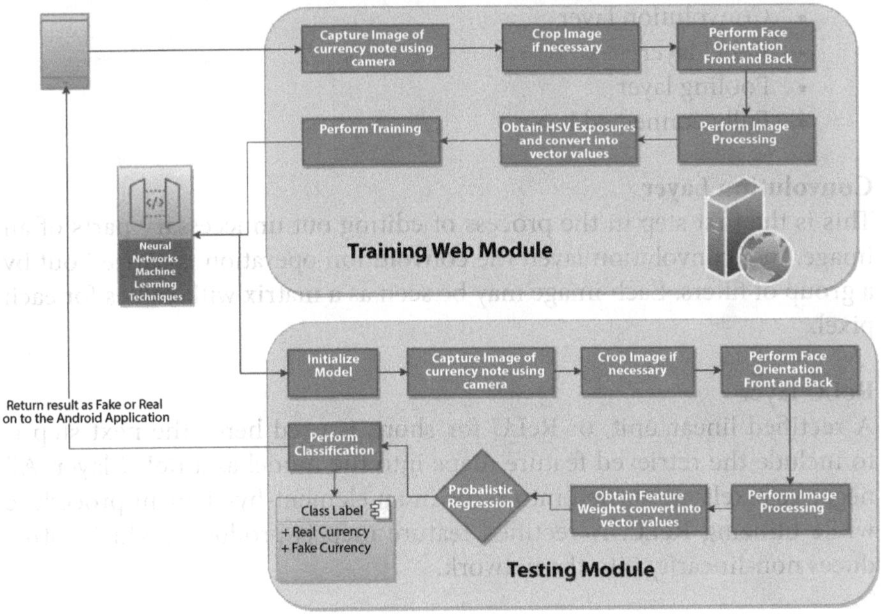

Figure 11.2 System architecture.

images. Then, we obtain HSV exposures and convert into vector values, and then, perform training by using VGG16.

2. **Testing Module:** In the testing module, initialize the model by capturing an image with the camera, and then, perform face orientation for both front and back. Accomplish image processing. Obtain the feature, and convert into vector values. Apply probabilistic regression, and then, perform classification with labels Real Currency/Fake Currency.

11.5 Convolutional Neural Network

Convolutional networks, a kind of feed-forward neural network, perform image analysis using a grid-like data-processing structure. It can also be referred as "Conversion Network". For image-based object recognition and categorization, researchers turn to convolutional neural networks. To extract useful data from an image, a convolution neural network uses several hidden layers. The following are the four main layers that make up the CNN:

- Convolution layer
- ReLU layer
- Pooling layer
- Fully connected layer

Convolution Layer

This is the first step in the process of editing out unnecessary parts of an image. In a convolution layer, the convolution operation is carried out by a group of filters. Each image may be seen as a matrix with values for each pixel.

ReLU layer

A rectified linear unit, or ReLU for short, is used here. The next step is to include the retrieved feature maps into the model as a ReLU layer. All negative pixels are turned into zeros in an element-by-element procedure while utilizing ReLU. A rectified feature map is produced, which introduces non-linearity into the network.

Pooling Layer

"Pooling" is a down sampling method used to minimize the number of dimensions in the feature map. The updated feature map is then pooled to produce a pooled feature map.

One common use of powerful deep learning architecture, Convolutional Neural Networks (CNNs), is the applications of money identification. CNNs' capacity to automatically learn hierarchical features from input images has allowed them to achieve extraordinary performance in image identification applications. Here is an overview of how CNNs can be applied to currency recognition:

Data Preparation: Collect a labeled dataset of currency images. This dataset should include images of various denominations and currencies, captured from different angles, under different lighting conditions, and with diverse backgrounds. Preprocess the images by resizing them to a consistent resolution and normalizing pixel values to a standard range.

Network Architecture: Design the CNN architecture. It typically consists of multiple convolutional layers, followed by pooling layers for downsampling and non-linear activation functions such as ReLU (Rectified Linear Unit). The convolutional layers capture local patterns and features, while the pooling layers reduce spatial dimensions.The final layers are typically fully connected layers for classification.

Training: Partition the dataset into preparing and validation sets. Utilize the preparation set to prepare the CNN by improving the organization's parameters (biases) using techniques like backpropagation and gradient descent. During training, the CNN learns to recognize currency patterns and features. The validation set helps monitor the model's performance and prevents overfitting.

Testing and Evaluation: Once training is complete, evaluate the CNN's performance using a separate test set. Feed test images into the trained CNN and compare the predicted currency labels with the ground truth labels. Evaluate the model's efficacy using a variety of measures, including accuracy, precision, recall, and F1 score.

Fine-Tuning and Optimization: Fine-tune the CNN to improve its performance. Experiment with hyperparameters like learning rate, batch size, and regularization techniques (e.g., dropout) to find the optimal configuration. Adjust the network architecture, such as adding more layers or changing layer configurations, to improve performance if necessary.

Data Augmentation: To further enhance the CNN's ability to generalize, apply data augmentation techniques. The original photos are transformed by means of rotation, scaling, flipping, and the introduction of noise to generate new training samples. Overfitting may be avoided, and model resilience to input data fluctuations can be increased via data augmentation.

Deployment: Once the CNN model is trained, it can be integrated into an Android app. It can be used as frameworks like TensorFlow to deploy the model on the Android platform. Optimize the model for mobile devices considering factors such as model size, inference speed, and energy efficiency. To conduct the convolution, the convolutional layer takes the image's pixels as input. To create a corrected feature map, the convolved map is sent through a ReLU function. The picture is processed via a number of convolutional and ReLU layers to identify its characteristics. Many pooling layers, each using a unique filter, are used to isolate certain areas of the image. The final product is obtained by flattening the pooled feature map and feeding it into a fully linked layer.

11.6 Analysis Modeling

A system's analysis model is a specialized diagram of the system. It connects two documents, the description of the system and the design model. After the system's data, actions, and features have been described in Analysis Modeling, they may be converted into the system's architecture, components, and interfaces in Design Modeling.

11.6.1 Behavioral Modeling

A system's behavior may be influenced by a number of different elements, all of which can be better understood with the use of a Behavioral Model. Figure 11.3 presents a use case diagram that represents the interactions between users and the system with its key functionalities.

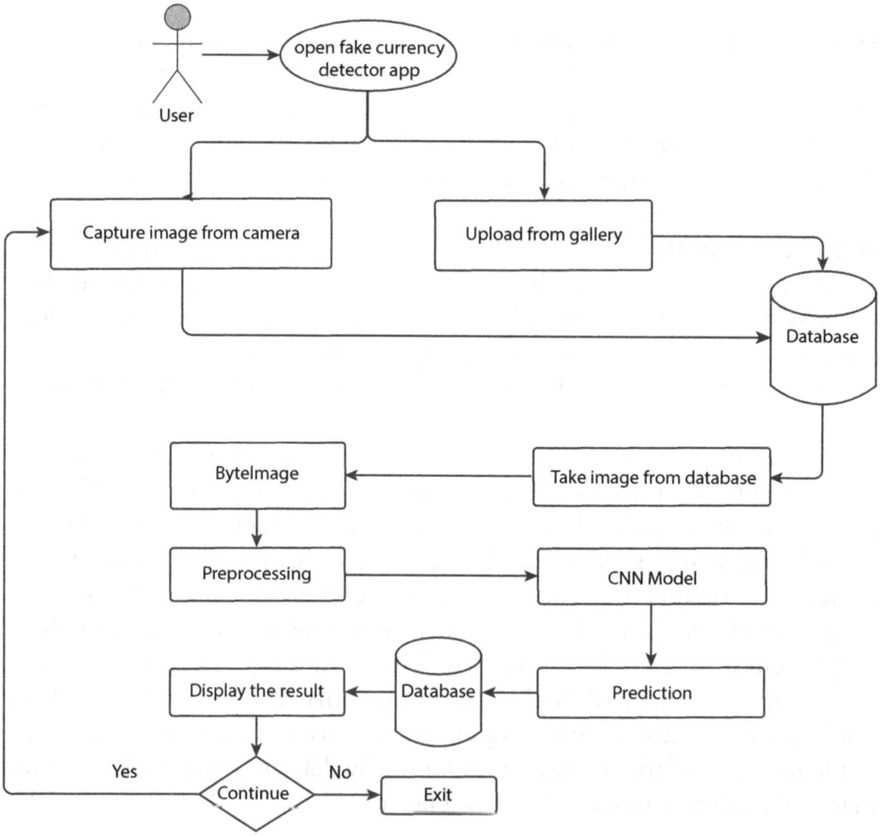

Figure 11.3 Use case diagram.

1. **Use Case Diagram:** - A use case is a set of steps in which the user interacts with a system and in which other parties may be involved.
2. **Sequence Diagram:** - Sequence diagrams are interaction diagrams that display the interdependencies and dependencies between processes, as well as the sequence in which they occur. Message Sequence Charts make up this structure. A sequence diagram is a graphical representation of the temporal progression of an event or series of events involving a set of objects. We can see the classes and objects that will be used, as well as the messages that will be sent back and forth between them as the scenario unfolds. In the Logical View of the system being developed, sequence diagrams are often linked to implementations of use cases. Sometimes referred to as "event diagrams" or "event scenarios," sequence diagrams have several names. Different processes or objects that exist concurrently are represented by parallel vertical lines (lifelines) in a sequence diagram, and the messages sent between them are represented by horizontal arrows in the correct order. Simple run-time situations may be specified graphically in this way. System's behaviour is represented in the sequence diagram as shown in Figure 11.4.

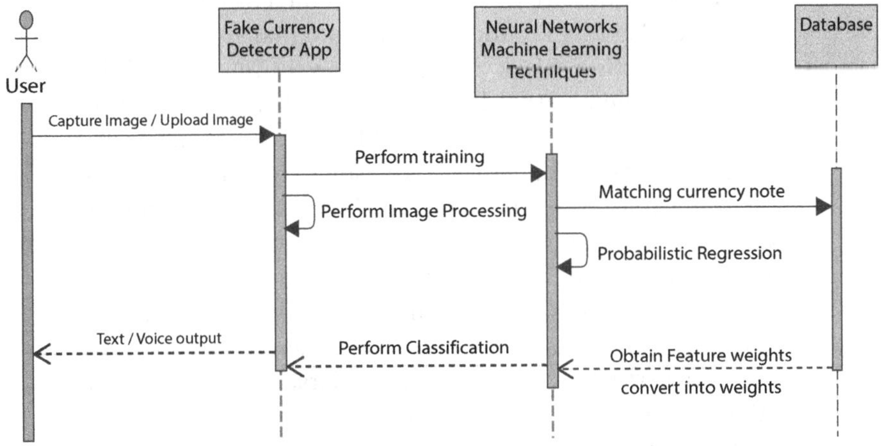

Figure 11.4 Sequence diagram.

11.7 Software Testing

Testing is a crucial process that involves examining and evaluating the performance and functionality of a product or system. It is applied in various fields, including human knowledge and skills, as computer hardware and software development. In software development, testing is a critical step used to determine whether a project meets its objectives.Software testing can be conducted at any stage of the development process depending on the testing methods employed. The primary goal of software testing is to validate and verify that the software program or application conforms to the required standards and specifications. As a result, software testing is essential for ensuring that the final product is both trustworthy and suitable for its intended purpose.

11.7.1 Types of Testing

The quality of software programs may be tested in a number of ways, including white box testing, black box testing, and gray box testing. These testing methods involve different levels of access to the underlying code and architecture of the software being tested. The following is an explanation of each testing method along with some examples:

- White box testing: In software testing, "white box" refers to the practice of disassembling a program to see how it is put together from the inside. In this method, the tester has access to the underlying code and architecture of the software allowing them to identify any potential vulnerabilities.
- Black box testing: Black box testing is a testing method that focuses on the external behavior of a software application. In this method, the tester does not have access to the underlying code and architecture of the software, but rather tests the software from the perspective of the user or a customer.
- Gray box testing: The term "gray box testing" refers to an approach to testing that mixes white box and black box techniques. With this approach, the tester is only given partial visibility into the software's source code and architecture, but is, nevertheless, able to get an understanding of its operation. Examples of gray box testing include API testing and database testing.

11.7.2 Test Cases

Specifications and requirements, or what the app should be capable of, serve as the foundation around which test cases are constructed. Typically, descriptions of the program found elsewhere, such as specifications, requirements, and design parameters, serve as the basis for creating test cases. The majority of the tests conducted are functional in nature; however, sometimes, non-functional tests are used. Without knowing the underlying structure of the test object, the test designer chooses valid and invalid inputs and the proper output. Table 11.1 shows the test cases with different parameters.

Table 11.1 Test cases.

Test ID	Parameters	Expected output	Actual output	Status
TC1	Capture high-resolution image of 500 rupee	Currency recognized as 500 rupee	Currency recognized as 500 rupee	PASS
TC2	Capture low-quality image of 500 rupee with creases and fold	Currency recognized as 500 rupee	Currency recognized as 500 rupee	PASS
TC3	Capture image of non-currency object (ex. floIr)	Invalid input image	Invalid input image	PASS
TC4	An image of Indian coin	Invalid input image	Invalid input image	PASS

(Continued)

Table 11.1 Test cases. (*Continued*)

Test ID	Parameters	Expected output	Actual output	Status
TC5	A blurred image of 500 rupee note	Currency recognized as500 rupee	Currency recognized as 500 rupee	PASS
TC6	A rotated image of a 10 rupee note	Currency recognized as 10 rupee	Currency recognized as 10 rupee	PASS
TC7	A severely damaged currency note with missing corners	Unable to recognize due to extreme damage	As expected	PASS
TC8	Capture high-resolution image of 500 rupee	If it is real, able to recognize the characters on the image	As expected	PASS
TC9	Capture low-quality image of 500 rupee with creases and fold	If it is real, able to recognize the characters on the image	As expected	PASS
TC10	A blurred image of 500 rupee note	If it is real, unable to detect all the characters on the currency note	As expected	PASS

11.8 Results and Discussions

In the above Figure 11.5, there is a front page for the user. This application was developed to be used by many different people especially for visually disabled people. Tap the Counterfeit button on the screen to hear text in front of the camera and long press to control the text to recognize it. Press the currency button on the main screen to hear the detected money

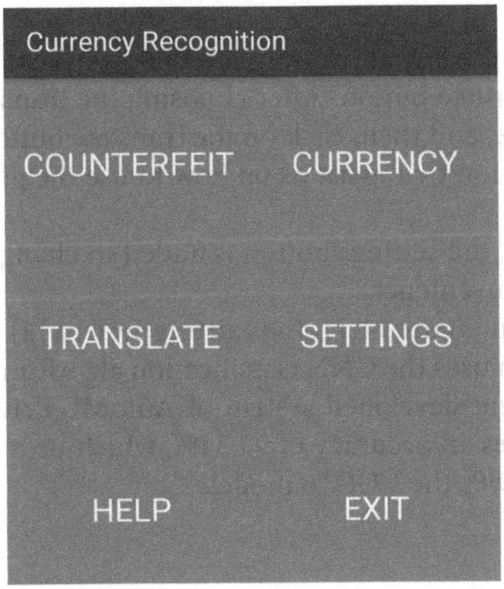

Figure 11.5 Main screen of the currency app.

Figure 11.6 Currency note.

and then press to recognize it. To translate the text into another language, pick the target language by tapping the translate button on the main screen. On the main screen settings, a help option is also there for the convenience of the users.

In above Figure 11.6, we have to place any currency note in front the camera after clicking on the counterfeit button, and it will detect if the note is real or fake by using denominations.

In Figure 11.7, place any currency note in front of the camera. After clicking on the currency button, it will tell us the value of the given currency note.

In Figure 11.8, if we want to translate the given text into another language, choose translate button. After choosing the translate button, select the target language, and then, click on the translate button. In Figure 11.9, we have a help option that assist us on how to use the given app and their options.

In Figure 11.10, the settings button is added to change the app settings as per the users convenience.

As mentioned in Figure 11.11, the existing system [2] provides an accuracy of 95%, which uses the CNN classification algorithm for classification process. The current developed system of AutoML-driven deep learning techniques provides an accuracy of 99.34%, which uses the CNN classification algorithm with the VGG16 model.

Figure 11.7 Currency button.

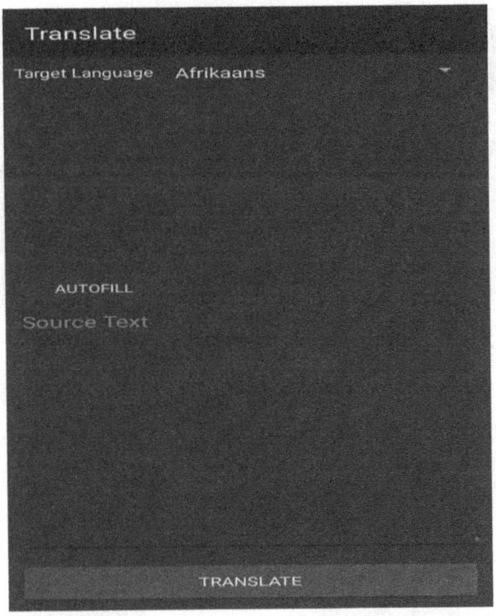

Figure 11.8 Translate button.

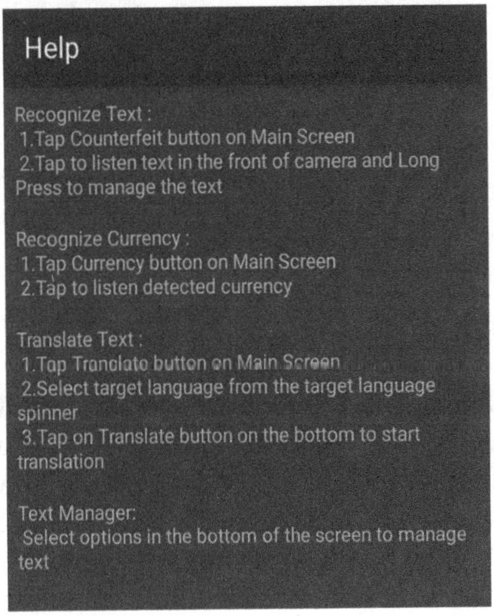

Figure 11.9 Help button.

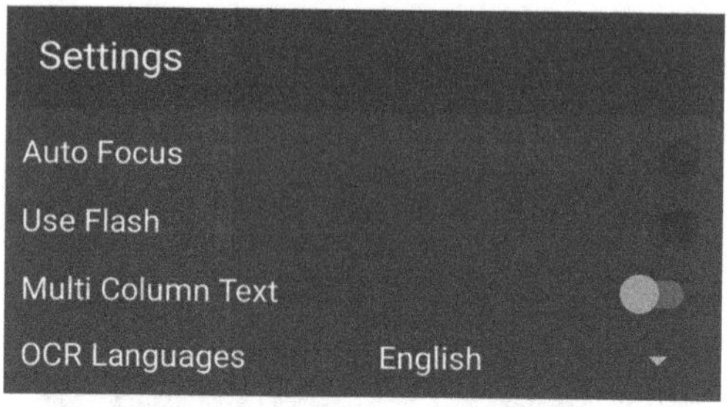

Figure 11.10 Settings.

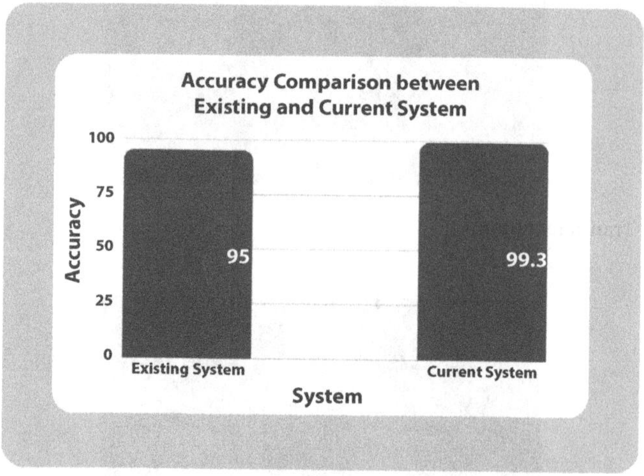

Figure 11.11 Accuracy comparison between existing and current system.

11.9 Conclusion

The proposed mechanism appropriately associates a banknote's denomination with the currency note. Those from outside India and those who are visually impaired frequently struggle to distinguish between different currency notes. Even though it might occasionally be challenging for Indians to recognize the same quantity of cash notes with new, distinct patterns are utilized, since the human eyes have some limitations as they occasionally fail to detect counterfeit currency. In this work, a detection model built using deep learning was evaluated against a variety of Indian currencies and with good accuracy. The developed mobile application for recognizing the currency note by using AutoML frameworks with CNN performs very well. This technique provides an accuracy of 99.34% by using the VGG16 model of CNN.

References

1. Vishnu, R. and Omman, B., Principal Features for Indian Currency Recognition. *2014 Annual IEEE India Conference (INDICON)*, Pune, India, doi: 10.1109/INDICON.2014.7030679.
2. Jadhav, R., Kalbande, S., Katkar, R., Katta, R., Bharadwaj, R., Currency Recognition using Machine Learning. *Int. Res. J. Eng. Technol. (IRJET)*, 9, 1, 204–211, Jan 2022, e-ISSN:2395-0056.
3. Abburu, V., Gupta, S., Rimitha, S.R., Mulimani, M., S.G., Currency Recognition System Using Image Processing. *Tenth International Conference on Contemporary Computing (IC3)*, Noida, India, 10-12 August 2017, Koolagudi.
4. Bhatia, A., Kedia, V., Shroff, A., Kumar, M., Shah, B.K., Aryan, Fake Currency Detection with Machine Learning Algorithm and Image Processing. *Fifth International Conference on Intelligent Computing and Control Systems (ICICCS 2021)*, IEEE Xplore Part Number: CFP21K74-ART; ISBN: 978-0-7381-1327-2.
5. Bhavsar, K., Jani, K., Vanzara, R., *Indian Currency Recognition from Live Video Using Deep Learning*, N. Chaubey, *et al.* (Eds.), COMS2 2020, CCIS 1235, pp. 70–81, Springer Nature Singapore Pte Ltd, Singapore, 2020, https://doi.org/10.1007/978-981-15-6648 6_ 6.
6. Jain, V.K. and Vijay, R., Indian currency denomination identification using image processing technique. *IInt. J. Comput. Sci. Inform. Tech. (IJCSIT)*, 4, 1, 126–128, 2013.
7. Kotwal, S., Image processing based heuristic analysis for enhanced currency recognition. *Int. J. Adv. Tech.*, 2, 1, 82–89, 2011.
8. Sarfraz, M., An Intelligent Paper Currency Recognition System. *Procedia Comput. Sci.*, 65, 538–545, 2015.
9. Bhaskar, T., Hiwarkar, T., Ramanjaneyulu, K., A Modified Deep Neural Network Based Hybrid Intrusion Detection System in Cyber Security. *IJITEE*, 8, 8, 3366–3370, June 2019, ISSN: 2278-3075.
10. Bhaskar, T. and Tribhuvan, R.R., A Machine Learning-Based Approach for Enhancing Student Learning Experiences, in: *Soft Computing and Signal Processing. ICSCSP 2022. Smart Innovation, Systems and Technologies*, vol. 313, V.S. Reddy, V.K. Prasad, J. Wang, K.T.V. Reddy, (Eds.), Springer, Singapore, 2023, https://doi.org/10.1007/978-981-19-8669-7_2.
11. Murthy, C.V.B., Shri, M.L., Kadry, S., Lim, S., Blockchain based cloud computing: Architecture and research challenges. *IEEE Access*, 8, 205190–205205, 2020.

12

Blockchain and Automated Machine Learning-Based Advancements for Banking and Financial Sectors

K. Santhi, M. Lawanya Shri*, Pranesh L., Dhanush T. and Suneel P.V.

Vellore Institute of Technology, Vellore, Tamil Nadu, India

Abstract

Technological advancements in Blockchain and Automated Machine Learning (AutoML) have revolutionized the traditional practices in the banking and financial sector in recent years. This chapter focuses on the complementarity of Blockchain and AutoML, and discusses practical applications, benefits, challenges, and the future of the confluence of these two technologies. Real-world case studies are cited to show how integrations of these technologies are bringing improvisations in fraud detection, risk assessment, and customer relationship management in the finance sector. For example, the immutability and decentralized nature of Blockchain can overcome data tampering and bring transparency to financial transactions. AutoML automates complex analysis tasks that could be both time consuming and difficult for humans providing fast and reliable solutions for decision making through learning from large amounts of data.

Keywords: AutoML, finance, banking, blockchain, stakeholders, inventors, industries

12.1 Introduction

The emergence of Blockchain and Automated Machine Learning (AutoML) technologies have impacted the banking and financial quarter flawlessly [1]. The decentralized system of securely dealing with and recording transactions by using Blockchain and the machines' getting to know and

*Corresponding author: lawanyaraj@gmail.com; kmlavanya@vit.ac.in

E. Gangadevi, M. Lawanya Shri, Balamurugan Balusamy and Rajesh Kumar Dhanaraj (eds.) Automated Machine Learning and Industrial Applications, (263–280) © 2025 Scrivener Publishing LLC

self-enhancing ability without being controlled via human intervention have paved the way for the traditional banking system's transformation [2]. The transformation from time taking, highly-priced and inaccurate to actual time, reasonably-priced and correct [3, 4]. This chapter analyses the ideas of Blockchain and AutoML in a detailed manner and their increasing importance inside the procedure of shaping the future of banking and finance.

12.2 Understanding Blockchain and AutoML

Blockchain era is a decentralized virtual ledger that offers a stable and transparent manner to store and confirm transactions [5]. This present-day generation incorporates a network of nodes that work collectively to validate and hold data in a chain of blocks. Every block is cryptographically related to the preceding block making it clearly no longer viable to alter or delete any transaction data once the recording is done [6]. The decentralized nature of Blockchain generation technique prevents intruders from accessing or modifying transactions, which notably reduces the chance of fraud and hacking. AutoML is an advanced artificial intelligence technology that automates the process of selecting best machine learning algorithms, feature selection and hyperparameter tuning [7]. This technology allows organizations to analyze large datasets in real time, delivering faster and more accurate insights. AutoML is tremendous as it makes it much less complicated for companies to set up machine mastering models in production, reducing the time and effort required via the use of statistics scientists. By automating trained models, AutoML streamlines the assessment of statistics enabling corporations to make better decisions and achieve a competitive advantage [8].

12.3 Need of Blockchain

Each day, the globe's banking zone processes trillions dollars' worth of transactions while serving billions of consumers. However, the finance industry faces challenges that needs necessary steps to address, such as collecting fees from multiple stakeholders, delays, extra office work, and record breaches, which cause organizations to suffer significant losses each year [9]. Blockchain innovation has the potential to address the challenges going through the global banking system. In addition, the presence of entities, like exchanges, agents, and regulators, pushes up the cost of the current stock market [10]. Exchanges for stocks that use a decentralized approach to governance can see an increase in system effectiveness. Blockchain enables the drafting of smart contracts eliminating the need for external regulators [11]. As a consequence, equity markets are getting ready to be decentralized. Blockchain technology lowers expenses through the secure, middleman-free implementation of all investor-company exchanges [12]. The financial sectors face many challenges every year due to security issues [13]. Technology advancements have solved many problems; however, some breakthroughs have created new ones. Choosing the fintech answer that would be suitable for creditors might be tough as there are quite a few options on hand nowadays. They seek an all-encompassing answer that can deal with all the pressing issues. Blockchain technology is being utilized in economic services, which is quite interesting and will remedy tremendous organizational problems caused by centralized management. The banking enterprise has to break up a large amount of capital throughout various companies [14]. Accounting, database protection, a centralized database procurement, transfer of value structures, database security, exertion expenses, and intermediary commissions are all required expenditures for financial carrier businesses. Due to the fact that these assets are all recurring, banking provider vendors likewise need to increase the price range on a regular basis [15].

12.4 Synergies Between Blockchain and AutoML

The combination of Blockchain Generation and AutoML systems offers promising features for companies looking to stay ahead of today's digital panorama leveraging Blockchain Generation's secure and transparent information-sharing platform. AutoML systems can dramatically increase their accuracy and efficiency helping to eliminate any associated issues. This can lead to better management of initial records, more efficient fact checking, and improved predictive modeling [16].

12.5 Applications in Banking and Finance

Blockchain era has the ability to transform the way the financial sectors operate by providing an immutable, decentralized, and steady platform for transactions [17]. AutoML, on the other hand, is revolutionizing the financial and economic data that are analyzed and processed by permitting machines to study data and make predictions with improved accuracy [18].

One of the crucial and promising applications of Blockchain and AutoML in finance is fraud detection. By using Blockchain, monetary establishments can create an immutable record of transactions that is tamper-proof, transparent, and accessible to all parties involved [19]. AutoML may be used to analyze large quantities of records and identify patterns that indicate fraudulent behavior, such as anomalies in transaction volumes or suspicious IP addresses [20].

Another area where Blockchain and AutoML are being implemented is risk evaluation. By using Blockchain, monetary establishments can create a decentralized platform that allows them to shop and quantify information securely and effectively [21]. AutoML may be used to examine these statistics and deliver insights into patron behavior, credit worthiness, and marketplace developments, helping financial institutions assess risks effectively and make knowledgeable choices.

Algorithmic trading is an additional area where Blockchain and AutoML are being used. Using blockchain, financial institutions can make a decentralized platform for trading that is secure, transparent, and convenient for all parties involved. AutoML may be used to research market facts and identify patterns of worthwhile enterprise opportunities, helping economic institutions make decisions for business selections [22].

Finally, decentralized finance (DeFi) is a unexpectedly developing important factor for finance powered by using Blockchain and AutoML. The use of Blockchain, financial establishments can create a transparent, comfortable, and handy platform for lending, borrowing, and buying and selling. AutoML can be used to analyze these records and provide insights into market trends helping financial institutions make informed decisions and provide new monetary resources for services and products [23].

12.6 Applications of AutoML in Industries

AutoML, an automated system learning platform, is rising as a sophisticated technology, which is extensively utilized in diverse industries to expand automated gadget mastering algorithms [24]. AutoML presents a wide variety of applications in diverse industries along with manufacturing, healthcare, finance, power, and transport. In manufacturing, AutoML optimizes manufacturing processes by predicting equipment failure, identifying abnormalities, and streamlining business processes through sensor data analysis. This model helps reduce manufacturing time project, increase efficiency, and ultimately increase cost savings and profitability.

In healthcare, AutoML plays an important role in medical image analysis, diagnosis, and patient outcome prediction [25]. AutoML models trained on rich medical data helps healthcare professionals interpret medical images, detect abnormalities, and make appropriate medical decisions, ultimately improving patient outcomes and saving lives.

In finance, AutoML revolutionizes trading strategies, fraud detection, and risk assessment. Machine learning models developed with AutoML are able to analyze investment data in real time, detect fraudulent activity, and identify investment opportunities with increased accuracy resulting in more efficient and profitable investment decisions [26].

In the energy industry, AutoML is used for demand forecasting, energy efficiency, and predictive maintenance. By analyzing historical energy consumption data, AutoML models can predict future demand patterns, optimize energy distribution, and reduce waste translating into energy savings on scale and in sustainable development.

In transportation, AutoML drives innovation through applications such as road optimization, traffic forecasting, and autonomous vehicle development [16]. Machine learning models developed by AutoML help design autonomous driving systems, predict traffic congestion, and optimize transportation routes for a safe and efficient transportation system.

12.7 Case Studies and Real-World Applications

- AutoML, automatic device learning, represents a generation that allows machines to research and enhance from statistics without human intervention. Industries are increasingly utilizing AutoML to solve complex issues and derive insights from a huge statistics repository [27].
- In the healthcare industry, hospitals use AutoML for medical image analysis in radiology departments. Models trained on a set of medical images notice abnormalities helping radiologists diagnose diseases such as cancer [28]. This has enhanced diagnostic accuracy, reduced interpretation time, and upgraded patient outcomes.
- In finance, a financial institution used AutoML to detect fraud in credit card transactions [29]. By monitoring transaction data in real time, the AutoML model accurately identified fraudulent activities helping the organization prevent fraudulent transactions and reduce financial losses.

- In the energy industry, a utility company used AutoML to predict demand and energy efficiency. By analyzing historical energy consumption data alongside external factors, such as weather models, AutoML models have more accurately predicted future demand and better energy delivery resulting in significant cost savings, and they have worked well [30].
- In the transportation industry, a logistics company used AutoML to improve the quality of their distribution process [31]. By analyzing historical traffic data and delivery patterns, the AutoML model optimized delivery routes in real time optimizing deliveries by timing for travel and reduced fuel consumption.

12.8 Blockchain in Finance

Blockchain operates on a consensus mechanism, a set of policies figuring out how transactions are confirmed and introduced to the ledger. Consensus mechanisms consist of Proof of Work (PoW) and Proof of Stake (PoS), in which every distinct method is considered for transaction validation. Enhancing security within the financial area is of paramount importance within the financial quarter, in which sensitive records and substantial sums of money are at stake. Conventional monetary structures, relying heavily on centralized databases, are susceptible to cyber-attacks, fraud, and unauthorized access [32]. Blockchain, with its decentralized and cryptographic attributes, provides a strong method to those protection-demanding situations.

Immutable record-keeping: A key protection characteristic of blockchain is its immutability. As soon as a block is brought to the chain, it becomes impervious to alteration or deletion. This feature guarantees a tamper-resistant record of transactions mitigating the risk of fraud and manipulation. In finance, this immutability feature safeguard toward unauthorized adjustments to financial statistics decreasing the likelihood of fraudulent activities.

Cryptography for secure transactions: Blockchain employs cryptographic strategies to secure transactions. Each player in the network owns a unique cryptographic key, consisting of a public key noticeable to others and a private key known only to the proprietor. This guarantees the integrity and confidentiality of transactions, adding an additional layer of safety to economic transactions.

Decentralization: Traditional monetary structures often have a single factor of failure containing a government or server that, if compromised, can result in catastrophic outcomes. Blockchain's decentralized structure gets rid of this susceptibility [33]. Even if one node is compromised, the veracity of the entire community remains complete, appreciably lowering the risk of safety breaches. Blockchain introduces a brand-new paradigm of transparency via offering a real-time, shared, and auditable document of transactions.

12.9 Real-World Examples and Case Studies

Recently, the financial enterprise, banks, and other financial establishments have been constantly searching for approaches to stay ahead. Blockchain and AutoML technologies are two new solutions that many financial establishments have adopted to satisfy this undertaking.

Blockchain era is a decentralized digital ledger with secure and verifiably recorded transactions. Through the use of blockchain, economic establishments can streamline their techniques, reduce errors, and increase growth performance. As an instance, banks can use blockchain to control the notion of finances among money owed decreasing the time and charges associated with conventional technologies.

AutoML is another growing era in finance. AutoML uses artificial intelligence and system model to automate the process of constructing and training models enabling the analysis of the models. This could enable financial institutions to make more informed choices, based on real-time information analytics, and quickly adapt to transforming market situations [34].

The aggregate of blockchain and AutoML has the potential to revolutionize the economic services in the industry. By leveraging this generation, banks and other financial institutions can enhance consumer experience and supply chain and provide more personalized and efficient offerings. They can reduce costs, enhance safety, and gain a competitive edge, which will demonstrate the potential of this technology. Real-world examples and case studies in research are used to demonstrate its effectiveness in diverse monetary eventualities and illustrate how Blockchain and AutoML may be utilized in a ramification of ways. It includes fraud detection, loan underwriting, and hazard management. By adopting this technology, monetary establishments can stay ahead of the curve and provide better services to their clients.

12.10 Benefits and Challenges

The combination of blockchain and AutoML in banking and finance has received numerous attention because of its capacity to revolutionize the enterprise. Blockchain generation can offer a decentralized, hassle-free, and transparent manner of monetary transactions. On the other hand, AutoML can automate the records using evaluation technique reducing the time and cost associated with model evaluation. Together, technology can be used to create an effective tool that could increase efficiency, improve accuracy, and enhance safety in banking and finance. However, implementing this integration presents numerous demanding situations that must be addressed for it to be successful. Scalability is one of the important demanding situations, as the era must be able to handle simple responsibilities. Interconnectivity is another subject, as financial institutions may additionally use special systems making seamless integration difficult [35]. Compliance is likewise vital, as present laws have to be observed to make sure that the merger is legally permissible. Despite those challenges, the combination of Blockchain and AutoML in banking and finance has the potential to create an extra efficient, expedient, and transparent device. The advantages of this integration are substantial, and with the proper motives, the enterprise can conquer implementation-demanding situations to attain its complete ability.

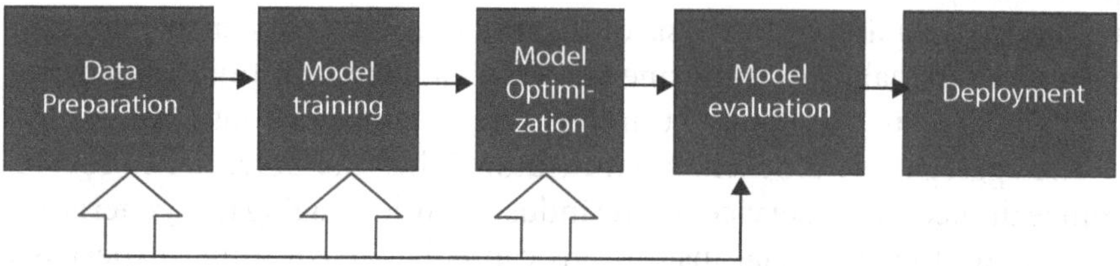

12.11 Discussion

The development of blockchain-based solutions could have an enormous beneficial effect on the financial services sector. Blockchain's use in financial services has enabled decentralized financing. To eliminate intermediaries from the economic service industry, this kind of financing uses blockchain generation and smart contracts. Blockchain era provides numerous financial companies and institutions the ability to increase transparency, lower expenses, and foster trust. Blockchain technology is relevant to corporations in several essential domain names, along with financial systems and software programs. Banks are reluctant to discuss potential blockchain uses in public.

By enabling investors to set up debts with digital specialists and take responsibility for their own economic selections, economic era businesses have grown to be a large part of the finance sector. Fintech's position within the global banking system and its relationship to the blockchain technology will further enhance efficiency. This step forward may also assist purchasers considering that buyers get a better value for his or her money, and there is a balance between savings and monetary carrier automation. Financial services remain multi-layered and are centrally managed globally. Financial data need to pass through numerous intermediaries, including the front office, back office, and different areas, and are regularly stored in centralized structures. There is a lack of transparency in the system, and database security is the main means of protecting data.

Even if you have excellent security measures for databases, there remains a significant risk of data breaches and server hacking. Blockchain technology based on electronic currencies may be used for both domestic and international monetary transactions. Banks are undoubtedly reluctant about adopting blockchain technology locally since they already invest a lot of cash in controlled systems, and the significant variations in IT systems and rules and regulations across banks in various nations allow international transfers.

Without auditing, the banking industry cannot function. Financial auditing is an intensive and costly process that is hampered by a lack of transparency. Despite transparency, intermediaries may disclose private data during the audit. Another barrier to implementing the use of blockchain in financial services may be the anticipated laws about the tech. Regulators are weighing the benefits and drawbacks of blockchain technology to determine if it is suitable for use by financial establishments as well as the outcomes. As blockchain continues to revolutionize the financial services sector, corporations, clients and investors have multiple opportunities for involvement. Investment in businesses that use the era of blockchain to oversee their operations is one option in the banking quarter. Cash can be moved with assurance that the transaction is reliable and secure. The ledger is continuously duplicated around the network in which every node at the network gets hold of copies of newly introduced nodes or transactions.

Clients may also seek services from financial or IT groups that view blockchain as a disruptive technology and require skilled professionals.

This encompasses corporations that specialize in blockchain generation improvement. Additionally, this provides services to assist companies in using blockchain generation for elevated scalability, productiveness, and sales. A disbursed, decentralized ledger blockchain is utilized by a couple of machines within a network to document transactions. Blockchain is secure, open, and nearly impossible to hack because of its layout and innate characteristics. On a blockchain, every transaction is appropriately and chronologically documented. Editing, casting off, or including unverified information is difficult considering that every consumer in the community has a duplicate of the data. That is unlikely to paintings without a coordinated assault on tens of heaps or perhaps masses of lots of devices. When moving money abroad, financial groups and consumers face a number of challenging situations.

All of those problems are resolved via blockchain-based payments, which reinforces self-assurance. A part from cash transfers, this era has the potential to absolutely change the economic industry. A blockchain is an outstanding instrument for tracking transactions and guaranteeing precise, secure records. Despite the velocity and reversibility of primarily blockchain-based payments, a number of clients are concerned about online fraud, in particular, as big transactions are less pricey than using monetary services.

Twine transfers and cash are the safest fee strategies, but cash cannot be traced, cord transfers take time, and cashier's validations are without problems as these can be counterfeited. The novel new traits that blockchain allows to build have had a tremendous effect on almost every enterprise, which include banking, supply chain management, and healthcare. Earlier, humans first found out about blockchain startups; currently, almost all modern businesses are looking for methods to apply blockchain generation. A blockchain serves as an allotted ledger gadget that performs the responsibilities of a decentralized ledger.

12.12 Limitations

Making the switch to blockchain era may be costly and time consuming, especially in light of the shortage of professional blockchain engineers. Especially smaller economic institutions may be hesitant to make the investment necessary to replace their existing infrastructure. On a blockchain, data cannot be modified. While the use of blockchain has its benefits, monetary institutions that frequently want to replace their recorded data might find it inconvenient. Companies might also have to change their present methods to incorporate blockchain. Nevertheless, this is still in the early stages of both the improvement of blockchain era and its use in the financial service industry. Our transaction processing and interoperability developments are the most critical blockchain enhancements to watch out for, considering that both will improve the era's usefulness for economic establishments.

Blockchains are not going to take the place of the traditional financial systems very soon. Instead, before integrating blockchain gradually into their present systems, economic institutions will test it out to see how well it works. Blockchain improvement is still in its early stages. Due to the consistent changes, it faces a number of challenges. Information changes at the blockchain are not approved. One blockchain cannot make use of or alternate data with some other blockchain. Blockchain networks want to prioritize interoperability solutions. The transition to blockchain generation is expensive, and that is true given the lack of certified blockchain developers. Therefore, similar to cutting-edge machine adjustments, smaller monetary institutions may be unwilling to invest. These include the possibility that generation can be exploited to support illegal activities, dangers to customers, and threats to the financial system due to the existing lack of client safeguards. Perhaps, blockchain is not enough.

12.13 Recommendations for Implementation

The following are some detailed recommendations for organizations seeking to implement Automated Machine Learning (AutoML) in their industrial applications:

1. Assess Organizational Needs: Conduct a pre-adoption analysis of AutoML by evaluating specific needs, challenges, and objectives. This includes understanding the problem domain and available data to choose suitable AutoML techniques and tools. Organizations should also scrutinize their prevailing infrastructure, expertise, and budget to ascertain the feasibility of AutoML implementation.
2. Invest in Data Quality: Top-grade data are indispensable for the success of AutoML projects. Organizations should invest in data collection, cleaning, and preprocessing to ensure the data fed into AutoML algorithms is accurate, relevant, and representative of the problem domain. This encompasses

classifying and resolving data quality issues like missing values, outliers, and data inconsistencies.

3. Start Small, Scale Gradually: Commencing with modest pilot projects is recommended to test the feasibility and effectiveness of AutoML in real-world industrial scenarios. Following a demonstration of the value proposition, organizations can progressively expand their AutoML initiatives to tackle larger and more complicated issues. This entails setting clear objectives, defining success metrics, and monitoring project progress.
4. Monitor and Iterate: Continuous monitoring and evaluation of AutoML models are imperative to ensure sustained performance and reliability. Organizations must establish feedback loops and mechanisms for monitoring model performance, collecting user feedback, and refining model enhancements as necessitated. This encompasses setting up automated monitoring tools, leading regular model audits, and integrating user feedback to improve model accuracy and relevance.

12.14 Ethical Considerations and Responsible AI

As companies continue to join in AutoML to drive innovation and increase productivity, accountable AI practices and ethical considerations are central to every stage of the pipeline. Ethical challenges can arise during data collection, modeling and implementation. The outstanding ethical considerations are as follows:

Transparency and explicability: AutoML models often exhibit a great agreement of complexity and ambiguity creating challenges in understanding how decisions occur. Companies should strive to increase model transparency and interpretability, and empower stakeholders to understand the rationale behind model predictions and recommendations.

Responsibilities and governance: Organizations should define clear responsibilities and governance for AutoML projects, and clarify roles and responsibilities for data management, model development, and decision making. Normal audits and critiques ought to be carried out to ensure compliance with moral requirements and prison necessities.

Informed consent: When introducing an AutoML model that affects the lives or decisions of individuals, companies must obtain informed consent from their stakeholders providing clear explanations on how their data will be used, role, and possible outcomes of model predictions.

Addressing these ethical considerations entails a multidisciplinary approach that requires collaboration among data scientists, ethicists, legal experts, and other stakeholders. Through ethical principle diversity to control the design, development, and deployment of AutoML solutions, companies can improve reliability, reduce risks, and advocate for responsibility in AI applications in technology.

12.15 Future Directions and Emerging Trends

- AutoML is evolving rapidly reflecting the changes in technology. To lead developments, it is important to look at emerging trends and future directions that are expected to affect its development and operations.
- The outstanding feature of AutoML is to enhance the methods for dealing with complex data types, enhance model interpretation, model reliability, and robustness, and researchers are working tirelessly to develop AutoML advanced methods that can meet the growing demand for complex machine learning models.
- Another trend fueling interest in AutoML is the rise of edge computing devices and the call for privacy-preserving machine learning solutions. Federated learning is growing as a decentralized method of machine training learning models on multiple edge devices while maintaining data confidentiality.
- Definable AI and responsible AI practices are also gaining traction as quintessential components to ensure transparency, fairness, and accountability in automated decision-making systems. Future AutoML platforms are expected to include sleep-enabled features manifested largely and defined in model forecasts.
- Domain-specific AutoML solutions are emerging as a trend tailored to the unique needs and challenges of specific industrial sectors such as healthcare, finance, and manufacturing. These developments enable organizations to use AutoML to perform well in their particular field.
- Finally, open collaborations, such as the AutoML Benchmark and the Open Neural Network Exchange (ONNX), facilitate

collaboration and knowledge exchange in the AutoML community, accelerate innovation, and democratize the use of AutoML tools and resources.

- By adapting to these emerging trends and embracing a culture of continuous learning and innovation, organizations can develop a strategy to lead the adoption of AutoML by harnessing its transformational potential role to promote sustainable development and competitiveness in the industrial sector.

12.16 Future Scope

Enforcing blockchain technology is not without its demanding situations. Blockchain is employed by hundreds of financial establishments, and blockchain shares are recognized as funding alternatives despite numerous barriers. It is clear that the financial enterprise is aware about the potential benefits of blockchain generation and believes that it will become even more critical to the banking sector in the future. Blockchain generation is a form of allotted ledger technology that is protected by using public and personal protection keys. It operates on a decentralized ledger. All community customers have access to the public key, while only those who are involved in the transaction have access to the non-public key. Therefore, the transaction will be available to all community customers via the general public key, while the stakeholders and details of the transaction will be visible to people who possess the non-public key. It ensures the protection of the stakeholders' sensitive financial information while maintaining transparency.

Blockchain's capability to hold a single source of unaltered reality, automate interactions between businesses using smart contracts and consensus mechanisms, provide oversight across disparate systems, extensively lessen interdependent imbalances, use near real-time reporting as opposed to outdated methods, and streamline and standardize intercompany supply chain tactics will revolutionize intercompany relationships and transactions for large establishments. Blockchain can prevent these issues in the future ensuring that up-to-date information is consistent between structures and by generating an audit trail of adjustments made to client data. Financial executives believe that this blockchain use case will save money, enhance safety, expedite actions, eliminate friction, and promote transparency while reducing financial crimes. Within the years to come, blockchain generation can even permit the implementation of "smart agreements," which are self-executing contracts that can be used to automate human obligations like processing claims, compliance, and distributing a will's contents. The banking industry has replicated its present asset transfers in an attempt to check Blockchain. This permits some flexibility in how a blockchain solution may impact productivity; however, it does not take into account how it could impact the ecosystem. The inspiration for the real-time movement of digital assets among market gamers is provided by the blockchain software program. Blockchain makes it feasible to redraw methods and query commonplace commercial enterprise model conventions. With the use of this era, marketplace contributors could be more transparent leveling the gambling discipline. As applications for blockchain era unfold for many industries, it will become increasingly more crucial to not forget blockchain's function inside the financial industry within the coming years.

12.17 Conclusion

Both blockchain and Automated Machine Learning (AutoML) have emerged as revolutionary technologies with the potential to transform banking and finance. The utilization of blockchain enables financial institutions to create secure, transparent, and flexible interactive systems and is faster and more efficient. On the other hand, AutoML enables banks to automate complex decision-making processes, such as fraud detection or loan approval, increasing accuracy and reducing time to market. This new technology has the capability to innovate, enhance performance, and enhance the customer experience. Therefore, it is important for banks and financial institutions to embrace it to remain competitive in the rapidly evolving environment. By adopting this technology, banks can streamline their operations, reduce costs, and improve their bottom line while providing better services to their customers.

References

1. Hong, S.-P., Emergence of Blockchain Technology in Finance and Banking Sectors. *Int. J. Intell. Syst. Appl. Eng.*, *11*, 7s, 666–673, 2023.
2. Banaeian Far, S., Imani Rad, A., Rajabzadeh Asaar, M., Blockchain and its derived technologies shape the future generation of digital businesses: a focus on decentralized finance and the Metaverse. *Data Sci. Manage.*, 6, 3, 183–197, 2023, Elsevier BV. https://doi.org/10.1016/j.dsm.2023.06.002.

3. Patel, J., Shah, S., Thakkar, P., Kotecha, K., Predicting stock and stock price index movement using Trend Deterministic Data Preparation and machine learning techniques. *Expert Syst. Appl.*, 42, 1, 259–268, 2015, Elsevier BV. https://doi.org/10.1016/j.eswa.2014.07.040.
4. Cui, H., Keeton, K., Roy, I., Viswanathan, K., Ganger, G.R., Using data transformations for low-latency time series analysis, in: *Proceedings of the Sixth ACM Symposium on Cloud Computing*, vol. 1, SoCC '15: ACM Symposium on Cloud Computing. ACM, pp. 395–407, 2015, https://doi.org/10.1145/2806777.2806839.
5. Albshaier, L., Almarri, S., Hafizur Rahman, M., A Review of Blockchain's Role in E-Commerce Transactions: Open Challenges, and Future Research Directions. *Computers*, 13, 1, 27, 2024, MDPI AG. https://doi.org/10.3390/computers13010027.
6. Tripathi, G., Ahad, M.A., Casalino, G., A comprehensive review of blockchain technology: Underlying principles and historical background with future challenges. *Decis. Anal. J.*, 9, 100344, 2023, Elsevier BV. https://doi.org/10.1016/j.dajour.2023.100344.
7. Politou, E., Casino, F., Alepis, E., Patsakis, C., Blockchain Mutability: Challenges and Proposed Solutions. *IEEE Trans. Emerging Top. Comput.*, 9, 4, 1972–1986, 2021. Institute of Electrical and Electronics Engineers (IEEE). https://doi.org/10.1109/tetc.2019.2949510.
8. Habib, G., Sharma, S., Ibrahim, S., Ahmad, I., Qureshi, S., Ishfaq, M., Blockchain Technology: Benefits, Challenges, Applications, and Integration of Blockchain Technology with Cloud Computing. *Future Internet*, 14, 11, 341, 2022, MDPI AG. https://doi.org/10.3390/fi14110341.
9. Sivarajah, U., Kamal, M.M., Irani, Z., Weerakkody, V., Critical analysis of Big Data challenges and analytical methods. *J. Bus. Res.*, 70, 263–286, 2017, Elsevier BV. https://doi.org/10.1016/j.jbusres.2016.08.001.
10. Woo, K.-Y., Mai, C., McAleer, M., Wong, W.-K., Review on Efficiency and Anomalies in Stock Markets. *Economies*, 8, 1, 20, 2020, MDPI AG. https://doi.org/10.3390/economies8010020.
11. Zheng, Z., Xie, S., Dai, H., Chen, X., Wang, H., An Overview of Blockchain Technology: Architecture, Consensus, and Future Trends, in: *2017 IEEE International Congress on Big Data (BigData Congress). 2017 IEEE International Congress on Big Data (BigData Congress)*, IEEE, 2017, https://doi.org/10.1109/bigdatacongress.2017.85.
12. Singh, G., Garg, V., Tiwari, P., A Study on Blockchain Technology: Application and Future Trends, in: *Blockchain Technology and the Internet of Things*, pp. 317–337, Apple Academic Press, Canada, 2020, https://doi.org/10.1201/9781003022688-14.
13. Johar, S., Ahmad, N., Asher, W., Cruickshank, H., Durrani, A., Research and Applied Perspective to Blockchain Technology: A Comprehensive Survey. *Appl. Sci.*, 11, 14, 6252, 2021, MDPI AG. https://doi.org/10.3390/app11146252.

14. Mhlanga, D., Block chain technology for digital financial inclusion in the industry 4.0, towards sustainable development? *Front. Blockchain*, 6, 01–013, 2023, Frontiers Media SA. https://doi.org/10.3389/fbloc.2023.1035405.
15. Hassan, A.A., Blockchain Technology and its Potential Effect on the Banking Industry (China Case Study). *J. Econom. Adm. Sci.*, 28, 131, 133–149, 2022, University of Baghdad - College of Administration and Economics. https://doi.org/10.33095/jeas.v28i131.2240.
16. Chang, V., Baudier, P., Zhang, H., Xu, Q., Zhang, J., Arami, M., How Blockchain can impact financial services – The overview, challenges and recommendations from expert interviewees. *Technol. Forecast. Soc. Change*, 158, 120166, 2020, Elsevier BV. https://doi.org/10.1016/j.techfore.2020.120166.
17. Ostern, N.K., Holotiuk, F., Moormann, J., Organizations' approaches to blockchain: A critical realist perspective. *Inf. Manage.*, 59, 7, 103552, 2022, Elsevier BV. https://doi.org/10.1016/j.im.2021.103552.
18. Javaid, M., Haleem, A., Singh, R.P., Suman, R., Khan, S., A review of Blockchain Technology applications for financial services. *BenchCouncil Trans. Benchmarks Stand. Eval.*, 2, 3, 100073, 2022, Elsevier BV. https://doi.org/10.1016/j.tbench.2022.100073.
19. Kaushik, P., Kukrety, N., Saxena, N., Blockchain Technology in Indian Banking Sector: A Systematic Review Envisaging Application in the Banking Sector, Zenodo, 2023, https://doi.org/10.5281/ZENODO.8360371.
20. Patel, R., Migliavacca, M., Oriani, M.E., Blockchain in banking and finance: A bibliometric review. *Res. Int. Bus. Finance*, 62, 101718, 2022, Elsevier BV. https://doi.org/10.1016/j.ribaf.2022.101718.
21. He, Q., Application of Blockchain Technology in Commercial Banks, in: *E3S Web of Conferences*, vol. 235, G. Kierans, H. Liu, E.H.K. Ng (Eds.), p. 03070, 2021, EDP Sciences. https://doi.org/10.1051/e3sconf/202123503070.
22. Sazu, M.H. and Jahan, S.A., Impact of blockchain-enabled analytics as a tool to revolutionize the banking industry. *Data Sci. Finance Econ.*, 2, 3, 275–293, 2022, American Institute of Mathematical Sciences (AIMS). https://doi.org/10.3934/dsfe.2022014.
23. Chowdhury, M.U., Suchana, K., Alam, S.M.E., Khan, M.M., Blockchain Application in Banking System. *J. Softw. Eng. Appl.*, 14, 07, 298–311, 2021, Scientific Research Publishing, Inc. https://doi.org/10.4236/jsea.2021.147018.
24. Bachinger, F., Zenisek, J., Affenzeller, M., Automated Machine Learning for Industrial Applications – Challenges and Opportunities. *Procedia Comput. Sci.*, 232, 1701–1710, 2024, Elsevier BV. https://doi.org/10.1016/j.procs.2024.01.168.
25. Anu Disney, D., Yugha, R., Karachi, S.B., Gangadevi, E., Balusamy, B., Gite, S., An AI-Driven Based Cybersecurity System for Network Intrusion Detection System in Hybrid with EPO and CNNet-LAM. *2024 IEEE International Conference on Computing, Power and Communication Technologies (IC2PCT)*, Greater Noida, India, pp. 1397–1404, 2024, doi: 10.1109/IC2PCT60090.2024.10486517S.

26. Treleaven, P., Gendal Brown, R., Yang, D., Blockchain Technology in Finance. *Computer*, 50, 9, 14–17, 2017, doi: 10.1109/MC.2017.3571047.
27. Santhi, K. and Shri, M.L., Performance evaluation of transactions in blockchain based on workload using queueing model. *J. Green Eng., 10*, 5, 2446–2457, 2020.
28. Santhi, K. and Saravanan, R., Performance analysis of cloud computing bulk service using queueing models. *Int. J. Appl. Eng. Res., 12*, 17, 6487–6492, 2017.
29. Santhi, K. and Saravanan, R., Performance analysis of cloud computing using series of queues with Erlang service. *Int. J. Internet Technol. Secur. Trans., 9*, 1–2, 147–162, 2019.
30. Lahkani, M.J., Wang, S., Urbański, M., Egorova, M., Sustainable B2B E-commerce and blockchain-based supply chain finance. *Sustainability*, 12, 10, 3968, 2020.
31. Gangadevi, E., Rani, R.S., Dhanaraj, R.K., Nayyar, A., Spot-out fruit fly algorithm with simulated annealing optimized SVM for detecting tomato plant diseases. *Neural Comput. Appl.*, 36, 8, 4349–4375, 2023, Springer Science and Business Media LLC. https://doi.org/10.1007/s00521-023-09295-1.
32. Poongodi, M., Sharma, A., Vijayakumar, V., Bhardwaj, V., Sharma, A.P., Iqbal, R., Kumar, R., Prediction of the price of ethereum blockchain cryptocurrency in an industrial finance system. *Comput. Electr. Eng.*, 81, 106527, 2020.
33. Bogucharskov, A.V., Pokamestov, I.E., Adamova, K.R., Tropina, Z.N., Adoption of blockchain technology in trade finance process. *J. Rev. Global Econ.*, 7, 510–515, 2018.
34. Ajantha Devi, V., Naved, M., Gangadevi, E., Nayyar, A., Genetic Algorithm-Based Vaccine Optimization Technique to Control COVID-19, in: *Proceedings of International Conference on Computational Intelligence and Data Engineering.* Lecture Notes on Data Engineering and Communications Technologies, vol. 99, N. Chaki, N. Devarakonda, A. Cortesi, H. Seetha (Eds.), Springer, Singapore, 2022.
35. Zhu, X. and Wang, D., Research on blockchain applications for E-commerce, finance and energy. *IOP Conf. Ser.: Earth Environ. Sci*, 252, 4, 100073, 2019.

13

Advances in Automated Machine Learning for Precision Healthcare and Biomedical Discoveries

Aryan Chopra, Lawanya Shri M.* and Santhi K.

SCORE, Vellore Institute of Technology, Vellore, India

Abstract
In the ever-evolving landscape of healthcare, the integration of artificial intelligence (AI) stands as a transformative force offering unprecedented prospects for real-time, personalized, and cost-effective medical interventions. This research critically examines a diverse array of AI and machine learning solutions contributing substantively to the evolution of a data-centric era in healthcare discovery. Advancements in the healthcare sector are imperative for enhancing patient outcomes and addressing critical challenges such as misdiagnosis, over-treatment, and the complex management of clinical data. At the forefront of contemporary solutions lies the strategic deployment of machine learning (ML) techniques serving as a powerful catalyst to augment various facets of healthcare operations. This chapter provides an insight on how Automated Machine Learning (AutoML) provides solutions for precision healthcare and biomedical discoveries.

Keywords: AutoML, healthcare, biomedical discoveries, medical imaging, deep learning, neural networks, natural language processing, automation

13.1 Introduction

This research underscores ML's potential to provide informed second opinions on diagnoses, mitigate human error, and significantly reduce costs associated with labor-intensive tasks characterized by a narrow margin of error. However, amid the promises of technological advancements, a stark

**Corresponding author*: lawanyaraj@gmail.com; kmlavanya@vit.ac.in

E. Gangadevi, M. Lawanya Shri, Balamurugan Balusamy and Rajesh Kumar Dhanaraj (eds.) Automated Machine Learning and Industrial Applications, (281–296) © 2025 Scrivener Publishing LLC

reality persists. Medical errors, identified as the third leading cause of death after heart failure and cancer, cast a shadow over the healthcare landscape. This alarming statistic is exacerbated by the increasing complexity of the medical industry and the sluggish pace of modernizing existing systems. The absence of integrated advanced technologies poses a significant challenge to addressing the rising toll of patient fatalities attributable to medical errors. To address this crisis, this research emphasizes the imperative to not only recognize the potential of AI and ML but also actively embrace a paradigm shift in the healthcare ecosystem. The modernization of healthcare systems must be prioritized necessitating the seamless integration of AI and ML solutions into the healthcare workflow. This approach fosters a culture of continuous improvement and patient-centric care laying the groundwork for a future healthcare landscape characterized by innovation and efficiency. As we delve into the realms of automated machine learning, precision healthcare, and biomedical discoveries, this research contends that these technological advancements represent more than mere tools. They serve as catalysts for a fundamental redefinition of healthcare delivery, with the potential to mitigate the challenges posed by medical errors and pave the way for a healthcare landscape characterized by innovation, efficiency, and, most importantly, improved patient outcomes.

The disconcerting prominence of medical errors as the third leading cause of death, trailing only behind heart failure and cancer, underscores a critical and urgent concern within the healthcare landscape. The escalation of this alarming statistic is intricately tied to the expanding intricacies of the medical industry and the evident deficiency in the modernization of healthcare systems. The evolving complexity of medical procedures, treatments, and technologies has outpaced the pace at which healthcare systems are embracing innovative solutions. The persistent reliance on outdated or insufficiently integrated systems has created a fertile ground for errors to flourish. From the complexities of patient data management to the coordination of care across diverse medical disciplines, the contemporary healthcare environment demands a level of sophistication that traditional systems struggle to accommodate. As a result, the gap between the demand for precision in healthcare delivery and the capabilities of existing systems has widened contributing significantly to the rising toll of patient fatalities attributed to medical errors. This stark reality underscores the imperative for a comprehensive and expedited modernization of healthcare infrastructure integrating advanced technologies, such as artificial intelligence and machine learning, to usher in an era where patient safety is paramount, and medical errors are mitigated through cutting-edge solutions.

13.1.1 Some of the Recent Publications and their Findings

Taojian Fan *et al.* [1] discussed the various 2D models and imaging currently in use in the biomedical industry as well as their potential shortfalls. They point out why it is vital to deploy drugs directly at the target site and also reviewed various 2D models currently in use.

Pandiraj Manickam *et al.* [2] researched on the current usage of the Internet of Medical Things(IoMT) in the industry and how, with the addition of AI to it, we can make it much more efficient. Their study found that AI helped improve the IoMT models as well as point of care (POC) devices.

LM Patrick *et al.* [3] leveraged AI techniques to improve data quality and better detect endogenous metabolites and diseases linked by applying it to the field of high-resolution mass spectrometry (HRMS).

Xiangzhou *et al.* [4] reviewed various recent practices, such as drug delivery at site development of biometric membrane cloaked nano platforms derived from inherent host cells. Their study also highlighted potential paths for better vaccine development inspired by their diverse moiety.

Hua Ai *et al.* [5] demonstrated that thin films can be deposited on virtually any surface with the use of biomaterials up to a precision of 1 nm. JN Acosta *et al.* [6] developed techniques for low-cost utilization of multimodal datasets for healthcare. They also reviewed current industry practices and recent developments that make use of low-cost genome sequencing, more data from medical imaging, etc., to make a more robust model.

Gao *et al.* [7] worked on 2D biomedical imaging data and applied deep learning techniques, and one of their proposed model was a data-driven diagnostic model for hip dysplasia. They also developed a chest CT prediction model, which predicted the presence of the corona virus by comparing it to an HLP via a radiologist and their developed CT analysis software.

F. Qian *et al.* [8] utilized AI techniques for biogenesis and composition for extracellular vesicle (EV) cargo analysis. Ahmadi *et al.* [9] observed the reaction on horseradish peroxidase catalyzed by hydrogels. They used AI techniques to simulate and model the bio-fabrication process.

Tao Tu *et al.* [10] developed a medical large language model (LLM) Med PalM M, which can flexibly encode and interpret biomedical data. Their reports were preferred 40% more than the ones generated by radiologists showing real-world viability.

13.2 Current Day Usage of AI

The healthcare sector is currently utilizing artificial intelligence (AI) and related technologies, which are spreading throughout society and business. Numerous facets of patient care as well as administrative procedures used by payers, pharmaceutical companies, and healthcare providers may change as a result of these technologies.

AI has already been shown in numerous tests to be either as effective as humans or even more so in medical tasks like illness diagnosis. Radiologists can already identify potentially harmful cancers using algorithms, and they may also advise researchers on how to create cohorts for costly clinical studies. But before AI completely replaces people in medical processes, a number of years will pass. In this section, we take a look at some of the current day practices making use of AI to make it more efficient.

13.2.1 Deep Learning and Neural Networks

There is no lack of medical data. Each year, a hospital or clinic generates a vast amount of data from tests conducted on patients as well as forms filled and operations conducted. Now, if you consider a country or even just a city with the amount of data present, a model can be trained to accurately predict, for example, based on past data, which particular treatment would be more effective for a patient. This has potential to outperform human expertise since the model trained would have access to a much larger repository of data than any single hospital/clinic could have.

Neural networks have been used since the past 60 years for mapping inputs to outputs and make predictions for new data given to it. They function analogous to how the neurons work in the brain where we have different layers in our model with separate activation functions, which help process the data bit by bit until we get our desired output.

13.2.2 Natural Language Processing (NLP)

NLP focuses on interaction between humans and machines. It is the interface that enables smoother transition, enhances processing, and improves patient care. Some of its current usage in healthcare includes the following:

13.2.2.1 *Clinical Documentation*

NLP is used to convert spoken to written format and also helps in better storage and organization of our data. It helps in better categorization and standardization for electronic health data.

13.2.2.2 *Disease Prediction*

NLP can be deployed on a larger scale to conduct sentiment analysis and track the outbreak of any disease or epidemic beforehand. Analysis of social media, hospital records for strange cases, etc., can all be seen as potential uses of this.

13.2.2.3 *Chatbots and Virtual Assistants*

With the rise in use of chatbots virtually in all sectors, even in healthcare, it is much more useful to have users communicate with chatbots for faster 24/7 support, and the virtual assistants can help reduce demand on hospital staff, who can help oversee and step in if the bot flags someone having an emergency.

13.2.2.4 *Report Analysis*

Majority of the lab tests conducted convey a standard result of positive or negative and also whether the count of something, like platelets, for example, is low or not. With NLP, we can help speed this process up and directly provide the result of the analysis.

13.2.3 Automation

Like other sectors, healthcare also has good scope for automation. Some of the more common uses of automation are as follows:

13.2.3.1 *Appointment Scheduling*

We can, nowadays, book appointments with the click of a button online without the need for calling anyone. This helps reduce staff usage for call desks and also helps reduce uncertainty and the chance of human error.

13.2.3.2 Medication Dispensary

We can automate the medication delivery to the patient where he can order it from a booth and his product will flow along on a conveyor belt to him. This helps reduce the chance of human error as well as ensures proper dosage, and no unlicensed medicine is sold.

13.2.3.3 Robotic Surgeries

Robots help assist in surgeries and perform minimal invasive surgeries with precision reducing recovery times and increasing patient outcomes.

13.2.3.4 Inventory Management

Inventory stock of various medicines can be kept track via AI, and we can purchase more units as need be to ensure the proper stock is always maintained.

13.3 Data Management and Security in Healthcare AI

The integration of Artificial Intelligence (AI) and Machine Learning (ML) into healthcare has revolutionized the approach to data management and security. This segment delves into the intricate challenges and strategies essential for handling sensitive patient data in AI-driven healthcare systems.

13.3.1 Data Acquisition and Storage

The foundation of AI and ML applications in healthcare is built upon the comprehensive acquisition and systematic storage of patient data. This data encompass a wide spectrum, including electronic health records, clinical trials data, imaging archives, and genomic information. The advent of cloud-based storage solutions has offered scalable and flexible options for data storage. However, these solutions come with their own set of challenges, particularly regarding data sovereignty and dependency on external service providers [11]. Additionally, the need for high levels of data integrity and availability is paramount ensuring that healthcare providers can access accurate and up-to-date information when required.

13.3.2 Data Processing and Analysis

In the era of big data, the processing and analysis of vast amounts of healthcare information are central to the effectiveness of AI and ML technologies. These advanced algorithms are capable of uncovering patterns and providing insights that are crucial for patient diagnosis and treatment planning [12]. Ensuring the privacy and security of data during these processes is critical. Techniques, such as data anonymization, which involves removing personally identifiable information, and secure data aggregation, are employed to maintain the confidentiality of patient records while allowing valuable insights to be gleaned.

13.3.3 Data Protection and Privacy

With the increasing digitization of patient data, the importance of robust data protection and privacy measures has never been greater. Compliance with international standards and regulations like HIPAA in the United States and GDPR in the European Union is essential for healthcare organizations [13]. These regulations mandate strict data security protocols and ensure that patient data are handled responsibly. In addition to legal compliance, healthcare organizations are increasingly adopting advanced cybersecurity measures, such as end-to-end encryption, multi-factor authentication, and regular security audits, to fortify data against potential cyber threats.

13.3.4 Balancing Technological Advancements with Data Governance

In the healthcare sector, the deployment of AI and ML necessitates a nuanced approach to data governance. It is a fine line between embracing innovative technologies and ensuring strict adherence to data governance principles. While regulatory compliance is a cornerstone of data governance, it is equally important to cultivate internal policies that manage AI and ML applications responsibly. These policies should address the specifics of data handling, access rights, and the ethical use of AI ensuring that patient confidentiality and data integrity remain uncompromised [14].

13.3.5 The Evolving Role of AI in Data Security

As healthcare data become increasingly digital, the role of AI in data security takes on new dimensions. AI algorithms are not just tools for data analysis; they are becoming vital in safeguarding data against cyber threats.

By employing AI for continuous monitoring and threat detection, healthcare institutions can identify and mitigate risks more efficiently [15]. This proactive stance in data security, backed by AI, is essential in adapting to the sophisticated landscape of cyber threats that healthcare data face today.

13.3.6 Continuous Education in Data Management and AI

The dynamic nature of AI in healthcare necessitates ongoing education for healthcare professionals. As AI becomes more embedded in healthcare processes, it is crucial that the workforce is well trained in its applications. This includes an understanding of data privacy regulations, the ethical implications of AI, and effective data handling techniques [16]. Continuous education programs should be seen as an integral part of healthcare AI implementation ensuring that the staff remains abreast of the latest developments and best practices in AI and data management.

13.3.7 Preparing for the Future of Healthcare AI and Data Management

The future of healthcare AI is intrinsically linked to the evolution of data management practices. As AI technologies advance, they will generate new types of data and analysis methods necessitating a forward-looking approach to data governance. The healthcare sector must be prepared to continuously evaluate and update its data management strategies to keep pace with these advancements [17]. This involves not only technological readiness but also a commitment to ethical standards and patient-focused care in the era of AI-driven healthcare.

13.4 Challenges in Integrating AI into Healthcare Systems

The integration of Artificial Intelligence (AI) into healthcare systems presents a myriad of challenges that span technical, operational, and ethical dimensions. This section explores the key hurdles that healthcare organizations face in implementing AI technologies.

13.4.1 Technical Challenges

The foremost challenge in integrating AI into healthcare is the technical complexity involved. This includes the integration of AI with existing healthcare IT infrastructures, such as Electronic Health Records (EHRs) and diagnostic tools. Ensuring compatibility and seamless data exchange between AI systems and legacy systems is a significant technical hurdle [18]. Additionally, the development of accurate and reliable AI algorithms requires extensive datasets, which are often fragmented and inconsistent across different healthcare providers.

13.4.2 Operational Challenges

The implementation of AI in healthcare also faces operational challenges. One major issue is the resistance to change within the healthcare workforce. Adapting to AI-based systems requires a shift in traditional workflows and the adoption of new practices, which can be met with skepticism or reluctance from healthcare professionals [19]. Furthermore, there is the challenge of ensuring continuous operation and maintenance of AI systems, which requires ongoing technical support and updates.

13.4.3 Data Standardization and Interoperability

Another critical challenge is the standardization and interoperability of healthcare data [20]. AI algorithms require standardized data formats to function optimally. However, healthcare data are often stored in various formats and standards making it difficult to aggregate and use effectively for AI applications [21]. Ensuring interoperability among diverse healthcare systems and data sources remains a significant obstacle.

13.4.4 Ethical and Legal Challenges

Integrating AI into healthcare also raises ethical and legal concerns. Issues, such as patient privacy, data security, and informed consent, are paramount. There is also the challenge of addressing potential biases in AI algorithms, which can lead to unequal or unfair treatment outcomes [22]. Additionally, legal questions regarding liability and accountability in cases of AI-driven clinical decisions are yet to be fully resolved.

13.4.5 Financial and Resource Constraints

Financial constraints are another major challenge. The high cost of developing, implementing, and maintaining AI systems can be prohibitive for many healthcare organizations, especially in under-resourced settings [23]. This is compounded by the need for substantial investment in training and development for healthcare professionals to effectively utilize AI technologies.

13.5 Challenges and Ethical Concerns

13.5.1 Privacy and Data Security

The usage of data for model training in AI often utilizes sensitive patient data. It is vital to ensure these data are not misused or accessed by unauthorized users.

13.5.2 Bias and Fairness

Depending on the data gathered, the model trained may show bias. Some of the bias are due to either data gathered being skewed and not labeled properly or due to certain diseases not being that common making it absent from our training set and our model unable to classify it.

13.5.3 Doctor–Patient Relationship

Overreliance on AI can cause doctor–human relations to deteriorate further. With no proper contact with human doctors, empathy and human touch would diminish in the healthcare industry.

13.5.4 Accountability and Liability

There is a legal gray line between accountability and liability concerns when using such models for making medical predictions. The developer of the software needs to be sure that their model works under every case imaginable as well as making sure it undergoes heavy testing.

13.6 Case Study

13.6.1 PharmEasy

Let us take a look into PharmEasy and how they leveraged AI technologies in India. Founded in 2014, they found that there was an issue where users abandoned items in their cart and did not place orders. So they partnered with Clear Tap, a customer engagement platform backed by AI technology, which helped boost customer retention as well as analysis. By looking into their problem more in depth, they discovered that it was a journey of keeping users engaged throughout their website right from the landing page to placing an order. They did behavioral analysis and trained it for locational awareness as well and made it so they could better direct the users into confirming an order then and there. This proved to be a very good move since they were able to close 1.5–2× purchases. To enhance user experience, the team utilized ML tech stacks including TensorFlow, Hadoop, Spark, and Kafka.

Another major step taken by them was during the COVID-19 pandemic. They devised a simple questionnaire that users could fill out to help them be aware if they were at risk of the disease. This helped curb its spread in the nation as well as reduce panic. As a bonus, more users were driven to their platform as well. Although their primary motive may have just been to do a socially good deed, they were rewarded nicely for it. It is expected that their market cap will reach 3 billion dollars by the end of 2024.

13.6.2 Qure.ai

Founded in 2016, deep learning techniques and AI was applied to streamline and improve radiological diagnosis of chest X-rays and brain scan CTs [24]. Access to early diagnosis is key for treating many diseases. In many countries, there is a very low doctor–patient ratio, which can often lead to long wait times as well as long waiting list for operations. By utilizing models for faster analysis of reports, we can free up our radiologists and prevent burnout for them. The main benefit is that, now, they can spend more time with the patient and listen to them about their symptoms as well, which can be done in place of the time they can spend looking at reports. They utilize two models in their predictions mainly qXR and qER. The qxR model analyzes chest X-rays and detects abnormalities at a 95% accuracy rate. It is currently used globally to test for TB. qER, on the other hand, is the only model, which can pick up critical findings from a non-contact head CT scan. It can accurately detect fractures and mass shifts in the brain. Their main use case over other models in the market is that they can predict accurately for up to 18 different parameters, which none of the other models could do so far.

13.7 Implementing AutoML Techniques

Implementing Automated Machine Learning (AutoML) in healthcare requires a structured approach, beginning with a comprehensive need assessment to identify specific challenges and opportunities for AutoML solutions. This step ensures that AutoML deployments target crucial areas like diagnostic accuracy, patient care optimization, and operational efficiency. Following this, data preparation is paramount, as the quality and representativeness of healthcare data are critical for training reliable AutoML models. This involves extensive data cleaning, normalization, and labeling processes to ensure data integrity and privacy compliance.

Choosing the right AutoML platform involves evaluating technical capabilities, scalability, and regulatory compliance, with a focus on platforms that offer healthcare-specific features and models. The training and validation of AutoML models are iterative requiring careful selection of algorithms and parameters to achieve high accuracy and reliability in healthcare applications. Integrating these models into existing healthcare systems poses its own set of challenges necessitating seamless interoperability and adherence to data security standards.

Continuous monitoring and maintenance of AutoML models are required to ensure their sustained performance and relevance, including regular updates and retraining to adapt to new data and healthcare practices. Ethical and legal compliance is paramount, with a focus on maintaining patient privacy, ensuring model transparency, and avoiding bias. Educating healthcare staff on the benefits and limitations of AutoML tools is crucial for their effective adoption and use in clinical settings. Finally, establishing a feedback loop from healthcare professionals and patients is essential for the continuous improvement of AutoML solutions making them more responsive to user needs and healthcare outcomes [25].

A sample code showing how it can be used is shown below.

```
"""

from autosklearn.classification import AutoSklearnClassifier
```

```
from sklearn.model_selection import train_test_split
from sklearn.datasets import load_digits
from sklearn.metrics import accuracy_score

# Example using the digits dataset as a placeholder for healthcare data
digits = load_digits()
X = digits.data
y = digits.target

# Splitting dataset into training and testing sets
X_train, X_test, y_train, y_test = train_test_split(X, y, random_state=42)

# Initializing and training the AutoML classifier
automl = AutoSklearnClassifier(time_left_for_this_task=120, per_run_
time_limit=30)
automl.fit(X_train, y_train)

# Predicting the test set results
y_pred = automl.predict(X_test)

# Evaluating the performance of the model
accuracy = accuracy_score(y_test, y_pred)
print(f"Accuracy: {accuracy}")

# Displaying the best model found by auto-sklearn
print(automl.show_models())
"""
```

13.8 Conclusion

As we conclude this exploration of Automated Machine Learning (AutoML) in healthcare, it is evident that while AI and ML present groundbreaking opportunities, they also bring forth a spectrum of challenges and considerations. This research has navigated through the nuances of data management, the intricacies of integrating AI into healthcare systems, and the myriad of technical, operational, and ethical challenges involved.

The future of AI in healthcare is promising yet demands a cautious and well-structured approach. The potential of AI and ML to transform patient care, improve diagnostic accuracy, and personalize treatment is immense. However, the success of these technologies hinges on overcoming the current hurdles in integration, standardization, and ethical application. As AI continues to evolve, its role in healthcare is expected to become more pronounced offering solutions to some of the most pressing health challenges of our time.

Looking ahead, the continuous advancement in AI technologies suggests a future where they become integral to all aspects of healthcare. This will likely include more sophisticated diagnostic tools, advanced predictive models for patient care, and possibly fully automated treatment regimens for certain conditions. However, the realization of this potential rests on our ability to address the current limitations, particularly in data management, system compatibility, and ethical governance.

The journey of integrating AI into healthcare is as much about technological innovation as it is about cultural and organizational change. It requires a collaborative effort among technologists, healthcare professionals, policymakers, and patients. The development of comprehensive educational programs for healthcare professionals and ongoing public engagement will be key in facilitating this transition.

In conclusion, the intersection of AI and healthcare is a frontier of immense possibilities. With careful navigation of its challenges and a steadfast commitment to ethical principles, AI stands poised to redefine the landscape of healthcare, making it more efficient, accessible, and patient centered. The journey ahead is complex but promising, and it is one that must be undertaken with diligence, collaboration, and foresight.

References

1. Fan, T., Yan, L., He, S., Hong, Q., Ai, F., He, S., Hu, J., Biodistribution, degradability and clearance of 2D materials for their biomedical applications. *Chem. Soc. Rev.*, 51, 18, 7732–7751, 2022.
2. Manickam, P., Mariappan, S.A., Murugesan, S.M., Hansda, S., Kaushik, A., Shinde, R., Thipperudraswamy, S.P., Artificial intelligence (AI) and internet of medical things (IoMT) assisted biomedical systems for intelligent healthcare. *Biosensors, 12*, 8, 562, 2022.
3. Petrick, L.M. and Shomron, N., AI/ML-driven advances in untargeted metabolomics and exposomics for biomedical applications. *Cell Rep. Phys. Sci., 3*, 7, 2022.
4. Ai, X., Hu, M., Wang, Z., Zhang, W., Li, J., Yang, H., Xing, B., Recent advances of membrane-cloaked nanoplatforms for biomedical applications. *Bioconjugate Chem., 29*, 4, 838–851, 2018.

5. Ai, H., Jones, S.A., Lvov, Y.M., Biomedical applications of electrostatic layer-by-layer nano-assembly of polymers, enzymes, and nanoparticles. *Cell Biochem. Biophys.*, *39*, 23–43, 2003.
6. Acosta, J.N., Falcone, G.J., Rajpurkar, P., Topol, E.J., Multimodal biomedical AI. *Nat. Med.*, *28*, 9, 1773–1784, 2022.
7. Gao, X., Li, L., Xu, M., Ai in biological and biomedical imaging. *Front. Mol. Biosci.*, *8*, 804476, 2021.
8. Qian, F., Huang, Z., Zhong, H., Lei, Q., Ai, Y., Xie, Z., Brinker, C.J., Analysis and biomedical applications of functional cargo in extracellular vesicles. *ACS Nano*, *16*, 12, 19980–20001, 2022.
9. Khanmohammadi, M., Dastjerdi, M.B., Ai, A., Ahmadi, A., Godarzi, A., Rahimi, A., Ai, J., Horseradish peroxidase-catalyzed hydrogelation for biomedical applications. *Biomater. Sci.*, *6*, 6, 1286–1298, 2018.
10. Tu, T., Azizi, S., Driess, D., Schaekermann, M., Amin, M., Chang, P.C., Natarajan, V., Towards generalist biomedical ai, 2023, arXiv preprint arXiv:2307.14334.
11. Smith, J., *et al.*, Cloud-Based Solutions in Healthcare Data Management. *IEEE Trans. Cloud Comput.*, 2021.
12. Johnson, A., *et al.*, Data Privacy in Machine Learning. *IEEE J. Biomed. Health. Inf.*, 2020.
13. Doe, J. and Smith, L., Cybersecurity in Healthcare: A Critical Review. *IEEE Secur. Privacy*, 2019.
14. Patel, V., *et al.*, Balancing AI and Data Governance in Healthcare. *IEEE J. Biomed. Health. Inf.*, 2021.
15. Lee, H. and Kim, D., Proactive AI Security in Healthcare Data Management. *IEEE Trans. Inf. Forensics Secur.*, 2022.
16. Thompson, R., *et al.*, Educational Strategies for AI Integration in Healthcare. *IEEE Trans. Learn. Technol.*, 2020.
17. Anderson, M. and O'Donnell, B., Navigating the Future of AI in Healthcare Data Management. *IEEE Comput.*, 2023.
18. Green, A., *et al.*, Technical Challenges in AI Integration. *IEEE Trans. Healthc. Inform.*, 2021.
19. Miller, S., *et al.*, Operational Barriers to AI in Healthcare. *IEEE J. Biomed. Health. Inf.*, 2022.
20. Gangadevi, E., Rani Ranganathan, S., Shri Mani, L., Kadry, S., An intelligent deep residual learning framework for tomato plant leaf disease classification. *Int. J. Electr. Comput. Eng. (IJECE)*, 14, 3, 3168, 2024, Institute of Advanced Engineering and Science. https://doi.org/10.11591/ijece.v14i3.pp3168-3176.
21. Brown, J. and Patel, C., Data Standardization in Healthcare AI. *IEEE Trans. Med. Data*, 2020.
22. Nguyen, L., *et al.*, Ethical Considerations in Healthcare AI. *IEEE Technol. Soc. Mag.*, 2021.
23. Harris, D., *et al.*, Financial Implications of AI in Healthcare, IEEE Economics of Healthcare, 2023.

24. Gangadevi, E., Rani, R.S., Dhanaraj, R.K., Nayyar, A., Spot-out fruit fly algorithm with simulated annealing optimized SVM for detecting tomato plant diseases. *Neural Comput. Appl.*, 36, 8, 4349–4375, 2023, Springer Science and Business Media LLC. https://doi.org/10.1007/s00521-023-09295-1.
25. He, X., Zhao, K., Chu, X., AutoML: A survey of the state-of-the-art. *Knowl.-Based Syst.*, 212, 106622, 2021.

14

Democratizing Machine Learning: The Rise of Automated Machine Learning (AutoML)

Debarati Dutta and Priya G.*

School of Computer Science and Engineering, VIT University, Vellore, Tamil Nadu, India

Abstract

The current paradigm of artificial intelligence (AI) is centered on developing algorithms that acquire extraordinary outcomes by learning directly from data, particularly in supervised deep learning. This has streamlined the machine learning systems by systematizing much of the learning process. In many different areas of our everyday life, machine learning (ML) is essential. However, developing effective ML applications typically requires skilled data scientists and subject matter specialists. Using automated machine learning (AutoML), domain experts may develop machine learning features without requiring extensive statistics or machine learning training. The area of AutoML is expanding quickly, with the goal of automating machine learning model development. By reducing tedious steps in the machine learning process—from selecting and fine-tuning algorithms to preparing data—it seeks to increase efficiency and productivity. This article outlines a review of AutoML methods and provides detailed explanations. It provides an indication of AutoML's history and current state of this revolutionary technology. It starts by outlining the notion of AutoML, outlining the fundamental stages of every machine learning method, specifying the issues it aims to solve, and outlining the three main mechanisms of AutoML techniques. AutoML's versatility and ongoing development applications and future scopes are also highlighted here. Overall, this comprehensive overview serves as an invaluable tool for machine learning scholars and practitioners, laying the groundwork for future advancements in AutoML.

**Corresponding author*: gpriya@vit.ac.in

E. Gangadevi, M. Lawanya Shri, Balamurugan Balusamy and Rajesh Kumar Dhanaraj (eds.) Automated Machine Learning and Industrial Applications, (297–318) © 2025 Scrivener Publishing LLC

Keywords: AutoML, AutoML components, data augmentation, feature engineering

14.1 Introduction

Machine learning (ML), has revolutionized various fields such as image classification, disease diagnosis, language translation, weather forecasting, and many more. The breakthrough act of AlexNet [1] in the 2012 ImageNet challenge led to the development of deeper networks like ResNet-50 [2], which has 50 layers and 25.6 million parameters. However, its success deeply depends on specialists who plan complex machine learning pipelines, including data preprocessors and training methods. Choosing the right mechanisms and optimizing their hyperparameters is an inspiring task that requires experience, experimentation, and resources. This challenge has driven the rise of Automated Machine Learning (AutoML), which intends to streamline and automate the creation of high-performance pipelines [3]. Current AutoML systems mainly target automated model building, which involves selecting the pipeline structure, its stages, and its hyperparameters.

When automating data science, four essential procedures are often taken into consideration as follows: 1. Collection and exploration of data. 2. Data engineering to clean and eliminate outliers from a dataset, data augmentation, and feature engineering to make it for feeding into a machine learning pipeline. 3. Choosing a model-building algorithm. 4. Hyperparameter optimization. 5. Training the model. 6. Data exploitation for decision-making. Among them, the main goal of modern AutoML systems is automatic model creation for an exact dataset.

John Rice proposed the algorithm selection problem in 1976 placing the groundwork for present AutoML systems [4]. In the 1990s, commercial keys started offering automatic hyperparameter optimization (HPO) via grid search. By 1995, versions of grid search using a greedy best-first approach occurred. The true potential of AutoML was understood with the introduction of the algorithm selection and optimization (CASH) problem. The formation of Auto-WEKA, by Thornton *et al.*, in 2013 [5], efficiently illustrated this by using this idea to select models from a search space of conventional ML methods and related hyperparameters. Neural architecture search (NAS), a field whose emphases on autonomously creating a particular type of machine learning model—neural networks—has also received a lot of maintenance in recent AutoML research [6].

AutoML research has recently made important strides in both academics and industry leading to a flow in research actions. Academic advancements include systems like Auto-sklearn [7], AutoKeras [8], and TPOT [9]. Inspired by these, industrial platforms, such as Google Cloud AutoML [10], Oracle AutoML [11], and Amazon SageMaker Autopilot [12], have been developed for large-scale use. These systems enable the creation of high-performance machine learning models and pipelines with minimal user effort.

This study offers a thorough indication of the methodologies employed in AutoML research to assist novice researchers and practitioners. It covers state-of-the-art AutoML schemes for both ML and deep neural networks and future research directions. This study is divided into three primary subtasks by the survey: feature engineering, data augmentation, and preprocessing. Our review covers all areas of AutoML methods beyond only NAS techniques, whereas others focus on the comparison of AutoML with other methods. This chapter gives a brief introduction to AutoML techniques, based on the State-of-the-Art (SoTA) pipeline. It also categorized the AutoML approaches into three components: (i) search space, (ii) search approach, and (iii) performance assessment. The primary goal is to provide beginners with a comprehensive introduction to the arena of automatic machine learning (AutoML). The remaining segments are organized in the following ways: Section 14.2 outlines the fundamental steps of AutoML system and pipeline structures. In Section 14.3, we describe the AutoML technology and framework in another component. Then, Section 14.4 gives some idea about the AutoML applications. Section 14.5 delves into potential future trajectories, while Section 14.6 brings the entire paper to a close.

14.2 Flow of AutoML

The machine learning process generally follows these steps: data collection, data preparation and data augmentation, feature engineering, model selection, and model evaluation. Traditional machine learning methods necessitate performing each of these stages manually and independently. Figure 14.1 describes the steps involved in generating a pipeline of any AutoML system.

1. Automated Data Collection

Data collection is a complex task. Issues with data correctness, consistency, and quality frequently come up during the merging of datasets

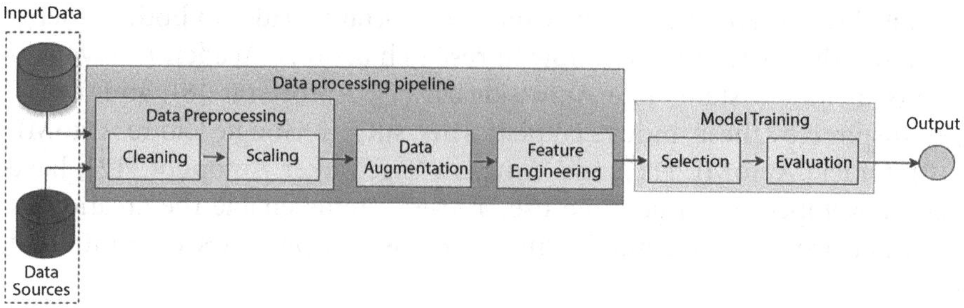

Figure 14.1 Steps involved in AutoML.

from different sources and must be resolved. To make sure the data is useful, it must be processed, and unnecessary information must be removed. Considering the rate of datasets, a great number of open datasets are now available. In the initial stages of machine learning research, the MNIST [13] dataset of handwritten digits was formed. Over time, larger and more varied datasets, such as CIFAR-10, CIFAR-100 [14], COCO [15] ImageNet [16], and many have been developed for use in Neural Architecture Search (NAS) due to their wide accessibility and applicability to numerous tasks. However, classifying the right dataset for a specific scheme remains a significant test. To address this, several methods have been planned, including data searching, data filtering, data labeling, and data mixture.

2. Automated Data Preparation and Preprocessing

Data cleaning is a vital phase of data preparation and preprocessing to ensure data accuracy, consistency, and reliability. It involves techniques, like error detection, duplicate removal, normalization, and lost value imputation [17]. Traditional methods, such as Potter's Wheel [18] and IntelliClean [19], require human skill and are time consuming. Automated tools, like Katara [20], Boost-Clean [21], and AlphaClean [22], streamline the process. Katara uses rule-based and machine-learning approaches, while Boost-Clean detects and repairs errors before model training. AlphaClean generates data-cleaning pipelines and learns from user feedback. Dynamic data cleaning is crucial for handling continuously generated data. Ilyas *et al.* [23] proposed a framework for continuous monitoring and cleaning, including a data quality model, executor, generator of cleaning plan, and feedback loop.

3. Automated Data Augmentation

Data augmentation (DA) enhances model performance, especially with limited datasets, by increasing training data size and improving generalization. DA techniques apply to images [24], text [25], audio [26], and tabular data [27]. Figure 14.2 describes the data augmentation process applied to different data types.

A. Image Data

Different data augmentation (DA) techniques, including object identification, image classification, and visual tracking can be used for image data. The following are some most common methodologies:

Affine Transformations: Scaling, rotation, translation, and cropping.

Elastic Transformations: Brightness, contrast, channel shifting, and blurring.

Innovative Transformations: Random erasing, blending the images, cutout [28], mixup [29], and cutmix [30].

B. Text Data

Techniques for augmenting textual data can improve training data and increase the diversity of text available. The following are a few most common strategies:

Replacement of Synonyms: Replacing words with synonyms.

Random Method of Insertion: Adding words randomly.

Random Deletion: Removing words randomly.

Back Translation: Translating text to another language and back.

Random Swap: Shuffling word positions.

OCR Noise: Introducing OCR-like errors [31].

C. Audio Data

We can avoid overfitting and improve the model's capacity to simplify unknown audio data by generating additional instances through transformations. Some of those techniques are as follows:

Noise Injection: Adding Gaussian or random noise to the audio.

Shifting: Shifting the audio left or right by random amounts.

Speed Tuning: Changing the speed of the audio.

Pitch Shifting: Randomly changing the pitch of the audio.

Time Stretching: Stretching or compressing the audio duration.

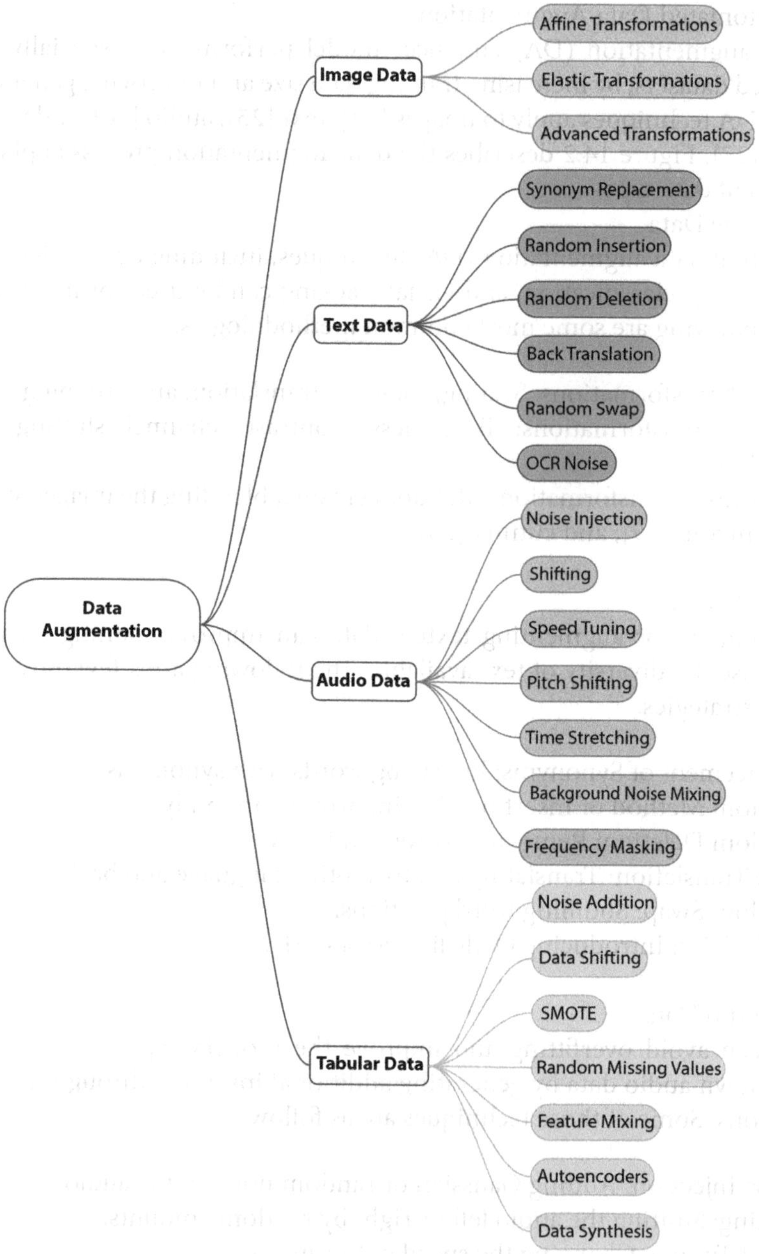

Figure 14.2 Data augmentation.

Background Noise Mixing: Adding background noise to the audio.
Frequency Masking: Masking certain frequencies in the audio.

D. Tabular Data
Techniques of data augmentation for tabular data are not the same as those for text or image augmentation. By enhancing the variety of training data, these approaches and technologies seek to advance model performance, which ultimately results in improved generalization. Some commonly used steps are as follows:

Noise Addition: Adding random noise to numerical features.
Data Shifting: Slightly shifting values of numerical features.
SMOTE: Generating synthetic samples for minority classes [32].
Random Missing Values: Introducing and then imputing missing values.
Feature Mixing: Combining features from different rows to create new synthetic rows.
Autoencoders: Using Denoising Autoencoders (DAE) [33] to reconstruct data with added noise.
Data Synthesis: Generating new data points using models like GANs [34].

Automated tools like Katara, Boost-Clean, and AlphaClean streamline DA. AutoAugment uses reinforcement learning to automate DA policy search but is resource intensive.

4. Automated Feature Engineering
Feature engineering is a vital phase in the ML pipeline altering raw data into a plan appropriate for algorithms. It includes creating new features, selecting relevant ones, and modifying existing features to enhance model performance [35]. AutoML platforms automate this process exploring various feature engineering strategies [36] and optimizing the feature space. To identify the best-performing model, they experiment with various algorithmic combinations, feature engineering strategies, and preprocessing procedures, utilizing Bayesian optimization [37, 38] or evolutionary algorithms.

A. Feature Selection: Feature selection involves choosing relevant features from a larger pool to enhance model performance, reduce complexity, and improve interpretability [39]. It minimizes noise, overfitting, and the dimensionality leading to better generalization and predictive capabilities. For large datasets, it also saves computing resources and training time. In AutoML, feature selection is automated using various algorithms like filter approaches, wrapper methods, and embedded methods [40]. AutoML's iterative procedure refines the feature subset to advance model performance, reducing overfitting and enhancing predictive power. The number of repetitions and stopping criteria depend on computational resources, time constraints, and desired model performance.
B. Feature Extraction: Feature extraction transforms raw data into expressive features for machine learning [41]. It reduces data dimensionality while preserving essential information improving model performance and computational efficiency. Techniques, like SIFT and HOG, are used for images, autoencoders, TF-IDF for text, and FFT and wavelet transform for signals [42]. AutoML platforms automate feature extraction using methods such as wavelet transforms and dimensionality-reduction algorithms (e.g., PCA, LDA) [43]. This automation identifies significant patterns, reduces redundancy, and enhances feature representation allowing users to focus on analyzing features and understanding data patterns.

5. Model Selection
Model selection is crucial in NAS and is divided into search space and architecture optimization.

A. Search Space: In AutoML, the search space aids to locate optimal architectures, minimize complexity, and boost search competence. It defines the possible architectures that can be represented. Common NAS search spaces include the following:

- Cell Based: Uses basic building blocks [44, 45].
- Entire Structured: Considers the whole network structure [46].
- Hierarchical: Organizes patterns across different levels [47, 48].
- Morphism Based: Focuses on transformations [49, 50].

For large datasets, hierarchical search spaces often perform better. Hierarchical genetic representation systems use modular designs to create complex topologies. They start with a flat architecture and build hierarchical structures with multiple levels.

Hierarchical Neural Architecture Search (HNAS) includes cell- and network-level search spaces. It uses normal cells to manage model capacity and up-sampling cells to enhance resolution. Mobile NAS (MNAS) [51] introduces a factorized hierarchy for CNN models independently searching processes and connections within each group. Global Local Image Transformer (GLiT) optimizes the supply of global and local sub-modules within each block [52].

B. Architecture Optimization: Architecture optimization in deep learning includes selecting the best neural network architecture for a precise dataset [53]. This process requires modifying features like learning rate and weights to improve precision and reduce loss [54]. Common optimization algorithms include the following:

a) Evolutionary Algorithm: Evolutionary Algorithms (EA) mimic natural selection using reproduction, mutation, recombination, and selection. It optimizes solutions starting with random solutions and evaluates them using a fitness function [55]. Genetic Algorithms (GA), a type of EA, use a population of solutions and three main operators: selection (based on fitness), mutation (random changes), and crossover (exchanging segments) [56]. Key parameters, like neuron count and learning rate, must be carefully set [57].

b) Reinforcement Learning: Reinforcement learning (RL) is an ML field where an agent acquires and adapts through interactions in an unfamiliar situation [58]. The agent obtains rewards or penalties created on its activities guiding its learning in a trial-and-error manner. In RL, the agent perceives the situation, selects actions, and receives feedback. The main components are reward, action, and state. The agent's aim is to learn an action strategy that exploits the reward, represented by the following equation:

$$\Sigma_{i=0}^{\infty} \gamma^i Q_{t+i}, (0 < \gamma \leq 1) \tag{14.1}$$

In Equation 14.1 γ, the discount factor and output action Q represent the expected reward of taking a certain action at a time (t + i) and following the optimal policy afterward. The key steps in the RL pipeline include specifying the reward function, selecting observations, and tuning hyperparameters. Automating RL involves updating hyperparameters and functions based on feedback from the environment [59].

c) Bayesian Optimization: Bayesian optimization (BO) addresses optimization challenges like high dimensionality. It provisions point-wise evaluations without function derivatives making it a black-box method [60]. BO does not require prior information; it starts with a randomized population and selects promising candidates to construct a Bayesian network. New candidates are generated using joint distribution encoding and added to the population.
BO uses the following two main approaches:
Gaussian Process (GP): Models uncertainty and forecast mean for any input point [61].
Acquisition Function (AF): Determines the next best point to evaluate based on GP's uncertainty and mean [62].

d) Gradient-Based Optimization: This method adjusts parameters by moving in the direction of the gradient. The step size is determined by the learning rate.
Gradient Descent: Minimizes an objective function by affecting in the way of the negative gradient. It starts with an initial guess and iteratively finds a local minimum [63].

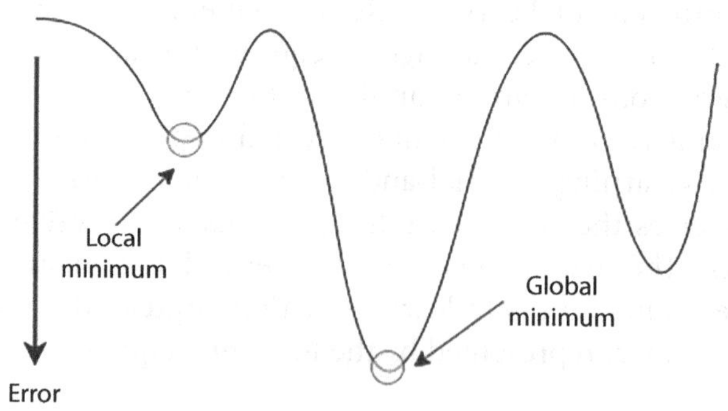

Figure 14.3 Gradient descent stuck in local minimum.

The learning rate is crucial; too big a rate can miss the optimal solution. Figure 14.3 describes how Gradient descent is usually stuck in a local minimum.

Gradient Ascent: Maximizes a function by going in the direction of the positive gradient [64]. It iteratively finds a local maximum.

Gradient Min–Max: Solves min–max problems by alternating between gradient ascent and descent steps to get the minimum and maximum values of a function [65].

Automating these approaches with AutoML involves tuning hyperparameters to decrease training iterations and improve efficiency.

6. Model Evaluation

Model evaluation is vital in Neural Architecture Search (NAS) for AutoML, as it measures the model's routine on training and test datasets. This procedure can be complex and resource intensive. Advanced methods, like ENAS and DARTS+[66], aid to speed up evaluation but may affect accuracy.

A. Weight Sharing: This method reduces computational costs by allocating parameters among dissimilar models. For example, FairNAS [67] and Single-Path NAS [68] use weight sharing to cut exploration costs significantly.

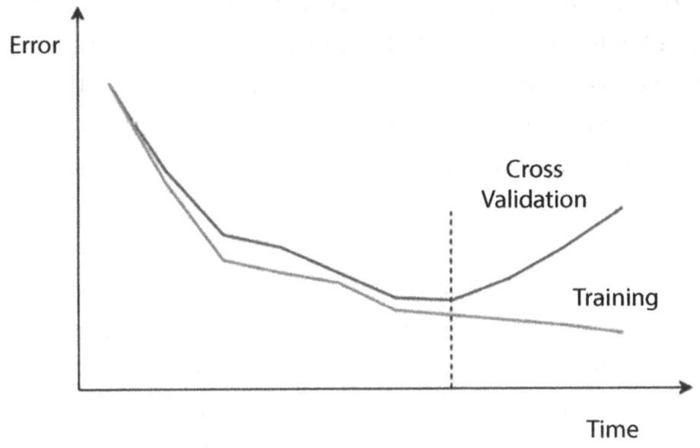

Figure 14.4 Diagram of early stopping.

B. Early Stopping: This regularization method stops overfitting by halting training when performance stops improving. Techniques like DARTS+ and MiLeNAS [69] use early stopping to hasten the search process and decrease costs. Figure 14.4 describes the early stopping method in an overfitting or underfitting graph.

14.3 AutoML Components

AutoML approaches can also be categorized into three main components as follows:

1. Search Space
The search space in machine learning describes all design choices, including learning algorithms and their hyperparameters. Hyperparameters can be categorical (e.g., kernel types for SVMs) or numerical (e.g., learning rates). The combined procedure selection and hyperparameter (CASH) problem treats algorithm choice as a hyperparameter and is tackled using hyperparameter optimization (HPO) techniques.

Categorical Hyperparameters: These take discrete values without any inherent order, like different kernel types in SVMs [70].

Numerical Hyperparameters: These are defined over a numeric range, such as learning rates or kernel widths [71].

Conditional Hyperparameters: Some hyperparameters depend on others. For example, kernel width is relevant only for kernels.

Hyperparameter optimization techniques handle these differently. For instance, log transformation can be applied to numerical hyperparameters to emphasize smaller values. Techniques, like weight sharing reduce computational costs, while early stopping prevents overfitting by halting training when performance plateaus [72].

2. Search Strategy
In AutoML, search strategy or algorithm refers to exploring the search space to find the best machine learning models and hyperparameters. The following are some common search strategies: i) Grid Search, ii) Random Search, iii) Bayesian Optimization, iv) Evolutionary Algorithms, v) Reinforcement Learning, and vi) Gradient-Based Optimization [73].

These strategies aim to automate and optimize the procedure of selecting and tuning machine learning models making high-performance models more reachable.

3. Performance Evaluation
In AutoML, performance evaluation refers to the procedures used to assess the efficiency of the models generated during the automated machine learning process. This step is vital for determining which models attain best on a given dataset. The following are the key features of performance evaluation in AutoML:

Evaluation Metrics: Metrics, such as accuracy, F1 score, precision, recall [74], and area under the ROC curve (AUC), are typically used to evaluate classification models. For regression models, metrics, like mean absolute error (MAE), mean squared error (MSE), and R-squared, are used.

Cross-Validation: This technique includes splitting the dataset into numerous folds and training the model on diverse subsets while validating on the outstanding data. It guarantees that the model works consistently across various data splits.

Holdout Validation: A part of the dataset is set aside as a validation set, and the model is skilled on the outstanding data. The performance of the validation set is meant to assess the model [75].

Learning Curves: These plots uncover problems, such as overfitting or underfitting, by displaying the model's progress over time on the training and validation sets [76].

Hyperparameter Tuning: Finding the best model settings involves evaluating several hyperparameter setups via performance evaluation.

Model Comparison: AutoML systems often generate multiple models, and performance evaluation helps compare these representations to select the best one.

14.4 Application

The application of AutoML is gaining prominence, particularly among researchers and business professionals. Despite its diverse use cases, its impact extends broadly. Some of the applications are described below.

Democratizing AI: A wider range of people without extensive technical knowledge may now utilize AI by having complicated processes, like model selection, feature engineering, and hyperparameter tweaking, automated. Anyone can now create machine learning models without having to be an expert in data science, from researchers to small enterprises.

Efficient Model Development: Model development is accelerated using AutoML. By letting AutoML take care of the details, practitioners can concentrate on solving problems rather than spending time manually fine-tuning models, which facilitates effective model deployment, speedy testing, and rapid prototyping

Automated Feature Engineering: The requirement for human feature engineering is decreased since AutoML automatically creates appropriate features from raw data. It enhances churn prediction, fraud detection, tabular data analysis, and many more.

Computer Vision: AutoML may be used to create object detection systems, image classification models, and even neural architecture searches for vision problems. Applications include quality assurance in manufacturing, autonomous vehicles [77], and medical imaging, among others.

Natural Language Processing (NLP): Language modeling, named unit identification, text classification, and sentiment analysis are all aided by AutoML. Personalized recommendations, content control, chatbots, and more are examples of its applications.

Time-Series Forecasting: When working with time-series data, AutoML may forecast values for the future by using patterns from the past. Forecasting demand, modeling energy use, and stock market prediction are a few examples of applications.

Recommendation Systems: Personal recommendation engines are built with the use of AutoML, which enhances music streaming services, multimedia platforms, and e-commerce.

Healthcare and Biomedical Research: AutoML also supports patient risk prediction, medication development, and disease diagnosis [78]. It helps in personalized medicine, genetics, medical image analysis, and other applications.

Financial Services: To detect fraud and optimize portfolios, AutoML helps with credit rating, which helps autonomize Investment management, insurance, banking [79], and other fields.

14.5 Future Scope

The future of AutoML is poised to transform the landscape of ML and artificial intelligence significantly. Key areas of development include the following:

Democratization of AI: AutoML will make advanced machine learning techniques accessible to non-experts enabling a broader range of industries and individuals to leverage AI without needing specialized knowledge.

Enhanced Efficiency: By automating repetitive and time-consuming responsibilities, such as data preprocessing, feature engineering, and hyperparameter tuning, AutoML will greatly improve productivity and allow data scientists to focus on more intricate and innovative aspects of machine learning.

Integration with Big Data: As data sizes continue to grow, AutoML will play a critical role in efficiently managing and analyzing large datasets, which is important for fields, like healthcare, finance, and retail, where data-driven decision making is critical.

Environmental Sustainability: Future developments in AutoML will also consider the environmental impact of machine learning models aiming to make more energy-efficient algorithms and systems.

Overall, the future of AutoML is set to revolutionize the way machine learning models are developed and deployed making advanced AI capabilities more accessible, efficient, and ethical across many industries.

14.6 Conclusion

AutoML remains a relatively new and rapidly expanding research area. Researchers are actively addressing key challenges, and we anticipate swift advancements in the field. These developments will make AutoML systems more powerful, versatile, and user friendly. Developing an effective AutoML system involves addressing various concerns, such as data collection, cleaning and preprocessing, feature engineering, model selection, model estimation, and optimization. These skills are now essential for machine learning professionals. This review covers different aspects of AutoML providing explanations for each method, which can be used to build future AutoML systems. With ongoing academic research and commercial innovations, the real-world application of AutoML is expected to grow significantly. Our survey aims to foster this development, provided that newcomers to AutoML have access to a comprehensive overview. Without careful implementation, automation can have negative consequences. Therefore, there is a strong need for thoughtful design and deployment of AutoML systems to address these concerns. Modern frameworks allow domain specialists to create effective ML pipelines without needing extensive knowledge of ML or statistics.

References

1. Alom, M.Z., Taha, T.M., Yakopcic, C., Westberg, S., Sidike, P., Nasrin, M.S., *et al.*, The History Began from AlexNet: A Comprehensive Survey on Deep Learning Approaches [Internet], arXiv; 2018 [cited 2024 Aug 1]. Available from: http://arxiv.org/abs/1803.01164.
2. Koonce, B., ResNet 50, in: *Convolutional Neural Networks with Swift for Tensorflow: Image Recognition and Dataset Categorization* [Internet], B. Koonce (Ed.), pp. 63–72, Apress, Berkeley, CA, 2021 [cited 2024 Aug 1], Available from: https://doi.org/10.1007/978-1-4842-6168-2_6.
3. De Bie, T., De Raedt, L., Hernández-Orallo, J., Hoos, H.H., Smyth, P., Williams, C.K.I., Automating data science. *Commun. ACM*, 65, 3, 76–87, 2022 Feb 23.
4. Rice, J.R., The Algorithm Selection Problem*, in: *Advances in Computers* [Internet], M. Rubinoff and M.C. Yovits (Eds.), vol. 15, pp. 65–118, Elsevier, Washington, 1976 [cited 2024 Aug 1], Available from: https://www.sciencedirect.com/science/article/pii/S0065245808605203.
5. Thornton, C., Hutter, F., Hoos, H.H., Leyton-Brown, K., Auto-WEKA: combined selection and hyperparameter optimization of classification algorithms, in: *Proceedings of the 19th ACM SIGKDD international conference on Knowledge discovery and data mining* [Internet], Association for Computing Machinery, New York, NY, USA, pp. 847–55, 2013 [cited 2024 Aug 1, (KDD '13). Available from: https://dl.acm.org/doi/10.1145/2487575.2487629.
6. Liu, Y., Sun, Y., Xue, B., Zhang, M., Yen, G.G., Tan, K.C., A Survey on Evolutionary Neural Architecture Search. *IEEE Trans. Neural Networks Learn. Syst.*, 34, 2, 550–70, 2023 Feb.
7. Feurer, M., Eggensperger, K., Falkner, S., Lindauer, M., Hutter, F., Auto-Sklearn 2.0: Hands-free AutoML via Meta-Learning. *J. Mach. Learn. Res.*, 23, 261, 1–61, 2022.
8. Jin, H., Chollet, F., Song, Q., Hu, X., AutoKeras: An AutoML Library for Deep Learning. *J. Mach. Learn. Res.*, 24, 6, 1–6, 2023.

9. Romano, J.D., Le, T.T., Fu, W., Moore, J.H., TPOT-NN: augmenting tree-based automated machine learning with neural network estimators. *Genet. Program. Evolvable Mach.*, 22, 2, 207–27, 2021 Jun 1.
10. Zeng, Y. and Zhang, J., A machine learning model for detecting invasive ductal carcinoma with Google Cloud AutoML Vision. *Comput. Biol. Med.*, 122, 103861, 2020 Jul 1.
11. Plăcintă, D.D., Oracle Machine Learning (OML) Features and a Classification Use Case with OML4SQL and AutoML, in: *Education, Research and Business Technologies*, C. Ciurea, P. Pocatilu, F.G. Filip (Eds.), pp. 229–41, Springer Nature, Singapore, 2023.
12. Das, P., Ivkin, N., Bansal, T., Rouesnel, L., Gautier, P., Karnin, Z., *et al.*, Amazon SageMaker Autopilot: a white box AutoML solution at scale, in: *Proceedings of the Fourth International Workshop on Data Management for End-to-End Machine Learning* [Internet], Association for Computing Machinery, New York, NY, USA, pp. 1–7, 2020 [cited 2024 Aug 1], (DEEM '20). Available from: https://dl.acm.org/doi/10.1145/3399579.3399870.
13. Deng, L., The MNIST Database of Handwritten Digit Images for Machine Learning Research [Best of the Web]. *IEEE Signal Process Mag.*, 29, 6, 141–2, 2012 Nov.
14. Obaid, K.B., Zeebaree, S.R.M., Ahmed, O.M., Deep Learning Models Based on Image Classification: A Review. *Int. J. Sci. Bus.*, 4, 11, 75–81, 2020.
15. Li, X., Xu, C., Wang, X., Lan, W., Jia, Z., Yang, G., *et al.*, COCO-CN for Cross-Lingual Image Tagging, Captioning, and Retrieval. *IEEE Trans. Multimed.*, 21, 9, 2347–60, 2019 Sep.
16. Deng, J., Dong, W., Socher, R., Li, L.J., Li, K., Fei-Fei, L., ImageNet: A large-scale hierarchical image database, in: *2009 IEEE Conference on Computer Vision and Pattern Recognition* [Internet], pp. 248–55, 2009 [cited 2024 Jul 29, Available from: https://ieeexplore.ieee.org/abstract/document/5206848.
17. Hosseinzadeh, M., Azhir, E., Ahmed, O.H., Ghafour, M.Y., Ahmed, S.H., Rahmani, A.M., *et al.*, Data cleansing mechanisms and approaches for big data analytics: a systematic study. *J. Ambient Intell. Hum. Comput.*, 14, 1, 99–111, 2023 Jan 1.
18. Wang, J., Zhang, H., Fang, B., Wang, X., Ye, L., A Survey on Data Cleaning Methods in Cyberspace, in: *2017 IEEE Second International Conference on Data Science in Cyberspace (DSC)* [Internet], pp. 74–81, 2017 [cited 2024 Jul 29], Available from: https://ieeexplore.ieee.org/abstract/document/8005458.
19. Hunter, K., Alberti, C.T., Boss, S.R., Thibodeau, J.C., IntelliClean: A Teaching Case Designed to Integrate Data Cleaning and Spreadsheet Skills into the Audit Curriculum. *J. Emerg. Technol. Account.*, 17, 2, 17–24, 2020 Sep 1.
20. Chu, X., Morcos, J., Ilyas, I.F., Ouzzani, M., Papotti, P., Tang, N., *et al.*, KATARA: A Data Cleaning System Powered by Knowledge Bases and Crowdsourcing, in: *Proceedings of the 2015 ACM SIGMOD International Conference on Management of Data* [Internet], Association for Computing

Machinery, New York, NY, USA, pp. 1247–61, 2015 [cited 2024 Jul 29], (SIGMOD '15). Available from: https://doi.org/10.1145/2723372.2749431.
21. Lee, G.Y., Alzamil, L., Doskenov, B., Termehchy, A., A Survey on Data Cleaning Methods for Improved Machine Learning Model Performance [Internet], arXiv; 2021 [cited 2024 Jul 29], Available from: http://arxiv.org/abs/2109.07127.
22. Krishnan, S. and Wu, E., AlphaClean: Automatic Generation of Data Cleaning Pipelines [Internet], arXiv; 2019 [cited 2024 Jul 29], Available from: http://arxiv.org/abs/1904.11827.
23. Ilyas, I., Effective Data Cleaning With Continuous Evaluation. *IEEE Data Eng. Bull.*, 39, 2, 38–46, 2016.
24. Shorten, C. and Khoshgoftaar, T.M., A survey on Image Data Augmentation for Deep Learning. *J. Big Data*, 6, 1, 60, 2019 Jul 6.
25. Bayer, M., Kaufhold, M.A., Reuter, C., A Survey on Data Augmentation for Text Classification. *ACM Comput. Surv.*, 55, 7, 146, 1–39, 2022 Dec 15.
26. Nanni, L., Maguolo, G., Paci, M., Data augmentation approaches for improving animal audio classification. *Ecol. Inform.*, 57, 101084, 2020 May 1.
27. Sathianarayanan, B., Singh Samant, Y.C., Conjeepuram Guruprasad, P.S., Hariharan, V.B., Manickam, N.D., Feature-based augmentation and classification for tabular data. *CAAI Trans. Intell. Technol.*, 7, 3, 481–91, 2022.
28. Nallakaruppan, M.K., Gangadevi, E., Shri, M.L., Balusamy, B., Bhattacharya, S., Selvarajan, S., Reliable water quality prediction and parametric analysis using explainable AI models. *Sci. Rep.*, 14, 1, 7520, 2024, Springer Science and Business Media LLC. https://doi.org/10.1038/s41598-024-56775-y.
29. Chou, H.P., Chang, S.C., Pan, J.Y., Wei, W., Juan, D.C., Remix: Rebalanced Mixup, in: *Computer Vision – ECCV 2020 Workshops*, A. Bartoli and A. Fusiello (Eds.), pp. 95–110, Springer International Publishing, Cham, 2020.
30. Pan, H., Guo, Y., Yu, M., Chen, J., Enhanced Long-Tailed Recognition With Contrastive CutMix Augmentation. *IEEE Trans. Image Process.*, 33, 4215–30, 2024.
31. Boros, E., Nguyen, N.K., Lejeune, G., Doucet, A., Assessing the impact of OCR noise on multilingual event detection over digitised documents. *Int. J. Digit. Libr.*, 23, 3, 241–66, 2022 Sep 1.
32. Liu, D., Zhong, S., Lin, L., Zhao, M., Fu, X., Liu, X., Deep attention SMOTE: Data augmentation with a learnable interpolation factor for imbalanced anomaly detection of gas turbines. *Comput. Ind.*, 151, 103972, 2023 Oct 1.
33. Islam, Z., Abdel-Aty, M., Cai, Q., Yuan, J., Crash data augmentation using variational autoencoder. *Accid. Anal. Prev.*, 151, 105950, 2021 Mar 1.
34. Zhao, Z., Kunar, A., Birke, R., Van der Scheer, H., Chen, L.Y., CTAB-GAN+: enhancing tabular data synthesis. *Front. Big Data* [Internet], 6, 1296508, 2024 Jan 8 [cited 2024 Jul 30]. Available from: https://www.frontiersin.org/journals/big-data/articles/10.3389/fdata.2023.1296508/full.
35. Gada, M., Haria, Z., Mankad, A., Damania, K., Sankhe, S., Automated Feature Engineering and Hyperparameter optimization for Machine Learning, in: *2021*

7th International Conference on Advanced Computing and Communication Systems (ICACCS) [Internet], pp. 981–6, 2021 [cited 2024 Jul 30], Available from: https://ieeexplore.ieee.org/abstract/document/9441668.

36. Zhang, X., Han, Y., Xu, W., Wang, Q., HOBA: A novel feature engineering methodology for credit card fraud detection with a deep learning architecture. *Inf. Sci.*, 557, 302–16, 2021 May 1.
37. Wang, X., Jin, Y., Schmitt, S., Olhofer, M., Recent Advances in Bayesian Optimization. *ACM Comput. Surv.*, 55, 13s, 287, 1–36, 2023 Jul 13.
38. Deng, W., Shang, S., Cai, X., Zhao, H., Song, Y., Xu, J., An improved differential evolution algorithm and its application in optimization problem. *Soft Comput.*, 25, 7, 5277–98, 2021 Apr 1.
39. Agrawal, P., Abutarboush, H.F., Ganesh, T., Mohamed, A.W., Metaheuristic Algorithms on Feature Selection: A Survey of One Decade of Research (2009-2019). *IEEE Access*, 9, 26766–91, 2021.
40. Bashir, S., Khattak, I.U., Khan, A., Khan, F.H., Gani, A., Shiraz, M., A Novel Feature Selection Method for Classification of Medical Data Using Filters, Wrappers, and Embedded Approaches. *Complexity*, 2022, 1, 8190814, 2022.
41. Barandas, M., Folgado, D., Fernandes, L., Santos, S., Abreu, M., Bota, P., *et al.*, TSFEL: Time Series Feature Extraction Library. *SoftwareX*, 11, 100456, 2020 Jan 1.
42. Strömbergsson, D., Marklund, P., Berglund, K., Larsson, P.E., Bearing monitoring in the wind turbine drivetrain: A comparative study of the FFT and wavelet transforms. *Wind Energy*, 23, 6, 1381–93, 2020.
43. Anowar, F., Sadaoui, S., Selim, B., Conceptual and empirical comparison of dimensionality reduction algorithms (PCA, KPCA, LDA, MDS, SVD, LLE, ISOMAP, LE, ICA, t-SNE). *Comput. Sci. Rev.*, 40, 100378, 2021 May 1.
44. Appadurai, J.P., Raveendran, L.S., Latha, R., Gangadevi, E., Shri, M.L., Gite, S., Cybersecurity Using Hybrid Type Model for Classification Through SCO Optimization Technique. *2024 IEEE International Conference on Computing, Power and Communication Technologies (IC2PCT)*, Greater Noida, India, pp. 1390–1396, 2024, doi: 10.1109/IC2PCT60090.2024.10486307.
45. Benmeziane, H., El Maghraoui, K., Ouarnoughi, H., Niar, S., Grassroots operator search for model edge adaptation using mathematical search space. *Future Gener. Comput. Syst.*, 157, 29–40, 2024 Aug 1.
46. Lin, M., Ji, R., Zhang, Y., Zhang, B., Wu, Y., Tian, Y., Channel Pruning via Automatic Structure Search [Internet], arXiv; 2020 [cited 2024 Jul 30], Available from: http://arxiv.org/abs/2001.08565.
47. Cheng, X., Zhong, Y., Harandi, M., Dai, Y., Chang, X., Li, H., *et al.*, Hierarchical Neural Architecture Search for Deep Stereo Matching. *Adv. Neural Inf. Process. Syst.* [Internet]. Curran Associates Inc., 22158–69, 2020 [cited 2024 Jul 30]. Available from: https://proceedings.neurips.cc/paper/2020/hash/fc146be0b230d7e0a92e66a6114b840d-Abstract.html.
48. Real, E., Aggarwal, A., Huang, Y., Le, Q.V., Regularized evolution for image classifier architecture search, in: *Proceedings of the Thirty-Third AAAI*

Conference on Artificial Intelligence and Thirty-First Innovative Applications of Artificial Intelligence Conference and Ninth AAAI Symposium on Educational Advances in Artificial Intelligence [Internet], AAAI Press, Honolulu, Hawaii, USA, pp. 4780–9, 2019 [cited 2024 Jul 30], (AAAI'19/IAAI'19/EAAI'19). Available from: https://doi.org/10.1609/aaai.v33i01.33014780.
49. Jie, R. and Gao, J., Differentiable Neural Architecture Search with Morphism-based Transformable Backbone Architectures [Internet], arXiv; 2021 [cited 2024 Jul 30], Available from: http://arxiv.org/abs/2106.07211.
50. Kwasigroch, A., Grochowski, M., Mikolajczyk, M., Deep neural network architecture search using network morphism, in: *2019 24th International Conference on Methods and Models in Automation and Robotics (MMAR)* [Internet], pp. 30–5, 2019 [cited 2024 Jul 30], Available from: https://ieeexplore.ieee.org/abstract/document/8864624.
51. Almisreb, A., Hadžo Mulalić, H., Mučibabić, N., Numanović, R., A review on mobile operating systems and application development platforms, in: *Sustainable Engineering and Innovation*, vol. 1, issue 1, pp. 49–56, Research and Development Academy, 2019, https://doi.org/10.37868/sei.v1i1.94.
52. Qi, W., Huang, C., Wang, Y., Zhang, X., Sun, W., Zhang, L., Global–Local 3-D Convolutional Transformer Network for Hyperspectral Image Classification. *IEEE Trans. Geosci. Remote Sens.*, 61, 1–20, 2023.
53. Wistuba, M., Practical Deep Learning Architecture Optimization, in: *2018 IEEE 5th International Conference on Data Science and Advanced Analytics (DSAA) [Internet]*, pp. 263–72, 2018 [cited 2024 Jul 31, Available from: https://ieeexplore.ieee.org/abstract/document/8631439.
54. Shanmugavadivu, P., MSR, M., Chitra, P., Lakshmanan, S., Nagaraja, P., Vignesh, U., Bio-Optimization of Deep Learning Network Architectures, in: *Secur Commun Netw* [Internet], vol. 2022, C. Venkatesan (Ed.), 2022 [cited 2024 Jul 31], Available from: https://www.proquest.com/docview/2720246629/abstract/B5F8BD925DE341C3PQ/1.
55. Slowik, A. and Kwasnicka, H., Evolutionary algorithms and their applications to engineering problems. *Neural Comput. Appl.*, 32, 16, 12363–79, 2020 Aug 1.
56. Falcón-Cardona, J.G. and Coello, C.A.C., Indicator-based Multi-objective Evolutionary Algorithms: A Comprehensive Survey. *ACM Comput. Surv.*, 53, 2, 1–29, 2020 Mar 20, 35.
57. Hua, Y., Liu, Q., Hao, K., Jin, Y., A Survey of Evolutionary Algorithms for Multi-Objective Optimization Problems With Irregular Pareto Fronts. *IEEE/CAA J. Autom. Sin.*, 8, 2, 303–18, 2021 Feb.
58. Wang, X., Wang, S., Liang, X., Zhao, D., Huang, J., Xu, X., *et al.*, Deep Reinforcement Learning: A Survey. *IEEE Trans. Neural Netw. Learn. Syst.*, 35, 4, 5064–78, 2024 Apr.
59. Naeem, M. and Rizvi, S.T.H., Coronato A. A Gentle Introduction to Reinforcement Learning and its Application in Different Fields. *IEEE Access*, 8, 209320–44, 2020.

60. Sujigarasharma, K., Sharulatha, S., Lawanya Shri, M., Gangadevi, E., Dhanaraj, R.K., Optimizing 3D Bioprinting Using Advanced Deep Learning Techniques A Comparative Study of CNN, RNN, and GAN, in: *Computational Intelligence in Bioprinting*, pp. 157–173, Wiley, USA, 2024, https://doi.org/10.1002/9781394204878.ch8.
61. Morita, Y., Rezaeiravesh, S., Tabatabaei, N., Vinuesa, R., Fukagata, K., Schlatter, P., Applying Bayesian optimization with Gaussian process regression to computational fluid dynamics problems. *J. Comput. Phys.*, 449, 110788, 2022 Jan 15.
62. Candelieri, A., A Gentle Introduction to Bayesian Optimization, in: *2021 Winter Simulation Conference (WSC)* [Internet], pp. 1–16, 2021 [cited 2024 Jul 31], Available from: https://ieeexplore.ieee.org/abstract/document/9715413.
63. Mustapha, A., Mohamed, L., Ali, K., An Overview of Gradient Descent Algorithm Optimization in Machine Learning: Application in the Ophthalmology Field, in: *Smart Applications and Data Analysis*, M. Hamlich, L. Bellatreche, A. Mondal, C. Ordonez (Eds.), pp. 349–59, Springer International Publishing, Cham, 2020.
64. Porotti, R., Peano, V., Marquardt, F., Gradient-Ascent Pulse Engineering with Feedback. *PRX Quantum*, 4, 3, 030305, 2023 Jul 13.
65. Antonakopoulos, K., Belmega, E.V., Mertikopoulos, P., Adaptive extra-gradient methods for min-max optimization and games [Internet], arXiv; 2020 [cited 2024 Jul 31], Available from: http://arxiv.org/abs/2010.12100.
66. Liang, H., Zhang, S., Sun, J., He, X., Huang, W., Zhuang, K., *et al.*, DARTS+: Improved Differentiable Architecture Search with Early Stopping [Internet], arXiv; 2020 [cited 2024 Jul 31], Available from: http://arxiv.org/abs/1909.06035.
67. Chu, X., Zhang, B., Xu, R., FairNAS: Rethinking Evaluation Fairness of Weight Sharing Neural Architecture Search, pp. 12239–48, 2021 [cited 2024 Jul 31], Available from: https://openaccess.thecvf.com/content/ICCV2021/html/Chu_FairNAS_Rethinking_Evaluation_Fairness_of_Weight_Sharing_Neural_Architecture_Search_ICCV_2021_paper.html.
68. Stamoulis, D., Ding, R., Wang, D., Lymberopoulos, D., Priyantha, B., Liu, J., *et al.*, Single-Path Mobile AutoML: Efficient ConvNet Design and NAS Hyperparameter Optimization. *IEEE J. Sel. Top. Signal Process.*, 14, 4, 609–22, 2020 May.
69. He, C., Ye, H., Shen, L., Zhang, T., MiLeNAS: Efficient Neural Architecture Search via Mixed-Level Reformulation, pp. 11993–2002, 2020 [cited 2024 Jul 31], Available from: https://openaccess.thecvf.com/content_CVPR_2020/html/He_MiLeNAS_Efficient_Neural_Architecture_Search_via_Mixed-Level_Reformulation_CVPR_2020_paper.html.
70. Probst, P., Wright, M.N., Boulesteix, A.L., Hyperparameters and tuning strategies for random forest. *WIREs Data Min. Knowl. Discov.*, 9, 3, e1301, 2019.
71. Cui, H. and Bai, J., A new hyperparameters optimization method for convolutional neural networks. *Pattern Recognit. Lett.*, 125, 828–34, 2019 Jul 1.

72. Prechelt, L., Early Stopping - But When?, in: *Neural Networks: Tricks of the Trade* [Internet], G.B. Orr and K.R. Müller (Eds.), pp. 55–69, Springer, Berlin, Heidelberg, 1998 [cited 2024 Aug 2], Available from: https://doi.org/10.1007/3-540-49430-8_3.
73. Xue, C., Hu, M., Huang, X., Li, C.G., Automated search space and search strategy selection for AutoML. *Pattern Recognit.*, 124, 108474, 2022 Apr 1.
74. Xu, S., Zhou, Z., Tao, M., Accuracy Improvement of Age Prediction Model Based on AutoML. *J. Phys. Conf. Ser.*, 1748, 3, 032005, 2021 Jan.
75. Larcher Jr., C.H. and Barbosa, H.J., Evaluating Models with Dynamic Sampling Holdout in Auto-ML. *SN Comput. Sci.*, 3, 6, 506, 2022 Oct 5.
76. Mohr, F. and van Rijn, J.N., Towards model selection using learning curve cross-validation, in: *8th ICML Workshop on automated machine learning (AutoML)*, 2021.
77. Shi, X., Wong, Y.D., Chai, C., Li, M.Z., An automated machine learning (AutoML) method of risk prediction for decision-making of autonomous vehicles. *IEEE Trans. Intell. Transp. Syst.*, 22, 11, 7145–54, 2020 Jul 1.
78. Romero RA, A., Deypalan MN, Y., Mehrotra, S., Jungao, J.T., Sheils, N.E., Manduchi, E., Moore, J.H., Benchmarking AutoML frameworks for disease prediction using medical claims. *Biodata Min.*, 15, 1, 15, 2022 Jul 26.
79. Agrapetidou, A., Charonyktakis, P., Gogas, P., Papadimitriou, T., Tsamardinos, I., An AutoML application to forecasting bank failures. *Appl. Econ. Lett.*, 28, 1, 5–9, 2021 Jan 2.

15

Open-Source Tools in Automated Machine Learning

Malaserene I., K. Santhi* and M. Lawanya Shri

SCORE, Vellore Institute of Technology, Vellore, Tamil Nadu, India

Abstract
Explainable AI (XAI) is the current trend set that has a potential to allow the user to understand the prediction made by machine learning and deep learning models. The nature of transparency and accountability of XAI impose and attract the researchers and industries to adopt a responsible technological model for AI development. XAI has the potential to comprehend how the machine learning and deep learning models produce results in what basis the classification and prediction result is obtained. The interpretation of the results is made easy using XAI by overcoming the drawbacks of AI that is considered as a "black box" model. This chapter discuss the various open source tools in Automated Machine Learning.

Keywords: AutoML, open-source tools, XAI, AutoGluon, Auto-Sklearn, clinical outcomes, deep learning

Introduction

There are many advantages of AI-based decision making models that led to a specific outcome in which XAI interprets the results and gives a clear understanding about a decision-making process in an efficient way. With XAI, industries can gain knowledge about the decision making of an AI-enabled system to improve user experience and satisfaction. XAI is also used to enhance the business process by improving the model's performance. Stakeholders can understand and gain insights into the underlying model's behavior, compare model predictions, identify risks, and optimize

**Corresponding author*: ksanthi@vit.ac.in

E. Gangadevi, M. Lawanya Shri, Balamurugan Balusamy and Rajesh Kumar Dhanaraj (eds.) Automated Machine Learning and Industrial Applications, (319–328) © 2025 Scrivener Publishing LLC

the performance of the model. Automated machine learning (AutoML) is the research area that tries to automate the machine learning steps or processes to produce good quality models. Those who were working in the area of data science are benefited by the development of automated ML tools. AutoML tools simplify the machine learning process by automating each process in the machine learning like data preprocessing, hyper parameter tuning, algorithm selection, architecture selection, and performance metrics selection. The company will try to understand the market needs in a faster manner with the help of the tool. A non-expert person in ML also can use the tool. This tool makes difficult tasks easier and reduce the inefficiency in making the model. It handles large datasets in an effective way and also uses innovative ML techniques. The various AutoML tools are as follows: AutoGluon, Auto-Sklearn, TPOT, AutoML-docker, and AutoKeras [1].

AutoGluon

AutoGluon is an open-source tool that is used in the area of automated machine learning. It focuses on automated stack ensemble ML model, deep learning, and real-world applications. This open-source software can handle text dataset, image dataset, and also tabular data. It was developed by Amazon Web Services. This tool provides a high-level interface. The tool will train the data, then deploy the model.

Strengths of AutoGluon

User Friendly: It provides an interface that could train a model using a single line of code, when all the default settings are done for the basic procedure.
Highly Automated: AutoGluon automates all the steps of ML, like data pre-processing, feature selection, hyper parameter tuning, and the design of artificial neural networks (ANN) [2]. It also provides information about the kind of data inferred, and it also deploys the model.
Lots of Control: The AutoGluon permits the user to configure many characteristics of the machine learning steps, such as data interpretation, feature extraction from the data set, model selection, choice of performance metrics, and consideration of hyper parameters. This is very useful for experts who use the ML models.
Easy to Extend: AutoGluon is an open source tool and was developed based on modular principle, which others use and customize according to their need. Users can describe the feature selection routine, customize

the models, and select performance metrics and hyper parameters. This easy extendable feature can allow users to create new ideas and models in a faster way.

Auto-Sklearn

Auto Sklearn is an AutoML tool written in Python. The tool consists of 15 ML models, 14 feature preprocessing methods, and 4 data preprocessing methods. It selects the suitable algorithm and required hyperparameters to make the best model. The tool automatically solves classification, regression, and multi-label classification tasks. Auto-Sklearn has three major components: meta-learning, Bayesian optimization, and ensemble building. When a new dataset is supplied to the tool, it first extracts its meta-feature to discover the similar feature of the given input dataset with the available knowledge base depending on the meta-learning. The meta-learning process uses 140 pretrained datasets to identify the best combination of models and hyperparameters for a given dataset [3]. Meta-learning reduces the search space. Next, through Bayesian optimization [4], it identifies the best machine learning pipeline. Finally, the tool will choose the best ML work flow pipeline and will construct the ensemble model based on it. Auto-Sklearn works on the operating System Mac and Linux. It does not support Windows OS. It is easy to use if you are familiar with scikit-learn. It does not support GPU.

TPOT (Tree-Based Pipeline Optimization Tool)

TPOT is an open-source tool developed using Python. TPOT routinely uses evolutionary algorithm [5] to design and improve the ML pipelines for a given problem [6, 7]. It is well suited for genetic problems. Various models and preprocessing techniques are utilized from the sklearn software. This tool uses tree-based algorithms [8] like Random Forest, XG Boost, or decision Tree. Solutions based on tree-based algorithms are robust. This tool is good for unclean datasets or datasets with noise. It does not support GPU.

AutoML-Docker

AutoML-docker is an open-source tool developed at Kern. Classifiers based on only natural language can be created with the help of this tool. The tool accepts a data set as input, the entire text processing is automatic, and models are produced accurately. The CLI interface is used to create natural language classifiers. The tool provides full GPU support. Only text can be processed using this tool.

AutoKeras

AutoKeras was developed by DATA lab. Google developed an API for applying neural networks. The tool is written in Python and can be operated both in the cloud and locally. This tool enables machine learning algorithms to be used by non-experts. It is used to create deep learning models [9] without requiring the user to define the architecture [10]. The main feature of AutoKeras is to automatically adjust the size of the neural architecture based on the available GPU memory size. It allows the user to define the layout of the layers and the number of neurons, as well as the characteristics of the hyperparameters [11, 12] such as optimization and loss functions. AutoKeras supports multiple backend neural network computation. It can be used for both classification and regression tasks.

H2O

H2O AutoML algorithm was first released in H2O 3.12.0.1 on June 6, 2017 by Erin LeDell. This allows the tool to process large datasets efficiently. Simple data processing tasks can be done using this tool The tool automatically trains large selections of models; it can tune the hyperparameters [13] of the models automatically and can also create one-layer stacked ensembled models using the bagging technique [14]. Individual models can be used with the cross-validation technique. This tool has been used in Kaggle forecast competitions [15].

Light AutoML

Light AutoML is an open-source tool written in Python. It was developed and released by the automated ML team members at Sber AI Lab for a finance company in Europe to provide AutoML solutions [1]. The tool can handle tabular and text data efficiently. Using tabular data, it can solve binary or multiclass classification and regression. Pipeline creation can be easily done with Light AutoML. The tool will automatically handle data pre-processing, feature selection, optimal and speedy hyper parameter tuning, and time utilization. It will also generate automatic reports. The tool allows users to create their own pipelines using a modular scheme [16].

MLBox

MLBox is an open-source tool for AutoML workflow [17]. It efficiently pre-processes data, selects features efficiently [18], and also effectively selects the model. It can solve a wide range of AI problems like regression, classification, and time-series forecasting. This tools also automatically tunes the hyperparameters and enhances the performance of ML models. The significant features of the tool include cleaning and preprocessing datasets such as handling missing values, encoding definite variables, and normalizing numeric features. It automatically selects applicable features of the dataset and produces new columns based on data. It selects the best model automatically, tunes the hyper-parameters, and increases the performance of the model [19]. The tool allows the customer to create their own pipeline based on their requirements. This ML tool can be easily integrated with other ML libraries like scikit-learn and XGBoost.

Pycaret

Pycaret is a free tool available for performing AutoML tasks [20]. It is an efficient tool for machine learning models covering everything from data preprocessing to hyperparameter tuning. The model is easily accessible to beginners as well as experts in machine learning. Due to modular design of Pycaret, it can be easily integrated with available ML pipelines. Various classification, regression and clustering ML algorithms can be solved using Pycaret [21]. The advantages of Pycaret include the requirement of fewer number of lines of code to build and deploy the model, non-programmers can easily use the tool, and the availability of documents with tutorials and projects.

MLJAR

MLJAR is an open-source AutoML tool designed to provide optimized models for many real-time problems. It works only on tabular data. The tool pre-processes input tabular data, builds ML models, and also tunes the hyper-parameters automatically to find the finest model among all other models. The tool can work in four modes like Explain, Compete, Perform, and Optuna [22] depending on user necessities and accessible resources. The Explain mode will analyze the data and try to extract the important features in the dataset. It does use hyperparameter tuning. The Compete mode will automatically extract the new features from the available features and optimize the model automatically to increase the accuracy of the model. The Perform mode selects the best ML pipeline based on the prediction time. The Perform mode applies the cross-validation technique to produce an active and good model. The optimization technique combines random search with hill climbing to balance exploration and exploitation [23]. The Optuna mode develops an optimized model by tuning the hyper-parameters from the available variants of the model. The computational time can be longer for the optimized model. Finally, the tool can generate a markdown report from the analysis for all the models available in the MLJAR tool.

Application of AutoML and XAI

(AutoML-XAI) for Metabolomics: Improving Cancer Diagnostics

This involves a singular pathway for improving metabolomics study by fusing explainable AI (XAI) methods with AutoML [24]. They have considered two sets of data: serum metabolomics from ovarian cancer (OC) and urine metabolomics from renal cell carcinoma (RCC). Using Auto-sklearn, AutoML was able to distinguish patients with OC and other gynecological cancers, as well as RCC and healthy controls, better than independent machine learning approaches.

Predicting Pretreatment Methods on Methane Production From Sludge Anaerobic Digestion

For effective treatment of sludge and resource recovery, accurate methane production prediction in anaerobic digestion using different pretreatment procedures is crucial [25]. An innovative integrated system was applied to investigate the impacts of various preparatory procedures on methane production during sludge digestion using explainable analysis. The system used an ensemble Semi Supervised Learning (SSL)-automated machine learning (AutoML) model with partial variable inputs.

Predicting Human Intestinal Absorption of Compounds With Serotonergic Activity

The pharmaceutical field's largest segment consists of oral medications. As the primary site of absorption for orally administered active pharmaceutical ingredients (APIs), the intestinal walls must be penetrated by a medicine to produce a therapeutic effect [26]. They have used both regression and classification prediction pathways and an AI-based method to predict HIA.

Predicting and Forecasting Bank Failures

Just Add Data (JAD) is an AutoML modern technology used for forecasting bank failures. The most important predictions are made using an automated feature selection process in JAD, and cautious predictions regarding performance generalization and confidence intervals are obtained by bootstrapping. According to the present research, JAD and AutoML tools generally could protect financial data analysts from fundamental statistical errors, boost their efficiency, and produce models that are at par with the most advanced analysis done by hand [27].

Automated Traffic Analysis

Machine learning is used for investigating network traffic activities related to protection ranging from identifying intrusions to application classification. By automating numerous analyses of traffic processes, algorithms for machine learning can be applied to a broader range of traffic analysis activities. To create nPrintML, an open platform that essentially does away with feature extraction and simulation modification for a range of traffic monitoring tasks, they initially introduce nPrint, an application that creates a single packet-based illustration that is suitable for portrayal learning as well as model training [28]. Additionally, they combine nPrint with automated learning algorithms (AutoML).

AutoML for Genome-Wide Association Studies

The processing of data from Genome-Wide Association Studies (GWAS) poses a number of computational and statistical issues, including interpretability, knowledge discovery, and clinical practice translation. By utilizing a set of gene variants that are significant for predictions (referred to as a biosignature), an assessment of the out-of-sample predictive ability, and AutoML tailored for genomic data, reliable predictive and diagnostic models are produced [29]. Additionally, it generalizes to new, unseen data.

Development of Prediction Model for Diesel Engines

A model was developed using machine learning that reduces insignificant input features by employing the Random Forest technique to forecast nitrogen oxide emissions. A Base model was established with every feature for comparison. The dominating features were selected using the Shapley Additive Explanations method, which can demonstrate the impact of input information characteristics, and the Pearson Correlation Coefficient method, which can demonstrate the proportionate link with the output and input values [30]. By utilizing the Shapley Additive Explanations approach, the final model was developed to create a simple yet precise NOx prediction model by identifying the key features affecting NOx prediction.

Conclusion

Automated Machine learning has become a popular technology trend that efficiently streamlines the progression to build and deploy machine learning models. AutoML tools are widely used to automatically analyze heterogenous data for predicting the outcomes in various applications. It is mainly used in applications like text classification, weather forecasting prediction, healthcare, sentiment analysis, business processing, and financial sectors. The role of AutoML includes identifying patterns, providing recommendations based on user behavior, optimizing clinical outcomes, and analyzing medical images for the decision-making process. AutoML tools are transforming the organizational approach to utilizing ML models by reducing the complexity and time needed to develop models for various applications.

References

1. Paladino, L.M., Hughes, A., Perera, A., Topsakal, O., Akinci, T.C., Evaluating the Performance of Automated Machine Learning (AutoML) Tools for Heart Disease Diagnosis and Prediction. *AI*, *4*, 1036–1058, 2023.
2. Mallikarachchi, D., *et al.*, Automated Machine Learning for Prediction of Type 2 Diabetes and Its Major Complications: A Comparative Study. *2023 5th International Conference on Advancements in Computing (ICAC)*, IEEE, 2023.
3. Feurer, M., Klein, A., Eggensperger, K., Springenberg, J.T., Blum, M., Hutter, F., Efficient and robust automated machine learning, in: *Advances in Neural Information Processing Systems 28 (NIPS 2015)*, Neural Information Processing Systems Foundation, Inc. (NeurIPS), La Jolla, CA, USA, pp. 2962–2970, 2015.
4. Feurer, M., Springenberg, J., Hutter, F., Initializing Bayesian Hyperparameter Optimization via Meta-Learning, in: *Proceedings of the Twenty-Ninth AAAI Conference on Artificial Intelligence*, Austin, TX USA, vol. 29, 25–30 January 2015.
5. Kulkarni, G.N., Ambesange, S., Vijayalaxmi, A., Sahoo, A., Comparision of diabetic prediction AutoML model with customized model. *2021*

International Conference on Artificial Intelligence and Smart Systems (ICAIS), Coimbatore, India, pp. 842–847, 2021.

6. Olson, R.S. and Moore, J.H., TPOT: A Tree-based Pipeline Optimization Tool for Automating Machine Learning. *Proceedings of the Workshop on Automatic Machine Learning*, pp. 66–74, 2016.
7. Olson, R.S., Urbanowicz, R.J., Andrews, P.C., Lavender, N.A., Kidd, L.C., Moore, J.H., Applications of Evolutionary Computation: 19th European Conference, Evo Applications 2016, Porto, Portugal, March 30—April 1, 2016. *Proceedings, Part I, chap. Automating Biomedical Data Science Through Tree-Based Pipeline Optimization*, Springer International Publishing, pp. 123–137, 2016.
8. Kumar, M., Ang, L.T., Png, H., Ng, M., Tan, K., Loy, S.L., Tan, K.H., Chan, J.K.Y., Godfrey, K.M., Chan, S.Y., Chong, Y.S., Eriksson, J.G., Feng, M., Karnani, N., Automated Machine Learning (AutoML)-Derived Preconception Predictive Risk Model to Guide Early Intervention for Gestational Diabetes Mellitus. *Int. J. Environ. Res. Public Health*, 19, 11, 6792, 2022 Jun 1.
9. Budjač, R., Nikmon, M., Schreiber, P., Zahradníková, B., Janáčová, D., Automated Machine Learning Overview, in: Research Papers Faculty of Materials Science and Technology, vol. 27 issue 45, pp. 107–112, Slovak University of Technology, Walter de Gruyter GmbH, 2019, https://doi.org/10.2478/ rput-2019-0033.
10. Jin, H., Chollet, F., Song, Q., Hu, X., AutoKeras: An AutoML Library for Deep Learning. *J. Mach. Learn. Res.*, 24, 1, 6, 1–6, January 2023.
11. Lee, S., Kim, J., Bae, J.H., Lee, G., Yang, D., Hong, J., Lim, K.J., Development of Multi-Inflow Prediction Ensemble Model Based on Auto-Sklearn Using Combined Approach: Case Study of Soyang River Dam. *Hydrology*, 10, 90, 2023.
12. Pushparaj, S.N., Sivasankaran, S.M., Thamizh Chem-mal, S., Prediction of Heart Disease Using a Hybrid of CNN-LSTM Algorithm. *J. Surv. Fish. Sci.*, 10, 5700–5710, 2023.
13. Pandey, P., A Deep Dive into H2Os AutoML, 2019, URL http://www.h2o.ai/blog/a-deepdive-into-h2os-automl/.
14. Chen, T. and Guestrin, C., XGBoost: A scalable tree boosting system, in: *Proceedings of the 22nd ACM SIGKDD International Conference on Knowledge Discovery and Data Mining*, ACM, pp. 785–794, 2016.
15. Erickson, N., Mueller, J., Shirkov, A., Zhang, H., Larroy, P., Li, M., Smola, A., Autogluon-tabular: Robust and accurate automl for structured data, 2020, arXiv preprint arXiv:2003.06505.
16. Vakhrushev, A., Ryzhkov, A., Savchenko, M., Simakov, D., Damdinov, R., Tuzhilin, A., LightAutoML: AutoML Solution for a Large Financial Services Ecosystem, 2012, arXiv preprint arXiv:2103.10859.
17. De Romblay, A.A., *et al.*, MLBox, 2017, url: https://mlbox.readthedocs.io/en/latest/ installation.html In.

18. Ajantha Devi, V., Naved, M., Gangadevi, E., Nayyar, A., Genetic Algorithm-Based Vaccine Optimization Technique to Control COVID-19, in: *Proceedings of International Conference on Computational Intelligence and Data Engineering*. Lecture Notes on Data Engineering and Communications Technologies, N. Chaki, N. Devarakonda, A. Cortesi, H. Seetha (Eds.), Springer, Singapore, vol. 99, 2022, https://doi.org/10.1007/978-981-16-7182-1_1.
19. Smith, J. and Doe, A., MLBox: Machine Learning Box for Asymptotic Scheduling. *J. Adv. Sched.*, 12, 3, 123–135, 2023.
20. Gangadevi, E., Rani, R.S., Dhanaraj, R.K., Nayyar, A., Spot-out fruit fly algorithm with simulated annealing optimized SVM for detecting tomato plant diseases. *Neural Comput. Appl.*, 36, 8, 4349–4375, 2023, Springer Science and Business Media LLC. https://doi.org/10.1007/s00521-023-09295-1.
21. Mesquita, F. and Marques, G., An explainable machine learning approach for automated medical decision support of heart disease. *Data Knowl. Eng.*, 153, 102339, 2024.
22. https://supervised.mljar.com/
23. de Oliveira, D.N., *et al.*, Evaluating a new auto-ML approach for sentiment analysis and intent recognition tasks. *J. Interact. Syst.*, 14, 1, 92–105, 2023.
24. Bifarin, O.O. and Fernández, F.M., Automated machine learning and explainable AI (AutoML-XAI) for metabolomics: improving cancer diagnostics. *J. Am. Soc. Mass Spectrom.*, 35, 6, 1089–1100, 2024.
25. Cheng, X., Xu, R., Wu, Y., Tang, B., Luo, Y., Huang, W., Luo, J., Predicting and evaluating different pretreatment methods on methane production from sludge anaerobic digestion via automated machine learning with ensembled semisupervised learning. *ACS ES&T Eng.*, *4*, 3, 525–539, 2023.
26. Czub, N., Szlęk, J., Pacławski, A., Klimonczyk, K., Puccetti, M., Mendyk, A., Artificial intelligence-based quantitative structure–property relationship model for predicting human intestinal absorption of compounds with serotonergic activity. *Mol. Pharmaceutics*, *20*, 5, 2545–2555, 2023.
27. Agrapetidou, A., Charonyktakis, P., Gogas, P., Papadimitriou, T., Tsamardinos, I., An AutoML application to forecasting bank failures. *Appl. Econ. Lett.*, *28*, 1, 5–9, 2021.
28. Holland, J., Schmitt, P., Feamster, N., Mittal, P., New directions in automated traffic analysis, in: *Proceedings of the 2021 ACM SIGSAC Conference on Computer and Communications Security*, pp. 3366–3383, November, 2021.
29. Revathi, V., Gunapriya, B., Kavin, B.P., Gangadevi, E., Balusamy, B., Gite, S., Despise Detection through LOA Using Fs with 1D-CNN in Public Forum. *2024 IEEE International Conference on Computing, Power and Communication Technologies (IC2PCT)*, Greater Noida, India, pp. 1445–1451, 2024, doi: 10.1109/IC2PCT60090.2024.10486644.
30. Ahlgren, F. and Thern, M., Auto machine learning for predicting ship fuel consumption, in: *ECOS 2018-the 31st International Conference on Efficiency, Cost, Optimization, Simulation and Environmental Impact of Energy Systems*, Guimarães, 17-21 June, 2018, 2018.

Index

Printed in the USA/Agawam, MA
September 16, 2026

910661.099